RICHARD BAKER'S

Companion to Music

A personal A-Z guide to classical music

BBC
BOOKS

RICHARD BAKER'S COMPANION TO MUSIC

Designed and produced by Parke Sutton Publishing Limited,
The Old Tannery, Barrack Street, Norwich NR3 1TS

Published by BBC Books,
a division of BBC Enterprises Limited,
Woodlands, 80 Wood Lane, London W12 0TT

First published 1993
Text copyright © Richard Baker 1993
ISBN 0-563-36414-9

Edited by Anne Priestley
Designed by Gillian Matthews
Picture research by Christine Cook
Typeset by PS Typesetting
Printed and bound in Great Britain by BPCC Paulton Books Ltd, Paulton

PRELUDE

I have had the pleasure of presenting music programmes for the BBC for a great many years now, and one of the challenges of the job is to cope with queries from listeners and viewers. Sometimes they are easily dealt with but often they are quite obscure and lead to much delving into the big musical reference books. So I thought I would put together a handy compendium of musical information based on the enquiries I have had in the past. I hope it may provide answers to some of the questions *you* might like to ask.

There is a very wide choice of books about music on the market and I would like to make it clear that this is not a comprehensive encyclopaedia on the subject. It is intended for the growing number of people who listen with pleasure to 'classical' music, whether in the concert hall or opera house, at home or in the car, on television, BBC Radio or Classic FM. People who know what they like and would like to know a little more. I have had in mind particularly the audience of Radio 2's long-running *Melodies for You*. Our repertoire in that programme ranges from symphonies to stage musicals, the only criterion being that the music we choose should be enjoyable and well performed. We are content to be guided in our selections by the great Sir Thomas Beecham. 'Good music,' he said, 'penetrates the ear with facility and quits the memory with difficulty.' There is no distinction in such a definition between a song by Schubert and a number by Jerome Kern. That is how it should be, in my opinion.

In this book you will, of course, find entries on all the great 'classical' composers (and, by the way, under 'Classical music' you will discover why the word should not really be applied to the whole range of serious music). On the other hand, there is a double-page spread on Jazz, and another on the Musical. There are references to many of the leading performers who are likely to feature in musical broadcasts of wide appeal, accounts of popular operas and ballets, and details of some of the world's major musical centres. You can read about well-known tunes such as 'Rule, Britannia' and 'Hark, the Herald Angels Sing' and, where a piece is better known than its creator, I have featured the title rather than the composer: *Rustle of Spring*, for instance, which prompts a mention of Christian Sinding.

It is my intention that the pointers provided will help when it comes to choosing recordings, in whatever form suits your circumstances. The most comprehensive guide to what is available on tape and CD is *The Classical Catalogue*, produced by General Gramophone Publications and updated each year. If you require more detailed musical information, the most exhaustive British work of reference is the twenty-volume *New Grove Dictionary of Music and Musicians* coupled with the four-volume *New Grove Dictionary of Opera*. One of the most useful single-volume works is Michael Kennedy's *Oxford Dictionary of Music*. Peter Gammond's *Oxford Companion to Popular Music* is very good on the lighter side of musical life.

I hope you will enjoy what follows and find it interesting. Before we embark on letter **A**, let me offer a few words of thanks: to my researchers Ross Winston and William Humphreys-Jones, to my editor Anne Priestley, and to Margaret Dowson, a former BBC colleague and good friend of many years' standing, who typed the manuscript impeccably.

Richard Baker

A

A

The note A, the sixth note above middle C on the **piano**, is generally used for the tuning of instruments. The A is given to an **orchestra** by the **oboe**, the woodwind instrument least affected by temperature variations. At the **Proms**, the audience loves to distract the players by singing a misleading A while the orchestra tries to tune.

ABBADO, *Claudio* (born Milan 1933)

Italian conductor of great distinction and disarming modesty. He made his début at **La Scala** in 1960 and was music director at La Scala 1968–86, with the **London Symphony Orchestra** (1979–88) and at the **Vienna** State Opera (1986–91). In 1989 he succeeded **Herbert von Karajan** with the **Berlin Philharmonic Orchestra**. Abbado has always encouraged young talent, and is founder and conductor of the European Community Youth Orchestra and Artistic Adviser to the still youthful Chamber Orchestra of Europe.

'ABIDE WITH ME'

Popular **hymn**, sung by the crowd at the FA Cup Final at Wembley and on other public occasions. Written by the Rev. Henry Francis Lyte (1793–1847) in 1820; the tune, 'Eventide', was composed for *Hymns Ancient and Modern* in 1861 by William Henry Monk (1823–89).

ACADEMY OF ST MARTIN-IN-THE-FIELDS

Highly accomplished and successful **chamber orchestra**, so named because it started in 1958 by giving concerts in the famous church in London's Trafalgar Square. Founded by **Sir Neville Marriner**, who remained director until 1978 when he was succeeded by Iona Brown. Extensive repertoire of recordings which has extended latterly into 'crossover' albums such as 'The Academy Plays Opera'. Awarded the Queen's Award for Exports in 1993, the first orchestra ever to receive it.

ADAGIO

Italian musical term meaning 'slow' (slower than andante, quicker than largo).

ADAGIO (ALBINONI)

Much-loved composition for organ and strings by the twentieth-century Italian musicologist Remo Giazotto, based on a fragment of manuscript by the Venetian Tommaso Albinoni (1671–1751), a prolific composer of operatic and instrumental music.

ADAGIO FOR STRINGS (BARBER)

Most famous composition of the American composer Samuel Barber (1910–81). Originally the slow movement of his String Quartet (1936), it was first performed and recorded in an orchestral version by the **New York Philharmonic Orchestra** under **Arturo Toscanini**.

ADAGIO OF SPARTACUS AND PHRYGIA (KHACHATURIAN)

Music for the pas-de-deux of the slave Spartacus and the Roman beauty Phrygia in the **ballet** *Spartacus* (1956) by **Aram Khachaturian**, better known in Britain as the TV signature tune for *The Onedin Line*.

'ADESTE FIDELES'

The music and original Latin words of this splendid Christmas **hymn** were probably written in the 1740s by John Francis Wade (1711–86), a Latin teacher and music copyist at Douai in France.

ADLER, *Larry* (Born Baltimore 1914)

World-famous virtuoso of the **harmonica** or, as he prefers to call it, the mouth-organ. Born in the USA, Adler made his home in Britain after being accused of Communist sympathies in the American witch-hunts of the late 1940s. The first player of his instrument to be taken seriously in the 'classical' music world, he has had works specially written for him by composers such as **Malcolm Arnold**, **Gordon Jacob**, **Darius Milhaud** and **Vaughan Williams**. His own compositions include the music for the film *Genevieve* (1954).

AIDA

Opera by **Verdi**, composed for the new Cairo Opera House, and first performed there on 24 December 1871, with immense success. Radamès is to be rewarded for his victory over the Ethiopians with the hand of the Egyptian princess Amneris in marriage, but he loves her Ethiopian slave Aida. Aida tricks Radamès into betraying a military secret, thus avoiding a further defeat for her people, and the general is condemned to be buried alive. However, Aida has concealed herself in the tomb before it is finally sealed, and the lovers die together. Familiar excerpts include the triumph scene with its ballet music; the tenor aria for Radamès, 'Celeste Aida'; Aida's arias 'Ritorna Vincitor' (Return Victorious) and 'O Patria Mia' (O My Country); and the final trio between Aida, Amneris and Radamès.

AIR DE BALLET (*ZÉMIR ET AZOR*) GRÉTRY

The first 'Air de Ballet', otherwise known as 'Pantomime', from the opera *Zémir et Azor* (1771) by the Belgian composer André Ernest Modeste Grétry (1741–1813) was adopted by **Sir Thomas Beecham** as one of his favourite 'lollipops'.

ALBÉNIZ, *Isaac* (Born Camprodón, Lérida, 1860; died Cambô-les-Bains 1909)

Important Spanish composer and pianist who helped create a national musical style, above all in **piano** music. At the age of four his playing ability amazed an audience in Barcelona and at seven he was rejected by the Paris conservatoire as too young. He ran away from home when he was ten to give concerts on his own in Castile, and at twelve stowed away on a ship leaving Cádiz for South America. Albéniz never settled for long, but in 1883 he married in Barcelona and met Felipe Pedrell who inspired him with the ambition to write music of authentic character. In the 1890s he spent much time in Paris, forming friendships with d'Indy, **Fauré**, **Debussy** and **Dukas**. He also spent three years in London setting the operatic librettos of the banker Francis Burdett Money-Coutts to music, not altogether successfully. The historical *Henry Clifford* (1895) was a failure, but the collaboration produced one successful opera in *Pepita Jiménez*, based on a Spanish novel. It was premiered in Barcelona in 1896. Albéniz spent most of the last nine years of his life in France, where he completed the four sets of piano pieces known collectively as *Iberia*. This was his masterpiece and includes, both in the original piano version and in orchestrations by Enrique Arbós and Carlos Surinach, some of Albéniz's best-known

pieces. His shorter piano works include a very popular Tango.

ALLEN, *Thomas* (Born Seaham Harbour, County Durham, 1944)

Hailed as the leading baritone of the day and perhaps the best British baritone ever. Made his début in 1969 as Figaro in *The Barber of Seville* with **Welsh National Opera**. Since then has been in increasing demand worldwide in an operatic and concert repertoire which extends from **Mozart** to Carl Orff's *Carmina Burana*. In 1986 Allen created the title role in the first British stage production of Busoni's *Doctor Faust* for **English National Opera**; he is also a notable interpreter of **lieder** and of English songs by **Vaughan Williams** and others. CBE 1989.

ALPHORN

The Swiss national instrument, but the name is also applied to similar instruments in other mountainous regions. Its sound is imitated in **Beethoven**'s 'Pastoral' Symphony, **Rossini**'s *William Tell* Overture and **Wagner**'s *Tristan und Isolde*. **Brahms** incorporated an alphorn melody in the last movement of his First Symphony and Leopold Mozart (Wolfgang's father) wrote a part for the alphorn in his *Sinfonia Pastorella* ('for two **violins**, **viola** and **bass** with a herdsman's horn which is not obligatory though it creates a good effect').

ALTO

Italian word meaning 'high'. The male alto voice (often called **countertenor**) was popular from the sixteenth to the eighteenth centuries; a twentieth-century revival of interest was prompted by the voice of **Alfred Deller**.

ALWYN, *Kenneth* (Born Croydon 1925)

English conductor often engaged by the BBC Concert Orchestra. He spent most of the 1950s with the Royal Ballet, then moved to Western Theatre Ballet. He was appointed conductor of BBC Northern Ireland Orchestra in 1969 and has worked a great deal in theatre, radio and television.

ALWYN, *William* (Born Northampton 1905)

English composer, painter and writer. Five

symphonies form the core of his output as a composer but he became more widely known for his **film scores**, which include *Odd Man Out* (1947), *The Fallen Idol* (1948) and *The Running Man* (1963). CBE 1978.

A MADEUS QUARTET

One of the world's most admired twentieth-century string quartets, especially in music by the Viennese masters from **Haydn** to **Brahms**. Its members were Norbert Brainin (**violin**), Siegmund Nissel (violin), Peter Schidlof (**viola**) and Martin Lovett (**cello**). Brainin, Nissel and Schidlof were Austrian Jews from Vienna who fled to Britain in 1938; Martin Lovett was born in London. Formed in London in 1947, the quartet enjoyed forty years of worldwide fame before it was disbanded in 1987 after Schidlof's death. Brainin was created CBE in 1960, the other members in 1973.

A MELING, *Elly* (Born Rotterdam 1938)

Dutch **soprano** whose beautiful voice is matched by a delightful personality. **Bach**, **Handel**, **Mozart**, **Schubert** and **Brahms** are often featured in her concerts and recordings, but early training with Pierre Bernac led to expert singing of the French song repertoire, and an easy command of English plus the right lightness of touch has led to successful recordings of **Gershwin**, **Ellington** and **Cole Porter**. Knight of the Order of Oranje Nassau in 1971.

A NDERSON, *Leroy* (Born Cambridge, Mass., 1908; died Woodbury, Conn., 1975)

Of Swedish descent, Anderson studied Scandinavian languages as well as music at Harvard. In the 1930s he became a freelance composer and arranger, often in association with **Arthur Fiedler**'s Boston Pops orchestra which he sometimes conducted. After service in the army in the Second World War, Anderson produced a number of very successful light orchestral pieces including 'Sleigh Ride' (1950), 'Blue Tango' (1952), 'The Typewriter' (1953) and 'Forgotten Dreams' (1955).

A NDERSON, *Marian* (Born Philadelphia 1902; died 1993)

Described by **Toscanini** as the possessor of a 'voice that comes once in a hundred years', Marian

The adventurous Isaac Albéniz: he was a transatlantic stowaway at the age of twelve.

Anderson was a great achiever in the cause of black equality. With the backing of Eleanor Roosevelt she gave a concert before 75 000 people in Washington in April 1939, and was the first black soloist to appear at the **Metropolitan Opera House**, New York (as Ulrica in **Verdi**'s *A Masked Ball* in 1955). Delegate to the United Nations 1957–8. Awarded US Congressional Medal on her seventy-fifth birthday. Popularly acclaimed for her glorious contralto singing of **spirituals.**

A NDRÉ, *Maurice* (Born Alès, France, 1933)

Trumpeter who started his working life at the age of fourteen as a miner. After winning first prizes in competitions at Geneva (1955) and Munich (1963), he is now one of the world's outstanding instrumentalists, using a four-valved piccolo **trumpet** specially made for him. Has recorded upwards of thirty

concertos and many other works, some written for him by contemporary composers.

A NSERMET, *Ernest* (Born Vevey, Switzerland, 1883; died Geneva 1969)

Originally a mathematics teacher, Ansermet took lessons in composition and studied the art of **conducting**. In 1915, with **Stravinsky**'s backing, he became conductor of Diaghilev's Russian ballet. His central achievement was the creation and direction for forty-eight years (1918–66) of the Orchestra of the Suisse Romande. With that orchestra he recorded a comprehensive repertoire ranging from the classics to contemproary composers; many of these recordings are now being reissued on CD. Conducted the first performance of **Benjamin Britten**'s *The Rape of Lucretia* at **Glyndebourne**, 1946.

A NTHEM

A song expressing a commonly shared loyalty – e.g., National Anthem; also, in church music, the Anglican equivalent of the Latin **motet**, performed by the choir without congregational participation. The 1662 Prayer Book laid down that, after the Third Collect, 'in Quires and Places where they sing here followeth the Anthem', and the practice has been widely followed ever since.

A RABESQUE (French and English), Arabeske (German)

A type of decoration in painting and architecture involving interwining leaves, flowers or geometrical designs in the Arab style. **Debussy**'s *Two Arabesques* of 1888 illustrate the application of the term to music which is decorative rather than emotional in quality. **Schumann**'s *Arabeske*, Op. 18, is perhaps less appropriately named.

A RGERICH, *Martha* (Born Buenos Aires 1941)

Argentinian pianist of great power and brilliance. Made her début at the age of five and was soloist with an orchestra when she was eight. Début in London 1964, winner of Warsaw International **Chopin** Competition 1965.

A RIA

Italian word derived from the Latin for air, or atmos-

phere, so originally applied to a style of performance rather than just a song or 'air'. An aria (almost always for solo voice) can be either simple or complex; in the seventeenth and eighteenth centuries it was commonly in ABA form, with the opening section repeated after a contrasting middle section. In **oratorio** and **opera** of that period an aria was often preceded by a **recitative**; in later works arias became much more varied in form and scale.

A RMSTRONG, *Sheila* (Born Ashington, Northumberland, 1942)

British **soprano** distinguished on the concert platform and opera stage; also fine exponent of Northumbrian and other folk-songs. Won **Kathleen Ferrier** Prize 1965. Gave first performance of John McCabe's *Notturni in Alba*, dedicated to her, in 1970. Acclaimed soloist in British choral works, took part in first recording of **Elgar**'s *The Apostles* (1973).

A RNE, *Thomas Augustine* (baptised London 1710; died London 1778)

Most famous for **'Rule, Britannia'** which formed part of the masque *Alfred*, produced by command of the Prince of Wales in 1740. Arne's sister became, as Mrs Cibber, one of the most famous actresses of her day, and Arne wrote a very large quantity of theatre music for productions involving her and others at Drury Lane and **Covent Garden**. Also worked periodically in Dublin. He was reputed to be 'a bit of a scoundrel', but was the most significant British composer of his time. As a later writer put it, 'he had neither the vigour of **Purcell**, nor the grandeur, simplicity and magnificence of **Handel**; he apparently aimed at pleasing, and he fully succeeded.'

A RNOLD, *Malcolm* (Born Northampton 1921)

English composer who started his professional life as a trumpeter. His output ranges from eight full-scale **symphonies** to much slighter pieces, but all reveal an outstanding gift for melody as well as outbursts of great dramatic power. Has written over eighty film scores, including *The Bridge on the River Kwai* which won him an Oscar in 1957. Among his most popular works are the sets of English, Scottish and Cornish Dances and the overture *Tam O' Shanter. A Grand, Grand Overture* for three vacuum cleaners, floor polisher, four rifles and orchestra, produced for the **Hoffnung** Music Festival in 1956, reflected a vigorous sense of humour. Knighted 1992.

ARRAU, *Claudio* (Born Chillán, Chile 1903; died Muerzzuschlag, Austria, 1991)

One of the twentieth century's most respected pianists, Arrau is famous as a **Beethoven** interpreter. Has given complete cycles of the thirty-two **sonatas**, and recorded the piano **concertos** three times. Studied at the Stern Conservatory in Berlin with Martin Krause 1912–18, and was on the staff of the Conservatory 1924–40, after which he founded his own **piano** school in Santiago. Subsequently made his home in New York, finally returning to Chile in 1984. Awarded West German Verdienstkreuz in 1970 at the Beethoven bicentenary celebrations.

ASHKENAZY, *Vladimir* (Born Gorky 1937)

Outstanding pianist and, latterly, conductor. Russian by birth but since 1972 Icelandic by nationality: he married an Icelandic wife. Shared first prize in the second **Tchaikovsky** competition in Moscow with **John Ogdon** 1962; left Russia 1963, settling first in England, then in Iceland and Switzerland. A masterly interpreter of an extensive range of solo **piano** works, he also performs much **chamber music**, particularly in partnership with the violinist **Itzhak Perlman** and the cellist **Lyn Harrell**. Now a very successful conductor, he has been music director of the **Royal Philharmonic Orchestra** since 1987.

ATHERTON, *David* (Born Blackpool 1941)

English conductor particularly noted for his sympathy with contemporary music. At twenty-seven was the youngest conductor ever to appear at **Covent Garden** (with **Verdi**'s *Il Trovatore*), and at the **Proms** (with **John Tavener**'s *In Alium*). Music director of the London Sinfonietta, specialising in modern works, 1968–73. Subsequent appointments include periods with the Royal Liverpool Philharmonic and the San Diego Symphony orchestras. Music director of the Hong Kong Philharmonic Orchestra from 1989.

AUBADE

The early-morning equivalent of the **serenade**. There is a well-known aubade in **Bizet**'s opera *The Fair*

Maid of Perth; **Ravel**'s Spanish-style *Alborada del Gracioso* may be translated 'Aubade of the Buffoon'.

AUGER, *Arleen* (Born Long Beach, California 1939)

Long recognised as one of the world's leading **sopranos**, Auger achieved popular international fame when she performed **Mozart**'s *Exultate, Jubilate*, which includes the famous 'Alleluia', at Prince Andrew's wedding in 1986.

'AULD LANG SYNE'

The words were published by Robert Burns in 1794, but they may well be traditional in origin. The tune is often attributed to the English composer William Shield (1748–1829), who included a version of it in the overture to his opera *Rosina* (1782), but the melody could be a Scottish folk-tune Shield heard in his native Northumbria. It is wrong to pronounce the 's' in Syne as 'z'.

'AUTUMN' (Chaminade)

Extremely popular **piano** solo by Cécile Chaminade, French pianist and composer (1857–1944). Wrote church music at the age of eight, and gave recitals including her own works when she was eighteen.

B

BACH SONS

Three of Johann Sebastian's sons achieved lasting fame in varying degrees. Wilhelm Friedemann (1710–84), a virtuoso organist, never really moved as a composer out of the shadow of his father. Carl Philipp Emanuel (1714–88) was an accompanist at the court of **Frederick the Great** 1738–67, then director of church music in Hamburg. He wrote an important treatise on keyboard playing and developed **sonata** form. Johann Christian (1735–82), the 'English' Bach, spent much time in London during the last twenty years of his life, founded an important series of concerts with his compatriot Carl Friedrich Abel, and greatly impressed the boy **Mozart** during his London visit, 1764–5. Master of the elegant, so-called 'galant' style.

*B*ACH

Johann Sebastian BACH

1685	Born in Eisenach
1700–3	Singer and violinist in Lüneburg
1703–17	Organist in Arnstadt
1707	Organist in Mühlhausen
1708–17	Court organist and chamber musician to Duke of Saxe-Weimar
1717–23	*Kapellmeister* to Prince Leopold of Anhalt-Cöthen
1723–50	Cantor at St Thomas's School, Leipzig
1750	Died in Leipzig

Johann Sebastian was the most famous member of a large family of musical Bachs, but there was nothing in his early life to suggest that his achievements would amount to what **Wagner** called 'the most stupendous miracle in all music'.

In Bach's own time, he was chiefly known as the greatest organist in Germany – fewer than a dozen of his massive number of works were published when he was alive. In 1829 **Mendelssohn** conducted the first performance of the *St Matthew Passion* since Bach's death and in 1850, spurred on by **Schumann**, the newly formed German Bach Society (*Bach Gesellschaft*) began the huge task of publishing all Bach's music. The job took fifty years.

Bach was, in fact, the last and greatest master of **polyphony**, a type of composition in which several different vocal or instrumental lines move in harmony with each other. Music of this type had flourished for at least two centuries before Bach's time so he was often criticised by contemporaries for being old-fashioned.

The image of Bach that comes across to us in portraits is of a thoroughly admirable, solid citizen, a little dull perhaps and a bit of a pedant. But you don't play the organ as Bach did, or write the kind of music that Bach wrote, without being fired by passion. After the death of his mother when he was only ten, Johann Sebastian went to live with his uncle Johann Christoph, a good musician who taught the boy the clavier. But that was not enough. Night after night for six months, the boy sat up copying by moonlight some keyboard music he'd come across in a locked cupboard of his uncle's. When he was fifteen he walked the 150 miles to Lüneburg to take up an appointment as a church chorister; from there he often walked thirty miles to Hamburg to listen to Johann Adam Reinken play the organ, and during his period as organist at Arnstadt he walked getting on for three hundred miles each way to hear the famous **Dietrich Buxtehude** play the organ at Lübeck.

Bach's productive career can be conveniently divided into three parts. The greater part of his organ music was composed before he was thirty-two years of age, before he entered the service of Prince Leopold of Anhalt-Cöthen. In his six years at Cöthen, Bach created mainly orchestral music, including the famous Brandenburg Concertos, and his period as Cantor of St Thomas's School at Leipzig gave rise to a long series of **cantatas** and other works involving voices, produced mainly for church use. During the Leipzig years, Bach also published a number of new and revised keyboard works under the title *Clavierübung*, which means 'keyboard exercise', and during the last three years of his life composed the challenging *Musical Offering* on a theme provided by **King Frederick the Great of Prussia**, and *The Art of Fugue*, which was intended to be the last word on fugal composition and was regarded as unplayable until the 1930s.

The choral forces at Bach's disposal in Leipzig were pathetically inadequate, but Bach stuck it out at St Thomas's School, consoled up to a point by a number of extramural activities and commissions from aristocratic patrons. He was, by the standards of the time, a prosperous musician.

Bach was a deeply committed Protestant and very much a family man. At the age of twenty-two he married his cousin Maria Barbara Bach, and when she died thirteen years later he married Anna Magdalena Wilcken, composing special pieces to encourage her keyboard studies. Bach fathered twenty children. Several of his sons became successful musicians, notably **Wilhelm Friedemann**, **Carl Philipp Emmanuel** and **Johann Christian**, the latter known as the 'English' Bach. But none of them comes near to rivalling their father's unique glory.

Favourite works

The BWV numbers refer to the *Bach Werke-Verzeichnis* (list of Bach's works) published in 1950. It runs to 1087 items.

CHURCH MUSIC

'Jesu, Joy of Man's Desiring' – the English title for a chorale from Bach's Church Cantata No. 147;
'Sheep May Safely Graze' – **recitative** and **aria** from a secular cantata about the pleasures of the chase (BWV208);
'Sanctus' – one of the shortest and most often-heard sections of the **Mass** in B minor, BWV232;
'Grief for Sin' – **contralto** aria from the *St Matthew Passion*, BWV244;
'Rejoice, be glad!' ('Jauchzet fröhlocket!') – opening chorus of the *Christmas Oratorio*, BWV248.

OTHER MUSIC

Toccata and Fugue in D minor, BWV565;
Violin Concerto in E major, BWV1052;
Concerto for Four Harpsichords in A minor, BWV1065;
Brandenburg Concerto No. 3 in G, BWV1048;
Italian Concerto in F major, BWV971;
'Air on the G String' – an arrangement of the **Air** from Bach's Orchestral Suite No. 3 in D, BWV1068;
Minuet and Badinerie – two movements from Bach's Suite No. 2 in B minor, BWV1067;
'Ave Maria' (Bach–Gounod) – **Charles Gounod** added his famous tune to the Prelude in C from Bach's 48 Preludes and Fugues (*The Well-Tempered Clavier*).

Morning Prayers – *a romantic image of the Bach family with J.S. at the keyboard.*

*B*ACH GOES TO TOWN' (Templeton) —————

Popular jazzy spoof in the style of **Johann Sebastian Bach** by the blind pianist and composer Alec Templeton (1919–63). He also wrote 'Mozart Matriculates', 'Mendelssohn Mows 'em Down', 'Beethoven in Tin Pan Alley'.

*I*L BACIO' (THE KISS) Arditi —————————

Florid waltz-song by the Italian Luigi Arditi (1822–1903). He travelled widely, but spent much of his working life as a conductor of concerts and **opera** in London.

*B*AGATELLE ————————————————

French word meaning 'trifle' applied by composers, starting with **Couperin,** to a slight piece, usually for keyboard. **Beethoven** wrote three sets of Bagatelles, Opp. 33, 119 and 126. The most famous, in A minor, has the title 'Für Élise'.

*B*AGPIPE ——————————————————

Bagpipes have been known for at least 3000 years and survive in various forms in many parts of the world. The tune is created on a reed-pipe or 'chanter' with finger-holes, the other pipes (drones) playing a single sustained note. Air is supplied to a reservoir made of skin, either by the mouth or by bellows. British bagpipes include the Scottish Highland bagpipe whose penetrating sound is best heard at a distance, the Irish Union or 'uilleann' pipe and the Northumbrian bagpipe, or small-pipe, whose sweet sound makes it suitable for use indoors.

*B*AÏLERO' (Canteloube) —————————

Most famous of the *Songs of Auvergne* collected and arranged by the French composer, Joseph Canteloube (born Annonay 1879, died Gridny 1957) between 1923 and 1930.

*B*AILEY, *Norman* (Born Birmingham 1933) ——

English **baritone** who trained at Rhodes University, South Africa, and at the **Vienna** Music Academy. Made his début at Vienna Chamber Opera 1959. Appeared with German **opera** companies 1960–7, at **Sadler's Wells** 1967–71. Played Hans Sachs in the Sadler's Wells production of **Wagner**'s *The Mastersingers*, 1968, and thenceforward regarded as a major Wagnerian performer. CBE 1977.

*B*AILLIE, *Isobel* (Born Hawick, Roxburghshire, 1895; died Manchester 1983) —————

After one of the Scottish **soprano**'s broadcasts a **BBC** listener wrote to ask who was the nightingale he had heard on the wireless the previous evening. For thirty years one of Britain's leading **oratorio** sopranos, she sang in **Handel**'s *Messiah* upwards of 1000 times, and continued to accept engagements into her eighties. As **Sir Henry Wood** said, 'I have never found her anything but note-perfect'. In later life, 'Bella' Baillie taught in Britain and the USA. DBE 1978.

*B*AKER, *George* (Born Birkenhead 1885; died Pontrilas, Herefordshire, 1976) —————

English **baritone** famous for the **Gilbert and Sullivan** opera recordings he made under **Sir Malcolm Sargent**'s direction in the late 1950s, though he never appeared on stage in these works. CBE 1971.

*B*AKER, *Janet* (Born Hatfield, Yorks., 1933) ——

English **mezzo-soprano** distinguished on concert platform and in **opera**. In 1962 an appearance as Dido in **Purcell**'s *Dido and Aeneas* at the Aldeburgh Festival led to a continuing association with **Benjamin Britten**; she sang the title role in his opera *The Rape of Lucretia* and Britten wrote the role of Kate for her in his television opera *Owen Wingrave* (1971). Her recital repertoire extends from **lieder** by **Schubert** and **Brahms** through a wide range of French and English song; she is a **Bach** singer of great eloquence and very memorable in **Mahler** and in **Elgar**'s *The Dream of Gerontius*. DBE 1976.

*B*ALAKIREV, *Mily* (Born Nizhny-Novgorod [now Gorky] 1837; died St Petersburg 1910) ————

Significant Russian composer who absorbed the nationalistic ideas of **Glinka** and in turn influenced a new generation of Russian composers. Balakirev was the sometimes despotic leader of the group known as the '**Mighty Handful**' or 'The Five', which included **Borodin**, César Cui, **Moussorgksy**, and **Rimsky-Korsakov**. Subsequently **Tchaikovsky** also came under his influence. In St Petersburg, Balakirev founded the Free School of Music to propagate his ideas, which included the collection and transcription of folk-song material. His best-known compositions include the sensationally brilliant oriental fantasy for **piano** *Islamey*, the symphonic poem *Tamara* and the Symphony No. 1 in C which took thirty years to complete. **Sir Thomas Beecham** conducted *Tamara* in the 1912 Diaghilev Russian ballet season in London, and in 1934 introduced the C major symphony to Britain, recording it memorably in 1955 with the **Royal Philharmonic Orchestra**. Beecham rightly described it as 'a tremendous work, a very exciting score'.

BALALAIKA

Russian guitar-like instrument with a triangular body normally fitted with three strings, one of which is usually employed to supply the melody.

BALFE, *Michael William* (Born Dublin 1808, died Rowney Abbey, Herts., 1870)

Chiefly famous as the composer of *The Bohemian Girl*, which was a sensational success at Drury Lane in 1843, and of the **ballad** 'Come into the Garden, Maud'. Balfe enjoyed a successful international career as a **baritone** in his earlier years, impressing **Rossini** so much that he was engaged to sing Figaro in *The Barber of Seville* in Paris in 1827. He also appeared at **La Scala** and sang Papageno in the first London production of **Mozart**'s *The Magic Flute* in 1838. *The Bohemian Girl* is still revived with success, and there is a good CD recording under the direction of **Richard Bonynge**.

BALLAD

A word of many meanings derived from the Latin *ballare*, to dance, but any association with dance has long since disappeared. In Elizabethan times, ballads were usually verses based on sensational or scandalous news of the day, set to well-known traditional tunes. Old British ballads, particularly Scottish ballads telling of tragic or heroic tales, were of great interest to German writers and composers such as Goethe, **Schubert** and **Schumann**, while the 'drawing-room ballad' kept Victorian ladies and gentlemen supplied with romantic sentiments. *The Beggar's Opera* of 1728 was the first and most popular example of ballad-opera, a type of musical play interspersed with popular tunes of the day. Today the word ballad is applied to many popular songs, especially of the moody, sentimental kind.

BALLAD OF MACK THE KNIFE'

Most popular number from *The Threepenny Opera* (*Die Dreigroschenoper*), with music by **Kurt Weill** and lyrics by Bertolt Brecht, first produced in Berlin in 1928 with prodigious success.

BALLADE

A form of medieval French song; also the name given by **Chopin** to four **piano** pieces which have the character of romantic **ballads** of the heroic type. The title was also used by **Brahms**, **Liszt**, **Grieg**, **Fauré** and others.

BALTSA, *Agnes* (Born Lefkas, Greece, 1944)

Greek singer propelled into international orbit by **Herbert von Karajan**, who called her 'the most important **mezzo-soprano** of our day'. Studied at Athens conservatoire; she won the **Maria Callas** Scholarship which enabled her to study in Germany. In 1969 made her début as Octavian in *Der Rosenkavalier* by **Richard Strauss** at the **Vienna** State Opera. Since then has appeared in most of the world's major opera houses in a wide range of mezzo roles.

BANJO

Guitar-type instrument, perhaps of African origin, associated with slaves in the New World. There are usually five or six strings of which the thumb string (or chanterelle) plays the melody.

BARBER OF SEVILLE, THE

There are at least eight **operas** based on Beaumarchais's play *Le Barbier de Séville* (1775), but by far the best known is **Rossini**'s *Il Barbiere di Siviglia*, first performed in Rome in 1816. Figaro, a barber, is privy to everyone's secrets, and for a price he will fix pretty well anything for anyone. He manages to outwit the elderly and tyrannical Dr Bartolo, who wants to marry his young ward Rosina, and to arrange her union with Count Almaviva, who is quite ready to reward Figaro suitably for his pains. Famous numbers include Figaro's 'Largo al Factotum' and Rosina's **aria** 'Una voce poco fà'.

BARBICAN, THE

Arts centre in the City of London, opened in 1982. It is the home of the **London Symphony Orchestra**, and also houses the Guildhall School of Music and Drama.

BALLET MUSIC

The alliance of dance with music dates from the beginning of recorded history, and the form of theatrical dance which we call ballet is allied to music ranging from tunes of the tum-ti-tum variety to new creations by major composers.

This was also true of ballet in its earliest form. Political stability was the message promoted by elaborate entertainments combining dance, music and spectacle at the French court in the sixteenth and seventeenth centuries. As with the earliest **operas**, these were often based on legends of antiquity adapted to present the reigning monarch in a flattering light. What is more, the king himself often headed a cast of aristocratic amateurs: Louis XIV danced in court ballets for twenty years, appearing typically as the god Apollo. The king retired as a dancer in 1670 when his figure was no longer quite what it was, but by then he had made ballet a business for professionals by founding the Royal Academy of Dance in Paris in 1661.

The eighteenth century brought a movement towards the so-called *'ballet d'action'*, which aimed to tell a human story in a straightforward, logical way. The most important reformer, Jean Georges Noverre (1727–1810), was engaged to arrange dances for David Garrick at Drury Lane, and learned much from his 'realistic' acting style. In 1788 **Mozart** became the first great composer to write for the ballet when Noverre commissioned him to compose *Les Petits Riens* (*The Mere Nothings*), and in 1789 Noverre created a ballet which has remained very popular to this day – *La Fille mal gardée*, featuring peasant characters instead of gods and grandees. The original production was accompanied by popular dance tunes of the day. Meanwhile, another choreographic reformer, the Italian Salvatore Viganò (1769–1801), had commissioned a ballet score from **Beethoven** – *The Creatures of Prometheus* (Vienna 1801).

Ballet in the early nineteenth century, like literature, was preoccupied with exotic tales and landscapes bathed in moonlight. *La Sylphide*, staged in Paris in 1832, was the first 'romantic' ballet. The ballerina Marie Taglioni (1804–84) made her name by using the 'pointe' technique (dancing on her toes) to establish the ethereal character of the Sylphide. In 1841, *Giselle* – also a story of love pursued beyond the grave – was created for another great dancer of the period, Carlotta Grisi (1819–99). This had one of the first highly-developed ballet scores, by Adolphe Adam (1803–56). France remained pre-eminent in ballet for most of the nineteenth century. The Parisian Arthur Saint Léon (1821–70) invented a system of dance notation and commissioned **Léo Delibes** to compose the fine *Coppélia*.

Saint-Léon also worked in St Petersburg, and in the last decade of the nineteenth century Russia took over the leadership of the ballet world, thanks largely to the French-born choreographer Marius Petipa (1818–1910). It was he who provided **Tchaikovsky** with a detailed step-by-step brief for *The Sleeping Beauty* (1890), and two further Tchaikovsky ballets followed: *The Nutcracker* (1892) and *Swan Lake* (1895). These three works represent the finest flowering of classical ballet, with inventive dancing matched by superb music.

Michel Fokine (1880–1942) had a more open approach to dance technique. Influenced by the American dancer Isadora Duncan (1877–1927) who had visited Russia in 1904, he produced the dreamy *Les Sylphides* to music by **Chopin**, and was the chief choreographer for the season of Russian ballet presented by Serge Diaghilev (1872–1929) in Paris in 1909. Diaghilev gathered around him a formidable array of talent; his company created an artistic sensation in Paris and subsequently in London, and he commissioned much important new music. Among **Igor Stravinsky**'s contributions were *The Firebird* (1910), *Petrouchka* (1911) and *The Rite of Spring*. **Maurice Ravel, Manuel de Falla, Francis Poulenc** and **Serge Prokofiev** all supplied Diaghilev with ballet scores though Prokofiev's ballet masterpieces *Romeo and Juliet* and *Cinderella* came rather later (1938 and 1945).

Though ballet was used as an instrument of propaganda in the Soviet Union, Russia's schools continued to produce great dancers, a number of whom defected to the West. British composers of ballet music include **Constant Lambert, Sir William Walton, Sir Arthur Bliss, Benjamin Britten** and **Sir Malcolm Arnold.**

In the USA, meanwhile, the pioneering work of Isadora Duncan led to freer forms of dance being developed. Martha Graham (b.1894) engaged major composers such as Samuel Barber, **Aaron Copland**, Paul Hindemith and **Gian-Carlo Menotti** to create music for her. George Balanchine (b.1904) introduced Broadway to the word choreography with his ballet sequence 'Slaughter on Tenth Avenue' in *On Your Toes* (1936), while Agnes de Mille scored a significant breakthrough into the light musical theatre with her dream ballet in *Oklahoma* (1943). The music in both cases was by **Richard Rodgers.**

At the present time there is wide diversity in the world of ballet: on the one hand, the neo-classical creations of Balanchine and others, set to conventional music; on the other, highly experimental works which sometimes dispense with music altogether. But whatever happens, it is inconceivable that the age-old marriage of rhythmic movement and music will ever be completely dissolved.

Margot Fonteyn and Rudolph Nureyev in a Royal Ballet production of Tchaikovsky's Romeo and Juliet *in 1965.*

Daniel Barenboim: equally accomplished at the piano keyboard and on the conductor's rostrum.

BARBIROLLI, *John* (Born London 1899; died London 1970)

'Glorious John', as he was called by **Vaughan Williams**, was one of the most outstanding British conductors of his generation. He first made his mark as a cellist, but in 1924 began to conduct his own string orchestra. He conducted the Scottish Orchestra for three seasons in the early 1930s and was invited to succeed **Toscanini** as permanent conductor of the **New York Philharmonic Orchestra**, a post he held for five years. In 1943 he returned to become permanent conductor, subsequently conductor-in-chief, of the **Hallé Orchestra**, and his period of twenty-five years in Manchester was the core of his career. Dubbed 'the last romantic', his touch was perhaps particularly inspiring in large-scale works by **Bruckner**, **Mahler**, **Elgar** and **Sibelius** as well as by his friend Vaughan Williams. He was adored by Promenaders at the **Royal Albert Hall** for his direction of 'Viennese Nights', though his approach to

Strauss waltzes was latterly apt to be wayward. Barbirolli's second wife was the oboist Evelyn Rothwell, who continues a distinguished career as adjudicator and teacher. Knighted 1949; Companion of Honour 1969.

BARCAROLLE

A piece which imitates the song of Venetian gondoliers and the gentle rocking rhythm of their boats. One of **Chopin**'s finest **piano** works is the Barcarolle in F sharp, and **Fauré** wrote a series of thirteen pieces with this title.

BARENBOIM, *Daniel* (Born Buenos Aires 1942)

Israeli pianist and conductor of major importance. Début in London 1955, in New York 1957. Conducting début 1962. Much associated with the **English Chamber Orchestra** as conductor and piano soloist, for example in **Mozart**'s concertos which he has recorded complete. Conductor at the Bastille Opéra 1975–90. Music director of **Chicago Symphony Orchestra** from 1991. Married the cellist **Jacqueline du Pré** in 1967.

BARITONE

Male voice lying between **tenor** and **bass**. In **opera**, baritones appear frequently as fathers, villains and best friends of the hero.

BAROQUE

A word which literally means 'bizarre'. It was first used in 1746 to disparage a kind of music which at that time was beginning to go out of fashion. Nowadays the term, also used to describe architecture of the period, in no way suggests disapproval; indeed, the **Early Music** Movement has made the music of the Baroque era extremely popular. The era extends from about 1580 to about 1750. Drama is one of the most important strands in the development of Baroque music. The period saw the growth of **opera** together with its religious equivalent, **oratorio**, and a great development of instrumental music which led on to those essentially dramatic musical forms, the classical **symphony** and **sonata**. The new style of composition spread from Italy, and early baroque masters included **Gabrieli** and **Monteverdi**. In the central Baroque years (1640–90) opera became widely popular in Europe, while solo and trio sonatas were developed along with the **concerto**: the German Heinrich Schütz (1585–1672), the Frenchman **Lully** and the Englishman **Purcell** were all prominently successful. Between the years 1690 and 1750 the **key** system as we know it today was regularised. In Italy a school of virtuoso violinists and **violin** composers grew up, but the balance of influence began to shift to Germany. Among the great masters of the later Baroque period are Alessandro and Domenico **Scarlatti**, **Couperin**, **Rameau**, **Telemann**, **J.S. Bach** and **Handel**.

*B*ARREL ORGAN

Strictly speaking, a kind of automatic pipe-organ used in English churches from about 1700 in which pins fixed in a hand-rotated barrel brought various notes into play.

*B*ARTERED BRIDE, THE (Smetana)

Several times revised by **Smetana**, the **opera** is a tale of village life in Bohemia. Mařenka loves Jeník but is required to marry the apparently simple son of Tobias Micha, Vašek. Jeník is persuaded to renounce Mařenka by the marriage broker for 300 crowns – on condition that she marries Micha's heir! Mařenka is heart-broken until Jeník reveals that he is Micha's long-lost eldest son, so all ends happily. The Overture, Furiant and Polka from the opera are extremely popular.

*B*ART, *Lionel* (Born London 1930)

An East End lad who studied at the St Martin's School of Art before making a career as composer and lyricist. For Joan Littlewood's Theatre Workshop at Stratford, East London, Bart wrote music and lyrics for Monty Norman's *Fings Ain't Wot They Used to Be* (1959) and scored a triumph with *Oliver!* (1960), which ran initially for 2618 performances and is constantly revived.

*B*ARTÓK, *Béla* (born Torontál district, Hungary, 1881; died New York 1945)

Generally considered Hungary's greatest composer; also a brilliant pianist. Bartók chose to study in Budapest rather than Vienna, and in 1904 heard his first true Hungarian folk-song (as opposed to the gipsy tunes used by **Brahms** and **Liszt**). This led to many years of folk-song collecting, often in collaboration with his friend **Kodály**, in Hungary and other East European countries. **Folk music** was a major influence on Bartók's own compositions which nonetheless were increasingly modern and uncompromising in character. The one-act opera *Bluebeard's Castle* and the **ballets** *The Wooden Prince* and *The Miraculous Mandarin* were important early works, while a series of six string quartets is at the heart of Bartók's legacy. Three brilliant piano **concertos** reflect his mastery of the **piano**, while an interest in percussive effects found expression in the *Music for Strings, Percussion and Celesta* of 1936, and the **Sonata** for two pianos and percussion (1937). In 1943 he was commissioned by the **Koussevitsky** foundation to produce one of his finest and most accessible works, the Concerto for Orchestra. Bartók's early *Allegro Barbaro* for piano has proved very popular; if some of his other music still presents a tough challenge to the ordinary listener, it is worth a bit of a struggle to get to know one of the twentieth century's most admirable spirits.

*B*ASS

The lowest male voice, apt for operatic roles which require great authority, and also exploited for its comic possibilities. The bass clef is the lower of the two sets of five lines on which keyboard music is commonly written. 'Bass' is also short for **double-bass**, the deepest-voiced instrument of the string family.

*B*ASSOON

Bass member of the double-reed family, dating from the seventeenth century. Used for comic effect in, e.g., *The Sorcerer's Apprentice* (**Dukas**); can also suggest mystery and magic, as in the opening of *The Rite of Spring* (**Stravinsky**).

*B*ATE, *Jennifer* (Born London 1944)

English organist of high international reputation and great versatility. Some thirty recordings have been issued, including the complete organ works of Messiaen (1908–92).

*B*AX, *Arnold* (Born Streatham 1883; died Cork 1953)

Prolific English composer who, at nineteen, read W. B. Yeats's 'The Wanderings of Oisin' after which, as he put it, 'The Celt within me stood revealed'. Some of his best compositions, like 'The Garden of Fand', were inspired by Irish legend. Wrote much **piano** music and seven large-scale **symphonies** which are now arousing revived interest. The *Overture to a Picaresque Comedy, Mediterranean*, and film scores for *Malta GC* and *Oliver Twist* are among his more popular music. Knighted 1937. Master of the King's Music, 1942–53.

*B*BC

The importance of the BBC in the musical life of Britain in the twentieth century is difficult to overestimate, for the BBC has promoted much new music and been a major employer of musicians. The very first music broadcast was given from Savoy Hill by an **orchestra** of nine players in 1922, and **opera** relays soon followed. In 1927 the BBC took over the **Proms**, and in 1930 the BBC Symphony Orchestra of 114 players was formed, to be followed by other major orchestras in Scotland, Wales and the English regions. Music education and 'music appreciation' have been prominent in BBC output, and popular record-based programmes have introduced the public to a wide repertoire of enjoyable classical music. The Third Programme, inaugurated in 1946, together with its successors the Music Programme (from 1964) and Radio 3 (from 1970), has done much to extend the range of music available to the public. Music has also been of major importance in BBC Television. Between 1936 and 1939 the infant Television Service at Alexandra Palace produced some thirty operas, and in the years since the war a huge number of studio-based and other concerts, operas and **ballets** have been presented. Television has proved a perfect medium for documentary material about music, and on the lighter side quizzes such as *Face the Music* and *My Music* have proved very popular.

*B*EAUX ARTS TRIO

American piano trio, originally consisting of Menahem Pressler (**piano**), Daniel Guilet (**violin**) and Bernard Greenhouse (**cello**), which made its début in 1955. Isadore Cohen took over as violinist in 1968.

*B*ECAUSE'

Hugely popular **ballad** published in 1902. Words by Edward Teschemacher, music by Guy d'Hardelot

(pen-name of French song-writer Helen Guy, 1858–1936, after she married and settled in England).

*B*EECHAM, *Thomas* (Born St Helens 1879; died London 1961)

Outstanding conductor who had no formal musical training and taught himself to conduct. He used his considerable private means in the cause of the art he loved, founding the Beecham Symphony Orchestra in 1909, and shortly afterwards he began a lifelong association with **opera** at **Covent Garden** and elsewhere. Beecham was responsible for the first London appearances of Diaghilev's Russian ballet. He championed a number of living British composers, notably **Delius**, and created two further orchestras, the **London Philharmonic** (1932) and **Royal Philharmonic** (1946). Beecham's famous sayings (authentic or apocryphal) include the following: 'Good music penetrates the ear with facility and quits the memory with difficulty'; 'All Festivals are bunk. . . . Festivals are for the purpose of attracting trade to the town. What that has to do with music, I don't know'; 'The English may not like music but they absolutely love the noise it makes'; 'All that matters in a concert is for the orchestra to begin together and end together – in between it doesn't matter much'. No great admirer of antique instruments, he likened the sound of the **harpsichord** to two skeletons copulating on a hot tin roof. Knighted 1916. Companion of Honour 1957.

*B*EGGAR'S OPERA, THE *(John Gay)*

First produced in 1728, *The Beggar's Opera*, which made use of sixty-nine popular tunes, started a vogue for ballad-opera. It was thought immoral in Victorian and Edwardian times but was revived with great success in 1920. There are several other twentieth-century versions, including a reworking by **Britten** (1948) and *Der Dreigroschenoper* (see **'Ballad of Mack the Knife'**).

*B*EL CANTO

Italian expression meaning 'beautiful singing'. In 1858 **Rossini** is reported to have said of Italian singing: 'Alas for us, we have lost our bel canto.' He was referring to a smooth and elegant style of singing which required evenness of tone throughout the range and the capacity to deliver rapid display passages. Rossini's own **operas**, and those of **Bellini** for instance, call for a bel canto approach; by the mid-nineteenth century a bigger and more dramatic style of opera singing was required.

BELLINI, *Vincenzo* (Born Catania 1801; died near Paris 1835)

'Bellini's music comes from the heart and it is intimately bound up with the text,' said **Wagner**, and there is no doubt that Wagner, and **Verdi** too, were influenced by Bellini's mastery of long, flowing and beautiful melodies. His first major operatic success was in 1827 at **La Scala** with *Il Pirata* (*The Pirate*). It was the start of a six-year partnership with the librettist Felice Romani which in 1831 produced Bellini's masterpiece, *Norma*. The most famous aria is 'Casta Diva' ('Chaste Goddess'). Chastity was not a guiding principle in the handsome Bellini's own life: he had a prolonged affair with Giuditta Turina, the wife of a Milanese merchant, and the resulting threat of legal action drove Bellini to seek refuge in London. He spent his last years in Paris where his last opera *I Puritani* (*The Puritans of Scotland*) was produced in 1835.

BENEDICT, *Julius* (Born Stuttgart 1804; died London 1885)

After early studies with **Weber** and conducting and composing in Naples, Benedict settled in London in 1835. While musical director at Drury Lane (1838–48) he conducted *The Bohemian Girl* (**Balfe**) and *Maritana* (**Wallace**), the first two **operas** of the so-called 'English Ring'. Benedict composed the third, *The Lily of Killarney* (1862). He adopted British citizenship and was knighted by Queen Victoria in 1871.

BENNETT, *Richard Rodney* (Born Broadstairs 1936)

British composer and pianist who now lives mainly in New York. A brilliant **jazz** pianist, he greatly enjoys sessions with other expert jazz musicians as a contrast to the isolated work of composition. Bennett has written five **operas**, and many other vocal and instrumental works which combine modern compositional techniques with accessibility. His ability to assume different styles has made him adept at film scores: *Far from the Madding Crowd* (1967) and

Murder on the Orient Express (1973) were among his successes in this medium. *Jazz Calendar* (1964) was a successful and popular **ballet** score.

BERCEUSE

French word meaning 'cradle-song' or 'lullaby'. The most famous instrumental example is **Chopin**'s Berceuse for **piano**, Op. 57.

BERGANZA, *Teresa* (Born Madrid 1935)

Spanish **mezzo-soprano** famous for her interpretations (often accompanied by her husband Felix Lavilla) of Spanish and other songs; her agile and subtly controlled voice makes her the perfect **Rossini** heroine on stage, though her repertoire also extends to early works by **Purcell** and **Monteverdi**. Début at **La Scala** 1957 in Rossini's *Le Comte Ory*; at **Covent Garden** 1960 as Rosina in Rossini's *The Barber of Seville*.

BERKELEY, *Lennox* (Born Boar's Hill, nr Oxford, 1903; died London 1989)

Distinguished English composer who studied in Paris 1927–32 with Nadia Boulanger. Berkeley's music, which includes the **operas** *Nelson* (1953) and *A Dinner Engagement* (1954), is marked by civilised elegance. Knighted 1974.

BERKELEY, *Michael* (Born London 1948)

Composer son of **Lennox Berkeley**, who was one of his teachers, together with **Richard Rodney Bennett**. Also well known as presenter of music programmes on radio and television.

BERLIN, *Irving* (Born Temun, Russia, 1888; died New York 1989)

Unable to read music, and only able to play the **piano** in the key of F sharp, Berlin was perhaps the most successful American popular song-writer of the twentieth century. His father's death in 1896 forced him to start work at eight years of age, and at sixteen he got his first regular job as a singing waiter. In 1907 his lyrics for *Marie from Sunny Italy* were published, and in 1911 he cashed in on the craze for ragtime with 'Alexander's Ragtime Band'. Wrote first complete Broadway score in 1914 (*Watch your Step*); founded his own music publishing company in

BEETHOVEN

Ludwig van BEETHOVEN

1770	Christened in Bonn
1784	Assistant court organist in Cologne
1787	Visited Vienna; met Mozart
1792	Left Bonn for Vienna: studied with Haydn
1802	*Heiligenstadt Testament* acknowledged incurable deafness
1815	Became guardian of nephew Karl
1824	Triumphant success of Ninth Symphony
1827	Died in Vienna

Beethoven is music's great hero. Powerfully influenced by the ideal of human equality which led to the French Revolution, he became a symbol of the nobility of humankind. Ludwig's father, a musician in the Elector's household, was a notorious drinker; his hard-pressed wife died when she was only forty, much to the grief of the young Beethoven who adored her. Ludwig showed early musical promise, and at the age of fourteen became a salaried professional as assistant court organist.

When he was sixteen, the young Beethoven paid his first visit to Vienna and there encountered **Mozart** who remarked, 'Keep your eye on him; one day he will give the world something to talk about.' The boy was summoned back to Bonn, however, to attend his dying mother, and at the age of nineteen found himself virtually head of the family.

At this stage the first of a series of aristocratic friends came to the rescue of the young Beethoven; Madame von Breuning welcomed him to her home, and Count Ferdinand von Waldstein became an intimate friend. With introductions from Waldstein to influential people, Beethoven returned to **Vienna** where he lived for the rest of his life.

The young man quickly found his feet in the Imperial capital and took lodgings in the house of Prince Karl Lichnowsky where he soon became a privileged member of the household. At this time Beethoven was chiefly recognised as a pianist but he worked hard perfecting his craft as a composer. **Antonio Salieri** gave him lessons, as did **Joseph Haydn** who found the young man difficult to deal with: 'the Grand Mogul' he called him. Already Beethoven was well aware of his own immense potential as a creative musician. 'Power', he declared, 'is the moral principle of those who excel others and it is also mine.'

At the turn of the century the thirty-year-old Beethoven seemed assured of a brilliant future as a **piano** virtuoso who incidentally composed. But he'd begun to realise his hearing was not all it might be, and by 1801 he had accepted the fact that his growing deafness was incurable. Advised by his doctors to live quietly for a time in the village of Heiligenstadt, near Vienna, he came near to total despair. The famous *Heiligenstadt Testament* expressed his sense of social isolation and the conviction that his life was virtually over. In that moment of black despair, however, he found courage in the idea of resignation to his fate; from then on he would live only to create music.

Beethoven's determination to transcend his deafness marks the transition between his first period as a composer and the second, which spanned the years until 1815. Now his work was marked by an altogether new grandeur. A **ballet** score on the subject of Prometheus who brought fire (and inspiration) to the human race was the turning point. Hugely impressed by Napoleon in the years following the French Revolution, Beethoven composed the great 'Eroica' Symphony in his honour, and then, on hearing that Napoleon had declared himself Emperor, tore out the title-page in fury. Beethoven's only **opera**, *Fidelio*, was a heroic tale of resistance to tyranny. It failed at first but at its revival in 1814, not long before Napoleon's final overthrow at Waterloo, it was a triumphant success and confirmed Beethoven's position in the musical world as a hero in his own right.

Then a new problem arose which almost put a stop to his creative work for several years. Beethoven's brother died, making him guardian of his nephew Karl. Conflicts over the will led to endless litigation, Karl proved an increasingly awkward young man and a more unsuitable guardian than Beethoven, despite his love for his nephew, can hardly be imagined. For all the splendour of his music, he lived in conditions approaching squalor, antagonising servants and bellowing out tunes whenever they happened to occur to him by day or night. Fortunately for Beethoven, whose notorious eccentricities once got him arrested as a tramp, his friends never deserted him; but this was no adequate consolation for the grief he felt over young Karl who, in 1824, attempted suicide. 'No man', said the suffering composer, 'has a right to take his own life as long as he can accomplish one good action.'

In the final phase of his creative life Beethoven achieved an almost spiritual profundity. After five years of labour he produced the immense *Missa Solemnis* as a monument to his faith in a supreme creative being. Then there was the huge Choral Symphony with its setting of Schiller's 'Ode to Joy', an affirmation of hope for humankind which triumphantly contradicted the composer's own bitter experiences. The symphony brought a great storm of applause at its first performance in 1824 but the composer could not hear it; he had to be turned round to take a bow. The late piano sonatas and the final group of string quartets take us into regions remote from all earthly struggles.

Beethoven's own struggle with life continued until 26 March 1827 when he died of what may have been cirrhosis of the liver. Friends, it is good to report, were with him to the last, despite the chaotic conditions of his lodgings. Schools were closed on the day of his funeral and a crowd of twenty thousand gathered to escort the coffin.

A brief anecdote sums up Beethoven's character: one day Frederick-William of Prussia sent him a gift and an awestruck friend remarked: 'It comes from a King,' to which Beethoven quietly replied, 'I too am a king.'

Engraving of Beethoven based on a romantic portrait of the master by Stieler.

Favourite works

SYMPHONIES All nine are universally familiar and popular, notably:
No. 3 ('Eroica');
No. 5 – with its opening 'fate' theme;
No. 6 ('Pastoral');
No. 7 – which Wagner called 'the apotheosis of the dance';
No. 9 – with its choral finale.

CONCERTOS
(piano) No. 3 in C minor; No. 4 in G;
No. 5 in E flat.
Violin Concerto in D.

SONATAS
(piano) No. 8 ('Pathétique');
No. 14 ('Moonlight');
No. 23 ('Appassionata').
(Violin and piano) Op. 24 in F ('Spring');
Op. 47 in A ('Kreutzer').

OTHER MUSIC
Op. 18 (six string quartets); Piano Trio in B flat, Op. 97 ('Archduke'); *Fidelio* (opera); and the charming bagatelle 'Für Élise'.

1919 and in the twenties put on the Music Box Revues at his own theatre as a rival to the Ziegfeld Follies, to which he also contributed songs such as 'A Pretty Girl is like a Melody'. Berlin's marriage in 1925 was the cue for one of his most enduring songs, 'Always'. A 1933 revue, *As Thousands Cheer*, featured 'Easter Parade', and then came the series of Astaire–Rogers films. The Second World War years produced 'This is the Army, Mr Jones' and Berlin's all-time best-seller 'White Christmas'. In 1946 came the hugely successful *Annie Get Your Gun* followed by *Call Me Madam* (1950).

BERLIN PHILHARMONIC ORCHESTRA

One of the best **orchestras** in the world, the Berlin Philharmonic established itself with a festive concert at the reconstructed Philharmonie in 1888. This hall was destroyed in the Second World War and replaced in 1963 with the new Philharmonie, one of the finest modern concert halls. Hans von Bülow was engaged as the orchestra's first chief conductor; successive major conductors have been **Nikisch** (1895–1922), **Furtwängler** (1922–45 and 1952–4), and **Karajan** (1954–89). **Abbado** was elected artistic director (chief conductor) in 1989.

BERLIOZ, *Hector* (Born La Côte-St-André, Isère, 1803; died Paris 1869)

Berlioz's genius had to wait until the twentieth century to be fully recognised, and many of his works require massive forces in their performance, such as the ***Requiem*** (1837), which calls for four **brass bands** as well as a large chorus and **orchestra**. A performance of *Hamlet* by Charles Kemble's company in Paris in 1827 gave him a passion both for Shakespeare and Kemble's Ophelia, the Irish actress Harriet Smithson. The dramatic **symphony** *Romeo and Juliet* expressed his love for Shakespeare, as did his last **opera**, *Beatrice and Benedict*, while Berlioz's obsession with Harriet Smithson resulted in the autobiographical *Fantastic Symphony*, written before he had even met the actress. Berlioz experienced failure with some of his most cherished works: the opera *Benvenuto Cellini* (1838), the dramatic cantata *The Damnation of Faust* (1846) and *The Trojans at Carthage* (1863), the second part of his masterpiece *The Trojans* (part one, *The Capture of Troy*, had to wait until 1890 for a production),

though his **oratorio** *The Childhood of Christ* was a great success in 1854. Berlioz was also a remarkable conductor; he wrote a treatise on **conducting**, and another very important treatise on instrumentation which he described as the musical equivalent of colour in painting. Among favourite works by Berlioz are the *Roman Carnival Overture* (derived from the opera *Benvenuto Cellini*), the *Symphonie fantastique*, the 'Royal Hunt and Storm' from *The Trojans*, the 'Shepherd's Farewell' from *The Childhood of Christ* and the Villanelle from the **song cycle** *Nuits d'Été*.

BERNSTEIN, *Leonard* (Born Lawrence, Mass., 1918, died New York 1990)

One of the most variously gifted and vital musicians of the twentieth century, Bernstein was a conductor, composer and pianist of brilliance, and a charismatic musical communicator. In 1944 he took over a concert with the **New York Philharmonic** at short notice from **Bruno Walter**; he was that orchestra's sole conductor 1958–69, and subsequently 'laureate conductor for life'. His association with the **Vienna Philharmonic** led to a noble series of **Beethoven** recordings, and he also appeared frequently with the **London Symphony Orchestra** and the Israel Philharmonic. As much at home in **jazz** and show music as in **Mahler**, Bernstein's compositions range from the moving *Chichester Psalms* (1965) and *Mass* (1970) to the ballet *Fancy Free* (1944) and a series of **musicals**, starting with *On the Town* that same year and continuing through *Wonderful Town* (1953), *Candide* (1956) to *West Side Story* (1957). Bernstein's best-known **film score** was *On the Waterfront* (1954). *West Side Story* contains a succession of memorable numbers, including 'Tonight' and 'Maria'. 'Glitter and be Gay' is perhaps the best known song in *Candide*.

BINGE, *Ronald* (Born Derby 1910; died Ringwood 1979)

English composer of light music whose successes include 'Elizabethan Serenade' (1952) and 'Cornet Carillon' (1961). Also pianist and arranger, notably with the **Mantovani** orchestra before and after the Second World War. Largely responsible for creating Mantovani's cascading string sound.

*B*IRMINGHAM, West Midlands _____

Birmingham's musical history is of high distinction. The Birmingham Festival, which ran triennially 1768–1912, gave rise to **Mendelssohn**'s *Elijah* (1846) and several major works by **Elgar**, including *The Dream of Gerontius* (1900). The City of Birmingham Symphony Orchestra has had a succession of fine conductors, among them **Sir Adrian Boult** (1924–30), Leslie Heward (1930–43), Rudolph Schwarz (1951–7), Hugo Rignold (1960–8), **Louis Frémaux** (1969–78) and latterly **Simon Rattle**, appointed in 1980. The impressive Town Hall, built in 1834, was the setting of Birmingham's major musical events until the opening in 1991 of its Symphony Hall. Birmingham is also the home of the Birmingham Royal Ballet and of the D'Oyly Carte Opera Company.

*B*IZET, *Georges* (Born Paris 1838; died Bougival, near Paris, 1875) _____

If Bizet had written only *Carmen*, his place would be assured in the musical history books. After winning the coveted Prix de Rome in 1857, Bizet spent three happy years in Italy, later producing a **symphony** based on his Italian impressions called *Roma*. His first important **opera**, *The Pearl Fishers*, was given with little success in 1863 (though it does contain a duet for **tenor** and **baritone**, 'Au fond du temple saint', which is universally popular); *The Fair Maid of Perth* (the Serenade is very well known) fared better in 1866, but *Djamileh* (May 1872) was yet another failure. The same year brought the first performance of Daudet's play *L'Arlésienne* with Bizet's music; again the production had little success, though the score was recognised as a work of genius. After five months of rehearsal, *Carmen* opened in March 1875 to a very mixed reception. The story was widely condemned as too obscene for the stage. Bizet did not live to learn of the opera's triumph in **Vienna** in October that year; suffering from acute depression, he died after two heart attacks at his home in June 1875. The curtain had just fallen on the thirty-third performance of *Carmen* at the Opéra-Comique, during which the singer of the role, Galli-Marié, felt such foreboding during the card scene when she foretells her own death that she fainted as she left the stage.

*B*JÖRLING, *Jussi* (Born Stora Tuna 1911; died Stockholm 1960) _____

Swedish tenor who started his professional life at the age of six as a member of his family's Björling Male Voice Quartet. Member of Royal Swedish Opera till 1938, after which he was in great demand worldwide, notably at the **Metropolitan**. A limited actor, but endowed with one of the most beautiful voices of the century. Notable complete recordings of *La Bohème* and *Madam Butterfly*. His 'Nessun dorma' is incomparably thrilling.

*B*LACK, *Stanley* (Born London 1913) _____

Versatile English musician who was pianist and arranger with various dance bands in the 1930s, and was conductor of the BBC Dance Orchestra 1944–52; he also conducts leading symphony **orchestras** around the world. As a composer he has written over 200 film scores.

*B*LADES, *James* (Born Peterborough 1901) _____

Exceptionally creative English percussionist who supplied the sound of the gong apparently struck by Bombardier Billy Wells as the trademark of the Rank Organization films. Principal percussionist of the **London Symphony Orchestra** and professor at the **Royal Academy of Music**. Delightful lecturer who has worked much with the handicapped. Recognised and encouraged the talent of **Evelyn Glennie**. OBE 1972.

*B*LISS, *Arthur* (Born London 1891; died London 1975) _____

Universally known for the March from the film *Things to Come* (1936), Arthur Bliss had an interesting career as a composer, from avant-garde in the 1920s to Master of the Queen's Music in 1953. He was adept at providing music for ceremonial occasions, such as the Investiture of the Prince of Wales in 1969, when his antiphonal fanfares, sounded from the tower of Caernarfon Castle, made a striking impression. Bliss's brother was killed in the First World War, and Bliss dedicated to his memory the **oratorio** *Morning Heroes* (1930). The composer's compassionate sense of drama also found expression in three remarkable **ballet** scores, *Checkmate* (1937), *Miracle in the Gorbals* (1944) and *Adam Zero* (1946). Knighted 1950; KCVO 1969; Companion of Honour 1971.

Billie Holiday was a great jazz and blues singer till drink and drugs sabotaged her career.

BLUES (see Jazz)

The blues as a musical form seems to have originated among American negroes in the early nineteenth century as a means of expressing their frustration and despair. The blues became essentially a twelve-bar pattern, accompanying a three-line verse, with the third and seventh notes of the scale slightly flattened to give 'blue notes'. W. C. Handy popularised this kind of lament with 'St Louis Blues' and 'Basin Street Blues' just before the First World War. Bessie Smith from Chattanooga ('the Empress of the Blues') helped to give the form worldwide currency in the twenties and thirties, and among more recent artists Billie Holiday made a reputation as a singer of blues

as well as pop numbers. Alongside the commercial success of the blues there has been much research into its folk origins, and much interest in 'authentic' performance.

LA BOHÈME

One of the world's most popular **operas**, adapted by Giacosa and Illica from the novel *Scenes of Bohemian Life* by Henri Mürger and set to music by **Puccini**. It was first performed in Turin in February 1896 under the musical direction of **Toscanini**. The story is set in Paris in about 1830. A group of young artists and writers are struggling to survive in their freezing attic. A neighbour, the seamstress Mimì, comes to ask for a light for a candle and she and the poet Rodolfo immediately fall in love. The story concerns the ups and downs of their relationship, and that of the painter Marcello with his flighty girlfriend Musetta. Rodolfo and Mimì love each other deeply and when she dies of consumption in his arms he is heartbroken. The opera has many favourite **arias** and duets, from the famous sequence in Act 1 beginning with Rodolfo's 'Your tiny hand is frozen', through Musetta's waltz song in Act 2, to the philosopher Colline's farewell to his overcoat in Act 4. **Leoncavallo**'s opera *La Bohème* was produced in 1897, but has never found the same favour as Puccini's work.

BÖHM, *Karl* (Born Graz 1894; died Salzburg 1981)

One of the outstanding conductors of the century, particularly in works by **Mozart**, **Wagner** and **Richard Strauss**, who was a close personal friend: Strauss dedicated his opera *Daphne* (1938) to Böhm. His vintage period was at Dresden Staatsoper 1934–42; he was subsequently director of Vienna Staatsoper 1942–4 and 1954–6. Böhm's many recordings include all Mozart's **symphonies** and three versions of his **opera** *Così fan Tutte*.

BOLET, *Jorge* (Born Havana 1914; died Mountain View, California, 1990)

American pianist of Cuban birth who has the strange distinction of conducting the Japanese première of *The Mikado* (while he was on military service in Japan in 1946). A great interpreter of **Liszt** and other romantic composers, in the grand tradition of virtuoso pianists.

BOLSHOI THEATRE

Moscow's famous 'great' theatre (*bolshoi* means 'great' or 'grand'), home of world-renowned **opera** and **ballet** companies. The seating capacity of the Bolshoi, at 2000, is slightly less than **Covent Garden**, but the stage is half as wide again.

BONYNGE, *Richard* (Born Sydney 1930)

Started as accompanist and vocal coach to **Joan Sutherland**, whom he married in 1954. Conducted many of her operatic appearances, beginning with *Faust* in Vancouver in 1963. Director of Australian Opera 1976–84. Specialist in vocal music of the **bel canto** period. Among his recordings are several rarely performed operas such as William Shield's *Rosina* and **Balfe**'s *The Bohemian Girl*.

BORODIN, *Alexander* (Born St Petersburg 1833; died St Petersburg 1887)

Borodin's life was divided between science and music: he became a professor of chemistry in his early thirties, and founded the first school of medicine for women in Russia. Music had to take second place; indeed, Borodin said he could only get down to composition when he had the excuse of a cold in the head. Not surprisingly his operatic masterpiece, *Prince Igor*, was left unfinished – it was later completed by **Rimsky-Korsakov** and **Glazounov**, though Borodin did compose the exciting and very popular Polovtsian Dances in that **opera**. In 1862 (the year of his appointment to his professorship) he met **Balakirev** and became a member of the '**Mighty Handful**'; of Borodin's three **symphonies** (the third was unfinished), No. 2 in B minor has remained a great favourite. His tuneful and appealing String Quartet in D contains a Nocturne whose melody was used for the song 'And this is my Beloved' in the musical *Kismet*, created by Robert Wright and George Forrest out of Borodin's works.

BOSKOVSKY, *Willi* (Born Vienna 1909; died Visp, Switzerland, 1991)

Willi Boskovsky is chiefly remembered as the conductor of the New Year concerts of the **Vienna** Philharmonic Orchestra 1954–79, and also for the series of recordings of Viennese light music which he made with the same **orchestra** at that time.

Pierre Boulez: outstanding twentieth-century composer, conductor, and pioneer of new musical techniques.

Boskovsky joined the Vienna Philharmonic in 1932 as a violinist and graduated to **conducting**, which he often did in the Strauss manner, violin in hand. Boskovsky was also a fine **chamber music** player, founder in 1947 of the Vienna Octet, and leader of the Boskovsky Ensemble.

BOSTON SYMPHONY ORCHESTRA

Founded in 1881, its vintage period was 1924–49 under the direction of **Serge Koussevitsky**, who commissioned many significant new works. Concerts on the lighter side were inaugurated in 1885 and from 1900, with the opening of the Symphony Hall, they became known as 'Pops'. **Arthur Fiedler**, who took over the Boston Pops in 1930, made them world-famous through numerous recordings.

BOULEZ, *Pierre* (Born Montbrison, Loire, 1925)

French composer and conductor of major significance. Studied composition with Messiaen among others, and once described his compositional method as 'organised delirium': many of his works call for improvisation by the players. He has made notable recordings of works by **Debussy**, **Stravinsky** and many others, and conducted the centenary production of **Wagner**'s *Ring* at Bayreuth in 1976. Chief conductor of the BBC Symphony Orchestra 1971–5 and of the **New York Philharmonic** 1971–7. Since 1976 he has directed a Paris institute devoted to research into new musical techniques involving electronics and other ingredients.

*B*OULT, *Adrian* (Born Chester 1889; died London 1983)

British conductor whose gentlemanly appearance and minimal gestures on the rostrum belied a passionate involvement with the music in hand. A great interpreter of **Elgar** and other English composers, he was also a fine **Wagner** conductor, and undertook many new scores: in 1934 he conducted the first British performance of Berg's *Wozzeck*. He was the first conductor of the BBC Symphony Orchestra (1930–50) and provided inspirational leadership to the **London Philharmonic** at a time when it had recruited many new young players (1950–7). He was also an influential teacher of the art of **conducting**. Knighted 1957; Companion of Honour 1969.

*B*RAHMS, *Johannes* (Born Hamburg 1833; died Vienna 1897)

The third of the three great German Bs – **Bach**, **Beethoven** and Brahms – who dominated concert programmes in the first half of the present century, and a model of how to combine romantic ardour with classical discipline. The young Brahms went on tour with the Hungarian violinist Reményi in the course of which he met another Hungarian **violin** virtuoso, Josef Joachim, who was to become a lifelong friend and was closely involved with the creation of Brahms's glorious Violin Concerto. When Brahms was twenty a crucially important meeting took place with Robert and Clara **Schumann**. Schumann hailed Brahms as the destined saviour of German music; Brahms responded with devotion both to Robert (died 1856) and to Clara who remained his closest woman friend until her death in 1896. The high hopes expressed by Schumann, implying that Johannes was Beethoven's heir, weighed heavily on the young composer, with the result that he worked

for fourteen years on his First Symphony before bringing it out in 1876. It proved to be a masterpiece, as were the three other **symphonies** that followed in 1877, 1883 and 1885. Meanwhile, Brahms, a magnificent pianist, had established himself as a composer with the first of his two piano **concertos** (1859), with two **serenades** written for the **orchestra** at Detmold and with songs written for a women's choir which he created in Hamburg. In 1868 the *German Requiem*, written in the wake of his mother's death, established him as one of the leading composers of the age. He responded to the award of an honorary degree by Breslau university in 1879 with the popular *Academic Festival Overture*. In the last few years of his life, Brahms produced a final series of **piano** pieces which includes some of his most touching compositions.

*B*RAIN, *Dennis* (Born London 1921; died Hatfield, Herts., 1957)

British **horn** player who set new standards of performance on his instrument. **Britten** composed his *Serenade* for **tenor**, horn and strings for **Peter Pears** and Dennis Brain. Wartime experience in the RAF Central Band led to appointments as principal of the **Royal Philharmonic** and **Philharmonia** orchestras. He was killed in a road accident, driving home overnight from an **Edinburgh Festival** concert.

*B*RANNIGAN, *Owen* (Born Annitsford, Northumberland, 1908; died Newcastle upon Tyne 1973)

Loved and respected British **bass**, as much at home in **opera** as in Northumbrian folk-songs. **Britten** wrote several roles with him in mind including Noye in *Noye's Fludde* and Bottom in *A Midsummer Night's Dream*.

*B*RASS, BRASS BAND

Family of wind instruments formerly made of brass, but sometimes constructed of other metals. Usually the brass section of a symphony **orchestra** consists of **horns**, **trumpets**, **trombones** and **tuba**, sometimes with other additions. The typical instruments of a brass band are **cornets**, **flugelhorns**, saxhorns, **euphoniums**, trombones and bombardons; the **saxophone** (not strictly a brass instrument) is sometimes included. Brass bands exist worldwide; in Britain they began to come into existence in the wake of the

Napoleonic Wars. Early brass bands which still survive include the **John Foster Black Dyke Mills Band** (1837) and Besses o' the Barn (1853); in all some 3000 bands involving 75 000 players are thought to exist in Britain today. A spur to maintain high standards is provided by the competition system. The National Brass Band Championship, with a final at the **Royal Albert Hall**, attracts some 500 bands every year. Many 'mainline' British composers have written for brass band, including **Elgar**, **Holst** and **Vaughan Williams**.

*B*REAM, *Julian* (Born London 1933)——————

The **guitar** was not taught at the **Royal College of Music** when Bream went there in the early 1950s and, from his London début in 1950, it was Bream who largely created a British following for the classical guitar; in that same year he took up the **lute**, and together with **Peter Pears** did much to revive interest in Elizabethan lute songs. Among composers who have written for Bream are **Benjamin Britten**, Alan Rawsthorne and **William Walton**. He plays guitar duets with **John Williams**. CBE 1985.

*B*RENDEL, *Alfred* (Born Wiesenberg 1931)———

Austrian pianist, acclaimed specially for his **Haydn**, **Mozart**, **Schubert** and **Beethoven**. A fastidious performer, he gives wonderful master-classes and is the author of many perceptive essays on music. Honorary KBE 1989.

*B*RITTEN, *Benjamin* (Born Lowestoft 1913; died Aldeburgh 1976) ————————————

Britten's folk-song arrangements including 'The Sally Gardens', 'The Foggy Dew' and 'The Ploughboy', made for **Peter Pears** and himself to perform, brought universal popularity to Britten. He began composing at the age of five, and when he went to the **Royal College of Music** in 1930 he also developed impressive skill as a pianist which made him an accompanist of great distinction. Wartime work included the popular *Ceremony of Carols* (1942) and the *Serenade* for **tenor**, **horn** and strings (1943). In 1945 Britten's **opera** based on an Aldeburgh story, *Peter Grimes*, reopened **Sadler's Wells Theatre**, and established him as the leading British stage composer since **Purcell** (whose music Britten loved: the famous *Young Person's Guide to*

Members of the quintet SCO Brass.

the Orchestra is based on a theme of Purcell). Britten settled in Aldeburgh where, in 1948, he began the Aldeburgh Festival for amateur local talent as well as for great names in the musical world. It was for the tiny Jubilee Hall at Aldeburgh that many of Britten's subsequent operas were originally conceived; and 'church parables' such as *Curlew River* and *The Burning Fiery Furnace* were first performed in Suffolk churches. Works such as *Let's Make an Opera*, *Noye's Fludde* and *Saint Nicholas* bear witness to Britten's eagerness to work with non-professionals and to communicate with a wide audience, perhaps above all children. The *War Requiem*, a masterpiece of our time, was first performed in 1962 in Coventry Cathedral with the German baritone **Dietrich Fischer-Dieskau** as one of the soloists. It made a formidable impact: when the recording was first issued in 1963, it sold 200 000

The Maltings at Snape, near Aldeburgh: now, thanks to Benjamin Britten, a superb concert hall.

sets in five months, an unprecedented figure for a contemporary work. Life peerage, 1976, the first ever given to a musician.

BRUCH, *Max* (Born Cologne 1838; died Friedenau, near Berlin, 1920) _____

German composer chiefly remembered today for his very beautiful Violin Concerto No. 1 in G minor and *Kol Nidrei*, an adagio on Hebrew melodies for **cello** and **orchestra**. His other works include a number of choral works and three **operas**. Bruch was conductor of the Liverpool Philharmonic Society 1880–3, and of the Scottish Orchestra 1898–1900, and took pride in the fact that his *Scottish Fantasy* for **violin** and orchestra was based on melodies he heard during his British travels.

BRUCKNER, *Anton* (Born Ansfelden, near Linz, 1824; died Vienna 1896) _____

Austrian composer rarely represented in programmes of popular classics, not through any lack of melodic

appeal (Bruckner has plenty of that) but because of the sheer scale of his creations, especially the nine **symphonies** on which his reputation chiefly rests. Bruckner started out as a teacher, but his musical studies resulted in an appointment as organist of Linz Cathedral in 1855. He was regarded very highly as an improviser and was invited to perform on the new **Royal Albert Hall** instrument in 1871. Bruckner's last twenty-eight years were spent in **Vienna**, at the Conservatoire, and he lived to enjoy the success of his Eighth Symphony when it was performed under **Hans Richter** in 1892. 'I know of only one who reaches up to **Beethoven**,' said **Wagner**, 'and that is Bruckner.'

BRYMER, *Jack* (Born South Shields 1915) _____

British clarinettist, formerly schoolmaster, who suddenly achieved prominence when **Beecham** appointed him principal in the **Royal Philharmonic Orchestra** in 1947, an appointment Brymer held for sixteen years. OBE 1960.

BUGLE _____

Small signalling horn made of copper or brass, in Britain normally shaped to the key of B flat. The bugle as a means of conveying orders or messages originated in Germany in the Seven Years War (1756–63).

BURROWS, *Stuart* (Born Pontypridd 1933) _____

A schoolmaster until he won the **tenor** solo competition in the Royal National Eisteddfod in 1959, Burrows went on to achieve notable success at **Covent Garden**, the **Vienna** State Opera, the **Metropolitan** and elsewhere, particularly in **Mozart** roles. A popular singer, too, of ballads.

BUTT, *Clara* (Born Southwick, Sussex, 1872; died North Stoke, Oxfordshire, 1936) _____

British **contralto** of stately appearance (she was 6 feet 2 inches tall), who gave many charity concerts during the First World War. Identified particularly with 'Land of Hope and Glory', which she sang all over the British Empire, she also gave the first performance of **Elgar**'s *Sea Pictures* at the Norwich Festival of 1899, dressed, according to Elgar, 'like a mermaid'. Married the **baritone** Kennerly Rumford, with whom she frequently gave concerts. DBE 1920.

*B*UTTERWORTH, *George* (Born London 1885; died Pozières 1916)

English composer who met **Cecil Sharp** and **Vaughan Williams** while at Oxford and was an enthusiastic collector of folk-songs and dances. Folk-tunes found their way into the orchestral idyll *The Banks of Green Willow*, and the rhapsody *A Shropshire Lad*, suggested by the poems of A. E. Housman, has the feel of **folk music.**

*B*UXTEHUDE, *Dietrich* (Born Oldesloe *c*. 1637; died Lübeck 1707)

Danish organist and composer chiefly famous for his influence on **J. S. Bach**. Composed many works for voices and for **organ**.

*B*YRD, *William* (Born Lincoln 1543; died Stondon Massey, Essex, 1623)

The leading English composer during the reigns of Elizabeth I and James I, Byrd joined the **Chapel Royal** as joint organist with **Thomas Tallis**. Tallis and Byrd were granted a monopoly of music publishing by the Queen, and in 1575 they produced a collection of thirty-four *Cantiones Sacrae* (sacred songs), one each for each year of her reign.

C

*C*ABALLÉ, *Montserrat* (Born Barcelona 1933)

Spanish **soprano** of ample figure and amazing vocal powers. After twelve years at the Barcelona Conservatoire awarded gold medal 1954. Learned repertory at Basle and Bremen operas, broke through to stardom in concert performance in New York 1965 of **Donizetti**'s *Lucretia Borgia*. Soon regarded as leading soprano of her day in rare Donizetti operas revived with her in mind, as well as many **Verdi** operas and others by **Bellini**, **Mozart**, **Puccini** and **Richard Strauss.** Many recordings, including session with pop star Freddie Mercury 1988. Enchanting interpreter of Spanish song.

*C*ADENZA

Passage, often improvised in earlier times, inserted towards the end of an operatic **aria** or instrumental movement designed to display the virtuosity of the performer; from **Mozart** onwards, written-out cadenzas were often supplied by composers, or by leading soloists. Cadenzas are usually unaccompanied, but effective accompanied cadenzas are also found, for example in **Elgar**'s Violin Concerto.

*C*ALIPH OF BAGHDAD, THE (Boieldieu)

Adrien Boieldieu (1755–1834) was dubbed 'the French **Mozart**' by his contemporaries. A master of melody, he created a long list of theatre works, mostly in the *opéra-comique* vein. *La Dame blanche* (*The White Lady*) was prodigiously successful in 1825, but Boieldieu's name is now most often remembered through the lively overture to *The Caliph of Baghdad* (1800).

*C*ALLAS, *Maria* (Born New York; died Paris 1977)

Born Maria Kalogeropoulos of Greek parents, she adopted Greek nationality in 1966, and is now acknowledged to have been one of the most celebrated operatic **sopranos** of all time. She made her début in Athens as Tosca in 1941; this was to become one of her most successful roles, displaying great dramatic acting as well as vocal brilliance. After appearing at the Verona arena in Ponchielli's *La Gioconda* in 1947 she was soon in demand throughout Italy in 'heavy' roles such as **Wagner**'s Isolde in *Tristan and Isolde* and Brünnhilde in *The Ring*, but in 1949 she appeared at short notice in the florid **bel canto** role of Elvira in **Bellini**'s *The Puritans*. From then on she appeared with huge success in earlier Italian **operas** as well as those of **Verdi** and **Puccini**. She made her **Covent Garden** and New York débuts (1952 and 1954) in Bellini's *Norma*, one of her most celebrated roles, and generated wild enthusiasm in London until her last appearance as Tosca in 1965. The vagaries of Callas's private life attracted huge publicity and, as the years passed, vocal faults such as a certain unevenness of tone, a tremolo on high notes, and some harshness in the middle register became more marked. Nevertheless, Callas is remembered by those who saw her at the peak of her form as incomparably great. There are many recordings which recall some of her faults, and many of her outstanding virtues. Drama, rather than purity of line, was perhaps her chief gift.

CAMDEN, *Archie* (Born Newark 1888; died Wheathampstead 1979) ──────────

English bassoonist who enjoyed a playing career of almost sixty-five years and set new standards of performance on his instrument. After almost twenty years with the **Hallé Orchestra,** he joined the BBC Symphony Orchestra in 1933. Later he devoted himself largely to solo work until his eightieth birthday. Of his sons, Kerry (b. 1936) has followed his father as a bassoonist, while Anthony (b. 1938) is a leading oboist. OBE 1969.

CAMPOLI, *Alfredo* (Born Rome 1906; died Princes Risborough 1991) ──────────

Violinist who made his London début at the age of ten and achieved great popularity on radio in the thirties with his own salon **orchestra.** After 1945, using only his surname, he re-established himself in the classical repertoire with success, especially in **Mendelssohn**'s E minor Concerto.

CANON ──────────

Word meaning 'rule', used to describe contrapuntal composition in which a melodic line is exactly imitated after an interval of time in another voice or voices. The influential **Baroque** composer Johann Pachelbel (1653–1706) is chiefly remembered for his haunting Canon (and Gigue) in D for three **violins** and **continuo.**

CANTATA ──────────

Italian word meaning 'sung'. Used to describe many extended solo songs in the seventeenth century. **Bach** wrote nearly 300 church cantatas, as well as secular works such as the 'Coffee' Cantata and 'Peasant' Cantata using solo voices with organ or orchestra; later cantatas were short **oratorios**, e.g., **Elgar**'s *King Olaf*, **Britten**'s *Cantata Academica*, etc.

CAPRICCIO ──────────

Italian word meaning 'whim' or 'fancy' – caprice in French and English. Famous examples include **Paganini**'s Twenty-four Capriccios for solo **violin,** the Capriccio in B minor for **piano** by **Brahms**, the *Capriccio espagnol* by **Rimsky-Korsakov**, the *Capriccio italien* by **Tchaikovsky** and an opera by **Richard Strauss** called *Capriccio* (1942).

CAPRIOL SUITE (Warlock) ──────────

Six-movement **suite** for string orchestra (1926) based by Warlock on dances from Thoinot Arbeau's *Orchésographie* (1589). Peter Warlock was a pseudonym (another was Bulgy Gogo) adopted by Philip Heseltine (1894–1930), composer and scholar much interested in **early music**, a dual personality who veered from sensitive introspection to bawdy exuberance.

CARL ROSA OPERA COMPANY ──────────

Important British **opera** company devoted to performing opera in English, which began operations in Dublin in 1875 and came to an end with *Don Giovanni* in 1960. Founded by the German Karl August Nicolaus Rose, whose wife Euphrosyne Parepa-Rosa was his first prima donna, the company introduced a large repertoire of operas to a wide public throughout Britain and provided many British singers with otherwise unobtainable operatic opportunities.

CARMEN (Bizet) ──────────

Now universally popular **opera**, produced in Paris in 1875, with a story at first regarded as scandalous (see **Bizet**). Don José, an army corporal, falls desperately in love with a flighty girl employed at the cigarette factory in Seville. Appointed to stand guard over her, he allows her to escape, resulting in military disgrace. Carmen loses interest in Don José in favour of the bullfighter Escamillo and, outside the bullring in Seville (while Escamillo enjoys a triumph within), José stabs Carmen to death. Famous numbers include Carmen's Habanera and Seguidilla, José's 'Flower Song' and Escamillo's 'Toreador's Song'. Nowadays the opera is more often performed with the original spoken dialogue than with the **recitatives** added by Ernest Guiraud. *Carmen* was reinterpreted in twentieth-century terms in Oscar Hammerstein's *Carmen Jones* (1943) which was filmed in 1954, and in 1991 was successfully revived at London's Old Vic Theatre.

CARMINA BURANA (Orff) ──────────

Popular choral work by the German composer and musical educator Carl Orff (1895–1982), based on poems from a manuscript dated 1280 found in the

Maria Ewing as Bizet's Carmen at Covent Garden in 1991, with Luis Lima as Don José.

monastery of Beuron in Austria. The poems, in medieval Latin, old French and old German, celebrate the joys of bed, board and bottle, and the music is tuneful and strongly rhythmic. First produced, with mimed stage action, Frankfurt 1937.

CARNEGIE HALL

Andrew Carnegie (1835–1918) was born in Dunfermline and made a huge fortune in the USA. Famous for his benefactions, notably to educational causes, he provided most of the funds to build New York's Music Hall (1891), renamed Carnegie Hall in 1898. With a capacity of 3000, it is New York's largest concert hall.

CARNIVAL IN PARIS

Most famous work of the Norwegian composer Johan Svendsen (1840–1911). Svendsen also composed a famous Romance for **violin** and **orchestra**, among many other works, and was a distinguished conductor.

CARNIVAL OF VENICE

'Le carnaval de Venise' was the tune of the popular song 'O Mamma Mia'. Paganini wrote a set of variations on the theme for unaccompanied **violin**, and Chopin wrote a **piano** piece based on it called *Souvenir de Paganini*.

CAROL

Word derived from the French *carole*, which signified a dancing song in medieval times. Originally a celebratory song for no particular season, but increasingly associated with Christmas, as were the *noëls* of France from the sixteenth century. Early carols were largely of traditional or folk origin but, after Dickens invented Christmas as we know it, new carols began to be written and still are.

CAROL SYMPHONY

Well-known work, based on popular **carol** tunes, by Victor Hely-Hutchinson (1910–47). Born in South Africa, he became Music Director of the **BBC** (1944–7) and also wrote charming settings of nonsense verses by Lewis Carroll and Edward Lear.

'CARO MIO BEN'

'My Well-beloved'. Very popular Italian **song** probably by Giuseppe Giordani (*c.*1753–98), a Neapolitan **opera** composer, but often wrongly attributed to Tommaso Giordani (1733–1806).

CARRERAS, *José* (Born Barcelona 1946)

One of the triumvirate of singers who currently rule the **tenor** roost in the world's great **opera** houses and performing arenas. Together with **Placido Domingo** and **Luciano Pavarotti**, Carreras took part in the prodigiously successful 'three great tenors' concert from the Baths of Caracalla in Rome on 7 July 1990, the eve of the World Cup Final, which was televised worldwide. The concert raised funds for the singers' favourite charities, including

Enrico Caruso as the tragic Canio in Pagliacci. *In real life he enjoyed practical jokes.*

the José Carreras International Leukaemia Foundation. In his early twenties he became the chosen leading man of the distinguished Catalan **soprano**, **Montserrat Caballé**, and made his début at **La Scala** in 1975, appearing in the 1978 production of *Don Carlos* which marked La Scala's bicentenary. A notable partner has been **Agnes Baltsa**: they have sung *Carmen* together over 120 times. Carreras was Tony in the celebrated recording of Bernstein's *West Side Story*, conducted by the composer: 'incredible, this singer', was Bernstein's verdict, though they did not always see eye to eye in matters of interpretation. In 1987, at the height of a brilliant career, Carreras contracted leukaemia. With great courage he fought back and made a remarkable

recovery, returning in 1988 to sing Italian and Catalan songs before a vast audience in his native city of Barcelona. Since that time he has devoted a significant part of his time to fund-raising for his own Leukaemia Foundation to help other sufferers from the disease.

CARUSO, *Enrico* (Born Naples 1873; died Naples 1921)

Prodigiously successful Italian **tenor**. His early career included the first performance of Giordano's *Fedora* in Milan in 1898, and the following year he triumphed in *The Elixir of Love* at **La Scala**. After appearing with **Dame Nellie Melba** in Monte Carlo in 1902, he made his début at **Covent Garden**, where he appeared again 1904–7 and 1913–14, but New York's **Metropolitan** was really his theatrical home – he made more than 600 appearances there in nearly 40 operas 1903–20. Caruso was a legendary eater, who could consume an entire plate of spaghetti at one gulp. He was a great practical joker: Melba recalled how, on one occasion, Caruso bent low over her while she was playing a death scene in Monte Carlo, making a small rubber toy he held in his hand squeak in her ear. He was also a cartoonist of talent, who resented it when Mark Twain failed to invite him to a cartoonists' dinner: 'perhaps he knows me only as a tenor', he sadly complained. Caruso's ringing, seductive tones made him the first and, arguably, still the foremost recording tenor. Before his premature death from pleurisy, Caruso earned up to a million pounds from records, many of which have been reprocessed and reissued with great success.

CASALS, *Pablo* (Born Vendrell 1876; died Puerto Rico 1973)

Great cellist renowned as much for his humanity as his musicianship; he identified strongly with the cause of democracy in Spain, and in particular in his native Catalonia. From an early age Casals experimented with new fingering and bowing techniques, achieving unparalleled mastery of his instrument. His unique quality can be heard on many historic records, notably in **chamber music** for piano **trio** in his famed partnership with the violinist **Jacques Thibaud** and the pianist **Alfred Cortot**, which began in 1905. Huge international success enabled him to spend $320 000 on founding his own

The very model of a modern multi-talented musician, Vladimir Ashkenazy has long been a front-rank pianist and is now highly regarded as a conductor.

With its perfect acoustics, Birmingham's Symphony Hall is a major factor in the city's development as an important musical centre. It was opened in 1991.

The John Foster Black Dyke Mills Band pictured in 1992: top prize-winners since 1855.

orchestra in Barcelona; between 1920 and 1939 it gave concerts for workers and others. In 1936, under threat of execution by the Franco regime, he moved to Prades, a Catalan village on the French side of the border, and there he settled, giving concerts for the Red Cross during the Second World War and making it the centre of his own Festival in 1950 to mark the bicentenary of **Bach**, whose unaccompanied **cello suites** he had rescued from oblivion. The monks of Montserrat, so closely identified with the Catalan cause, perform some of the religious choral music written by Casals.

CASTRATO

Literally 'castrated', an Italian word for a practice which seems to have originated in Italy and was widely practised there and elsewhere in the seventeenth and eighteenth centuries, in order to preserve a boy's **soprano** voice.

CAVALLERIA RUSTICANA (Mascagni)

Rustic Chivalry, one-act **opera** by Pietro Mascagni (1863–1945) which won a competition in 1889 and was produced with fabulous success in Rome in 1890; often performed with Leoncavallo's *Pagliacci*, making a pair of operas referred to as 'Cav' and 'Pag'. The peasant girl Santuzza loves Turiddù, but he has abandoned her in favour of Alfio's wife Lola, his former love. Santuzza betrays Turiddù to Alfio, the two men fight off-stage and Turiddù is killed. Famous numbers include the Easter Hymn and the orchestral intermezzo.

CAVATINA

In eighteenth-century **opera**, a short **aria**, without the often customary repetition of the first section: 'Porgi amor' in **Mozart**'s *The Marriage of Figaro* is a cavatina. Joachim Raff's 'Cavatina' is an instrumental example of the form.

CECILIA, *Saint*

Patron saint of music, commemorated annually on 22 November. A Christian martyred probably in the second or third century AD, she was not associated with music at all until the late fifteenth century, after which she was often portrayed inappropriately playing an organ.

Playing Dvořák while smoking a pipe: no problem for Pablo Casals in Prague, 1937.

CELESTA

Keyboard instrument in which steel bars are hit by hammers, giving a bell-like sound. Patented in 1886 by Auguste Mustel in Paris, where **Tchaikovsky** heard it and later used it for the 'Dance of the Sugar-Plum Fairy' in his **ballet** *The Nutcracker* (1892).

CELLO

Short for violoncello, the bass member of the **violin** family. Descended from the bass violin, the modern cello originated in the late seventeenth century: it was usually played gripped between the knees, the spike which supports it today being a later addition. The cello is one of the most expressive of all instruments and has inspired a vast repertoire of music from the unaccompanied **suites** of **J. S. Bach** (rediscovered by **Casals**) to twentieth-century masterpieces such as **Britten**'s Cello Symphony (1963).

CHAMBER MUSIC

*I*f you are one of those who think the term 'chamber music' is forbiddingly highbrow, you are in good company. That no-nonsense Antipodean **Percy Grainger** insisted on calling his small-scale pieces 'room music'.

But Grainger's protest went largely unregarded and we are stuck with Chamber Music as the generic description of a very large number of works written over the centuries for performance by a few people in more or less intimate surroundings indoors. Resistance to the idea of chamber music should be quickly overcome, for it embraces some of the most beautiful and appealing compositions ever written, as my father discovered for one. He was essentially musical but had very little formal education in music or anything else. When he came to work in London, however, he was taken to one of the the free chamber music concerts given at a meeting house off Moorgate, and from then on he was hooked. After the venue was changed to Conway Hall in Red Lion Square, he took me along sometimes and I too became a convert.

I suppose the phrase 'chamber music' most often conjures up what Laurence Durrell described as 'the cool fern-like patterns of a string quartet'. But the string quartet – two violins, viola and cello – is no more than 250 years old, and the beginnings of chamber music can be traced back to the period of the Renaissance in Italy, when a great deal of music was written for cultivated amateurs to perform in their own homes.

In the period from the sixteenth to the mid-eighteenth century, three categories of music were recognised – for the Church, for the theatre and chamber music. The latter covered any secular music which might be performed in a private household, whether vocal or instrumental, solo or ensemble, including music for small **orchestra**. A popular form was the Trio Sonata; hundreds of examples have survived by such composers as **Corelli, Purcell, Vivaldi, Telemann, Bach** and **Handel**. Typically these were written for two **violins** with **continuo**

accompaniment provided by a **harpischord**, small **organ** or **lute**, and a **cello** or bass **viol**.

In the early eighteenth century composers began to experiment with music for strings without keyboard accompaniment, and in the mid-1750s **Joseph Haydn** produced his first twelve string quartets. He was to write eighty-three string quartets in all, including the famous 'Emperor' Quartet, Op. 76 No. 3, so-called because the slow movement is a set of variations on the tune Haydn wrote in 1797 as an Austrian national **anthem**.

Mozart declared that he learned from Haydn how to compose string quartets; he wrote twenty-three in all, dedicating a set of six to Haydn. However, Mozart composed a huge amount of chamber music for groups other than the string quartet; among his best-loved works in this genre are the Oboe Quartet, K370, and the Clarinet Quintet, K581.

Beethoven was another copious producer of chamber music. Of his ten piano trios (**piano**, violin, cello) the best known is the one in B flat, Op. 97, dedicated to the Archduke Rudolph, and therefore known as the 'Archduke'. Beethoven's ten **sonatas** for violin and piano include the so-called 'Spring' Sonata in F, Op. 24, and the 'Kreutzer' in A, Op. 47, dedicated to the violinist and composer Rudolph Kreutzer. The seventeen Beethoven string quartets range from the six delightfully accessible works of Op. 18 to some of the most profound music ever written, for example the Quartet in C sharp minor, Op. 131, and the last quartet of all, Op. 135.

The sociable **Schubert** turned out a great quantity of music for home consumption. Some of it is on the lighter side, such as the 'Trout' Quintet for piano, violin, **viola**, cello and **double bass**. Then there are the glorious melodies of the Piano Trio in B flat, D898, the deeper appeal of the String Quartet in D minor, and the great String Quintet in C, D956. Following in the wake of Beethoven's tuneful Septet, both Schubert and **Mendelssohn** enlarged the range of chamber music works by producing octets.

By this time the pendulum had swung from private performances by amateurs to semi-public or public appearances by professionals. The improvement of the piano coupled with advances in the standard of playing led to many chamber works involving the piano by Mendelssohn, **Schumann, Brahms, Dvořák** and others. But the string quartet was not neglected. Dvořák's 'American' in F, Op. 96, is one of the most tuneful works in the medium; and the Quartet No. 1 in E minor ('From My Life') by **Bedřich Smetana** is one of the supreme examples of the quartet as confessional. **Tchaikovsky**'s String Quartet No. 1 in D, Op. 11, has a slow movement whose theme became a popular song, and the Nocturne in **Borodin**'s String Quartet No. 2 in D went straight into *Kismet* as the number 'And This is My Beloved'.

Around the turn of the twentieth century **Debussy** and **Ravel** both produced string quartet masterpieces, and as the century has developed many other leading composers have found the medium rewarding, among them **Béla Bartók** and **Janácek, Shostakovich** and **Benjamin Britten.** More unusual combinations of wind and strings have also been devised, beginning with **Schoenberg**'s *Pierrot Lunaire* of 1912, and **Stravinsky**'s *The Soldier's Tale* written during the First World War.

Though chamber music may originally have been intended for performance in the home, it is now more generally to be heard on concert platforms. A twentieth-century example is **William Walton**'s *Façade*, first heard in the privacy of the Sitwell home in Chelsea in 1922 but subsequently often given in public. With its one or two narrators and six or seven instrumentalists, this is music of such complexity that a conductor is required – a long way from a kind of music-making which traditionally has been regarded as a 'conversation among equals'.

The Coull String Quartet performing at Packwood House, near Birmingham, 1987.

CHABRIER, *Emmanuel* (Born Ambert 1841; died Paris 1894)

Universally known for the rhapsody *España* (1883) which was inspired by a Spanish holiday and made his name as a composer; the *Joyeuse marche* of 1890 is hardly less well known. But Chabrier also wrote a number of operas, the best known being *Gwendoline* (1886) and *Le roi malgré lui* (1887), and a number of piano pieces which reveal advanced harmonic ideas. Francis Poulenc said the *Pièces pittoresques* of 1881 were 'as important for French music as the Preludes of **Debussy**'. Chabrier worked in the Ministry of the Interior 1861–80, and only decided to become a full-time composer after he had heard **Wagner**'s *Tristan und Isolde* in Munich in 1879. A lively wit often surfaced in Chabrier's music: the *Bourrée fantasque*, for **piano**, based on a dance from his native Auvergne, was, said Chabrier, 'rather amusing – I've counted 113 different sonorities in it'.

CHACONNE

Instrumental piece constructed over a repeated motif in the bass part ('ground bass'). A famous chaconne is the one which closes the Second Partita for solo **violin** in D minor by **Bach: Purcell**'s Chacony in G minor for strings is well known, and the last movement of the Fourth Symphony of **Brahms** is a passacaglia, a form very similar to the chaconne.

CHAILLY, *Riccardo* (Born Milan 1953)

Italian conductor, son of composer Luciano Chailly. Assistant conductor at **La Scala** when he was nineteen; conducted *Madam Butterfly* in Chicago when he was twenty-two. Subsequently music director (1982) of the Berlin Radio Symphony Orchestra; succeeded **Bernard Haitink** with the **Concertgebouw** Orchestra of Amsterdam 1988.

CHALIAPIN, *Fyodor* (born Kazan 1873; died Paris 1938)

Great Russian **bass** singer of outstanding acting ability. Closely identified with the title role of **Moussorgsky**'s *Boris Godounov*; created the title role in **Massenet**'s *Don Quichotte* (Don Quixote) 1910.

CHAPEL ROYAL

Not a building but a body of clergy and musicians employed to provide religious services for the king or queen. Dating back to the twelfth century, it consisted of thirty-two gentlemen and twelve children in Tudor times, and under James I it included musicians of great distinction such as **William Byrd**, **Orlando Gibbons** and **John Bull**. Another great period was under Charles II, who revived the Chapel after Cromwell and employed **Henry Purcell** as his composer-in-ordinary. **Arthur Sullivan** was trained in the Chapel Royal as a boy. The Chapel Royal still exists to provide Sunday services at St James's Palace and elsewhere.

CHARPENTIER, *Marc-Antoine* (Born Paris c.1645; died Paris 1704)

French composer whose importance rivalled that of **Lully** in late seventeenth-century France. One of his settings of the Te Deum, in D major, opens with a prelude which is familiar as the Eurovision signature tune.

CHERKASSKY, *Shura* (Born Odessa 1911)

Russian-born American pianist who plays in the tradition of the great nineteenth-century virtuosi. Tiny of stature and notoriously eccentric (he must always be led to the platform for his performance by precisely the same route he followed at rehearsal), he is a master interpreter of large-scale romantic works; his many recordings also include some enchanting miniatures.

CHICAGO SYMPHONY ORCHESTRA

Third-oldest symphony **orchestra** in the USA and one of the most outstanding, it was founded in 1891 by Theodore Thomas. The conductorship of **Sir Georg Solti** from 1969 brought the orchestra great international acclaim. Solti was succeeded by **Daniel Barenboim** in 1991.

CHILDREN'S OVERTURE, A (Quilter)

A sequence of nursery tunes, inspired by Walter Crane's *Baby's Opera*, composed by Roger Quilter (1877–1953) in 1919. Quilter was generous with his private income and helped to found the Musician's Benevolent Fund.

CHOPIN, *Frédéric* (Born near Warsaw 1810; died Paris 1849)

Chopin represents for many people the essence of romanticism, all sighs and soulful yearning, yet his

Frédéric Chopin, darling of the Romantic salon, admired the formality of Mozart and Bach.

own musical allegiances were quite different: he modelled himself to a great extent on **Bach** and said 'play **Mozart** in memory of me'. His youthful compositions were in the brilliant style favoured at the time, culminating in the two piano **concertos** in E minor and F minor, both written before he was twenty. The publication of Chopin's Variations on Mozart's 'Là ci darem la mano' had already prompted **Robert Schumann** to exclaim in print: 'Hats off, gentlemen, a genius'. In 1837 illness forced the cancellation of a secret engagement to the teenaged Maria Wodzińska: it was followed by Chopin's first visit to Britain and the beginning of his ten-year relationship with Aurore Dudevant (the novelist Georges Sand). After her break with him in 1847 Chopin's precarious health declined rapidly; when he died, 3000 people attended his funeral after a performance of Mozart's *Requiem* in the Madeleine church. Many of Chopin's most popular compositions have attracted nicknames, among them the 'Minute' Waltz, Op. 64, No. 1

(though it is hard to play it in less than a minute and a half), the 'Raindrop' Prelude, Op. 28, No. 15, and the 'Revolutionary' Study, Op. 10, No. 12. Chopin's Polish allegiance also found expression in his noble polonaises and numerous mazurkas. Among Chopin's larger works for the **piano**, the four Ballades have remained extremely popular, as have the Berceuse, Op. 57, and the Barcarolle, Op. 60; the Sonata in B flat minor, Op. 35, contains the famous funeral march, associated with the collapse of Chopin's engagement to Maria Wodzińska.

CHOPSTICKS

Quick waltz tune played for fun on the **piano** with the right hand held vertically, striking the notes with the little finger. Basis of a collection of pieces called *Paraphrases* by **Borodin**, Cui, Liadov, **Rimsky-Korsakov** and **Liszt**.

CHORD

Any combination of notes played or sung simultaneously; sequences of chords are the basis of the harmonic structure of music.

CHRISTMAS CONCERTO

In the late seventeenth and early eighteenth centuries there was a vogue in Italy for instrumental works intended for church use on or near Christmas Day. The best-known Christmas concerto is **Corelli**'s Concerto Grosso, Op. 6, No. 8.

CHRISTOFF, *Boris* (Born Plovdiv 1918)

Bulgarian **bass**, hailed as Chaliapin's successor and one of the great singing actors of the age. Became famous for his interpretation of the title role in **Mussorgsky**'s *Boris Godounov*, which he first sang at **Covent Garden** in 1949. Specially at home in the Russian repertoire, he has also been a fine **Verdi** and **Wagner** singer, making a notable success in the powerful monologue of King Philip in Verdi's *Don Carlos*.

CHROMATIC

From the Greek *chromatikos*, meaning 'coloured'. The chromatic scale consists of twelve semitones as opposed to the seven notes of the diatonic scale. Instruments which can produce all the semitones are said to be chromatic.

CHORAL MUSIC

*T*hese are the days of bring-it-and-sing-it *Messiahs*, *Elijahs* and **Verdi** Requiems – a great formula for making music if you happen to have a voice but no particular aptitude or training for singing beyond a desire to enjoy it. Choral Music, which I take to mean vocal music in which each harmonic line is shared by a number of voices, has long been a means of involving the relatively unskilled in the creation of satisfying sounds. This, of course, is not to ignore the multitude of amateur and professional choirs which have been in existence no doubt as long as music itself.

The Christian Church from its earliest days encouraged choral singing as a way of glorifying God: an earthly echo, if you like, of the celestial angelic hosts. It remains true that probably the best early training for singers is to be found in a cathedral choir school, though the opportunity was open until recently only to boys. Now, not before time, Salisbury Cathedral has started a pioneer scheme which offers a choir school education to girls.

In medieval times church music mostly took the form of **plainchant**, performed in unison by the members of monastic institutions. By the year 1400 or thereabouts, however, choral song blending a number of different melodic lines in simultaneous harmony (**polyphony**) was becoming widespread in churches and elsewhere. By the end of the fifteenth century, the now familiar division of a chorus into **soprano**, **alto**, **tenor** and **bass** sections had been developed, and certain forms of religious choral music had become established, such as settings of the **Mass** (including the **Requiem**, or Mass for the dead) and other ecclesiastical texts such as the *Magnificat*, *Te Deum* and *Stabat Mater*. Choral music in church at this period was always unaccompanied: if an **organ** was available, it was used in alternation with the choir.

Accompanying instruments were introduced in the sixteenth century, a golden age of choral music marked in England by the achievements of such men as **William Byrd, Orlando Gibbons** and **Thomas Tallis.** All of them produced masterly works for church use, including in Tallis's case an amazing **motet** in no fewer than forty parts – *Spem in Alium*. Italian masters of the period included **Giovanni Palestrina** and the Venetians **Andrea and Giovanni Gabrieli**. The Gabrielis experimented with motets using up to four choirs placed in different parts of the church: the effect in the great dark spaces of St Mark's Cathedral in Venice could be highly dramatic.

In the year 1610 **Claudio Monteverdi** composed the religious work *Vespers* which, thanks to the **Early Music Movement**, has become widely popular in recent years. From the early years of the seventeenth century, Monteverdi also introduced a choral element into that new-fangled invention **opera.** While motets, **anthems** and settings of the Mass continued to be written for religious use, choral writing henceforth found an increasing place in secular music-making. This was notably the case in the operas of French masters such as **Lully** and **Rameau**, and the odes written by **Henry Purcell** to celebrate royal occasions; nor were the **cantatas** of such men as **Telemann, Bach** and **Handel**, which often involved choral elements, confined to religious subjects.

Closely related to opera was **oratorio**, a means of telling (mostly religious) stories by musical means in the theatre or concert hall as well as the church. Devised in Italy around the end of the sixteenth century, the form was brought to perfection in Britain by Handel. It was mainly with the object of performing these works (above all *Messiah*) that the amateur choral movement came into being in Britain in the eighteenth century. The first of a series of massive Handel commemorations was held in London in 1784; **Joseph Haydn** was inspired by one of these events to write another staple of the choral society repertoire, *The Creation*. The **Three Choirs Festival**, bringing together a large chorus from the cities of Hereford, Worcester and Gloucester, had come into

The Tallis Scholars have inherited the tradition of church choral music.

existence as early as 1724, to be followed in 1768 and 1770 by the largely choral festivals of **Birmingham** and Norwich.

By the time the **Huddersfield Choral Society** (still one of Britain's leading large choirs) had been formed in 1836, **Beethoven** had endorsed the use of large choirs in the concert hall with his Ninth Symphony and Choral Fantasia, and soon afterwards (in 1846) **Mendelssohn** created *Elijah* for Birmingham. That was a work very much in the Handelian tradition, but Mendelssohn was also responsible for reviving interest in Johann Sebastian Bach, whose great choral works now found their way back into favour in Germany and elsewhere. Among other favourite oratorios in Victorian England were **Sullivan**'s *The Golden Legend* of 1886 and Sir John Stainer's *The Crucifixion* written the following year. The choral tradition in Britain has continued to be nourished by a series of important works, from **Elgar**'s *The Dream of Gerontius*, written as the twentieth century opened, through the *Sea Symphony* of **Vaughan Williams** to **Sir William Walton**'s *Belshazzar's Feast* and *Morning Heroes* by **Sir Arthur Bliss.** In other countries large choruses featured in works by **Berlioz, Brahms, Mahler,** **Stravinsky, Debussy** and **Ravel**, while Carl Orff's ***Carmina Burana***, written in the 1930s, has proved a worldwide winner.

As the present century has progressed, some composers have preferred to write for a well-trained chamber choir rather than for massive forces, and works by such people as Vaughan Williams, **Holst, Kodály, Britten** and **Poulenc** often feature as test pieces for choral competitions. Such major events as the annual Llangollen International **Eisteddfod** bear witness to a worldwide passion for choral singing in the late twentieth century. The repertoire extends way beyond the 'classical' mainstream: a male-voice choir from the Welsh valleys or a children's choir from Bratislava are just as likely to choose Negro **spirituals** or folk-song arrangements for their programmes as works by the great composers.

Choral music, in fact, whether performed by massive forces or a small carefully selected group, is the music, you might say, of human-kind.

Muzio Clementi, Mozart's teenage keyboard rival. Later he became a piano-maker and Beethoven's publisher.

CHUNG, *Kyung-Wha* (Born Seoul 1948)

Korean violinist, first member of a highly talented family to make a major international reputation. In 1967 won Leventritt Award in USA jointly with **Pinchas Zukerman**. Plays **Beethoven**'s triple concerto and trios with her sister, the cellist Myung-Wha Chung (born 1944), and brother, pianist Myung-Whun Chung (born 1953). Myung-Whun Chung now conducts, and was appointed to succeed **Daniel Barenboim** at the Bastille Opéra in Paris in 1989.

CILEA, *Francesco* (Born Palmi 1866; died Varazze 1950)

His opera *L'Arlesiana* (1897), based on the play by Daudet for which **Bizet** wrote famous incidental music, contains a beautiful **aria**, the 'Lamento di Federico', which helped to make the young **Caruso** famous; *Adriana Lecouvreur* (1902) includes a lovely aria for the actress heroine of the piece, 'Io son l'umile ancella' ('I am the humble handmaid').

CLAQUE

A group of people who are paid (usually by leading singers) to applaud in certain opera houses and concert halls. The practice is happily extinct in Britain but survives at the **Metropolitan** in New York and some leading houses in continental Europe including the **Vienna** State Opera and **La Scala.**

CLARINET

Single-reed woodwind instrument with cylindrical bore invented around 1690 but subsequently much improved, notably by the application to the clarinet of the new system of keywork and fingering devised for the flute by Theobald Boehm (1794–1881). The clarinet family is extensive, but the soprano instrument pitched in the key of B flat is the most widely used today.

CLASSICAL MUSIC

The term 'classical music' is often used to describe the whole range of serious music, but it really only should be applied to the period between about 1750 and 1830. The Classical period in music was preceded by the **Baroque** and followed by the **Romantic**, though all such labels are apt to be arbitrary and a matter of convenience.

CLASSIC FM

Radio station specialising in classical music. It began broadcasting 7 September 1992 and soon enjoyed a widespread public response.

CLAVICHORD

Small keyboard instrument in which the strings are made to sound when struck by a metal 'tangent'. Invented in the early fifteenth century, it was in common use in the home until the arrival of the **piano.**

CLEMENTI, *Muzio* (Born Rome 1752; died Evesham, Worcs., 1832)

English pianist, composer, publisher and piano-maker of Italian birth. At the age of fourteen he was adopted by an English traveller, Peter Beckford, who 'bought Clementi of his father for seven years' and brought him home to Dorset. There the boy studied and composed and, once free of the Beckford connection, began life as a touring virtuoso: in 1781 in Vienna, the Emperor Leopold II staged a keyboard contest between Clementi and **Mozart**. He went into business as a music publisher and **piano** manufacturer, subsequently touring Europe to promote his wares as well as his own keyboard and orchestral compositions. In 1807 he entered into a publishing agreement with **Beethoven.** Clementi was subsequently revered (not quite accurately) as 'the father of the pianoforte'; his studies (*Gradus ad Parnassum*) and his 100 piano sonatas remain important in the development of piano technique.

CLEVELAND ORCHESTRA

Important American symphony orchestra founded in 1918 in the city of Cleveland, Ohio. Principal conductors of the orchestra have included the Hungarian-born **George Szell**, who was in charge 1946–70 and brought it great international renown, and Lorin Maazel.

CLOCHES DE CORNEVILLE, LES (Planquette)

Operetta (1877) by Robert Planquette (1848–1903) whose overture remains very popular. The story is built around the legend that the bells of the village of Corneville in Normandy will only ring out again when the rightful lord of the manor returns to his property. The success of the work was such that Planquette was able to build himself a villa in Normandy which he gratefully named 'Les Cloches'.

COATES, Eric (Born Hucknall, Notts., 1886; died Chichester 1957)

One of the most enduringly popular of English composers of light music. Works which continue to be heard often include the 'Three Bears' Fantasy of 1926, the 'London Bridge' March (1934), the 'Dambusters' March written for the film of that name in 1955, and the 'Three Elizabeths' Suite (1944). But all his achievements were eclipsed by the runaway success of the 'Knightsbridge' March from the **London Suite** of 1933. It was chosen as the signature tune of the **BBC**'s radio magazine programme *In Town Tonight*, and within two weeks 20 000 enquiries about it had been received at Broadcasting House.

CODA

Italian word meaning 'tail', applied to the concluding passage of a piece of music which may or may not have an integral connection with the preceding material.

COHEN, Harriet (Born London 1895; died London 1967)

English pianist famous for her playing of **Bach**, and of twentieth-century composers; her close friend **Sir Arnold Bax** wrote a number of works for her. CBE 1938.

COHEN, Robert (Born London 1959)

One of the leaders of a remarkable generation of British cellists. Son of violinist Raymond Cohen and pianist Anthya Rael, Robert made his London solo début at the age of twelve.

COLERIDGE-TAYLOR, Samuel (Born London 1875; died Croydon 1912)

Brought up in near-poverty by his English mother after his father, a doctor from Sierra Leone, decided to return to Africa, Samuel Coleridge-Taylor gained the patronage of Colonel Walters of the Royal West Surrey Regiment, who paid for the boy to go to the **Royal College of Music**. There in 1898 his setting of Longfellow's *Hiawatha's Wedding Feast* created a sensation, and the Hiawatha trilogy was given a run of large-scale performances in the **Royal Albert Hall** every year from 1924 to 1939. Next to *Hiawatha*, with its beautiful **tenor** solo 'Onaway, awake beloved', the *Petite Suite de Concert* (1910) is perhaps Coleridge-Taylor's best-remembered composition.

'COLONEL BOGEY' (Alford)

Best-known march (1914) of Kenneth Alford, the pen name (his mother's maiden name) of Frederick Joseph Ricketts (1881–1945). The stirring tune of Colonel Bogey was whistled to great effect in **Malcolm Arnold**'s arrangement for the film *The Bridge on the River Kwai* (1957).

COLORATURA

Word derived from the German *Koloratur* (colouring), describing decorative ornamentation in singing, whether written or improvised. Most often applied to soprano voices.

COMPACT DISC

Mode of presenting recorded material on a disc 4.7 inches (approx. 12 centimetres) in diameter, covered with acrylic plastic to prevent damage. The system was pioneered by Philips and Sony and introduced to the market in 1983. A small, high-powered laser directs an infra-red light on to the rotating disc, reading sound signals expressed in binary code from billions of microscopic pits on the surface of the disc. These are arranged in a spiral 2.5 miles (4 kilometres) long. This technology eliminates the hiss and other unwanted surface noises associated with older forms of recording. A decade after the introduction of compact discs, mini-disc systems are now being offered. These can be used for recording as well as playback and in time may rival the compact disc in popularity.

CONCERTGEBOUW

The main concert hall of Amsterdam, built in 1888, home of the magnificent Royal Concertgebouw Orchestra. The **orchestra** became internationally famous under the direction 1895–1945 of William Mengelberg, and continues to enjoy a high reputation under his successors who have included Eduard van Beinum (1945–59) and **Bernard Haitink** (1961–88).

CONCERTINA

Small instrument with bellows opened and closed by the hands. It has hexagonal ends fitted with buttons to activate the small metal reeds which make the notes. The English concertina was invented by Charles Wheatstone (1802–75).

CONCERTO

Word now commonly understood to mean a work in which a solo instrument or instruments is accompanied by orchestra. Two main types of concerto developed in the seventeenth century, for church and secular use ('concerto da chiesa', which was serious and to some extent solemn, and 'concerto da camera', which often meant a suite of dances); these could involve voices or instruments or both. In the early eighteenth century the 'concerto grosso' was developed, most famously by **Corelli** and **Handel**, for a group of solo instruments with orchestral accompaniment. **Bach**'s Brandenburg Concertos were of this type, but Bach also developed the solo concerto as we know it today. Most concertos consist of three movements, quick-slow-quick, but there are many exceptions.

CONCIERTO DE ARANJUEZ (Rodrigo)

The world's most famous **guitar** concerto written in 1939 by the Spanish composer Joaquín Rodrigo (b. 1901), blind from the age of three. He also arranged the work for harp. The music evokes the courtly elegance of old Spain.

CONDUCTING

Means of directing a performance involving a number of performers by use of gesture, with or without a small stick or baton. In the fifteenth century the Sistine Chapel choir was controlled by a man with a roll of paper called a *sol-fah*, and in 1687 **Lully** died of gangrene after striking himself on the foot with the long staff he used to beat time on the floor, but most musical performances were directed from the keyboard or by the leading violinist until the early nineteenth century. **Beethoven**, it seems, used a baton. **Berlioz** was one of the first to conduct from a full score, instead of the first violin part, and Ludwig Spohr (1784–1859) added cue letters to scores to aid rehearsal. **Wagner** was perhaps the first conductor to become famous for interpretive genius in his own and other people's music, and he was succeeded by other great composer–conductors, notably **Richard Strauss** and **Mahler**. The good conductor must have total knowledge of the work in hand and be able, through clarity of gesture and force of personality, to convey his or her intentions to all involved in the performance. Seasoned players are quick to see through conductors who do not know their business.

CONSORT

John Bullokar's *English Expositor* (1616) defines a consort as 'a company of Musitions together'; they could consist of voices or instruments or both.

CONTINUO

Abbreviation for 'basso continuo' (literally 'continuous bass'), a type of accompaniment most frequently associated with **Baroque** music. The **bass** line is often supplied by an instrument such as a **cello** or **bassoon**, while a keyboard player fills in the harmonic structure on the basis of figured indications.

CONTRALTO

The lowest type of female voice, generally of a rich tonal quality. In the 16th century the abbreviation 'contr'alto' was sometimes used to describe the male 'contratenor altus' (high countertenor).

COOPER, *Imogen* (Born London 1949)

English pianist, daughter of critic and music author Martin Cooper. Studied at Paris Conservatoire and with **Alfred Brendel**; won **Mozart** Prize in 1969.

COOPER, *Joseph* (Born Bristol 1912)

Pianist taught by Egon Petri and **Claudio Arrau** who turned with great success to lecturing and broadcasting. He was for many years the genial host of BBC's *Face the Music*.

COPLAND, *Aaron* (Born Brooklyn, New York, 1900; died Westchester, New York, 1990)

Copland was the son of Russian Jews who emigrated to America. After studies in Paris with the famous Nadia Boulanger, Copland returned home to write extremely avant-garde music. His Symphony for Organ and Orchestra (1925) was daringly modern but, as time passed, Copland, who is widely regarded as the first 'great' American composer, decided he wanted to reach a wider public without debasing his style. This resulted in such enduringly enjoyable works as *El Salón México*, inspired by Mexican popular tunes, *A Lincoln Portrait* (1942), and a series of **ballet**s, *Billy the Kid* (1938), *Rodeo* (1942), and *Appalachian Spring* (1944), which won him the Pulitzer Prize. The Third Symphony (1946) and the opera *The Tender Land* also won critical acclaim.

COR ANGLAIS

Tenor member of the **oboe** family, with the reed inserted in a bent metal tube; the instrument frequently has a bulbous end. It has a plaintive voice, displayed to great effect in **Sibelius**'s *The Swan of Tuonela*.

CORELLI, *Arcangelo* (Born Fusignano 1653; died Rome 1713)

Corelli won international fame as a violinist and composer. He spent most of his life in Rome, where he greatly flourished and died a rich man with an extensive art collection. The rapid growth of music publishing in his lifetime brought Corelli's church and chamber **sonatas** wide currency and his twelve concerti grossi (including the **Christmas Concerto**) were very influential.

CORNET

Valved brass instrument, with a sound somewhere between **trumpet** and **horn**, of great importance in brass and military bands and capable of the utmost brilliance and beauty of tone.

CORTOT, *Alfred* (Born Lyon 1877; died Lausanne 1962)

French musician, famous for his interpretations of **Chopin**'s piano music and as the pianist member of the finest **trio** of the day, with violinist **Jacques Thibaud** and cellist **Pablo Casals**. The trio was active 1905–44 and there are many recordings.

COTRUBAS, *Ileana* (Born Galati 1939)

Among the roles in which this Romanian **soprano** excelled were Tatyana in **Tchaikovsky**'s *Eugene Onegin*, Violetta in *La Traviata*, Gilda in *Rigoletto* and Mimì in *La Bohème*.

COUNTERPOINT

Word derived from the Latin *punctus contra punctus*, point against point. In music it means setting melodic lines of equal interest against each other.

COUNTERTENOR

High male voice much used in music of the Renaissance and reintroduced in the twentieth century thanks to the talent of **Alfred Deller** and his successors.

COUPERIN, *François* (Born Paris 1668; died Paris 1733)

Most brilliant member of a distinguished family of French musicians, hence known as 'Couperin le Grand' (Couperin the Great). He occupied a position of high importance at court, producing for the king's entertainment a series of *Concerts royaux* (royal suites) which are among his best-known works.

Couperin created some 230 pieces for the harpsichord, many with descriptive titles: 'Le Rossignol-en-amour' ('The Nightingale in Love'), 'Les petits Moulins-à-vent' ('The Little Windmills') and 'Le Moucheron' ('The Gnat') are among the best known.

COVENT GARDEN

In 1732, on the site of a former convent garden, John Rich, who had made a fortune with John Gay from *The Beggar's Opera*, built a new theatre; three of **Handel**'s operas were produced there, but in 1808 it was destroyed by fire. Its successor, which became the Royal Italian Opera in 1847, met a similar fate in 1856. Frederick Gye opened the present theatre in 1858. It acquired its present title, the Royal Opera House, Covent Garden, in 1892, and is now the home of the Royal Ballet as well as the Royal Opera.

COWARD, *Noël* (Born Teddington 1899; died Jamaica 1973)

Without any formal music training, Coward started composing at fifteen and showed amazing ability to create memorable tunes and piquant harmonies. Coward's style as a performer of his own material was literally inimitable, but many of his satirical and sentimental numbers have survived him. 'Mad Dogs and Englishmen' and 'The Stately Homes of England' may be very much of their period but their wit is still enjoyable, while 'Some Day I'll Find You' and 'I'll See You Again' continue to haunt us.

CRAIG, *Charles* (Born London 1920)

British **tenor** who, as a chorister at **Covent Garden**, was spotted by **Sir Thomas Beecham** who paid for his training for two years. He recorded the title role in **Verdi**'s *Otello* in English in 1983.

CREED

There have been innumerable settings of the Christian creed over the centuries, but the one in the second liturgy by the Russian composer Alexander Grechaninov (1864–1956) is specially famous.

CRESPIN, *Régine* (Born Marseilles 1927)

French **soprano** who in the 1960s made an outstanding recording of the **song cycle** *Les Nuits d'Été* by **Berlioz**. Achieved international fame in

Wagner operas; also, notably, in French roles such as Dido in *The Trojans* by Berlioz.

CROOKS, *Richard* (Born Trenton, New Jersey, 1900; died Portola Valley, California, 1972)

American **tenor** who acquired a popular following similar to that of **John McCormack** for his singing of popular ballads, often of a religious type, such as 'The Holy City', 'The Star of Bethlehem' and 'Nazareth'. He also enjoyed an operatic career which began in Hamburg in 1927 and continued mainly at the **Metropolitan** in New York until 1946.

CROSS, *Joan* (Born London 1900)

A student of **Gustav Holst**, Joan Cross played a significant role in the development of **opera** in English. She was principal **soprano** of **Sadler's Wells** Opera 1931–46 and directed the company 1943–5. In 1948 with Anne Wood she founded what was to become the National School of Opera. Closely associated with **Benjamin Britten** and the English Opera Group, Britten composed several roles with her in mind, including Ellen Orford in *Peter Grimes* and Elizabeth I in *Gloriana*. CBE 1951.

CRUCIFIXION, THE (Stainer)

Oratorio, first performed at St Marylebone Church, London, in 1887, which became immensely popular in late Victorian and Edwardian times. The composer, Sir John Stainer (1840–1901), was a notable organist of St Paul's Cathedral and a leading figure in the Victorian musical establishment.

CRYSTAL PALACE

The world's first prefabricated building, the Crystal Palace, was designed by Joseph Paxton and erected in Hyde Park for the Great Exhibition of 1851. In 1854 the building was dismantled and re-erected at Sydenham in South London where, from 1855 to 1901, it housed a famous, adventurous series of Saturday evening concerts under the direction of August Manns. From 1859 to 1912 the Handel Festival was held in the Crystal Palace every three years. The Palace burned down in 1936.

CUCKOO, THE (Daquin)

Written in 1735 for harpsichord, *The Cuckoo (Le Coucou)* is much the best-known composition of

Louis-Claude Daquin (1694–1772). A child prodigy, he became organist of the French Chapel Royal in 1739.

CURZON, *Clifford* (Born London 1907; died Lucerne 1982)

British pianist whose scrupulous attention to detail and impeccable sense of style earned him a very high reputation with the public and fellow-professionals, especially perhaps as a **Mozart** and **Schubert** interpreter. Studied in Berlin with **Artur Schnabel** and in Paris with **Wanda Landowska** and Nadia Boulanger. Knighted 1977.

CYMBALS

Modern orchestral cymbals are usually made of a copper and tin alloy; a pair of these plate-shaped discs are commonly clashed together to produce a bright, percussive sound.

CZECH PHILHARMONIC ORCHESTRA

Formerly the orchestra of Prague National Opera, the Czech Philharmonic started its independent life in 1901 and achieved international fame under the conductorship (1919–41) of Václav Talich.

CZERNY, *Karl* (Born Vienna 1791; died Vienna 1857)

Best known to generations of piano students as the composer of thousands of studies for their instrument, Czerny was himself one of the finest pianists of his time. Czerny dedicated his *Complete Theoretical and Practical Piano Forte School*, Op. 500, to Queen Victoria – he had played piano duets with her in 1837.

D

'DANCE OF THE HOURS' (Ponchielli)

Ballet episode, concerned with the conflict between darkness and light, which occurs during a ball scene in the opera *La Gioconda* (1876) by Amilcare Ponchielli (1834–86).

DAVIES, *Peter Maxwell* (Born Manchester 1934)

After early studies in Manchester he spent three years as Head of Music at Cirencester Grammar School (1959–62). This awakened an interest in working with young people which has remained important. Davies created his own performance group, the Fires of London, in 1970. Since 1970 Davies has lived for much of his time in Orkney; the chamber opera *The Martyrdom of St Magnus* is one of many works which draw on Orcadian themes. Knighted 1987.

DAVIES, *Walford* (Born Oswestry 1869; died Wrington, Somerset, 1941)

Composer of the RAF March Past, written when he was Director of Music to the RAF from 1917, and of the 'Solemn Melody', composed while he was organist and choirmaster of the Temple Church (1898–1928). Knighted 1922.

DAVIS, *Andrew* (Born Ashridge, Herts., 1944)

British conductor who has been Musical Director at **Glyndebourne** since 1988 and is Chief Conductor of the BBC Symphony Orchestra. Music Director of the Toronto Symphony 1975, and their Conductor Laureate since 1988. Brilliantly sang his own Gilbertian parody at the Last Night of the Proms, 1992.

DAVIS, *Colin* (Born Weybridge 1927)

British conductor, formerly clarinettist. Music Director of **Sadler's Wells** Opera (1959–65) and Principal Conductor of the BBC Symphony Orchestra. Music Director of the Royal Opera (1971–86) and of the Bavarian Radio Symphony Orchestra from 1983. Knighted 1980.

DAWSON, *Peter* (Born Adelaide 1882; died Sydney 1961)

Australian bass-baritone who rivalled **Caruso** as a pioneer in the recording industry: he made his first records in 1904 and sold 13 million worldwide. He made his début at **Covent Garden** in 1909 but decided opera involved 'too much work for too little money' and thereafter concentrated on concert and recording work. Dawson was loved and admired by colleagues and audiences alike.

DANCE MUSIC

Music has been associated with dancing since time immemorial. Many major composers have written dance music, and the rhythms of the dance have in their turn inspired compositions intended for the concert platform or drawing room. The individuals connected with dance music are too numerous to mention but here is a list of some of the most important dance forms which have invaded the world of 'classical' music.

ALLEMANDE A French word meaning 'German (dance)'. A treatise on dancing published in 1588 describes the allemande as 'a plain dance of a certain gravity'. Much used by seventeenth- and eighteenth-century composers, notably **J.S. Bach**, in keyboard and other **suites** of pieces.

BOLERO Lively Spanish dance said to have been invented around 1780. **Ravel**'s *Bolero* of 1928 is the most famous orchestral use of the dance, and there's a delightful operatic bolero ('Mercè, Dilette Amiche') in **Verdi**'s *The Sicilian Vespers*.

COUNTRY DANCE The English name for dances performed on the village green by two lines of people facing each other; it became in French 'contredanse' and in German 'Contretänz'. No. 7 of **Beethoven**'s twelve *Contretänze* is used in the finale of his 'Eroica' Symphony.

CSÁRDÁS Often misspelt 'czárdás'. Hungarian dance with slow (*lassú*) introduction and fast (*friss*) main section invented in the early nineteenth century. Some of **Liszt**'s Hungarian Rhapsodies follow this pattern. Rosalinde sings a famous csárdás during the party scene in *Die Fledermaus*; another occurs in *Coppélia* (**Delibes**).

DARGASON Popular English country-dance tune used by **Gustav Holst** in his Suite No. 2 for military band and the *St Paul's Suite*.

FANDANGO Spanish courtship dance said to have been originated by eighteenth-century muleteers.

Used by **Mozart** in *The Marriage of Figaro* and other composers in search of Spanish atmosphere, for example **Rimsky-Korsakov** in his *Spanish Caprice*.

FARANDOLE A dance of ancient origin from Provence in which the participants dance through the streets in a chain, linking hands or handkerchiefs. Adds southern French atmosphere to **Bizet**'s music for *L'Arlésienne*.

GALLIARD Derived from the vigorous *gagliardo* which dates from late-fifteenth-century Italy, the galliard was often linked in **baroque** dance suites with the slow pavan. **Vaughan Williams** includes the 'Pavan and Galliard of the Sons of the Morning' in his Masque for Dancing, *Job*. See also **Pavan**.

GALOP Hectic ballroom dance first popular in Vienna in the 1820s. **Schubert** composed galops, followed by **Lanner** and the **Strauss family**. The dance was a favourite in Denmark where **Hans Christian Lumbye** composed, for example,'The Copenhagen Steam Railway Galop'. It also appears in **operettas** by **Offenbach** and **piano** pieces by Liszt.

GAVOTTE Originally from the Pays de Gap whose inhabitants are known as *gavots*, a more refined gavotte became popular at the court of Louis XIV. Often occurs in the dance-suites of Bach and others, and adds old-world feeling to **Prokofiev**'s 'Classical' Symphony of 1917.

GIGUE The jig, to give it is English name, was a spirited dance first known in England in the fifteenth century. Much used in dance suites by Bach, **Handel** and others. A movement of **Debussy**'s *Images* is called 'Gigues'.

HABANERA Dance devised in the Cuban capital, Havana, which later became popular in Spain and elsewhere. **'La Paloma'** by Sebastian Yradier is a well-known habanera, and a song by Yradier inspired Bizet's famous Habanera in *Carmen*.

HORNPIPE This ancient British dance involved dancing on the spot, which is perhaps why sailors adopted it in the limited space available to them at sea. **Purcell, Arne** and Handel were among many composers who wrote hornpipes.

MAZURKA Invented by the Mazurs of Mazovia near Warsaw in the sixteenth century, the Mazurka later acquired aristocratic dignity. **Chopin** wrote fifty mazurkas expressing a variety of emotions.

MINUET Dainty, small steps marked this extremely popular court dance which originated at the court of Louis XIV. Much used by **Lully, Couperin,** Bach and Handel in keyboard and other suites, it constituted the third movement of most eighteenth-century symphonies.

PAVAN Sedate dance whose early name, *padovana*, suggests it came from Padua. Much used by English Elizabethan composers such as **Byrd** and **Dowland.** More recent examples include **Fauré**'s stately *Pavane* and Ravel's *Pavane pour une infante défunte.* See also **Galliard.**

POLKA Introduced in Prague in 1837, this energetic Bohemian dance became all the rage in nineteenth-century ballrooms. Innumerable polkas were composed by the Strauss family and others, and the dance made its stage début in **Smetana**'s *The Bartered Bride* (1866). Another famous operatic polka occurs in Weinberger's *Schwanda the Bagpiper* (1927).

POLONAISE Stately processional dance of aristocratic origin in seventeenth-century Poland. Vehicle for patriotic sentiment in thirteen piano pieces by Chopin; much used in **ballet** and **opera**, for example in **Tchaikovsky**'s *Eugene Onegin.*

QUADRILLE Type of square dance devised in Napoleonic France and subsequently very popular in ballrooms. Much operatic and other music was arranged for quadrilles, some of it quite incongruously. **Chabrier** quarried his *Souvenirs de Munich* from **Wagner**'s *Tristan*

A typically energetic rendition of the Spanish fandango.

and Isolde, and Fauré and **Messager** based their *Souvenirs de Bayreuth* on Wagner's ***Ring.***

SARABANDE Fast and slow versions existed of this dance imported from Latin America in the sixteenth century. Standard slow movement in dance suites by Purcell, Bach, Handel and others. Appears in **Benjamin Britten**'s *Simple Symphony* (1934).

WALTZ Revolving dance for couples which developed in the late eighteenth century and became the most popular of all ballroom dances. It inspired innumerable compositions by the Strauss family and others, and became universally beloved. Among symphonic waltzes, those by Tchaikovsky are perhaps especially popular and Ravel's *La Valse* is a brilliant twentieth-century tribute to the hectic spirit of the waltz.

Claude Debussy: one of the twentieth century's most original and influential musical creators.

DEBUSSY, *Claude* (Born St Germain-en-Laye 1862; died Paris 1918)

One of the most significant twentieth-century composers. A rebellious student at the Paris Conservatoire, he won the coveted Prix de Rome in 1884 with his **cantata** *The Prodigal Son*. From 1893 to 1902 he was occupied with his **opera** *Pelléas et Mélisande*, which introduced a quite new kind of declamatory singing against a seamless orchestral background, and in 1894 made a strong but controversial impression in the concert hall with the famous *Prélude à l'après-midi d'un faune*. Debussy's ability to create pictures in music, as in his three-movement portrait of the sea in various moods, *La Mer*, has led to his being identified with the methods of his impressionist painter friends, but underlying all Debussy's music is a formal, almost classical sense of structure. Other favourite orchestral works include the three Nocturnes (*Nuages,*

Fêtes and *Sirènes*) and the *Danse sacrée et danse profane* with **harp** soloist. Debussy wrote a great deal of **piano** music; much-loved pieces include 'Clair de lune' from the *Suite bergamasque*, the two early Arabesques, 'The Girl with the Flaxen Hair' ('La Fille aux cheveux de lin') from the Preludes for piano, and the *Children's Corner* suite which includes the 'Golliwog's Cake Walk'.

DELIBES, *Léo* (Born St Germain-du-Val 1836; died Paris 1891)

French composer chiefly remembered for the **ballet** scores of *Coppélia* (1870) and *Sylvia* (1876), and for two numbers from the **opera** *Lakmé* (1883): the 'Bell Song' and the so-called 'Flower Duet', sung by Lakmé and her handmaid Mallika and adopted by British Airways as the theme tune of television commercials. In his early years Delibes wrote fourteen operettas for **Offenbach**'s theatre, Les Bouffes Parisiens, and assisted **Gounod** to produce the vocal score of *Faust*.

DELIUS, *Frederick* (Born Bradford 1862; died Grez-sur-Loing 1934)

On Hearing the First Cuckoo in Spring (1912) establishes Delius in most people's minds as a sound-poet of the countryside. The son of a German-born wool merchant in Bradford, he left the family business to grow oranges in Florida. He went to Leipzig to study music in 1886, where he was befriended by **Grieg**, and then lived a Bohemian life in Paris, settling down in 1897 at the village of Grez-sur-Loing with the painter Jelka Rosen, whom he married in 1903. After the First World War Delius gradually became blind and paralysed as the result of a syphilitic infection, but during his last years his young assistant from England, Eric Fenby, was able to note down from the composer's painfully given instructions several important works. A popular early work is the dance 'La Calinda' from the **opera** *Koanga*, inspired by experiences in Florida; Delius's masterpieces begin with *Paris* (1899) and continue through *Sea Drift* (1903–4), a great choral setting of words by Walt Whitman, to the fine incidental music for James Elroy Flecker's *Hassan* (1923). Delius's operas have resisted revival, though orchestral excerpts are often played, including the Prelude to *Irmelin* and the 'Walk to the Paradise Garden' from *A Village Romeo and Juliet*.

José Carreras, one of the 'top three tenors', in Verdi's Stiffelio, Royal Opera, 1993.

Andre Previn conducting the LSO in London's Barbican Hall. Previn is one of music's polymaths: conductor, composer and pianist.

London's Royal Opera House, Covent Garden, showing the colonnaded frontage in Bow Street. The present building dates from 1858; there are controversial plans for refurbishment and expansion.

DELLER, *Alfred* (Born Margate 1912; died Bologna 1979)

British countertenor whose unusual talent revived interest in the use of the high male voice in music. In 1946, Deller sang **Purcell** on the opening night of the **BBC** Third Programme, and was thereafter in increasing demand. **Benjamin Britten** wrote the role of Oberon for Deller in his **opera** *A Midsummer Night's Dream*, and in 1963 he founded the informal Stour Music Festival in Kent. OBE 1970.

DEL MAR, *Norman* (Born London 1919)

While principal conductor (1948–56) of the English Opera group, Del Mar conducted the first performance of Britten's *Let's Make an Opera* (1949). Noted for adventurous repertoire and expertise on **Richard Strauss.** CBE 1975.

DEL MONACO, *Mario* (Born Florence 1915; died Mestre nr Venice 1982)

Power rather than subtlety was the strong point of Del Monaco's magnificent tenor voice: he excelled as Radamès in **Verdi**'s *Aida*, and sang the title role in the same composer's *Otello* 427 times by his own reckoning.

DE LOS ANGELES, *Victoria* (Born Barcelona 1923)

Spanish **soprano** who entranced London and the world in the post-war period. After studying at the Barcelona Conservatory, she went on to sing **Puccini** with the great tenor **Gigli** in Madrid, making her **Covent Garden** début in 1950. Audiences were dazzled by de los Angeles's rich, almost exotic, Spanish voice, and her exquisite interpretations of the roles of Madam Butterfly and Mimì (*La Bohème*). She has also been an accomplished **Wagner** singer, particularly in the role of Elisabeth in *Tannhäuser*, and has championed the music of her compatriot **Falla.**

'DEPUIS LE JOUR', *Louise* (Charpentier)

Beloved soprano **aria** sung by Louise in the **opera** of that name by Gustave Charpentier (1860–1956), expressing how happy she has been since she decided to set up home in Montmartre with the artist Julien, much to the disgust of her respectable working-class parents. The 'scandalous' theme of this

early example of operatic *verismo* (realism) helped to account for its success. By 1950 it had been performed 950 times and is much the most famous of Charpentier's works.

DESCANT

Commonly a high **soprano** line, either written out or improvised, sung to complement the singing of a **hymn** tune by a choir or congregation. But the word descant (or discant) can also refer to a form of medieval part-writing, the art of composing or singing **choral music**, or the **soprano** part in such music.

'DEVIL'S TRILL' Sonata (Tartini)

Nickname for a violin **sonata** in G minor by Giuseppe Tartini (1692–1770), a celebrated violinist who invented a new **violin** bow and founded an influential school of violin-playing at Padua in 1728. The legend attaching to the most famous of Tartini's many compositions is that the devil visited the composer in a dream and demanded his violin. On it he played a solo so beautiful that when he woke up Tartini tried to reproduce what he had heard.

DI STEFANO, *Giuseppe* (Born nr Catania 1921)

Di Stefano's vocal promise was spotted by a fellow student at a Jesuit seminary in Sicily. A frequent partner of **Maria Callas** at **La Scala** and elsewhere, he also shared her farewell concert tour in 1973–4. He was highly praised for the subtlety and beauty of his voice in the early fifties, but lost favour with many critics when he turned to heavier roles and the voice became 'rougher and less elegant' (Harold Rosenthal).

DIVERTIMENTO

Italian for 'diversion' or 'amusement', hence a work (usually in several movements) designed for entertainment, indoors or outdoors. **Mozart** wrote 25 divertimenti, sometimes called cassations or **serenades.**

DIVERTISSEMENT

The French equivalent of **divertimento**, but with a theatrical connotation. Divertissements often occur as episodes of stage entertainment in **opera** and **ballet**. The highly entertaining 'Divertissement' of Jacques Ibert (1890–1962) is an orchestral suite derived from his incidental music for the play *An Italian Straw Hat* (Eugène Labiche).

*D*OHNÁNYI, *Christoph Von* (Born Berlin 1929) ⎯

After musical studies in Munich, he won the **Richard Strauss** conducting prize in 1951. Music Director of the **Cleveland Orchestra** from 1984. Grandson of **Ernö Dohnányi**.

*D*OHNÁNYI, *Ernö* (Born Bratislava 1877; died New York 1960)

Regarded in his day as the greatest Hungarian pianist and composer after **Liszt**. His most famous composition is the cheerfully satirical version of 'Twinkle, twinkle, little star', *Variations on a Nursery Theme* (1913), for **piano** and **orchestra**.

*D*OLMETSCH FAMILY

Arnold Dolmetsch, born in Le Mans in 1858, a Swiss violinist, musicologist and instrument-maker, pioneered the twentieth-century revival of interest in **early music** and early instruments. He settled in Haslemere, Surrey, in 1917, where he established his workshop and, from 1925, an annual festival at which he and other members of the family would perform old music on instruments of their own manufacture. Dolmetsch **recorders**, in particular, sold to a worldwide market. Arnold Dolmetsch died in Haslemere in 1940, and the family activities are now carried on by his son Carl (born 1911), a virtuoso of the **recorder** who was made CBE in 1954.

*D*OMINGO, *Placido* (Born Madrid 1941)

Together with **Pavarotti** and **Carreras**, one of the 'three great tenors' at the present time. Domingo is admired almost as much for his talent as an actor as for his superbly controlled and projected voice. He has recorded no fewer than fifty complete **operas** together with many solos and ensembles which demonstrate extraordinary versatility. The fact that he is at home in lighter repertoire should perhaps come as no surprise, since he was the son of parents who were performers of *Zarzuela* (the Spanish equivalent of **operetta**). When he was eight the family moved to Mexico, and Domingo made his operatic début in Monterey as Alfredo in *La Traviata* when he was nineteen. As a member of Israeli National Opera 1962–5 he sang 300 perfor-

mances of twelve different roles, most of them in Hebrew. He first sang at the **Metropolitan** in New York in 1968, at **La Scala** in 1969 and at **Covent Garden** in 1971. Since then he has appeared in most of the world's major opera houses on many occasions and his performances have frequently been televised. Three of his most celebrated interpretations have been filmed: as Alfredo in *La Traviata*, in the title role in **Verdi**'s *Otello* and as Don José in *Carmen*. Since 1973 Domingo has developed an international reputation as a conductor and in 1992 he was Artistic Consultant to the World Fair in Seville. Meanwhile, his range of operatic roles continues to expand beyond the Italian and French repertoire he has made his own; he scored a great success in 1991 in New York as **Wagner**'s *Parsifal*.

*D*ON GIOVANNI

Opera by **Mozart**, with libretto by Lorenzo da Ponte, first produced in Prague in 1787; the most famous of many operas based on the legend of the Spanish libertine Don Juan. Comedy is interwoven with high drama, and the score contains a series of great numbers which have become popular outside the opera house. Among them are 'Madamina' or the so-called 'catalogue-song', in which Leporello enumerates his master's conquests – no fewer than 1003 in Spain alone; Don Ottavio's two beautiful **tenor** arias, 'Il mio tesoro' and 'Dalla sua pace'; the duet in which Don Giovanni tries to seduce the peasant girl Zerlina, 'Là ci darem la mano'; and Donna Anna's vengeance **aria**, 'Or sai chi l'onore'. In recent years *Don Giovanni* has been the subject of a number of innovative theatre and television productions of varying success.

*D*ONIZETTI, *Gaetano* (Born Bergamo 1797; died Bergamo 1848)

Italian composer of a comic masterpiece, *Don Pasquale* (1843) which rivals **Rossini** at his best, and a number of tragic **operas** which have provided the great singers of his own and succeeding generations with outstanding vocal opportunities. After being forced to enlist in the Austrian army by parents opposed to a musical career, Donizetti produced between 1818 and 1830 some thirty operas widely produced in Italy. International recognition came with *Anna Bolena* (1830). *L'Elisir d'Amore* (1832) disclosed his gift for comedy and *Lucrezia Borgia* (1833) and *Lucia di Lammermoor* (1835) consolidated his reputation. A period in Paris 1840–4 produced *The Daughter of the Regiment* and *La Favorita*. Donizetti's last years were clouded by illness – he became paralysed and mentally unbalanced as a result of syphilis. 'Una Furtiva Lagrima' ('A Furtive Tear') from *The Elixir of Love* is regarded as a high test of the **tenor**'s skill; the Mad Scene from *Lucia di Lammermoor* is a great showpiece for **coloratura soprano**, and the **Quartet** from the same opera is one of the best-known ensemble pieces in the operatic repertoire. Apart from a total of seventy-five stage works, which include the curiously named *Emilia di Liverpool*, Donizetti also wrote string quartets.

*D*ONNA DIANA (Reznicek) ───────────

Opera by Emil von Rezniček (1860–1945) produced in Prague (1894). The **overture** is a sparkling orchestral composition which has remained very popular.

*D*ONOHOE, *Peter* (Born Manchester 1953) ───────

A period of study in Paris with Yvonne Loriod prompted a lasting interest in the works of her husband Olivier Messiaen, but Donohoe's piano repertoire is wide-ranging, and includes other twentieth-century music, including the **concertos** by **Béla Bartók**. After early apprenticeship as an orchestral pianist, Donohoe leapt to international fame when he was joint winner of the Moscow **Tchaikovsky** Competition in 1982.

*D*ORATI, *Antal* (Born Budapest 1906; died Gerzensee nr Berne 1988)───────────

Conductor of Hungarian birth who became an American citizen in 1947. First made his name as conductor of the Ballets Russes de Monte Carlo. His many recordings include a fine complete series of **Haydn** symphonies with the Philharmonia Hungarica, consisting of Hungarian refugees.

*D*OUBLE BASS ─────────────────

Largest and lowest-voiced instrument of the string family. Essential to the symphony **orchestra** and widely used in **dance music** and **jazz**, the double bass has a repertoire of some 200 solo **concertos**.

Placido Domingo: still very much a top tenor, and a successful conductor too.

*D*OWLAND, *John* (Born London 1563; died London 1626)───────────────────

Rejected for a court appointment with Queen Elizabeth I, Dowland became famous as a lutenist and singer throughout Europe before returning to London in 1606. One of the finest of English composers, he published eighty-seven songs; among the best known are 'Fine knacks for ladies', 'Weep you no more, sad fountains' and 'In darkness let me dwell'.

*D*OWNES, *Edward* (Born Birmingham 1924) ─────

British conductor identified with adventurous repertoire in concert hall and opera house. Expert in the Russian language, he has conducted his own translations of operas by **Shostakovich** (at **Covent Garden**) and **Prokofiev**. In 1980 Downes was appointed Principal Conductor of the BBC

Antonin Dvořák: among the world's supreme melodists, he also had a mania for train-spotting.

Philharmonic, based in Manchester, and in 1991 became Associate Music Director and Principal Conductor at Covent Garden. Knighted 1991.

'DOWN IN THE FOREST'

Popular parlour song, the only composition of Sir Landon Ronald (1873–1938) to survive. He was Principal of the Guildhall School of Music 1910–38, an important conductor, and influential in the early years of the gramophone.

DRUM

Percussion instrument which comes in an almost infinite variety of sizes and shapes, most often sounded by striking with the hand or a stick.

DULCIMER

A shallow box with strings stretched over it which are normally struck by hammers but can sometimes be plucked. A larger version, the Hungarian cimbalom, stands on its own legs.

DU PRÉ, *Jacqueline* (Born Oxford 1945; died London 1987)

British cellist, student of William Pleeth, who won all the awards at the Guildhall School of Music and made her recital début when she was sixteen using a **Stradivarius** instrument presented to her anonymously. Toured widely and made memorable recordings, notably of the **Elgar** and **Schumann** concertos and **Beethoven**'s duo sonatas (with Stephen Bishop-Kovacevitch) before multiple sclerosis put an end to her performing career in 1972, though she continued to teach. Married **Daniel Barenboim** in 1967. The beautiful quality of her playing, her appealing personality and her sad fate combine to make the memory of Jacqueline du Pré inspiring and moving. OBE 1976.

'DUSK' (Armstrong Gibbs)

Slow waltz (published in 1940s), most commercially successful work of Cecil Armstrong Gibbs (1889–1960). His songs include many settings of poems by Walter de la Mare, among them the popular 'Five Eyes'.

DUTOIT, *Charles* (Born Lausanne 1936

Swiss conductor. With the **Montreal Symphony Orchestra**, whose Music Director he became in 1977, Dutoit has recorded with great flair and expertise a large number of major orchestral works.

DVOŘÁK, *Antonin* (Born Nelahozeves, Bohemia, 1841; died Prague 1904)

Dvořák was the son of a village butcher and his student years in Prague meant financial struggle. Played the **viola** in the **orchestra** of the new Provisional Theatre, on one occasion under **Wagner**'s direction and often under **Bedřich Smetana**. In 1873 a patriotic **cantata**, *The Heirs of the White Mountain*, attracted attention; three times Dvořák won an Austrian State Prize (Bohemia was part of the Austro-Hungarian Empire at that time) awarded by a jury which included **Brahms**. Brahms recommended Dvořák to the publisher Simrock, who brought out his *Moravian Duets* and *Slavonic Dances* in 1878. From this point Dvořák's international fame rapidly grew. In 1884 he paid the first of nine visits to Britain where he was presented in 1891 with an honorary doctorate of music at Cambridge. In his last years Dvořák was director of the Prague Conservatoire. Of Dvořák's nine **symphonies**, Nos. 8 and 9 ('From the New World') are the best known and most loved; his Cello Concerto in B minor is one of the most beautiful ever written; other orchestral works include the lovely String Serenade in E and the popular overture, *Carnival*. The two sets of *Slavonic Dances*, whether in their original **piano** form or in orchestral arrangements, are universally played, and the most popular of his **chamber music** works is the String Quartet in F, Op. 96 ('American'). The 'Song to the Moon' is a beautiful **aria** from Dvořák's **opera** *Rusalka*.

E

*É*COSSAISE

Ballroom dance in 2/4 time popular in Europe in the early nineteenth century. Though the word means 'Scottish', the Écossaise seems to have been no more than a French notion of what a Scottish dance should be.

*E*DINBURGH FESTIVAL

The Edinburgh Festival, which is held annually, was started in 1947 at the suggestion of Rudolph Bing, with the idea of finding an additional platform for **Glyndebourne** Opera, and of renewing cultural contact with the world at large after the Second World War. The appearance of **Bruno Walter** and the **Vienna Philharmonic** at the first Festival established its standing at the highest international level, and this status has by and large been maintained over the years. The Festival runs for three weeks in late August and early September, and is greatly enriched by many hundreds of events in the Festival Fringe.

*E*ISTEDDFOD

Welsh word meaning 'session' applied to competitive festivals devoted mainly to music and literature. The National Eisteddfod of Wales has been held annually

since 1880; the International Eisteddfod, which attracts individuals and groups from all over the world, has been held every year at Llangollen since 1947.

*E*LDER, *Mark* (Born Hexham 1947)

Mark Elder served his conducting apprenticeship with **Raymond Leppard** at **Glyndebourne**. Principal Conductor for **English National Opera** 1979–93. CBE 1989.

*E*LECTRONIC MUSIC

Attempts were made to produce electronic sounds as early as the 1890s, but it was the invention in the 1960s of synthesisers, such as the one developed by the American Robert Moog, which made possible the creation of a wide variety of artificially generated sounds; with the aid of digital computer synthesis, elaborate compositions can be put together. Electronic sound has proved extemely effective in the creation of unusual atmospheres in films, television and radio, and leading composers have been drawn to it.

*E*LLIS, *Osian* (Born Ffynnongroew, Flintshire, 1928)

Welsh harpist and persuasive advocate of the Welsh art of *penillion* singing. A number of composers have written works for him; these include the Suite for Harp, Op. 83 by **Benjamin Britten**. CBE 1971.

*E*LLIS, *Vivian* (Born Hampstead 1903)

British composer and writer who started his career as a concert pianist after studying with **Myra Hess**. His first major theatrical hit was *Mr Cinders* (1929) which included the popular 'Spread a Little Happiness'. Outstanding among many other successes was *Bless the Bride* (1947) which ran for 886 performances. The orchestral 'Coronation Scot' (1948) became familiar as the signature tune of radio's *Paul Temple* series.

'*E*MPEROR'S HYMN'

Tune composed (or adapted) by **Haydn** in 1797 as the national anthem of Austria, and used as a theme for variations in his String Quartet Op. 76, No. 3 (the 'Emperor' Quartet). Adopted in 1922 as the anthem of the German Federal Republic.

*E*ARLY MUSIC

*W*hat do we mean when we talk about 'early music'? I put the phrase in inverted commas because there is so much argument about where it begins and ends. Certainly it starts with the music of medieval times, going back 800 years or so, and these days some would claim it embraces music of the day before yesterday. In fact, use of the term 'early music' denotes an attitude of mind more than anything else. This is best shown by musicians in the Early Music Movement who are devoted to discovering hitherto unknown works or rethinking well-established pieces and performing them as nearly as possible in the manner the composer had in mind. Of course all this presents formidable problems of research, and the further you go back into musical history the more difficult it is to be sure of what really happened. The truth is that in the performance of really early music there has to be a large element of guesswork. None the less, it is a fact that nowadays **Christopher Hogwood** and his Academy of Ancient Music sell more records worldwide than **Luciano Pavarotti** so there is clearly great popular appeal in the performance of music of the past on instruments of the period (or, much more often, modern copies).

This interest in the 'authentic' performance of old music is a relatively new phenomenon. It was hardly evident at all until the late nineteenth century, grew slowly in the early decades of the present century, and has only taken hold of the musical public in the years since the Second World War. I was brought up on arrangements by people like **Sir Thomas Beecham, Sir Hamilton Harty** and **Leopold Stokowski** of works by **Bach** and **Handel.** These used the full resources of the modern symphony **orchestra** and it was generally felt that the best effect would be gained from Handel's *Messiah* by having the largest available chorus. The argument employed was that if past composers had been alive today they would have been only too pleased by the improvements now available. As for individual instruments, wouldn't Bach have been delighted by the sonority of the concert grand **piano** instead of having to make do with a tinkling **clavichord**?

The belief that what is newest in music must be best goes back a long way. In 1477 the composer Johannes Tinctoris declared that the only music worth listening to was written in the last forty years. Baron von Swieten prompted **Mozart** to rearrange Handel's *Messiah* in the style fashionable in Mozart's day, never doubting that such a rearrangement would be an improvement. When **Mendelssohn** revived Bach's *St Matthew Passion* in Berlin in 1829 after a century of neglect, there is no evidence that he attempted what we would now regard as an 'authentic' performance.

The first steps in a more scholarly approach to the music of the past seem to have been taken in Britain during the last decade of the nineteenth century. In 1899 an important treasury of early English keyboard music was published, the *Fitzwilliam Virginal Book*; meanwhile, the crucially influential musician and craftsman **Arnold Dolmetsch**, born in Le Mans, had made his home in London. Dolmetsch combed the libraries of the **Royal College of Music** and the British Museum for early musical manuscripts and soon began making reproductions of old instruments. His first **lute** was completed in 1893, his first clavichord in 1894, and in 1896 he made a **harpsichord**. During the First World War he settled at Haslemere in Surrey where he set up a workshop and established a centre for perform-ances of early music. These were given largely by members of his own family on instruments of his own creation. That tradition is still maintained under the supervision of Arnold's son, Carl.

Another very important figure in the early twentieth century was **Wanda Landowska**. She started life as a pianist but decided that the seventeenth- and eighteenth-century music which attracted her sounded better on the harpischord. So she had a special instrument made, with a sound loud enough to fill a modern concert hall. It had an iron frame and extra bass strings, with various special tonal effects, and so effective was it that **Manuel de Falla** and **Poulenc** wrote new harpsichord concertos for Landowska to play.

In the 1930s the Early Music Movement gathered momentum. Musicians such as Paul Sacher, Nadia Boulanger, Adolph Busch and Boyd Neel regularly performed pre-classical repertoire, and August Wenzinger with his Schola Cantorum in Basle was an important exponent of performance on early instruments.

After the Second World War, the **BBC** Third Programme quickly began extending public appreciation of music from earlier times.

In America, Noah Greenberg's New York Pro Musica, established in 1952, began giving virtuoso performances of medieval and Renaissance music and in Vienna in 1953 **Nikolaus Harnoncourt** established the Vienna Concentus Musicus.

1968 brought the début of the Early Music Consort of London, founded by the twenty-one-year-old **David Munrow.** Expert on a whole range of early wind instruments, Munrow seduced many listeners into the enjoyment of early music, and his *Pied Piper* programme on Radio Three from 1970 to 1976 was well named. The record industry was not slow to cash in on this promising area of revenue and there was a rapid growth of 'authentic instrument' recordings in the 1970s. The 1980s brought movement into ever more recent repertoire: authentic instrument recordings of works by **Beethoven,** Mendelssohn and **Berlioz** – and the trend towards the twentieth century continues.

So what has the Early Music Movement accomplished? Most of all it has made available to us a whole range of 'new' old music, and made it live in a way we can enjoy today.

An evening's entertainment in Sussex with the Duke of Sussex, Mrs Billington and friends, circa 1788.

A Country Concert, or, An Evening's Entertainment in Sussex.

E LGAR

Edward ELGAR

1857	Born in Broadheath, near Worcester
1889	Married Caroline Alice Roberts
1899	Great success of *Enigma Variations*
1900	Poor first performance in England of *Dream of Gerontius*
1901	*Pomp and Circumstance* March No. 1; *Dream of Gerontius* acclaimed in Germany
1904	Elgar knighted: Elgar festival at Covent Garden
1908	Success of Symphony No. 1
1910	Violin Concerto
1919	Cello Concerto
1920	Death of Lady Elgar
1931	*Nursery Suite*
1934	Died in Worcester

*E*lgar once said,'There is music in the air, music all around us, the world is full of it, and you simply take as much as you require.' As a boy he tried to write down the song of the reeds by his beloved River Teme. Elgar never had any formal instruction in composition, with the result that once he found his own voice it was quite unlike anyone else's. He also happened to give expression to the spirit of England at a particular period.

He succeeded his father as organist of St George's Roman Catholic Church in Worcester, played and taught the **violin** locally and did some conducting. All the time he was busily composing and an orchestral **serenade** of his was performed in Birmingham when he was twenty-nine. Three years later Caroline Alice Roberts, the daughter of a Major-General, came to him as a **piano** pupil; their wedding took place in 1889. Her family considered she had married beneath her and they never changed their mind, despite Elgar's high honours in later years.

Alice had a little money of her own and this enabled the young couple to live in London for a while near the Crystal Palace which offered concerts where the Elgars were able to listen to the latest musical creations. Edward had managed to sell a few salon pieces to publishers, including the popular *Salut d'Amour*, but his new **overture** *Froissart* aroused no interest in London so the couple returned to Worcestershire, setting up house in Malvern. Elgar's only ambition was to compose: teaching, he said, was like 'turning a grindstone with a dislocated shoulder'.

In the 1890s Elgar's reputation as a composer grew with **choral** works such as *The Black Night, The Light of Life* and *King Olaf*; and the *Imperial March* composed for Queen Victoria's Diamond Jubliee in 1897 brought him wider fame. The Queen accepted the dedication of the **oratorio** *Caractacus* the following year. None the less, Elgar suffered periods of deep depression. Outwardly a cheerful countryman, inwardly he felt himself to be an outsider.

In fact Elgar was never without companionship and in 1899 he dedicated his first really important orchestral work, the *Enigma Variations*, to his 'friends pictured within'. Each variation was a portrait of a different person in the Elgar circle, including his wife and himself. The 'enigma' concerned the main **theme**. Concealed within it, he said, there was another theme that was never heard, and this tantalising riddle continues to exercise scholars and others. 'Pop Goes the Weazle' and **'Auld Lang Syne'** are among the alternative tunes suggested; recently that master of the hidden melody, **Joseph Cooper**, has convincingly put forward the case for a theme in the slow movement of **Mozart**'s 'Prague' Symphony. Elgar is known to have loved Mozart and this symphony in particular; what is more, it was included in the concert when the *Enigma Variations* was first performed.

The *Enigma Variations* was a turning-point for Elgar and English music. Even in Germany they began to wonder if this country was really 'the land without music', and when Elgar's great oratorio *Dream of Gerontius* was performed at the Lower Rhine Festival of 1901, **Richard Strauss** declared that Elgar was the first progressive English musician. Two more great religious choral works followed – *The Apostles* (1903) and *The Kingdom* (1906).

Meanwhile, Elgar was growing in stature as a public figure. The year 1901 brought the first of the *Pomp and Circumstance* marches with its great tune that Elgar knew would 'knock 'em flat'. A year later the tune was incorporated into a Coronation Ode for King Edward VII, with patriotic words by A.C. Benson, and **'Land of Hope and Glory'** was born. The Overture *Cockaigne*, also written in 1901, gave expression to the spirit of London, heart of the British Empire, and in 1904 there was a three-day Elgar festival at Covent Garden which coincided with the award of a knighthood to the composer.

The years before the First World War brought a series of major works: the two symphonies (1908 and 1910), the Violin Concerto written for **Fritz Kreisler** (1910) and the symphonic study *Falstaff* (1913). During the war he turned out a number of patriotic pieces and some music for the theatre. Very different indeed was the elegiac Cello Concerto he wrote when the war was over: a deeply moving farewell to a vanished generation, a vanished age.

The Cello Concerto was also destined to be Elgar's last major work. The death of his wife in 1920 was a shattering blow and his creative impulse seems to have died with her. His life alternated between London clubs and the Worcestershire countryside. He conducted an important series of recordings of his own works, found companionship in his dogs (and the friendship of George Bernard Shaw), became **Master of the King's Music** in 1924 and was created a baronet in 1931. That year a late revival of creative energy produced the *Nursery Suite*, dedicated to the Duchess of York and her two daughters, and in 1932 Elgar conducted a historic recording of the Violin Concerto with the sixteen-year-old **Yehudi Menuhin** as soloist. Two years later, with his projected third symphony no more than sketched, Elgar died at home in Worcester at the age of seventy-six.

Elgar enjoyed country life and was often to be seen cycling, kite-flying and hunting.

Favourite works

'Land of Hope and Glory'; Trio of *Pomp and Circumstance* March No. 4; *Wand of Youth* suites; *Cockaigne* Overture; Cello Concerto; Violin Concerto (in particular, movements 1 and 2); *Enigma Variations*, *Dream of Gerontius*; *Falstaff*; Symphony No. 1 (slow movement); *Serenade for Strings*; 'Where Corals Lie' (from *Sea Pictures* cycle).

ENGLISH CHAMBER ORCHESTRA

Name taken in 1960 by the Goldsbrough Orchestra originally formed by Arnold Goldsbrough for the performance of **baroque** music. A Mozart-sized **orchestra** of first-rate players, it had no regular conductor until **Jeffrey Tate** was appointed in 1985.

ENGLISH NATIONAL OPERA

Lilian Baylis opened the new **Sadler's Wells** Theatre in 1931. In 1945, Sadler's Wells was reopened with the world première of **Benjamin Britten**'s *Peter Grimes*. In 1968 the company took a lease on Britain's largest theatre, the Coliseum, presenting highly acclaimed productions of **Wagner**'s *The Mastersingers* and the ***Ring*** cycle, and **Prokofiev**'s *War and Peace*. In 1974 the company adopted the name English National Opera. Since then the company has presented over twenty productions a year, and each season is planned to include a newly commissioned opera from a British composer.

ENTR'ACTE

A musical interlude performed during an interval, or sometimes during the action, of a theatrical entertainment. There are three famous Entr'actes in **Schubert**'s incidental music for the play *Rosamunde, Princess of Cyprus*.

'ENTRY OF THE LITTLE FAUNS' (Pierné)

By far the best-known composition of the French organist, composer and conductor Gabriel Pierné (1863–1937), from the ballet *Cydalise et le Chèvre-pied* (*Cydalise and the Satyr*), 1923.

ESPAÑA (Chabrier)

Most popular work of the French composer Emmanuel Chabrier (1841–94). Written after a Spanish holiday, it was an instant success in Paris in 1883.

'ETERNAL FATHER, STRONG TO SAVE'

'The Sailor's Hymn'. Words by William Whiting (1825–78). Tune by John Bacchus Dykes (1823–76), sometime precentor of Durham Cathedral.

ÉTUDE

French word for 'study'. A piece of music written primarily to exercise a performer (usually a pianist) in a particular aspect of technique; but the finest Études (such as those by **Chopin**, **Debussy** and **Liszt**) are also satisfying works of art.

EUPHONIUM

The tenor member of the **tuba** family: it first appeared in Germany about 1830 and with its warm, melodious sound is an indispensable component of brass and military bands.

EVANS, *Geraint* (Born Pontypridd 1922; died Aberystwyth 1992)

After studies at the Guildhall School of Music and in Hamburg and Geneva, Evans made his début at **Covent Garden** in 1948 and became one of the world's leading operatic baritones. His best roles include **Verdi**'s Falstaff, **Mozart**'s Figaro and Papageno (*The Magic Flute*), Alban Berg's Wozzeck, Beckmesser in *The Mastersingers*, **Donizetti**'s Don Pasquale and Dulcamara in *The Elixir of Love*, also by Donizetti, in which he made his Covent Garden farewell in 1984. Knighted 1969.

F

FADO

Portuguese word derived from the Latin *fatum*, meaning fate. Type of Portuguese solo song which became popular in the cafés and cabarets of Lisbon from the 1850s; it can include improvised words and music, sometimes topical in character.

'FAERY SONG' (Boughton)

Haunting **tenor** song from the music drama *The Immortal Hour* by Rutland Boughton (1878–1960). Under the influence of **Wagner**, Boughton wanted to establish an English Bayreuth at Glastonbury for the performance of works based on Arthurian legends. *The Immortal Hour* was produced at the first Glastonbury Festival in 1914 and in 1922 enjoyed a long London run.

FALKNER, *Keith* (Born Sawston 1900) —————

British bass-baritone and administrator. After being a chorister at New College School, Oxford, he studied at the **Royal College of Music**, and in Paris, Vienna and Berlin. Notable **oratorio** singer and recitalist specialising in English song. Professor of singing at Cornell University 1950–60 and highly regarded Director of the Royal College of Music 1960–74. Knighted 1967.

FALL, *Leo* (Born Olomouc 1873; died Vienna 1925)

Austrian composer of twenty operettas, and conductor. After conducting and playing in Berlin, Hamburg and Cologne he settled in Vienna where most of his major successes were first staged. They include *The Dollar Princess* (1907), *The Rose of Stamboul* (1916) and *Madame Pompadour* (1922)

FALLA, *Manuel de* (Born Cádiz 1876; died Alta Gracia, Argentina, 1946) ———————————

Spanish composer who was inspired by the example of **Grieg** to express the spirit of his country in musical terms that would be universally understood. Though he did not use actual folk tunes, much of his work can be described as 'imaginary folk art'. After early studies in Cádiz and Madrid, Falla had some success with light theatre pieces in the *zarzuela* style and won a competition with his **opera** *La vida breve* (*The Short Life*) (1904–5). This had to wait till 1913 for its first performance, which took place in Paris: Falla had moved to the French capital in 1907 and soon formed important friendships with **Debussy**, **Ravel** and **Dukas**. He returned to Madrid at the outbreak of the First World War, and there, in 1915, his *Seven Popular Spanish Songs* and *El amor brujo* (*Love the Magician*), a stage work with dances and songs, were first heard. The 'Ritual Fire Dance' from *El amor brujo* is one of Falla's best-known pieces; the three-movement *Nights in the Gardens of Spain* (1916) for **piano** and **orchestra** has also remained very popular, with its vivid impression of Granada where Falla settled in 1919. In that year Falla enjoyed perhaps his greatest success when the Diaghilev company staged his **ballet** *The Three-Cornered Hat*, based on a Spanish folk-tale, in London. The Miller's Dance is very well known. After the First World War Falla produced another major work for piano and orchestra (*Fantasia Bética*), a puppet opera inspired by an episode in *Don Quixote*,

and a harpsichord concerto for **Wanda Landowska**. For twenty years he worked at a vast **oratorio**, *Atlántida*, which was never completed. Deeply depressed by the Spanish Civil War, and suffering from ill health, Falla spent his last years in Argentina.

FALSETTO————————————————————

A type of **soprano** voice produced by adult males, bypassing the normal operation of the vocal chords. Much used in church music from early times, and elsewhere for comic effect.

FALSTAFF ———————————————————

Shakespeare's immortal fat knight appears in a number of **operas**, including Nicolai's *The Merry Wives of Windsor*, *Sir John in Love* (*Vaughan Williams*), and – most memorably – **Verdi**'s comic masterpiece *Falstaff*, first produced in Milan in 1893 when the composer was eighty. **Elgar**'s symphonic study *Falstaff* was first performed in Leeds in 1913.

FANTASIA ———————————————————

Italian word meaning 'fantasy' or 'fancy'. In musical terms, a Fantasia is a work in which imagination is generally more in evidence than strict formal construction. The word has been used to describe musical compositions since the sixteenth century; more recent Fantasias sometimes bring together a string of tunes, such as **Henry Wood**'s *Fantasia on British Sea Songs*. Walt Disney's film *Fantasia* (1940) used cartoons to illustrate well-known orchestral pieces played by the **Philadelphia Orchestra** conducted by **Leopold Stokowski** and thus brought serious music to a very wide audience.

FARNON, *Robert* (Born Toronto 1917) —————

Canadian composer and arranger who has latterly made his home in Guernsey. After a period as trumpeter in the CBC orchestra and as conductor of the Canadian army band in the Second World War, he settled in Britain and developed a prolific creative career. He wrote scores for many films starring Anna Neagle, and for the film *Captain Horatio Hornblower* (1951). Among the most familiar of many short orchestral pieces are 'Journey into Melody' (1947), 'Jumping Bean' (1948), 'Peanut Polka' (1951), 'Westminster Waltz' (1956) and 'Colditz March' (1972).

*F*AURÉ, *Gabriel* (Born Pamiers, Ariège, 1845; died Paris 1924) _____

Influential French composer, regarded as the finest master of French song: 'Après un rêve' ('After a Dream'), is perhaps the most famous of his many works for voice. Fauré's early training at the École Niedermeyer in Paris qualified him for a career as organist and choirmaster, and he held a number of such posts (he called them 'mercenary jobs') to support himself as a composer. His most beloved work, the *Requiem*, which includes the famous 'Pie Jesu' for boy **soprano**, occupied him for twenty years. Fauré wrote a number of **Nocturnes**, **Barcarolles**, **Ballades** and **Impromptus** among other pieces for **piano** and had the distinction of being told by **Liszt** that his piano music was too difficult. The description cannot be applied to the *Dolly Suite* for piano duet, written for the daughter of Emma Bardac, with whom Fauré enjoyed a happy liaison before she became Mme **Debussy**. In the early years of the present century, Fauré frequented the intellectual salons of Paris and was a friend of Proust, who drew inspiration from Fauré's music in creating his fictional composer Vinteuil. Fauré was director of the Paris conservatoire 1905–20, where his fierce passion for reform won him the nickname 'Robespierre'. Fauré's **opera** *Penelope* (1900, revised version 1913) is highly regarded, and his other theatre works include incidental music for the play *Pelléas et Mélisande* (1898) and the delightful *Masques et Bergamasques* (1919).

*F*AUST _____

The importance of Faust in music derives from the great poetic drama of that name which occupied the poet Goethe from 1770 almost until his death in 1832. **Wagner**, **Liszt** and **Berlioz** were among the many composers drawn to the story of Faust's downfall through the agency of Mephistopheles, but the most famous musical interpretation of the story was **Gounod**'s opera *Faust*, first staged in Paris in 1859. This concentrates on an episode in Goethe's poem describing how Faust, granted a second period of youth by Mephistopheles in exchange for his immortal soul, seduces and abandons the innocent Marguerite. The opera contains many famous musical passages, including Marguerite's 'Jewel Song', 'Even Bravest Heart may Swell', sung by Marguerite's

brother Valentine, and Faust's salute to Marguerite's cottage 'All Hail thou dwelling pure and lowly'. There is also the famous waltz which accompanies the 'Kermesse' scene.

*F*ERRIER, *Kathleen* (Born Higher Walton, Lancs., 1912; died London 1953) _____

British **contralto** whose spectacular rise to world fame in no way spoiled her unaffected, humorous and lovable personality. After studies with **Roy Henderson** among others she made her London début in *Messiah* in 1943 and rapidly established a national reputation in **Bach**, **Handel** and as the Angel in **Elgar**'s *The Dream of Gerontius*. **Benjamin Britten** created the leading role in *The Rape of Lucretia* (1946) with her in mind, and the following year she followed up this operatic début with her first performances (at **Glyndebourne**) as Orpheus in **Gluck**'s *Orpheus and Eurydice*. She was only able to sing two of four scheduled performances in this role at **Covent Garden** in 1953 before her tragically premature death from cancer. Ferrier's international reputation started with her appearance in **Mahler**'s *Song of the Earth* under **Bruno Walter**'s direction at the first **Edinburgh Festival** in 1946: Walter also trained and accompanied her in recitals of German **lieder**. **Sir John Barbirolli** was another major influence on her career. Fine though she was in music of high spiritual value, she loved to relax her audiences, whenever the chance offered, with lighter material. CBE 1953.

*F*IDELIO _____

Beethoven's only **opera**, first produced in **Vienna** in 1806 but subsequently revised. It was based on a play called *Leonora, or Conjugal Love* by Brouilly, which also inspired long-forgotten operas by Gaveaux, Paer and Mayr. Florestan, a Spanish nobleman, is a political prisoner and Leonora, his wife, decides to rescue him, disguised as the boy Fidelio. Famous passages from the opera include the delightful **quartet** in Act 1 and Leonora's **aria** 'Abscheulicher' ('Accursed One'). Beethoven wrote four **overtures** for the opera. The one called *Fidelio* now normally prefaces performances of the opera. The third of the three so-called *Leonora* overtures is often used as an interlude before the final scene.

FIEDLER, *Arthur* (Born Boston, Mass., 1894; died Boston 1979)

Son of an Austrian-born violinist, Arthur Fiedler studied **piano**, **violin** and **conducting** in Berlin before joining the **Boston Symphony Orchestra** as violinist and later violist. In 1924 he formed the Boston Sinfonietta of twenty-five players which toured widely, and in 1930 took over the Boston Pops Orchestra which he directed with huge success for forty years. Many recordings are available, in a wide repertoire including film and show music.

FIELD, *John* (Born Dublin 1782; died Moscow 1837)

After a sensational début in Dublin as a pianist at the age of nine, Field was apprenticed for seven years to **Clementi** in London, where he was employed to demonstrate Clementi's **pianos**. He accompanied Clementi on a European tour ending in St Petersburg, where Field settled in 1803, remaining in Russia for most of the rest of his life. In the Russian capital, 'not to have heard Field was regarded as a sin against art and good taste'. Field composed numerous works for piano with and without **orchestra**. In advance of **Chopin** he invented the term '**Nocturne**' to describe some of his best-known compositions.

FIFE

Small flute with a narrow bore and shrill sound. Long established in military bands, it was often used, like the bugle, to convey orders to troops as well as for marching.

FILLE MAL GARDÉE, LA

Much-loved ballet first staged in Bordeaux in 1789, when the score consisted of popular French tunes. Ferdinand Hérold (1791–1833) provided a new score for the Paris production of 1828, with newly composed music but also using some of the original tunes and with various arrangements from **Donizetti** and **Rossini** operas, and it is generally this version which is heard today. In 1960 Frederick Ashton created an important new production for the Royal Ballet with music by **John Lanchbery**, based on Hérold's score but with other additions including the very popular 'Clog Dance', based by Lanchbery on a tune from the original 1789 score.

A young soldier plays the fife in Manet's painting The Fifer *(1866).*

FILM SCORES

The first complete score specially created for a film was written as early as 1908, but it was in the 1940s that the film score really came into its own. In Britain, **Vaughan Williams** wrote a score for *Scott of the Antarctic* which became his *Sinfonia Antartica*, and the transfer of film themes to the concert platform and recording market began with Richard

*F*ILM MUSIC

*W*hen **Igor Stravinsky** first went to California he received an invitation to visit the all-powerful head of MGM, Louis B. Mayer.

'They tell me you are the greatest composer in the world,' said Mayer. 'How much money would you ask to compose a film score?'

'$100,000 dollars,' replied Stravinsky.

'If you are the greatest composer in the world, you're worth the money,' said Mayer. 'Now – how long would it take you to compose an hour of music?'

'One year,' said Stravinsky, after a moment's thought.

The conversation was over. 'Goodbye, Mr Stravinsky,' said Mayer.

This little episode neatly illustrates two points. The realisation by film producers that a prestigious musical name can help to sell a movie, and the instant fluency that is required of the film composer.

What an interesting relationship has grown up in the twentieth century between the cinema and the musical world! As early as 1895, when Auguste and Louis Lumière demonstrated their *cinématographe* in a basement café in Paris, a pianist was employed, mainly to drown out the noise of the machine. Solo pianists, organists, small instrumental groups and in some cases large orchestras were increasingly employed to accompany films in the silent era. Sometimes musicians were supplied by film companies with suggestions for suitable music to accommodate the varying moods of a story; often they relied on their own ingenuity. Orchestral conductors, using a baton with a light on the end, had to keep a sharp eye on the screen to watch for changes of shot, and hope their musicians would be able to shift quickly from one piece of music on their stands to the next. The first complete score actually created for a film was written by **Camille Saint-Saëns** for *The Assassination of the Duc de Guise* in 1908, and in 1915, for his classic *The Birth of a Nation*, D.W. Griffith collaborated with Joseph Carl Breil to produce a carefully synchronised score adapted from the symphonic repertoire, including **Wagner**'s *Ride of the Valkyries*. Another important early film which required a full symphony **orchestra** to perform the score (by Edmund Meisel) was Eisenstein's *Battleship Potemkin*, and during the 1920s a number of famous composers wrote music for the silent screen, including Jacques Ibert *(The Italian Straw Hat)*, Paul Hindemith (*Krazy Kat at the Circus*), and **Dmitri Shostakovich** (*The New Babylon*).

In 1927, when Al Jolson shouted 'You ain't heard nothing yet, folks, listen to this!' and launched into his hit tune 'Mammy' in *The Jazz Singer*, the talkies were born. Very soon it was realised, as the composer Bernard Herrmann has put it, that music could not only supplement what the technicians have been able to do in films, but supply what they have been unable to do. Original scores were soon in demand for early cartoons as well as feature films, and tunes such as 'Felix Kept on Walking' for Pat Sullivan's *Felix the Cat* and 'Who's Afraid of the Big Bad Wolf' from Walt Disney's 1933 Silly Symphony *Three Little Pigs* became international favourites – foreshadowing a link between the screen and the hit parade which was to prove a gold-mine for future film-makers.

The mid-thirties saw the rise of the symphonic film score, by men such as **Erich Korngold** and Max Steiner. When he was only nine, Korngold had been hailed in Vienna as a genius by **Gustav Mahler.** His numerous film credits include *Deception*, for which he created a one-movement cello concerto, and *Anthony Adverse*, the themes of which found their way into a violin concerto. The Viennese Max Steiner made a huge impact in 1933 with his score for *King Kong* and supplied music for many other screen classics, including *Gone With the Wind* (1939).

Meanwhile, composers who had made their name elsewhere were recruited to the cinema: **Aaron Copland** and Virgil Thomson in the States, **Prokofiev** in Russia with *Lieutenant*

Kijé (1934) and *Alexander Nevsky* (1938). In Britain, the music of **Arthur Bliss** played an integral part in *Things to Come* (1936), **Benjamin Britten** contributed scores to the documentaries *Coal Face* and *Night Mail* and **William Walton**, with *Escape Me Never* (1934), began a career as a film composer which was to culminate in his superb work for Laurence Olivier in *Henry V* (1944) and *Hamlet* (1948).

The 1940s have been referred to as the Golden Age of Film Music, while the influence of **jazz** and pop was at its greatest during the 1960s and 1970s – at the same time as 'classical' themes also began to be used to great effect. Alas, the catalogue of illustrious names and credits from the 1940s to the present day is too long to include here. For those readers particularly interested, however, they appear under the entry **Film scores.**

In the history of the talkies, composers and producers have often argued about the need for any music at all. On one occasion Alfred Hitchcock announced his intention of doing without music for a scene showing a lifeboat at sea. 'After all,' he demanded, 'where is the music coming from in the middle of the ocean?' When the remark was reported to composer David Raksin, he replied, 'Ask Hitchcock where the camera comes from, and I'll tell him where the music comes from!'

No one can deny that the contribution made by music to the cinema has been incalculably great; and it could be said the cinema has done much for the world of music, not only as an employer of talent. Would the commemoration of the death of **Mozart** in 1991 have been quite so popular and widespread if it had not been for the worldwide success of Peter Shaffer's *Amadeus*?

The impact of silent films was often enhanced by an inventive pianist.

Addinsell's pastiche of **Rachmaninov** (*Warsaw Concerto*) written for *Dangerous Moonlight* (1941). Hollywood responded in 1945 with the concerto in *Spellbound*. This won an Oscar for Miklós Rózsa, whose 'Dragnet' theme for *The Killers* in 1946 remains one of the best known of all film motifs, though perhaps David Raksin's *Laura* theme of 1944 is a competitor. Another film theme which achieved huge popularity was created by the zither player Anton Karas for Carol Reed's *The Third Man* (1949). Bernard Herrmann, whose numerous credits include a long series of collaborations with Alfred Hitchcock, first made his mark with *Citizen Kane* for Orson Welles in 1941; Alfred Newman was appointed music director for 20th Century-Fox in 1940, and produced many remarkable scores of which *The Song of Bernadette* (1943) was his own favourite; Franz Waxman provided memorable music for *Rebecca* (1940) and Dmitri Tiomkin, later to write the *High Noon* theme and win an Oscar for *The High and the Mighty* (1954), made a great impact with Selznick's *Duel in the Sun* (1946). Franz Waxman opened the 1950s by winning Oscars for *Sunset Boulevard* (1950) and *A Place in the Sun* (1951); Alex North entered the lists with *A Streetcar named Desire* (1951) and *Viva Zapata!* (1952), and in 1956 George Duning attracted great attention with a love theme played as a counterpoint to 'Moonglow' in the film *Picnic*. In Britain, **Malcolm Arnold** rose to prominence as a film composer, making a particular impact in *The Bridge on the River Kwai* (1957) with his use of the **Colonel Bogey** tune. **Richard Rodney Bennett** is another important British film composer, contributing scores, for example, to *Far from the Madding Crowd* (1967) and *Murder on the Orient Express* (1974). In the 1960s and 1970s the influence of **jazz** and pop music invaded the cinema and many of the old guard in Hollywood felt overtaken by events. Films like *The Graduate* (1967), *Easy Rider* (1969) and *Midnight Cowboy* (1969) were signs of the times, but another trend emerged too. This was the use of 'classical' themes in movies, like **Mozart**'s Piano Concerto No. 21 in *Elvira Madigan* (1967), **Richard Strauss**'s *Also Sprach Zarathustra* in *2001 – A Space Odyssey* (1968) and **Mahler**'s fifth symphony in *Death in Venice* (1971). There were also many classical themes in *A Clockwork Orange* (1971). The catalogue of names and credits continues to roll. **John Williams**, who scored *Close Encounters* in 1977 and *Raiders of the Lost Ark* in 1981, more recently gave us *JFK* (1991) and *Hook* (1991). David Grusin composed *On Golden Pond* (1981), Maurice Jarre contributed *Dr Zhivago* (1965) and *Lawrence of Arabia* (1962), **Henry Mancini** was responsible for *Breakfast at Tiffany's* (1961), not to mention the *Pink Panther* theme (1963); Elmer Bernstein brought the big band sound into *The Man with the Golden Arm* (1956), John Barry memorably scored *Out of Africa* (1985) and *Dances with Wolves* (1990); Stanley Myers contributed a much-loved theme tune in *The Deer Hunter* (1978). Another remarkable British figure is George Fenton whose 1980s' credits include *Gandhi* (1982) which won an **Ivor Novello** award and *Dangerous Liaisons* (1988), while in 1991 he composed *The Fisher King* for Terry Gilliam. In recent years the prolific Carl Davis has, in addition to his other work, created a special niche for himself as the composer of orchestral scores to accompany revivals of classic silent movies, starting in 1980 with Abel Gance's *Napoleon*.

FINZI, *Gerald* (Born London 1901; died Oxford 1956) ————————

A song writer of high distinction, he created beautiful settings of Hardy and **Shakespeare**, among others, and his orchestral works include a delightful clarinet **concerto**. Established the Newbury String Players 1939.

FISCHER-DIESKAU, *Dietrich* (Born Berlin 1925) —

German **baritone** and one of the supreme singers of the twentieth century. He made his début in **Brahms**'s *German Requiem* in Freiburg in 1947 and has since appeared in most of the world's major opera houses and concert halls. Fischer-Dieskau is specially celebrated as a recitalist with a repertoire of over 1000 songs by **Schubert**, **Schumann**, Brahms, **Wolf**, **Richard Strauss** and others. He was one of the singers for whom **Britten** wrote his *War Requiem* (1962).

FLAGEOLET ————————————————

Small wind instrument related to the **recorder** family. Invented in 1581 in Paris, it became popular in Britain in the seventeenth century: Samuel Pepys and his wife both learned to play it.

Sir Geraint Evans, the greatly beloved baritone, loaded with love potions as the quack doctor Dulcamara in Donizetti's The Elixir of Love *(Covent Garden, 1984).*

The Edinburgh Festival offers infinite variety in the arts. Here festival-goers surge up the Royal Mile to watch the 1991 Tattoo at the Castle.

*F*LAGSTAD, *Kirsten* (Born Hamar, Norway, 1895; died Oslo 1962)

Flagstad spent nearly twenty years performing a variety of light **soprano** roles in Scandinavia before singing Isolde for the first time in Oslo in 1932. Débuts at Bayreuth, the **Metropolitan** and **Covent Garden** soon followed, and by the late 1930s she was established as the world's leading **Wagner** soprano. Subsequently she appeared as Dido in **Purcell**'s *Dido and Aeneas* in the tiny Mermaid Theatre built by Sir Bernard Miles in the garden of his north London home. In 1953 she bade farewell to the operatic stage in the same role at the new Mermaid Theatre in the City of London.

*F*LEDERMAUS, DIE (Johann Strauss)

Most famous and successful operetta of **Johann Strauss**, first produced in 1874 in **Vienna** where it has retained special status: on New Year's Eve it is regularly performed at both the State Opera and the Volksoper. The story tells of romantic intrigue at a fashionable masked ball given by Prince Orlofsky, but in due course all the many misunderstandings are resolved and everyone joins in a final toast to King Champagne. Favourite numbers include the often-performed Overture, Rosalinde's Csárdás, Adèle's taunting 'Mein Herr Marquis' and the so-called Watch Duet.

*F*LÜGELHORN

Family of brass instruments widely used in European bands. A flügelhorn in B flat, with the same compass as the **cornet**, is found in British **brass bands.**

*F*LUTE

Important family of wind instruments in which the player's breath causes a column of air to vibrate inside a tube made of wood or metal. Two main types of flute have existed since the Middle Ages: the transverse type held sideways, in which the player blows across a round mouth-hole, and the end-blown type such as the **flageolet** or **recorder**. With its elaborate system of keys and levers, the modern transverse flute is largely based on the metal instrument produced by Theobald Boehm in 1847.

Stephen Foster, American creator of immortal popular songs. He sold 'Old Folks at Home' for a few dollars.

*F*OSTER, *Stephen* (Born Lawrenceville, 1826; died New York 1864)

American composer of many songs which have entered into the folk heritage of the USA. At the age of twenty-five Stephen Foster sold the song 'Old Folks at Home' outright for fifteen dollars to E.P. Christy of Christy's Minstrels fame, and allowed him to pass it off as his own work. Increasing success allowed Foster to bargain for royalties, and if an unstable character had not inclined him to drink he might have made a substantial fortune. As it was, he died in poverty after a fall in a cheap Bowery hotel. Foster's minstrel songs include 'Camptown Races', 'Oh, Susannah' and 'Old Black Joe'; for drawing-room use he wrote 'Jeannie with the Light Brown Hair' (1854), 'Come where my Love lies Dreaming' (1855) and 'Beautiful Dreamer' (1864), among many other favourites.

*F*OLK MUSIC

*A*ddressing the inaugural meeting of the Folk Song Society in 1898, Sir Hubert Parry said that folk music expressed 'the quiet reticence of our country folk, courageous and content, ready to meet what chance shall bring with a cheery heart'. He was speaking at a time when there was an upsurge of interest in traditional forms of music in many countries, prompted perhaps by the relentless growth of industrialised society and the feeling that something vital was likely to be lost in the process – the kind of unsophisticated artistic creation which stems from the disappearing values of country life. It was, of course, a rosy-tinted romantic view but those passionate early twentieth-century folk music collectors were on to something. 'Folk' is now a major, money-making strand of the popular music scene.

As to what is, or what deserves to be called, folk music – the arguments on that score still rage unabated. In some parts of the world, such as Africa and the Pacific Islands, no distinction seems to exist between folk and art music. Elsewhere a wavy line is drawn between works which are carefully crafted and written down, and the relatively spontaneous creations of untutored amateurs whose songs have been passed on orally from generation to generation (and often altered in the process). In the case of instrumental music, tunes that have been invented or adapted by gifted players are inherited by succeeding generations who make their own changes both to the material itself and to the manner of performance. There's nothing fixed or final about music such as this.

The impulses which have prompted the creation of folk music are as varied as the music itself. Rhythms of work and play, annual rituals of seed-time and harvest, human ceremonies associated with birth, death and marriage, the need to dance, a love of stories and a desire to laugh have all at one time or another inspired poets and musicians. Because of the relative difficulty of communication, their creations often had a marked local character, identified strongly with one particular region or group, and this tendency has persisted into the twentieth century in music associated with particular ethnic, social or political groups. Football fans, for example, have never stopped creating new football songs or amending old ones.

A great deal of borrowing has always gone on in the world of music, and serious composers have been indebted to folk music for centuries. A Provençal folk song, 'L'Homme armé' was the basic tune used in many settings of the **Mass** from the fourteenth century onwards; the Elizabethan composer **William Byrd** wrote keyboard variations on English folk tunes such as 'Sellinger's Round' and 'The Woods So Wild' and John Gay wrote new words for many a traditional tune in ***The Beggar's Opera*** (1727). By the late eighteenth century, an interest in the 'simplicity' of country folk and former times had become fashionable, and this interest embraced folk music and poetry. Thomas Percy's *Reliques of Ancient Poetry* (1765), containing the texts though not the tunes of traditional ballads, was very influential. **Thomas Moore** (1779–1852) added words of his own to traditional Irish tunes in the ten volumes of *Irish Melodies* he published 1807–34: the best known of them include 'The Last Rose of Summer' and 'The Minstrel Boy'. Robert Burns and Sir Walter Scott performed a similar service for Scottish folk tunes, while the Edinburgh publisher George Thomson commissioned **Haydn, Beethoven** and **Weber** to make arrangements of British folk tunes. Though his contributors were so distinguished, Thomson established a regrettable precedent for the drawing-room versions of folk songs, invariably featuring the parlour **pianoforte**, which were so popular in Victorian times.

But by the end of the nineteenth century a more scholarly approach to folk music was evident, for example in Frank Kidson's *Traditional Tunes* of 1891, and the monumental study of English and Scottish ballads by the American Francis J. Child. The foundation of the Folk Song Society (later to be absorbed into the English

Kathryn Tickell, a leading exponent of the Northumbrian small-pipes, at the Cambridge Folk Festival, 1991.

Folk Dance and Song Society) was supported by **Elgar** and **Stanford** as well as Hubert Parry, and a small army of folk song collectors went out into the field to note down folk material before, as was feared, it would vanish for ever. **Vaughan Williams** netted over 800 tunes, while **Cecil Sharp** (1859–1924), working in both Britain and the United States, amassed no fewer than five

thousand. **Percy Grainger** was also an enthusiastic recruit, using the recently invented phonograph to record and analyse singing styles. Among collectors in other countries, **Béla Bartók** and **Zoltan Kodály** were active in Hungary, while in France Joseph Canteloube's arrangements of folk songs from the Auvergne (though hardly 'authentic') have become hugely popular, especially the haunting **'Baïléro'**. In Britain **Benjamin Britten**'s folk song arrangements of the 1940s were variably received, though 'The Foggy Dew' and 'The Ploughboy' were extremely successful.

During the First World War, the working-class writer Alfred Williams made a remarkable collection in the Upper Thames area of the songs people actually sang and an interest in proletarian culture led A.L. Lloyd into collecting industrial songs. Social protest became identified with folk performers both in Britain and the USA from the 1930s onwards: many names come to mind, from Alan Lomax (an important collector) and Burl Ives through Bob Dylan, Joan Baez and Judy Collins to counterparts in Britain such as Ewan McColl, Alex Campbell, the Boys of the Lough and the Chieftains. Folk clubs, mixing amateur and professional performers in both traditional and new music, have sprung up everywhere. Mixed types of music have also been developed, such as 'Bluegrass' or the largely British 'Folk-Rock' in which bands like Fairport Convention, Steeleye Span and Pentangle present traditional material in the electrically amplified form popular with many young audiences.

So is folk music dead, or very much alive and vigorously kicking? The answer probably depends on your definition of the term. I once interviewed Kathryn Tickell who is the foremost player of the Northumbrian small-pipes. In her highly successful band she combines that ancient traditional instrument with the accordion, an acoustic guitar and electric bass. The tunes the band use come from all over and the versions they play begin with improvisation. 'Authenticity' for them matters less than what works, and above all the spirit of their music-making. It's a developing process and as long as that process continues, folk music is alive, even if it happens to flourish in an urban night-club.

FRANCK, *César* (Born Liège 1822; died Paris 1890)

Belgian-born composer and organist who became a French citizen and in his later years was one of the most influential French musicians of his time. A virtuoso on both **piano** and **organ**, **Liszt** heard him and compared his skill as an improviser to that of **Bach**. Recognition as a composer was slow to come, but Franck wrote several works which have remained perennial favourites, among them the appealing Violin Sonata (1886), the *Symphonic Variations* for piano and **orchestra** (1885) and the sombre but splendid Symphony in D minor (first performed in 1889). All these works reflect Franck's invention of 'cyclic form' whereby a theme recurs in modified shape at various points in a score.

FREDERICK THE GREAT, KING OF PRUSSIA (Born Berlin 1712; died nr Potsdam 1786)

Frederick was an accomplished performer on the flute and a composer of real ability. When **J.S. Bach** visited him in 1747, the king provided a theme on which Bach created his *Musical Offering*. **C. P. E. Bach** was employed from 1740 as chief harpsichordist at the royal court, though he was not favoured as a composer because Frederick's musical tastes were extremely conservative.

FRÉMAUX, Louis (Born Aire-sur Lys 1921)

French conductor. Music Director of the Monte Carlo Orchestra 1956–65, of the City of Birmingham Orchestra 1969–78 and of the Sydney Symphony Orchestra 1979–82.

FRENI, *Mirella* (Born Modena 1935)

Italian **soprano** who combines great charm and acting skill with high vocal talent. Enchanting in light roles such as Nanetta in **Verdi**'s *Falstaff*, she has also triumphed in heavier roles such as Cio-Cio San in *Madam Butterfly* and Desdemona in Verdi's *Otello*.

FRICSAY, *Ferenc* (Born Budapest 1914; died Basle 1963)

Hungarian conductor who studied with **Kodály** and **Bartók**. Fricsay conducted major orchestras in Britain and the USA, but two sustained periods with the Berlin Radio Symphony Orchestra were central to his career.

FRIML, *Rudolf* (Born Prague 1879; died Los Angeles 1972)

The son of a baker, Friml studied composition at the Prague Conservatoire and was for six years accompanist to the violinist Jan Kubelik before settling in the USA in 1906. In 1912, following a quarrel with **Victor Herbert**, the singer Emma Trentini commissioned Friml to write the score of *The Firefly*, which included the celebrated 'Donkey Serenade' and was the first of Friml's many stage works. Among the most successful were *Rose Marie* (1924) and *The Vagabond King* (1925). From 1925 Friml established himself in Hollywood where he was active as composer, arranger, pianist and conductor almost to the end of his long life.

FRÜHBECK DE BURGOS, *Raphael* (Born Burgos 1933)

Spanish conductor of German parentage. After studies in Spain and Germany he was conductor of the Spanish National Orchestra 1962–78, and his many overseas engagements have included appearances and recordings with London's **Philharmonia**.

FUGUE

Derived from the Latin word *fuga*, meaning flight or pursuit, the Fugue in musical terms is chiefly characterised by the statement of the main theme (or subject) of the piece by all the parts or 'voices' involved, each entering successively in imitation of each other. The greatest masters of Fugue remain **Bach** and **Handel**, who added to the complexity of the form by creating double fugues with two subjects.

'**F**UNICULÌ, FUNICULÀ'

The opening in 1880 of a funicular railway up Mt Vesuvius inspired this popular song by Luigi Denza (1846–1922), a Neapolitan composer who settled in London in 1879 and became professor of singing at the **Royal Academy of Music** in 1898.

FURTWÄNGLER, *Wilhelm* (Born Berlin 1886; died Baden-Baden 1954)

Furtwängler turned to **conducting** when his early works as a composer made little impact, and he brought a composer's creative mind to the rostrum. This led to a freedom of interpretation which has often been contrasted with the more literal approach of his leading contemporary **Toscanini**. Furtwängler was identified above all with the **Berlin Philharmonic**, which he directed 1922–45 and 1948–54.

G

*G*ABRIELI, *Andrea and Giovanni*

Andrea Gabrieli was born in Venice about 1510 and became organist of St Mark's Cathedral in 1566, remaining there till his death in 1586. His most famous works, often employing separated choirs to take advantage of the Cathedral's remarkable acoustics, were written for state occasions in St Mark's. Andrea's nephew Giovanni, who was born in Venice about 1555 and died there in 1612, was among his pupils and became organist at St Mark's in 1585. He built on Andrea's experiments, employing instruments as well as voices to achieve magnificent antiphonal effects with two or more groups answering each other from different points in the great church.

*G*ALLI-CURCI, *Amelita* (Born Milan 1882; died La Jolla, Calif., 1963)

Largely self-taught, Galli-Curci became the leading **coloratura soprano** of her time. A star of the **Metropolitan** in New York for many years, she continued to appear in concert until her retirement in 1937.

*G*ALWAY, *James* (Born Belfast 1939)

With his 18-carat gold **flute** 'Jimmie' Galway is a Pied Piper who has led a whole generation of young musicians to take up the instrument, but few indeed can aspire to imitate his uniquely rounded and rich tone. After studies in London and Paris (with **Jean-Pierre Rampal**) he graduated via the Royal Shakespeare Theatre, **Sadler's Wells**, **Covent Garden** and the BBC Symphony to the position of principal flute in the **London Symphony Orchestra**. Then in 1969 he was propelled into international orbit when **Karajan** chose him as principal flautist of the **Berlin Philharmonic**. In 1975 Galway left Berlin to pursue a solo career

which has brought him show-biz stardom as well as the highest respect for his musical talents. At the end of the 1970s a bad accident threatened to stop his activities, but he recovered and remains one of music's most charismatic performers.

*G*AMELAN

A type of instrumental ensemble found in Indonesia which delights the listener with its assortment of tuned and untuned percussion instruments (chimes, gongs, **marimbas**, **xylophones** and **drums**). Often used to accompany singing, dancing or dramatic performances. A very popular gamelan has been established at the **Royal Festival Hall** in London.

*G*AVOTTE (*Mignon*)

The most familiar piece by the French composer Ambroise Thomas (1811–96). *Mignon* (1866), based on Goethe's *Wilhelm Meister*, was his greatest operatic success.

*G*EDDA, *Nicolai* (Born Stockholm 1925)

Swedish **tenor** of great elegance and versatility. His Russian father, choirmaster of the Russian Orthodox church in Leipzig, gave him an early acquaintance with a rich ecclesiastical repertoire. This has remained important to him in a career which has included most of the principal tenor roles in **opera** at many leading opera houses. Gedda sings with equal facility in Russian, German, French, Italian and English, as well as the Scandinavian languages.

*G*ERMAN, *Edward* (Born Whitchurch, Shropshire, 1862; died London 1936)

Born German Edward Jones, Edward German made his name as a composer with incidental music for period plays, notably Shakespeare's *King Henry VIII* (1892) and Anthony Hope's *Nell Gwynn* (1900). His greatest single triumph was *Merrie England* (1902), a light opera set in the time of Queen Elizabeth I. Having completed **Sullivan**'s unfinished work *The Emerald Isle*, *Merrie England* established German as his successor. Knighted 1928.

*G*ERSHWIN, *George* (born Brooklyn 1898; died Hollywood 1937)

Gershwin once asked **Ravel** to give him lessons. The story goes that Ravel then asked Gershwin how much he earned each year from his compositions. 'About a hundred thousand dollars', said Gershwin. 'In that case', said Ravel, 'you give *me* lessons'. Born of Russian immigrant parents, Gershwin was a prodigious creator of melody and a gifted pianist. He had his first big hit in 1919 with 'Swanee' – Al Jolson's record boosted sheet music sales to over two million. Many more successful songs (many with lyrics by his brother Ira), and musical shows for the theatre and cinema followed. *Lady be Good* (1924), *Funny Face* (1927) and *Strike up the Band* (1930) were among the most successful. *Of Thee I Sing* (1931) was the first **musical** to win a Pulitzer Prize. As Gershwin's encounter with Ravel suggests, he had ambitions in the world of serious music. In 1924 Paul Whiteman commissioned him to write *Rhapsody in Blue* with its piquant mixture of **jazz** and 'classical' techniques. The Piano Concerto in F followed in 1925, and the tone poem *An American in Paris* (1928) was another large-scale concert work. Gershwin's masterpiece was the **opera** *Porgy and Bess*, first produced in 1935 in New York to a mixed reception. Now widely performed, it is the only American opera to be accepted into the international repertoire.

GEWANDHAUS ORCHESTRA

One of Europe's leading **orchestras**, 180 strong, it took its name from the Gewandhaus (Cloth Hall) in Leipzig where it performed from 1781. Its current maestro (since 1970) is **Kurt Masur**.

GHIAUROV, *Nicolai* (Born Velingrad 1929)

Bulgarian **bass**, prominent internationally since the late 1950s. One of the finest singers in the **Chaliapin** tradition, he is best known for the title role in **Moussorgsky**'s *Boris Godounov*.

GIBBONS, *Orlando* (Born Oxford 1583; died Canterbury 1625)

Gibbons was a versatile composer, best known today for **madrigals** such as 'The Silver Swan' and **anthems** including 'O Clap Your Hands' and 'This is the Record of John'.

GIBSON, *Alexander* (Born Motherwell 1926)

Scottish conductor. Musical Director of the **Scottish National Orchestra** (1959–84) and founding Musical Director of **Scottish Opera** (1962–87). Knighted 1977.

GIESEKING, *Walter* (Born Lyons 1895; died London 1956)

Distinguished German pianist who excelled in the mainstream Germanic repertoire but is particularly remembered for his refined interpretation of French music. His complete recordings of the **piano** music of **Debussy** and **Ravel** have, perhaps, never been surpassed.

GIGLI, *Beniamino* (Born Recanati 1890; died Rome 1957)

Very popular and successful Italian **tenor**, regarded as the heir of **Caruso**. For sheer beauty of sound he was unmatched in his day, though he had a tendency to 'play to the gallery' with over-sentimental touches and his acting ability was of quite a low order. Gigli's **La Scala** début took place in 1918 under **Toscanini** as Faust in Boito's *Mefistofele*. This remained a favourite among his sixty stage roles, but he is perhaps remembered best as Rodolfo in *La Bohème* (the role he sang in his last **Covent Garden** appearance in 1946 opposite his daughter Rina as Mimì), the Duke in *Rigoletto* and Cavaradossi in **Puccini**'s *Tosca*. The enthusiasm which attended Gigli's concert and recital appearances foreshadowed the immense popular success of **Pavarotti** in the television age. Gigli's many recordings include some delightful renderings of Neapolitan songs.

GILELS, *Emil* (Born Odessa 1916; died Moscow 1985)

One of the leading pianists of his time, a master interpreter of the mainstream repertoire, particularly noted for his **Beethoven**, but a champion too of **Prokofiev**, whose Eighth Piano Sonata is dedicated to him.

GISELLE

'Fantastic **ballet**' in two acts with music by the Frenchman Adolphe Adam (1803–56), whose best known work it is. After its Paris première in 1841, *Giselle* became universally popular. Its leading role is regarded as a great challenge to the classical ballerina.

*G*IULINI, *Carlo Maria* (Born Burletta 1914) _____

Italian conductor of high distinction. Closely associated with **Maria Callas**, and with the directors Luchino Visconti and Franco Zeffirelli. In 1958 he began a fruitful relationship with the **Philharmonia Orchestra** in London and conducted a memorable Visconti production of **Verdi**'s *Don Carlos* to mark the centenary of **Covent Garden.** After the 1967 Visconti production of *La Traviata* at the same house, Giulini announced that he would thenceforth concentrate on the concert repertoire, to which he has brought all his consummate skill and unassuming integrity.

*G*LASGOW ORPHEUS CHOIR _____

Mixed choir whose exceptionally well-drilled sound was the creation of Sir Hugh Roberton (1874–1952). He conducted the choir throughout its fifty years of existence (1901–51). Perhaps the most famous of many recordings is 'All in an April Evening'.

*G*LAZOUNOV, *Alexander* (Born St Petersburg 1856; died Paris 1936) _____

Russian composer, pupil of **Rimsky-Korsakov**, who scored a big success with his First Symphony at the age of sixteen. Influenced at first by Russian **folk music**, his style later became more cosmopolitan. Under the Soviets he was made a 'People's Artist of the Republic' but left Russia for good in 1928. Most popular work is the **ballet** *The Seasons* (1899) with its 'Waltz of the Cornflowers and Poppies' and the autumn 'Bacchanale'. The ballet *Raymonda* (1897) and the Violin Concerto in A minor (1904) are also well known, and other works include the engaging Saxophone Concerto (1934).

*G*LEE _____

A cheerful form of part song for male voices, popular in England between about 1750 and 1830. Many 'glee clubs' were formed, and the term is often still used in the USA.

*G*LINKA, *Mikhail* (Born nr Smolensk 1804; died Berlin 1857 _____

Russian composer, often termed 'the father of Russian music'. A trip to Italy (1830–3), where he heard works by **Bellini** and **Donizetti**, fired Glinka

George Gershwin, whose creative gifts often found expression in brilliant piano improvisations.

with the desire to write a Russian **opera**. After a year of study in Berlin, he composed *A Life for the Tsar* (1836) and *Russlan and Ludmilla* (1842) which was even more truly Russian in style. Through his operas, and works such as the **fantasia** *Kamarinskaya* (1848), based on two folk-songs, Glinka exerted a powerful influence over **Balakirev**, **Borodin**, **Rimsky-Korsakov** and **Tchaikovsky.**

*G*LOCKENSPIEL _____

Percussion instrument made of graduated metal bars arranged in two rows and struck by hand with small, hard beaters. A close relation is the **celesta**, in which the bars are struck through the medium of a keyboard.

GILBERT and SULLIVAN

W. S. GILBERT and Arthur SULLIVAN

1836	William Schwenk Gilbert born in London
1842	Arthur Seymour Sullivan born in London
1875	*Trial by Jury*
1877	*The Sorcerer*
1878	*HMS Pinafore*
1879	*The Pirates of Penzance*
1881	*Patience*
1882	*Iolanthe*
1884	*Princess Ida*
1885	*The Mikado*
1887	*Ruddigore*
1888	*The Yeomen of the Guard*
1889	*The Gondoliers*
1900	Sir Arthur Sullivan died
1911	Sir William Schwenk Gilbert died

W.S. Gilbert and Arthur Sullivan had individual talents of a high order and worked with other collaborators, but it is their work together as that composite creature 'Gilbert and Sullivan' which has earned them both immortality.

The two men could hardly have been more different: Sullivan the darling of high society, knighted by Queen Victoria when he was only forty-one; Gilbert cantankerous and cross-grained, obliged to wait for King Edward VII to award him a knighthood in 1909.

Gilbert was called to the Bar, earning less than a hundred pounds from his two years as a barrister. Sullivan graduated from being a chorister in the **Chapel Royal** to win the **Mendelssohn** scholarship at the **Royal Academy of Music**. He continued his studies in Leipzig where his incidental music for *The Tempest* brought him an ovation at the age of nineteen. Gilbert meanwhile had put his spare time to good use, winning attention with comic verses signed 'Bab' and with the production in 1866 of his burlesque *Dulcamara*.

Both men, therefore, had a record of achievement behind them when they first met in 1869. Sullivan accepted the suggestion that he should set Gilbert's libretto *Thespis* to music. The piece opened and closed within a month, mainly because it was far too long.

At the request of Richard D'Oyly Carte, the young manager of the Royal Theatre in Soho, they tried again with Gilbert's one-act legal **operetta** *Trial by Jury*. Sullivan completed the score in three weeks, and the piece opened in a double bill with **Offenbach**'s *La Périchole* in March 1875. It was an instant success and ran for a year.

In his early thirties, Sullivan was already regarded as the most significant figure in British music. However, he did not think it beneath his dignity to work with Gilbert on a new piece for D'Oyly Carte's specially formed Comedy Opera Company. This was *The Sorcerer* which opened in 1877 to rather mixed notices and ran for 175 performances. Its successor *HMS Pinafore* was ready to open almost as soon as the run ended: it was the first out-and-out hit of the partnership.

Pinafore, in pirated versions, was soon making Gilbert and Sullivan famous in the United States, and *The Pirates of Penzance* opened in New York on New Year's Eve 1879. Gilbert decided to satirise the aesthetic movement in his next libretto, *Patience*, which was assured of success in the States when D'Oyly Carte was able to arrange a transatlantic lecture tour for Oscar Wilde to coincide with the opera's opening.

By this time D'Oyly Carte had made enough money to build a brand new theatre, the Savoy. *Patience* was moved there in the middle of its run in 1881. The House of Lords was Gilbert's target in *Iolanthe*, a satire much enjoyed by the Prime Minister, Mr Gladstone.

After *Princess Ida*, which lampooned higher education for women, Sullivan began to show signs of restlessness; he wanted to compose a serious theatre work in which music had the primary role. But he agreed when Gilbert suggested a new piece to cash in on the craze for things Japanese, and *The Mikado* proved the greatest success of the partnership.

It took a promise on Richard D'Oyly Carte's part to build a new theatre specially to house Sullivan's opera *Ivanhoe* before he would agree to a further piece for the Savoy. This was *The Gondoliers*, one of the greatest hits of the series, and the last major success. *Utopia Ltd* (1893) and *The Grand Duke* (1896) were lacking in the partners' former inspiration.

No wonder. The triumvirate of Gilbert, Sullivan and D'Oyly Carte was terminally shaken by a quarrel as to who should pay for a new carpet in the theatre. There was, however, a move towards reconciliation just before Sullivan died, and when his memorial was erected it bore an inscription of lines by Gilbert from *The Yeomen of the Guard*:

'Is life a boon?
If so, it must befall
That death, whene'er he call
Must call too soon.'

Gilbert survived his partner by over ten years.

Postscript

For half a century after the death of Gilbert, the D'Oyly Carte Opera Company exercised a monopoly in the professional production of the Gilbert and Sullivan operas, but after the expiry of Gilbert's copyright, other companies were free to produce the operas as they thought fit. One of the most successful of these productions was Joseph Papp's *The Pirates of Penzance* (1980), in which the music was reorchestrated by William Elliott with Linda Ronstadt. Jonathan Miller's *Mikado* (1986) is an example of the innovative Gilbert and Sullivan successes of **English National Opera**. The D'Oyly Carte Opera Company ceased operations in 1982 but was revived in 1988. Now, thanks to the support of **Birmingham** City Council and British Midland, the company tours extensively from a permanent base at the Alexandra Theatre, Birmingham. Whether the operas stand their best chance of survival in traditional-style productions or in updated versions remains a matter of sharp controversy among Gilbert and Sullivan enthusiasts.

Jonathan Miller's production of The Mikado *for English National Opera, 1986.*

*G*LOVER, *Jane* (Born Helmsley, Yorks., 1949) ———

Not the first successful woman conductor but, thanks to media exposure, probably the best known. At first a musicologist specialising in the Italian **Baroque** period and a lecturer at Oxford University (1976–84), she made her conducting début at the 1975 Wexford Festival with her own edition of Cavalli's *Eritrea*. Chorus Master at **Glyndebourne** (1980) and Director of Glyndebourne Touring Opera (1982–5). Artistic Director of the London Mozart Players (1984–92), in succession to Harry Blech, and currently Principal Conductor of the Huddersfield Choral Society. Jane Glover has also become a very successful TV presenter.

*G*LUCK, *Christoph* (Born Erasbach, Bavaria, 1714; died Vienna 1787) ———

German composer famous for his operatic reforms. After studies in Prague and Italy he began producing Italian **operas**, and in 1745–6 two of his stage works were produced in London. There he met **Handel**, who remarked that Gluck knew no more **counterpoint** than his (Handel's) cook. Settling in **Vienna**, Gluck at first turned out French comic operas, and conventional works in the established style of Italian *opera seria*. However, in 1761 he produced a new kind of 'action' ballet in *Don Juan* which influenced **Mozart** in *Don Giovanni*, and the following year he collaborated with the librettist Ranieri Calzabigi in *Orpheus and Eurydice* which brought a new kind of noble simplicity, dramatic cohesion and emotional truth to opera. The great lament of Orpheus – 'Che Farò?' ('What shall I do?') – and the 'Dance of the Blessed Spirits' remain very popular. *Alceste* (1767) and *Paris and Helen* (1770), composed on similar principles, were less well received, and Gluck decided to try his luck in Paris in 1773, where his fortunes were mixed. Gluck returned to Vienna in 1779 and lived out his last years in grand style. He suffered a series of strokes and died after defying doctor's orders by drinking a glass of liqueur after dinner.

*G*LYNDEBOURNE ———

In 1934 John Christie and his wife, the **soprano** Audrey Mildmay, opened an **opera** house at their country home, Glyndebourne, near Lewes in Sussex. Initially Fritz Busch (conductor) and Carl Ebert

(producer) concentrated on operas by **Mozart**, but the repertoire is now much more extensive and, since 1968, Glyndebourne Touring Opera has taken the almost invariably distinguished productions around Great Britain in the autumn. The high standards of Glyndebourne derive from the spotting of brilliant international talents before they are established. A new horseshoe-shaped auditorium is due to open in 1994.

*G*OBBI, *Tito* (Born Bassano del Grappa, nr Venice, 1913; died Rome 1984) ———

Italian operatic **baritone**, and from 1965 **opera** director. After initially studying law, Gobbi made his singing début in Italy in 1935, and emerged as a major international star after the Second World War. He sang more than 100 roles but was specially famous as the evil Scarpia in *Tosca*, as Iago in **Verdi**'s **Otello** and in the title role of the same composer's *Falstaff*. He appeared in twenty-six films, not all of them operatic, and published two books, including a volume of autobiography.

'*G*OD BLESS THE PRINCE OF WALES' ———

Song published in 1862 with words translated from the Welsh by John Ceiriog Hughes and music by Brinley Richards (1817–85).

'*G*OD SAVE THE QUEEN (KING)' ———

The origin of both the words and music of the national **anthem** are obscure. Its adoption as a national song seems to date from 1745 when it was sung in theatres at the time of the landing of the Young Pretender. Some twenty countries have followed Britain in using the tune over the years; **Beethoven** wrote a set of piano variations on it 'to show the English what a blessing they have' in their anthem. In the USA it is sung with words written in 1831 by the Rev. Samuel Francis Smith ('My country, 'tis of thee') under the title 'America'.

*G*ODOWSKY, *Leopold* (Born nr Vilnius 1870; died New York 1938) ———

American virtuoso pianist and composer of Lithuanian birth. His paraphrases of **Strauss** waltzes are well known, as is the nostalgic and charming 'Alt Wien' ('Old Vienna').

*G*OMEZ, *Jill* (Born New Amsterdam, British Guiana, 1942) ——————————

British **soprano**. Made her **Covent Garden** début in **Tippett**'s *The Knot Garden* (1970). Her recordings include a selection of Cabaret Classics and an album of Latin American songs ('South of the Border').

'*G*O NOT, HAPPY DAY' ——————————

Probably the best-known song of Frank Bridge (1879–1941). Written in 1916, it is in a more accessible idiom than some of Bridge's later works which were more avant-garde.

*G*OODALL, *Reginald* (Born Lincoln 1901; died nr Canterbury 1990) ——————————

British conductor who conducted the first performance of **Britten**'s *Peter Grimes* at **Sadler's Wells** (1945). His conducting of *The Mastersingers* for Sadler's Wells Opera in 1968 revealed him as a great Wagnerian. Knighted 1985.

'*G*OODBYE' ——————————

Intensely sentimental song, with words by G. J. Whyte-Melville, composed in 1881 by the Italian composer Paolo Tosti (1846–1916), who had settled in London the previous year as singing-master to the royal family. British subject 1906, knighted 1908.

*G*OODMAN, *Benny* (Born Chicago 1909; died New York 1986) ——————————

American clarinettist equally at home in **jazz** and the classical repertoire. He commissioned and gave the premières of works by **Bartók**, **Copland** and Hindemith, and performed with many leading **orchestras** and **chamber** groups; his recordings include **Mozart**'s Clarinet Concerto and Clarinet Quintet. As a jazz musician, Goodman made his début in 1921 at the age of twelve. The famous band he formed in 1934 pioneered a new form of jazz which earned Goodman the title 'King of Swing'.

*G*OOSSENS FAMILY ——————————

Well-known Belgian–British musical dynasty. Eugène (1845–1906) was born in Bruges but settled in London in 1873: Principal Conductor of **Carl Rosa Opera** (1889–93), subsequently lived in Liverpool. He was the father of another Eugène (1867–1958)

Benny Goodman: dubbed 'King of Swing', he was also master of the classical clarinet.

who was Principal Conductor of the Carl Rosa company (1899–1915). The latter's five children all became distinguished musicians. The **horn** player Adolphe died of war wounds in 1916; Eugene (1893–1962) was **Beecham**'s associate conductor (1915–20), conducted widely in Britain and the USA in the twenties and thirties and in 1947 became conductor of the Sydney Symphony Orchestra, for which work he was knighted in 1955; Marie (born 1894) was active as a leading harpist until well into her nineties (OBE 1984); Léon (1897–1988) was regarded as the finest oboist of the day, giving his instrument a new status and inspiring new works by many leading composers; Sidonie (born 1899) was principal harpist of the BBC Symphony Orchestra for fifty years from its foundation in 1930, and returned as soloist at the **Proms** 1991 (OBE 1981).

GLENNIE

Evelyn GLENNIE

1965	Born in Aberdeen
1973	Hearing difficulties began
1978	Joined Cults Percussion Ensemble
1982	Entered Royal Academy of Music
1984	Won Shell Percussion Scholarship
1985	BBC-TV documentary: *A Will to Win*. Won top graduation prize at RAM
1986	Studied in Japan with Keiko Abe
1989	Gave first-ever solo percussion recital at Proms

*I*n the course of her life, Evelyn Glennie has received many awards. In 1989, for instance, Junior Chamber International voted her one of the Ten Outstanding Young People of the World. She attracts such accolades because she has battled against the worst disability a musician can suffer to become one of the world's leading instrumentalists, an extraordinary achievement accomplished with infectious charm and good humour.

Evelyn is the daughter of a farmer from a remote part of Aberdeenshire. Her childhood was a happy one, lived to a great extent out of doors. She picked out tunes on the piano at an early age and plucked away for hours on a toy guitar she'd seen in a local shop window.

At the age of eight she began to have trouble with the sound on television and in her diary posed the question: 'I wonder if I'm losing my hearing?' For the time being she told no one of these troubles, began piano lessons and within a year had been awarded the highest marks in the Trinity College of Music Grade One exam.

Evelyn's hearing continued to deteriorate and, at the age of eleven, a specialist advised her parents to send her to the Aberdeen School for the Deaf. But Evelyn thought she would be cut off from music there and went as originally planned to Ellon Academy, which had a strong music department. There, equipped with powerful hearing aids, Evelyn flirted briefly with the **clarinet** before deciding she wanted most to be a percussionist.

She was encouraged by Ron Forbes, her **percussion** teacher, and soon found she worked best by discarding her hearing aids and learning to control her movements to achieve the right volume of sound. Gifted with perfect pitch, she discovered she could tune her tympani by feeling the slackness or tension of the skin. 'I can also tell the quality of a note by what I feel,' she wrote in her autobiography *Good Vibrations*. 'I can sense musical sound through my feet and lower body, and also through my hands.'

Evelyn found playing percussion in the school **orchestra** extremely boring. She wanted to be a soloist, or at any rate play with a group which offered her instruments more prominence; the chance came with the Cults Percussion Ensemble, later the Grampian Schools Percussion Ensemble, which appeared with great success for several years at the Schools Proms in London. Already she was dreaming of a professional career in music, and this unlikely ambition for one so profoundly deaf took a major step forward in 1981. Ann Rachlin, founder of the **Beethoven** Fund for Deaf Children was hugely impressed by Evelyn Glennie's performance at the Schools Prom and, after an exacting audition with veteran percussionist **James Blades**, the sixteen-year-old was urged to seek admission to one of the major music schools. In September 1982 she was admitted to the **Royal Academy of Music**.

By this time the press had begun to take an interest in Evelyn as a phenomenon, and she was in great demand on radio and television after being named Scot of the Year by **BBC** Radio Scotland. Two years later BBC Television made a full-scale documentary about her in the series *A Will to Win*, and Evelyn has continued to attract media interest ever since. Sometimes, she feels, for the wrong reasons. She would like to be taken

Evelyn Glennie in concert, demonstrating her 'four mallet' technique.

seriously simply as a musician, yet also realises that such publicity, though unwelcome to her, may encourage other young people with hearing problems.

At the Royal Academy, Evelyn continued to find orchestral work irksome. Her ambition to be a soloist was reinforced by hearing a master class given by the **marimba** player Keiko Abe; this inspired Evelyn to develop a prodigious 'four-mallet' technique of her own and in 1986, with the help of a grant from the Countess of Munster Trust, she fulfilled her determination to study with Keiko Abe in Japan.

Meanwhile, Evelyn had won the prestigious Shell Percussion Scholarship; she had also graduated from the Royal Academy with the highest honours. 1986 brought an important début at the Wigmore Hall in London. Together with the duo pianists **Bracha Eden** and **Alexander Tamir**, she took part in **Béla Bartók**'s Sonata for Two Pianos and Percussion,

a work Evelyn was to record the following year with **Murray Perahia** and **Sir Georg Solti** at the keyboards.

The word unique is overworked but it can legitimately be applied to Evelyn Glennie. Her extraordinary skills have prompted a number of composers to create new works for her, and she also includes in her programmes pieces of her own composition. Her arrangements of familiar compositions originally written for other instruments, such as **Kreisler**'s *Tambourin Chinois*, **Saint-Saëns**'s Introduction and Rondo Capriccioso, and Monti's Csárdás are guaranteed to bring the house down. Evelyn Glennie loves the whole business of human communication; through her chosen language of music, she is an outstanding exponent of that art.

*G*ÓRECKI, *Henryk* (Born Czernice, Poland, 1933)

Polish composer educated in Katowice, near Oświecim (Auschwitz). His third symphony ('Symphony of Sorrowful Songs'), written in 1976, is in part the setting of a poem written on the wall of a Gestapo prison by an 18-year-old Polish girl. The London Sinfonietta recording of the work has achieved phenomenal popularity, rising to the top of both classical and pop charts in 1993.

*G*OTTSCHALK, *Louis Moreau* (Born New Orleans 1829; died nr Rio de Janeiro 1869)

Very successful American pianist who also composed tuneful music, much of it reflecting his upbringing by his French Creole mother. Compositions include 'Le Bananier' ('The Banana Tree'), 'The Banjo' and 'Souvenir de Puerto Rico', as well as two **symphonies** and a short **opera**. A youthful prodigy praised for his playing by **Chopin**, Gottschalk toured widely, giving 1000 concerts in one three-year period.

*G*OULD, *Glenn* (Born Toronto 1932; died Toronto 1982)

Canadian pianist famous for his brilliance and eccentricity – he was noted for singing along with his playing. In 1964 gave up concerts in favour of recording, in order to achieve more perfect performances.

*G*OUNOD, *Charles* (born Paris 1818; died nr Paris 1893)

French composer. After winning the Prix de Rome at the Paris Conservatoire when he was twenty-one, Gounod spent three years in Italy, where he discovered the music of **Palestrina**. Returning to Paris, he worked as an organist and concentrated on composing sacred music. His fourth **opera**, *Faust*, produced in Paris in 1859, brought him international celebrity: it remains one of the world's most popular operas. In the same year the famous 'Ave Maria' appeared, with words added to Gounod's *Meditation*, based on the first Prelude of **Bach**'s '48' (the Well-tempered Clavier). *Romeo and Juliet* (1867) was also a major operatic success. In 1870, Gounod escaped the Franco-Prussian war by going to England where he remained for four years, establishing a disastrous liaison with an amateur singer, Georgina Weldon. Gounod's popularity in Britain was rein-

forced by the **oratorios** *The Redemption* (1881) and *Mors et vita* (1885), both produced for the Birmingham Festival.

*G*RAINGER, *Percy* (born Brighton, Melbourne, 1882; died White Plains, New York, 1961)

Australian-born composer and pianist of exuberant and eccentric character. From 1905 was very active in the English Folk Song Society, collecting some five hundred songs with the aid of wax cylinder recording. Befriended by **Delius**, who based his *Brigg Fair* on a Grainger folk-song arrangement, and by **Grieg**, whose piano concerto Grainger recorded on a piano-roll. In 1914 he went to America and in 1918 became a US citizen. During a visit to Australia (1934–5) he established the Grainger Museum in Melbourne, bequeathing his skeleton to the museum 'for possible display': the offer was not taken up. Grainger's light pieces such as 'Handel in the Strand', 'Shepherd's Hey', 'Country Gardens' and 'Mock Morris' have remained very popular at the expense of more ambitious works. Resolutely Anglo-Saxon in his approach, he replaced Italian marks of expression in his scores with English words – for example, 'Louden lots' in place of 'molto crescendo'.

*G*RAMOPHONE

Device for reproducing recorded sound. The first practical machine was constructed in 1877 by the American Thomas Edison: it was called the 'phonograph' and used wax cylinders ('phonograms'). By 1888 the German-born American Emil Berliner had introduced the use of shellac plates which could easily be reproduced by using a master copy as a stamper. The patented title for his machine was 'grammophone' (later, 'gramophone'). Commercial recording now began: **Caruso**'s 1903 recording of 'Vesti la giubba' from ***Pagliacci*** was the first million-seller. In 1925 came the advent of electric recording which involved the conversion of sound waves into electrical energy. There remained the problem of the short playing time of 78 rpm records; this was solved in 1948 when the Columbia Co. in the USA introduced the long-playing (LP) record made of vinyl and revolving at $33^{1}/_{3}$ rpm. This gave some twenty-three minutes of playing time per side, with obvious advantages for the classical repertoire. The smaller 45 rpm records were mainly used for popular music. In 1958

Stephane Grappelli: supreme master of the jazz violin for over sixty years.

war, this was premiered at the **Metropolitan** in New York in 1916. An engagement to play at the White House meant that Granados missed a ship going directly to Spain. Instead he boarded the SS *Sussex* which was torpedoed in the English Channel. The orchestral **Intermezzo** from the opera *Goyescas* and the twelve Spanish Dances composed between 1892 and 1900 are his best-known works. One of his military marches for piano duet was the signature tune for some years of *Baker's Dozen* on **BBC** Radio 4.

*G*RAND CANYON SUITE

Orchestral **suite** in the symphonic **jazz** idiom by Ferde Grofé (1892–1972). He first won fame in 1924 as the orchestrator, for Paul Whiteman's band, of **Gershwin**'s *Rhapsody in Blue*.

*G*RAPPELLI, *Stephane* (Born Paris 1908)

French violinist, one of the pioneers of the use of the **violin** in **jazz**. After only four years of formal training (1924–8), Grappelli (originally spelt Grappelly) started playing jazz and in 1934 with the guitarist **Django Reinhardt** formed the Quintette du Hot Club de France which lasted five years and made many classic jazz recordings. Since then Grappelli's career has taken him all over the world: in 1988 he gave an eightieth birthday concert in New York's **Carnegie Hall**. Since 1973 he has done much playing and recording with **Yehudi Menuhin** and subsequently with **Nigel Kennedy**.

'*G*REENSLEEVES'

English traditional tune first referred to in 1580 and mentioned twice in **Shakespeare**'s *Merry Wives of Windsor*. Basis of the beloved *Fantasia on Greensleeves* by **Vaughan Williams**.

*G*REGORIAN CHANT

A type of unison **plainsong** identified with Pope Gregory I (*c*.540–*c*.604) which became the standard form of ritual melody in the early Western Christian Church until the rise of harmonised singing in the tenth century.

*G*RIEG, *Edvard* (Born Bergen 1843; died Bergen 1907)

Norway's foremost composer. Born into a well-to-do family of Scottish descent (originally Greig), Grieg's

stereo records and equipment began to be introduced. The 'compact tape cassette', introduced in 1965, soon rivalled, then outstripped, the sales of vinyl discs. From 1979 digital recording led to the gradual replacement of the vinyl LP by the **compact disc**.

*G*RANADOS, *Enrique* (Born Lérida 1867; died at sea, English Channel, 1916)

Spanish composer and pianist who studied composition in Barcelona and later the **piano** in Paris under Bériot (who also taught **Ravel**). In 1898 Granados's *zarzuela* 'Maria del Carmen' was a success, but full recognition awaited the appearance in 1911 of his piano **suite** *Goyescas*, inspired by the paintings of Goya: a Paris performance led to an invitation to compose an **opera** based on the suite. Owing to the talent as composer and pianist was recognised by the famous Norwegian violinist Ole Bull, at whose suggestion he went to study in Leipzig. There he came under the influence of **Mendelssohn** and **Schumann**, but it was the **folk music** of his native Norway which chiefly interested him. The première of his Piano Concerto in 1869 won him international acclaim. **Liszt** played it through at sight when Grieg and he met in Rome. In 1874 the Norwegian government granted Grieg an annuity, and that year he composed incidental music for Ibsen's *Peer Gynt*. Grieg travelled widely, often visiting England where he befriended **Delius** and **Grainger**. Grieg's music has great freshness and charm, and a strong flavour of Norwegian folk-tunes.

*G*ROVES, *Charles* (Born London 1915; died London 1992)

Beloved British conductor of great modesty but substantial achievement. Notable periods with the BBC Northern Orchestra 1944–51, Bournemouth Symphony Orchestra 1951–61, Royal Liverpool Philharmonic 1963–77 and **English National Opera** 1978–9. Knighted 1973.

*G*RUBEROVÁ, *Edita* (Born 1946)

Spectacularly gifted Czech **soprano**. Joined the **Vienna** State Opera 1970 and has since established a high-level international career, specialising in **coloratura** roles such as *Lucia di Lammermoor*.

*G*RUMIAUX, *Arthur* (Born Villers-Perwin 1921; died Brussels 1986)

Belgian violinist whose playing had exceptional purity, elegance and strength. Many **concerto** recordings, and famous sets of **Beethoven** and **Mozart sonatas** with the pianist Clara Haskil.

*G*UEDEN, *Hilde* (Born Vienna 1917; died Klosterneuberg 1988)

Austrian **soprano** specially noted for her **Mozart** and **Richard Strauss** roles. Leading member of **Vienna** State Opera 1946–73.

*G*UI, *Vittorio* (Born Rome 1885; died Florence 1975)

Italian conductor especially associated with **Mozart**, **Brahms** and **Rossini**, several of whose lesser-known

operas he revived. Helped found the Florence Maggio Musicale Festival 1933; conducted at **Glyndebourne** 1952–64.

*G*UILMANT, *Alexandre* (Born Boulogne 1837; died Meudon, Paris, 1911)

French organist and prolific composer for his instrument. Organist of La Trinité in Paris for thirty years from 1871; Professor of **Organ** at the Paris Conservatoire. Pioneer of organ recitals from 1878 and, with **Widor**, of the organ **symphony**.

*G*UITAR

Stringed instrument whose fingerboard has frets against which the fingers of one hand are pressed to create different notes, while the strings (normally six made of nylon – formerly gut – in the modern classical guitar) are plucked by the fingers of the other hand. Popular in France, Italy and Spain in the sixteenth and seventeenth centuries; in the nineteenth attracted composers such as **Paganini**, **Weber**, **Schubert** and **Berlioz.**

*G*URNEY, *Ivor* (Born Gloucester 1890; died Dartford 1937)

English composer of eighty-two songs, mainly settings of his own poems or those of A.E. Housman. Gassed and shellshocked in the First World War, he suffered a breakdown in 1922.

*G*YMNOPÉDIES

Three haunting and very popular piano pieces by the whimsical French composer Erik Satie (1866–1925). The title refers to dances performed in ancient Greece by naked men and boys in honour of Apollo.

H

*H*AENDEL, *Ida* (Born Chelm, Poland, 1923)

Polish-born violinist who became British 1940. Made a great impression 'as a little girl in a short frock and socks' on **Sir Henry Wood**, who conducted her London début in 1937 in **Beethoven**'s Concerto. CBE 1991.

A Shakespearean rogue set to music – Claudio Desderi stars with Remy Corazza as Dr Caius in the 1988 Glyndebourne production of Verdi's Falstaff.

The concert harp. Beautiful in itself, it was regarded by Victorian men as a vehicle for displaying shapely feminine arms. Jane Lister keeps hers covered.

HAHN, *Reynaldo* (Born Carácas 1875; died Paris 1947)

French composer of Venezuelan birth. Hahn created an operetta masterpiece in *Ciboulette* (1923) and wrote the song 'Si mes vers avaient des ailes' ('If my verses had wings') when he was only thirteen.

HAITINK, *Bernard* (Born Amsterdam 1929)

Dutch conductor of great distinction, who prefers a few sustained commitments to worldwide guest appearances. In 1961, jointly with Eugen Jochum at first, he was appointed the youngest-ever Principal Conductor of the **Concertgebouw** Orchestra, an office he held until 1988. Chief Conductor of the **London Philharmonic** 1967–79; appointed Music Director at **Glyndebourne** 1977, and of the Royal Opera at **Covent Garden** in 1988. Honorary KBE 1977.

HALL, *Nicola* (Born Ipswich 1969)

British **guitar** prodigy who gave her first concert aged nine. Many competition prizes; in 1989 nominated 'Commonwealth Musician of the Year'.

HALLÉ ORCHESTRA

Major symphony orchestra based in Manchester. It was founded in 1858 by Sir Charles Hallé (1819–95), German-born pianist and conductor who settled in England in 1848. Hallé remained Principal Conductor (and proprietor) of the **orchestra** until his death, after which it was run by the non-profit-making Hallé Concerts Society. **Sir Hamilton Harty** was Principal Conductor 1920–33; in 1943 the orchestra was reconstituted, and **Sir John Barbirolli** was Principal Conductor until his death in 1970. He was succeeded by **James Loughran** (1971–83) and Stanislaw Skrowaczewski (1971–91). The current Principal Conductor is Kent Nagano.

HAMMOND, *Joan* (Born Christchurch, New Zealand, 1912)

Soprano who played violin for three years in the Sydney Symphony Orchestra before making her operatic début in Sydney in 1929. She appeared in the leading opera houses and concert halls of London, **Vienna**, New York, Moscow and Leningrad (where she sang Tatiana in *Eugene Onegin* in Russian). She has a strong, vibrant voice: her record of 'O My Beloved Father' from **Puccini**'s *Gianni Schicchi* sold more than a million copies and won her a golden disc in 1969. DBE 1974.

HANDLEY, *Vernon* (Born Enfield 1930)

English conductor, formerly assistant to **Sir Adrian Boult**. From 1962 took charge of the Guildford Symphony Orchestra, making it a fully professional body. Principal Conductor of the **Ulster Orchestra** (1985–9).

'HARK, THE HERALD ANGELS SING'

The words of this great Christmas **hymn** have undergone many changes since Charles Wesley's version of 1743; the music was taken by Dr W. H. Cummings from a tune in a choral work written by **Mendelssohn**.

HARMONICA

Term once applied to an arrangement of musical glasses, or glass bowls, of variable pitch (the Glass Armonica); now up-market term for the mouth-organ, invented in the 1830s.

HARMONIUM

Small reed organ perfected by Alexandre Debain in Paris in the 1840s. The reeds are actuated by a current of air supplied by the treadle bellows operated by the feet of the performer. The volume of sound is determined by the pressure of air. Harmoniums were extremely popular for domestic and church use in former days, and in cinemas in the silent film era.

HARMONY

The simultaneous sounding of notes to give a pleasing effect. Harmony (the means by which melodies may be accompanied by a succession of **chords**) is one of the main subjects of study of a would-be composer.

HARNONCOURT, *Nikolaus* (Born Berlin 1929)

Austrian conductor and musicologist of great importance in the **Early Music** movement. In 1953 created the Vienna Concentus Musicus for the performance of music from the twelfth to the eighteenth centuries on authentic instruments.

*H*ANDEL

George Frideric Handel was born Georg Friederich Händel in Halle, 100 miles south-west of Berlin. He was the son of a barber-surgeon who tried to steer his son into the law, but the boy's talent for music was too strong and at seventeen he was taken on for a probationary year as organist of Halle's Calvinist Cathedral. From there he moved to Hamburg where he played second **violin** in the only public **opera** house in Germany and composed four operas, among them the successful *Almira* (1705).

For a composer ambitious to succeed in opera, a visit to Italy was essential, and in 1706 Handel accepted an invitation to join the retinue of Prince Ferdinand de'Medici, heir to the Grand Duke of Tuscany. In Italy he attracted several other patrons and wrote an **oratorio**, operas and a huge amount of other music including over one hundred **cantatas**. Thus, by the time he was twenty-five, Handel had wide experience and an established reputation. In 1710 he was appointed *Kapellmeister* to the Elector of Hanover, who accepted the composer's immediate demand for a year's leave. Handel used the time to establish himself in London, where his opera *Rinaldo* was a great success. After this Hanover seemed dull,

and in 1712 Handel was granted leave to travel to London again, provided he returned 'within a reasonable time'. He never went back. For Queen Anne he composed a *Te Deum* and *Jubilate* to mark the Treaty of Utrecht, and was granted a royal pension of £200 a year; as a house guest of Lord Burlington he settled into a brilliant circle which included Alexander Pope and John Gay.

In 1714 Queen Anne died, to be succeeded by Handel's employer the Elector of Hanover as King George I. Far from punishing the young composer for being absent without leave, the king paid him half a year's salary from the Hanover treasury and raised his royal pension to £600. In 1717 Handel provided the music for the king's famous water party on the River Thames; George I was so delighted he commanded three performances in the course of that one evening.

In 1718 Handel became music director of an Italian opera company at the King's Theatre known as the Royal Academy of Music, and for the next decade London became the operatic capital of Europe. The Royal Academy, however, ceased operations in 1728 and Handel had a struggle to continue at the King's Theatre until 1737. Happily there were consoling successes in other directions. In 1727 four **anthems** by Handel added splendour to the coronation of King George II, and in 1732 a **masque** on the biblical story of Esther was performed privately. It was such a success that Handel wanted to transfer it to the King's Theatre but, owing to the Bishop of London's ban on theatrical representation of a sacred subject, Handel had to dispense with the stage action. This apparent disappointment bore fruit in the birth of English oratorio, and was to lead to the creation of some of the composer's greatest works.

From 1735 Handel began putting on spring seasons of oratorio with the added attraction of organ concertos performed by himself, and after suffering a stroke in 1737 (from which he recovered well) his operatic activities declined. The composer's prospects in London were looking gloomy when the Lord Lieutenant of

Ireland invited Handel to write something for Dublin. The result was *Messiah*, first performed in April 1742. Thereafter Handel's fortunes in London recovered: other great oratorios followed, including *Samson* (1743), *Judas Maccabeus* (1746) and *Solomon* (1748). In 1749 Handel wrote the music for a royal fireworks display to celebrate the peace of Aix-la-Chapelle and, although the fireworks misfired, the music was considered a great success. But in January 1751 Handel was forced to break off the composition of his last oratorio *Jephtha* when he found the sight of his left eye was failing. By 1753 he had lost all sight, and composed little during his last years though he continued to play the **organ** and organise oratorio performances.

Three thousand people attended Handel's funeral in Westminster Abbey in 1759 and he left the large sum for those days of £20,000, much of it bequeathed to charity.

Favourite works

STAGE WORKS 'O Ruddier than the Cherry' from *Acis and Galatea*; 'Se pietà di me non senti' and 'Da tempeste il legno infranto' from *Julius Caesar*; 'Ombra mai fu' (Handel's *Largo*) from *Xerxes*.

ORATORIOS *Messiah*. Also *Israel in Egypt* (known for its great double-choruses); *Judas Maccabeus* ('See the Conquering Hero Comes'); *Samson* ('Total Eclipse'); *Jeptha* ('Waft Her, Angels'); *Solomon* ('The Arrival of the Queen of Sheba' and the Nightingale Chorus).

CORONATION ANTHEM *Zadok the Priest*.

ORCHESTRAL WORKS *Water Music* Suites and *Music for the Royal Fireworks*. Also eighteen *concerti grossi* of Op. 3 and Op. 6; Organ Concerto No. 13 in F ('The Cuckoo and the Nightingale').

Handel's Fireworks Music *accompanied the spectacular display in Green Park. Unfortunately the pavilion caught fire . . .*

HARP

Widespread family of instruments of very ancient origin. A graduated set of strings of variable length is stretched over an open frame, one side of which is made into a sounding-box. The strings are normally plucked.

HARPER, *Heather* (Born Belfast 1930)

British **soprano** at home in a wide range of music but much associated with **Britten**'s music: she was a notable Ellen Orford in *Peter Grimes*, and was one of the original soloists in the *War Requiem* 1962. CBE 1965.

HARPSICHORD

A wing-shaped keyboard instrument in which the strings are plucked by leather or quill plectrums operated by the depression of the keys. The Italian equivalent ('Clavicembalo') was referred to as early as 1397. The harpsichord was of great importance as a solo instrument and in most instrumental ensembles until the rise of the **piano**. It was then almost totally abandoned until the **Dolmetsch** family and others revived interest in it; it is now widely used in appropriate music.

HARRELL, *Lynn* (Born New York 1944)

American cellist. Principal cellist (and youngest player) **Cleveland Orchestra** (1965–71). Teaches at **Juilliard School**, New York. Principal, **Royal Academy of Music,** from 1993. Plays frequently with **Ashkenazy** and **Perlman.**

HARRISON, *Beatrice* (Born Roorkee, India, 1892; died Smallfield, Sussex, 1965)

British cellist. In a famous radio broadcast of 1924, she played her **cello** in her Surrey garden to the accompaniment of nightingales.

HARTY, *Hamilton* (Born Hillsborough, Co. Down, 1879; died Brighton 1941)

Irish composer, conductor and pianist, best known for his period (1920–33) as Principal Conductor of the **Hallé Orchestra**. His opulent arrangements of **Handel**'s *Water Music* and *Fireworks Music* became very popular. Knighted 1925.

HARWOOD, *Elizabeth* (Born Barton Seagrave, Northants., 1938; died Fryerning, Essex, 1990)

British lyric **soprano** whose talent and engaging personality took her to regular Salzburg Festival appearances under **Karajan** from 1970, and success at **La Scala** and the **Metropolitan**.

THE HAUNTED BALLROOM

The waltz from this **ballet** score is the best-known composition of Geoffrey Toye (1889–1942). The ballet, choreographed by Ninette de Valois, was staged at **Sadler's Wells** in 1934.

'HEART OF OAK'

Song written in 1759 for Garrick's pantomime *Harlequin's Invasion*. Best-known composition of William Boyce (1711–79), successful organist and composer who became Master of the King's Musick, 1755.

HEIFETZ, *Jascha* (Born Vilnius 1901; died Los Angeles 1987)

Widely regarded as the finest violinist of his time, certainly the most astonishing technician. A child prodigy who played **Mendelssohn**'s Concerto in E minor at the age of six, he was admitted to the St Petersburg Conservatoire at nine and made a sensational début in Berlin in 1912. He left Russia for the USA in 1917 and became an American citizen in 1925. Worldwide acclaim followed, but he reduced his appearances after the Second World War. From 1962 he taught at the University of Southern California. His seventieth birthday was celebrated by a television film in which he played **Bach**, and **Bruch**'s *Scottish Fantasy*, with all his old mastery.

HENDERSON, *Roy* (Born Edinburgh 1899)

British **baritone** who sang **Mozart**'s *Figaro* at the opening of **Glyndebourne** Opera (1934). Notable in **Delius**'s *Sea Drift*, which he recorded. Founded (1936) Nottingham Oriana choir.

HENDRICKS, *Barbara* (Born Stephens, Arkansas, 1948)

Black American **soprano** of high achievement. She sang Mimì in a 1988 film of *La Bohème*, and her many recordings include a delightful selection of Negro spirituals.

*H*ENRY VIII, *King* (Born Greenwich 1491; died Windsor 1547)

Henry VIII employed about fifty-eight musicians at court, and was himself a talented performer and composer. He played the **organ**, **lute** and virginals, and thirty-four of his compositions have survived.

*H*ERBERT, *Victor* (Born Dublin 1859; died New York 1924)

American composer of Irish birth. In 1886 he married the **soprano** Thérèse Foerster in Vienna, and went to New York, where she sang at the **Metropolitan Opera** and he played the **cello** in the **orchestra**. In 1894 Herbert was soloist with the **New York Philharmonic** in his Second Cello Concerto, which prompted **Dvořák** to compose his masterpiece in that form. Conductor of **Pittsburgh Symphony Orchestra** (1898–1904). Wrote over forty operettas, starting with *Prince Ananias* (1894) and including *Naughty Marietta* (1910, filmed 1935): 'Ah, Sweet Mystery of Life' appeared in that show.

*H*ESS, *Myra* (Born London 1890; died London 1965)

British pianist. After studies with the influential **Tobias Matthay** at the **Royal Academy of Music**, she made her début in 1907 in **Beethoven**'s Fourth Piano Concerto. This remained central in a repertoire which included **Mozart**, **Schumann**, **Brahms**, **Beethoven**, **Scarlatti** and **Bach**. Her **piano** transcription of Bach's 'Jesu, Joy of Man's Desiring' (and her recording of it) is extremely well known. In the Second World War she established and frequently performed at a series of lunchtime concerts at the National Gallery which made a vital contribution to the morale of all who attended. DBE 1941.

*H*ICKOX, *Richard* (Born Stokenchurch, Bucks., 1948)

Much recorded British conductor who created the Richard Hickox Orchestra (later the City of London Sinfonia), 1972. Musical Director of **London Symphony Orchestra** Chorus since 1976; appointed Associate Conductor of LSO 1985. With Simon Standage in 1990 he created Collegium Musicum 90. He has several guest conductorships and has been Principal Guest Conductor of Bournemouth Symphony Orchestra since 1992.

Christopher Hogwood with his Academy of Ancient Music at the Palace of Haydn's patron, Prince Nikolaus Esterházy.

*H*OFFNUNG, *Gerard* (Born Berlin 1925; died London 1959)

British artist, wit and **tuba** player of German Jewish birth. He specialised in grotesque but good-humoured cartoons of musicians and musical instruments, and combined a wicked sense of fun with his ability as a self-taught tuba player to present light-hearted Hoffnung Music Festivals in London, starting in 1956. Many leading musicians took part, and specially composed spoofs included **Sir Malcolm Arnold**'s 'Grand, Grand Overture for three vacuum cleaners, floor polisher, rifles and orchestra'.

*H*OGWOOD, *Christopher* (Born Nottingham 1941)

British harpsichordist, conductor and musicologist. Influenced at Cambridge by **Raymond Leppard** and Thurston Dart, he was a founder member (1967) of **David Munrow**'s Early Music Consort. In 1973 founded the Academy of Ancient Music which has performed and recorded much eighteenth-century music on period instruments, including all **Mozart**'s symphonies. Artistic Director of the Handel and Haydn Society of Boston, Mass. (1986) and Music Director of the St Paul Chamber Orchestra, Minneapolis (1988–92).

H AYDN

Joseph HAYDN

1732	Born in Rohrau, Lower Austria
1740	Joined choir of St Stephen's Cathedral, Vienna
1749	Left choir; freelance musician in Vienna
1761	Entered service of Esterházy family
1781	Met Mozart
1790	Retired from service with Esterházy family
1791–2	First visit to England
1794–5	Second visit to England
1798	First performance of *The Creation*
1801	First performance of *The Seasons*
1809	Died in Gumpendorf near Vienna

Joseph Haydn's musicians called him 'Papa' Haydn, and there is nothing in the life story of this genius to contradict the image of a thoroughly benevolent, modest and lovable man.

Haydn was the son of a wheelwright and a cook, born just on the Austrian side of the border with Hungary. There was not much money to spare in the family and from a very early age young Joseph learned the virtues of hard work and thrift. At the age of five he went to live with his cousin in the nearby town of Hainburg, where he sang in the church choir and learned the rudiments of music. The choirmaster of St Stephen's Cathedral in Vienna, Georg Reutter, on a visit to Hainburg, gave the boy an audition and at the age of eight, Joseph joined the choir school of St Stephen's, remaining there for nine years. He learned a good deal about the performance of church music and absorbed some general education but Reutter was too busy to pay attention to the boy's early efforts at composition. 'In those days,' Haydn wrote later, 'I thought everything was all right if only the paper was chock full of notes.' When his voice was near to breaking Reutter suggested it should be preserved by making him a **castrato** but fortunately his father refused permission for the operation. So, at the age of seventeen, Haydn was dismissed from the choir, with a beating by way of bonus for having mischievously cut off the pigtail of the chorister in front of him. He hadn't a penny in his pocket, but he could play the **violin** tolerably well and this enabled him to find casual work with the parties of serenaders who went round Vienna at night.

Gradually, thanks to his work as a violinist, an early commission to compose an **opera** about a desert island shipwreck, and a growing number of pupils with aristocratic connections, the young man's fortunes began to improve. In 1759 he was engaged as *Kapellmeister* to Count Morzin. One of the conditions of his contract was that he should not marry, but in 1760 Haydn decided to risk dismissal by making Maria Anna Keller his wife. It was to prove a disastrous liaison and the frigidity of their childless marriage drove Haydn into a series of other relationships. Meanwhile, Morzin disbanded his **orchestra** and Haydn was free to accept the invitation of Prince Paul Anton Esterházy to join his household. He was twenty-nine years of age.

The Esterházys were the grandest of the Hungarian families which owed allegiance to the Habsburg Empire. When Paul Anton died in 1762, his brother Nicholas acceded to the title; he was a man of refined musical taste who played a curious cello-like instrument called the baryton, for which Haydn composed about 150 works. Nicholas was also interested in architecture. This interest, combined with a passion for duck shooting, resulted in the completion, in 1766, of a palace almost as grand as Versailles on the site of a former hunting box. The Prince called the palace Esterház and in this isolated, unhealthy spot, Haydn and his team of musicians had to spend an increasing part of each year; visits to the Prince's other palace at Eisenstadt or to his town house in Vienna became fewer and further between. For Haydn as a composer there were consolations. 'My Prince was satisfied with all my works,' he wrote; 'I could experiment. I was cut off from the world, there was no one near me to torment me or make me doubt myself, so I had to become original.' But most of the musicians found Esterház a dreary place, especially after the Prince forbade them to bring their wives there, and on more than one occasion Haydn prompted the Prince to hasten their return to Vienna.

During his thirty years with the Esterházy family, Haydn turned out music at a tremendous rate – **symphonies**, **serenades**, **divertimentos**, **quartets**, **trios**, **sonatas**, vocal pieces – and by the 1770s his fame had spread throughout Europe. In 1781 he met **Mozart**. The respect felt by the two men for each other ripened into friendship and Haydn hailed his much younger colleague as the greatest musician known to him alive or dead. When, in September 1790, Prince Nicholas died, he left Haydn a pension of 1000 florins a year on the sole condition that he retained the title of *Kapellmeister* to the family. Otherwise he was free, and in 1791 when the London concert promoter Johann Peter Salomon came to Vienna with an invitation to England, Haydn accepted.

Now nearly sixty, Haydn prospered hugely in England, arousing the audience at Salomon's concerts 'to such a degree of enthusiasm as almost amounts to frenzy' with a series of specially written new symphonies and other works. He was awarded an honorary degree at Oxford and befriended by the royal family. An attachment developed between Haydn and an attractive widow, Rebecca Schroeter, and that was one reason, no doubt, why Haydn accepted Salomon's invitation to visit England again in 1794. Once again he was fêted on all sides, and returned to Vienna with his already great reputation further enhanced. He also took with him the memory of hearing **Handel**'s *Messiah* at Westminster Abbey. This was an overwhelming experience for Haydn and led to the composition in his last years of two **oratorios**, *The Creation* and *The Seasons*, both based on English texts. Other works of Haydn's last years were the 'Nelson' **Mass**, 250 arrangements of Scottish and Welsh **songs**, and a series of string quartets.

Joseph Haydn, 1732–1809.

Haydn's last public appearance was at a performance of *The Creation* in March 1808, when the enfeebled old man had to be carried to his seat. The French bombardment of Vienna in May 1809 hastened his final illness and on the 31st of that month he died at the age of seventy-seven. His strong faith in God was unshaken to the end, and to those around his bedside he said, 'Cheer up, children, I'm all right.'

Favourite works

SYMPHONIES No. 94 in G ('Surprise'); No. 100 in G ('Military'); No. 101 in D ('Clock'); No. 104 ('London').

OTHER MUSIC Op. 76, No. 3 in D (string quartet, including 'Emperor's **Hymn**'); Trumpet Concerto; *The Creation* (including 'With Verdure Clad').

*H*OLLIGER, *Heinz* (Born Langenthal, Berne 1939)

Highly accomplished and original Swiss oboist and composer. As a player he has experimented with new sounds such as double trills and glissandos: many contemporary composers have written for him.

*H*OLST, *Gustav* (Born Cheltenham 1874; died London 1934)

British composer and teacher of Swedish descent. Studied composition and the **trombone** at the **Royal College of Music** where, in 1895, he met his lifelong friend **Vaughan Williams**: they established the practice of criticising each other's works before publication or performance. In 1907 he was appointed Director of Music at St Paul's Girls' School in Hammersmith, where he had a sound-proofed music-room in which he could compose at weekends. He retained this post to the end of his life, but also taught elsewhere, for example at Morley College where in 1911 he gave the first performance of **Purcell**'s *The Fairy Queen* since 1697. *The Planets*, composed during the First World War and first performed privately under **Boult** in 1918, and *The Hymn of Jesus* which followed in 1920, made him famous and popular as a composer, but Holst disliked and distrusted his new-found celebrity. Apart from *The Planets*, Holst's best-known works include the **ballet** music from the **opera** *The Perfect Fool* (1923), the Suites in E flat and F for military band (1909 and 1911) and the St Paul's Suite for Strings (1912–13) composed for his school pupils.

'*H*OME SWEET HOME'

Almost a national folk song; its inclusion in **Henry Wood**'s *Fantasia on British Sea Songs* is odd since it has no nautical connections. Composed (1821) as a 'Sicilian air' by Sir Henry Bishop (1786–1855).

*H*ORN

The orchestral French horn (it was invented in France) is essentially a coiled tube of brass over 11 feet (about 3.5 metres) long. Valves make it possible to play any note of the chromatic scale, but it is one of the most difficult of all instruments to play well.

*H*ORNE, *Marilyn* (Born Bradford, Penn., 1934)

American **mezzo-soprano** who dubbed the singing voice of Dorothy Dandridge in the film *Carmen*

Jones (1954). Frequently partnered **Dame Joan Sutherland** in nineteenth-century **operas**, e.g. *Norma* (**Bellini**).

*H*OROWITZ, *Vladimir* (Born Kiev 1903; died New York 1989)

Russian-born pianist, became American citizen 1942. His international fame was established with concerts in Berlin in 1925. In 1928 made his New York début with **Beecham** conducting, and in 1933 took part in **Toscanini**'s **Beethoven** cycle with the **New York Philharmonic**, marrying Toscanini's daughter Wanda that year. Ill health and nervous strain prompted several long periods of retirement from which Horowitz occasionally emerged to astonish the world, making recordings in New York in 1985 and returning

and is engaged in recording the complete piano works of Liszt.

HOWARTH, *Elgar* (Born Cannock, Staffs., 1935) __

British conductor, composer and trumpeter. Director of the London Sinfonietta from 1973. Has also composed and conducted for brass bands, e.g. Grimethorpe Colliery Band 1972–6.

HOWELLS, *Herbert* (Born Lydney, Glos., 1892; died London 1983) _____

English composer whose works are highly esteemed. Succeeded **Holst** (1936) as Director of Music at St Paul's School, Hammersmith. He was an influential professor of composition at the **Royal College of Music** into his eighties. Wrote many church compositions, but his most famous work is *Hymnus Paradisi* (1938) written to express his grief for his son who died at the age of nine of meningitis. CBE 1953, CH 1972.

HUDDERSFIELD CHORAL SOCIETY_____

The most famous of Yorkshire's choral societies, founded in 1836, and mainly recruited from Nonconformist churches. From 1881 gave regular concerts in Huddersfield Town Hall, but the Society has since toured widely at home and abroad. Conductors have included Henry Coward and **Sir Malcolm Sargent** (who both held office for over thirty years). The current Principal Conductor is **Jane Glover** and the Chorus Master is Jonathan Grieves Smith who succeeded former King's Singer Brian Kay in 1993.

HUGHES, *Owain Arwel* (Born Cardiff 1942) _____

Welsh conductor. Studied with **Boult** and **Kempe** in London and **Haitink** in Amsterdam. Frequent conductor of **Hallé Orchestra** and many guest appearances with **English National** and **Welsh National Opera** companies.

HUMMEL, *Johann Nepomuk* (Born Pressburg (now Bratislava) 1778; died Weimar 1837) _____

Austrian musician regarded as one of the finest pianists of his time, a rival of **Beethoven**, with whom

in 1986 to the USSR for a performance televised worldwide. Horowitz was probably the most prodigious pianistic technician of the twentieth century and, although his interpretations sometimes seemed wayward, he generated nerve-tingling excitement.

HOTTER, *Hans* (Born Offenbach-am-Main 1909) __

Austrian bass-baritone of German birth. A great favourite at **Covent Garden**, at the **Metropolitan**, at Bayreuth and elsewhere, he was the leading Wagnerian bass-baritone of his generation.

HOWARD, *Leslie* (Born Melbourne, Victoria 1948)

Adventurous Australian **piano** virtuoso and scholar who has completed an unknown **sonata** by **Tchaikovsky**, edited **Liszt**'s Third Piano Concerto he enjoyed a stormy friendship. A brilliant child prodigy, Hummel lived and studied with **Mozart** (1785–7) before touring Europe with great success in his boyhood. Succeeded **Haydn** in the Esterházy household (1804–11) and was *Kapellmeister* in Weimar 1819–37: the position allowed him time to tour and compose. A conscientious and agreeable man, he enjoyed the friendship of many leading figures of his time; **Schubert** dedicated his last three piano **sonatas** to Hummel.

*H*UMPERDINCK, *Engelbert* (Born Siegburg 1854; died Neustrelitz 1921)

Not to be confused with the pop singer Arnold George Dorsey, born in Madras in 1936, who adopted the name Engelbert Humperdinck after finding it in a music dictionary. The real E.H. was a German composer who befriended and assisted **Wagner** at Bayreuth and elsewhere and held a variety of academic appointments. Much influenced by Wagner and by German **folk music**, his enchanting fairy-tale **opera** *Hansel and Gretel*, premiered at Weimar in 1893 and conducted by **Richard Strauss**, was an instant success. Another fairy-tale opera *Königskinder* (New York 1910) has also held the stage.

*H*URDY-GURDY

Not a barrel organ or street piano, but a portable medieval stringed instrument like a **viol**, with a resined wheel operated by a handle at one end to act as a bow, while different notes are produced by depressing keys in a box mounted on the instrument.

*H*URFORD, *Peter* (Born Minehead 1930)

British organist, renowned interpreter of **Bach** and of eighteenth-century French music. Master of the Music (1958–79) at St Albans Abbey. Founded International Organ Festival at St Albans (1963).

*H*YMN

The Greek *hymnos* was a song in praise of a god or hero, and hymns have featured in Christian worship from early times. Famous congregational collections include *Hymns Ancient and Modern* (1861), *The English Hymnal* (1906) and *Songs of Praise* (1925).

I

*I*DYLL

A poem or prose work describing an idealised, peaceful country life, hence a musical piece of similar character – e.g. **Wagner**'s *Siegfried Idyll*.

'*I*'LL SING THEE SONGS OF ARABY'

Frederick Clay (1838–89) sold the copyright of this enormously popular ballad from his **cantata** *Lalla Rookh* (1877) for five pounds. A friend of **Arthur Sullivan**, Clay introduced him to **W.S. Gilbert** in 1869.

*I*MPROMPTU

Title used by **Schubert**, **Chopin**, **Schumann** and others to describe pieces of music with the character of spontaneous invention, though they are, in fact, carefully crafted.

'*I*N A MONASTERY GARDEN'

Descriptive composition (1915) by the Birmingham-born Albert Ketèlbey (1875–1959) who also wrote 'In a Persian Market' (1920).

*I*NCIDENTAL MUSIC

From the days of ancient Greek drama it has been realised that music can add greatly to the effect of a play. **Purcell** contributed incidental music to many plays; among the most famous incidental scores since then have been those of **Mendelssohn** for *A Midsummer Night's Dream*, **Grieg** for Ibsen's *Peer Gynt* and **Bizet** for Daudet's *L'Arlésienne*.

*I*NTERMEZZO

In earlier times a light-hearted interlude in a serious **opera** or play; later a bridging passage between scenes, e.g. the Intermezzo from Mascagni's ***Cavalleria Rusticana***.

*I*RELAND, *John* (Born Bowdon, Cheshire, 1879; died Washington, Sussex, 1962)

The song 'Sea Fever' (1913), a setting of words by John Masefield, is the best-known single composition of this British composer and pianist, but the Piano

Concerto in E Flat (1930) and *A London Overture* (1936) are extremely attractive and often played.

ISRAEL PHILHARMONIC ORCHESTRA

Founded by the Polish violinist Bronislaw Huberman as the Palestine Symphony Orchestra, it gave its first concert in 1936 under **Toscanini**. Music directors have included **Jean Martinon**, Paul Kletzki and **Zubin Mehta**. Since 1951 has toured extensively from its base in Tel Aviv.

ISTOMIN, *Eugene* (Born New York 1925)

American pianist of Russian parentage. Appeared at Prades Festival 1950 with **Pablo Casals** and in 1975 married Casals' widow, the cellist Marta Casals. Chiefly known as pianist in **trio** with **Isaac Stern** and Leonard Rose.

IVES, *Charles* (Born Danbury, Conn., 1874; died New York 1954)

Unconventional, experimental, avant-garde American composer. One of his numerous works is *The Unanswered Question* (1906), in which the conductor cues in the various instruments as he thinks fit.

J

JACOB, *Gordon* (Born London 1895; died Saffron Walden 1984)

British composer, teacher, writer and conductor. Became an influential professor at the **Royal College of Music**, 1926–66, where his pupils included **Malcolm Arnold**. CBE 1968.

JANÁČEK, *Leoš* (Born Hukvaldy, Moravia, 1854; died Moravská Ostrava, 1928)

Not until he was in his sixties did Janáček become established as the outstanding twentieth-century Czechoslovak successor to **Smetana** and **Dvořák**. The staging of his **opera** *Jenůfa* (1904) in Prague in 1916 signalled the start of Janáček's international fame, and his operas (*Jenůfa*, *Katya Kabanová*,

The Cunning Little Vixen, *The Excursions of Mr Brouček*, *The Makropoulos Affair* and *The House of the Dead*) are now widely performed. Other famous works include the *Glagolitic Mass*, based on ninth-century Old Slavonic texts.

'JERUSALEM'

Unison chorus composed in 1916 by Hubert Parry (1848–1918) to William Blake's words. Adopted as the anthem of the Women's Institute, and now established as the finale of the Last Night of the **Proms**.

JEW'S HARP

Simple instrument of ancient origin (and no verifiable Jewish connection), which consists of a small metal frame with a vibrating metal strip. The frame is held in the teeth and notes are produced by varying the shape of the mouth.

JO, *Sumi* (Born Seoul, 1960)

Korean **coloratura soprano**. Brilliant in such roles as Olympia, the doll, in *Tales of Hoffman* and the Queen of the Night in **The Magic Flute**.

'JOHN BROWN'S BODY'

John Brown was an anti-slavery campaigner hanged in the American Civil War. His name was shared by an amateur singer in the Massachusetts Infantry and is well known through the now familiar words to the tune of an 1850s revivalist **hymn**.

JOHN FOSTER BLACK DYKE MILLS BAND

The Black Dyke Mills Band was formed in 1837 near Bradford, with the mill-owner John Foster as a member. In 1855 Foster rescued the band from difficulties and took it over, employing the members at his mill and providing uniforms and instruments. In 1860 the band won the first **Crystal Palace** contest, and since then has received a long series of national and international awards. It changed its name in 1987 to the John Foster Black Dyke Mills Band to mark the 150th anniversary of its foundation.

JOHNSON, *Emma* (Born Barnet, Herts., 1966)

British clarinettist who won the **BBC** Young Musician of the Year Award 1984 and has now established a very successful international career.

JAZZ

Attempts to define jazz have defeated better brains than mine, and maybe the composer and **piano** entertainer 'Fats' Waller (1904–43) came as near as anyone when he declared that jazz 'ain't what you do but the way that you do it'.

The word itself is fascinating. It was derived from a Black slang obscenity, 'jass', which referred originally to the sex act and later by extension to anything exciting. When Johnny Steiner's band were appearing in Chicago in 1916, a drunk member of the audience leapt to his feet and exclaimed, 'Jass it up boys!' The story goes that he was hired to utter this cry every night, and the band soon became known as Stein's Dixie Jass Band, and subsequently as the famous Original Dixieland Jazz Band.

Jazz, with its excitement, strong rhythms and large element of improvisation, emerged partly from the music of the slaves in the southern United States. But deep-rooted African traditions merged with the popular music-making of Whites as well as Blacks in America. 'Minstrel shows', performed largely by 'blacked-up' Whites, became hugely popular from the 1850s, and in 1859 the song 'Dixie' by the White northerner Daniel Emmett was so universally sung by both sides in the Civil War that the southern USA began to be referred to as Dixieland. The 'minstrel' tradition led on to Ragtime which became all the rage in the low dives of St Louis in the 1890s, thanks to the inspired rhythmic piano-playing of **Scott Joplin** (1868–1917) and others.

In the wake of the American Civil War there was a glut of discarded military band instruments, and a craze among Black musicians for marching bands arose. Towards the end of the nineteenth century, in the bustling seaport of New Orleans, this brash music, with the addition sometimes of **piano**, **drums** and **banjo**, moved into the bordellos and bars of the city's red-light district, Storyville. There, though not exclusively there, jazz was born. After the clean-up of Storyville, it moved north to Chicago to become the multi-racial music of the twenties. Another kind of music arose to give expression to distinctively Black emotions: the **Blues** which, as the critic Paul Oliver neatly wrote, is 'both a state of mind and the music which gives expression to it'. Dividing lines have always been hard to draw in the world of popular music: the blues influenced jazz, and vice-versa. Tin Pan Alley, too, was a tributary to the developing stream of jazz: in 1915 a tune of **Jerome Kern**'s, 'Magic Melody', used the jazz idiom and is credited with introducing the jazz world to a new kind of harmonic freedom.

Any list of Great Names in Jazz usually starts with Buddy Holden (1877–1931) who created a sensation in New Orleans with cornet playing they said could be heard fourteen miles away. Louis Armstrong (1901–71), the charismatic 'Satchmo', first played the **trumpet** in Storyville. Triumphing later in Chicago and New York, he has been called the first inspirational genius of jazz. Another major figure who learned his trade in New Orleans in the early days was the highly individual and inventive Jelly Roll Morton (1890–1941).

A key figure in what was known as the 'Chicago style' in the twenties was the **cornet** player Bix Beiderbecke (1903–31). He never learned to read music, though he sat behind a music desk (on which he propped a whodunnit) for the sake of appearances in Paul Whiteman's band. Whiteman (1890–1967), creator of 'symphonic jazz', commissioned **George Gershwin** to write his *Rhapsody in Blue* for a New York concert in 1924. Whiteman was a pioneer in the development of 'big band jazz'. This involved carefully prepared and orchestrated arrangements, though star soloists would be given 'breaks' to do their own brilliant thing. Duke Ellington (1899–1974) was installed with his all-Black band at the famous Cotton Club in Harlem from 1927, and Chicago-born **Benny Goodman** (1909–86) inaugurated the era of Swing with a trans-US tour in 1935. Among Goodman players who formed their own bands were trumpeter Harry James (1916–83), drummer Gene Krupa (1909–73), and trombonist **Glenn Miller**

(1904–44) whose American Air Force band in the Second World War became the most famous dance band in the world.

Nearer perhaps to the original spirit of jazz was the music created by great soloists such as pianists George Shearing (b.1919), Art Tatum (1909–56) and Oscar Peterson (b.1925), and a generation of singers grew up who applied instrumental jazz techniques to the voice, including Ella Fitzgerald (b.1918) and Billie Holiday (1915–59). In 1920 a record called 'Crazy Blues' brought the blues into the sphere of commercial music, paving the way for the success in this field of Bessie Smith (1895–1937). After the Second World War a new kind of 'cool' jazz that became known as Bebop was developed by saxophonist Charlie 'Bird' Parker (1920–55) and trumpeter 'Dizzy' Gillespie (b.1917) among others. The sax players Ornette Coleman (b.1930) and John Coltrane (1926–67) were prominent in a movement towards greater spontaneity known as 'free jazz', and in 1970 the album *Bitches Brew*, led by trumpeter Miles Davis (1926–91) ushered in the age of 'rock jazz'. At the present time many varieties of music related to jazz are performed by many different musicians, and there have been numerous nostalgic attempts to revive the bygone spirit of New Orleans, Chicago and the era of Swing.

If the boundaries between different kinds of popular music have tended to dissolve, so has the dividing line between jazz and 'classical' music. **André Previn** and **Nigel Kennedy** are just two examples of performing musicians who are happy in either camp, and many twentieth-century composers including **Igor Stravinsky**, **Claude Debussy**, **Constant Lambert**, **William Walton**, **Leonard Bernstein** and **Richard Rodney Bennett** have been influenced by jazz.

In fact it could be said that jazz, in its infinitely various forms, is the authentic musical voice of the twentieth century.

The Count Basie Band with Count Basie at the piano and soloist Sonny Payne on drums.

JONES, *Gwyneth* (Born Pontnewynydd 1936)

Welsh **soprano** who sang with **Welsh National Opera** and at **Covent Garden** before establishing a major international career, especially in **Wagner**. Sang Brünnhilde in the centenary *Ring* at Bayreuth 1976. CBE 1976. DBE 1986.

JONES, *Philip* (Born Bath 1928)

British trumpeter who, after a varied orchestral career, founded in 1951 the Philip Jones Brass Ensemble and remained its director until 1987.

JOPLIN, *Scott* (Born nr Marshall, Texas *or* Shreveport, LA, 1868; died New York 1917)

Known as the 'King of Ragtime' in his lifetime, Scott Joplin's genius was not fully recognised until the scholar Joshua Rifkin pioneered authentic-style performances of his music in the 1970s. Joplin settled in Sedalia, Missouri, where the Maple Leaf Club gave its name to Joplin's famous 'Maple Leaf Rag' (1899). 'The Entertainer', along with other numbers, became very popular through being used in the film *The Sting*.

JOYCE, *Eileen* (Born Zeehan, Tasmania, 1912: died Limpsfield 1991)

Australian pianist and harpsichordist who studied in Leipzig on the recommendation of **Percy Grainger**. She became highly popular after her **Proms** début in 1942.

JUDD, *Terence* (Born London 1957; died Beachy Head 1979)

Extremely talented British pianist who won the National Junior Piano Competition aged ten and the British **Liszt** Competition at nineteen. Fortunately made some recordings before his tragically premature death at twenty-two.

JUILLIARD SCHOOL

Based in the **Lincoln Centre**, the Juilliard School has departments for drama and dance as well as being one of the world's most distinguished music academies. Home of the internationally famous Juilliard Quartet.

K

KABALEVSKY, *Dmitry* (Born St Petersburg 1904; died Moscow 1987)

Russian composer, pianist and writer. He is best known in the West for his orchestral music, especially the **overture** to the **opera** *Colas Breugnon* (1938) and the Galop from the **suite** *The Comedians* (1940).

KÁLMÁN, *Emmerich* (Born Siófok, Hungary, 1882; died Paris 1953)

Kálmán had early training in law, but his operetta *The Gay Hussars* (1908) was a hit throughout Europe. Kálmán moved to **Vienna**, where he wrote the highly popular operettas, *The Gipsy Princess* (1915), *Countess Maritza* (1924) and *The Circus Princess* (1926).

KARAJAN, *Herbert von* (Born Salzburg 1908; died Anif 1989)

Austrian conductor who was so dominant that he was dubbed 'Music Director of Europe'. He joined the Nazi party in 1934, and was briefly banned after the war for his political affiliations. He resumed his career in 1947 with the **Vienna** Symphony Orchestra, making his début with London's **Philharmonia** the same year. Artistic Director of the Vienna State Opera 1957–64 and **La Scala** 1948–68. Founded the Salzburg Easter Festival 1967. But at the core of his worldwide activities was the **Berlin Philharmonic Orchestra**, whose principal conductor he became in 1955, resigning only three months before his death; with them he recorded **Beethoven**'s symphonies four times. The Herbert von Karajan Foundation, created in 1969, organises a biennial competition for young conductors.

KARR, *Gary* (Born Los Angeles 1941)

Probably the world's best-known **double bass** player, who has revived much of the existing solo repertoire for the instrument and commissioned new music from Henze and Schuller among others.

'KELTIC LAMENT'

From the *Keltic Suite* (1911) by the British composer and cellist John Foulds (1880–1939). Best-

Herbert von Karajan, 'Music Director of Europe', ruled the Berlin Philharmonic for nearly forty years.

known piece from a large output of works which also includes the *World Requiem* (1921).

*K*EMPE, *Rudolph* (Born Niederpoyritz, Saxony, 1910; died Zürich 1976) ————

German conductor highly esteemed by performers and public alike. Recorded complete orchestral works of **Richard Strauss**. Conducted **Wagner**'s *Ring* at Bayreuth and **Covent Garden**. Succeeded **Beecham** with **Royal Philharmonic Orchestra** and in 1975 appointed Principal Conductor of BBC Symphony Orchestra.

*K*EMPFF, *Wilhelm* (Born Jüterbog, 1895; died Positano, Italy, 1991) ————

German pianist whose international stature grew rapidly after his London recital début in 1951. Highly regarded interpreter of **Beethoven** and **Schubert**, and editor of the piano works of **Schumann**.

*K*ENNEDY, *Nigel* (Born Brighton 1956) ————

British violinist who has made an extraordinary public impact with his punk hairdos, earrings and unconventional clothes, which have helped him to make a particularly strong impact with the young. 'Nige', as he likes to be called, initially studied piano at the **Yehudi Menuhin** School. When he was sixteen he went to the **Juilliard School** in New York and made his London début in 1977. His recording of **Vivaldi**'s *The Four Seasons* achieved unprecedented sales of over 600,000 and helped him to become one of the hottest musical box-office attractions worldwide. He is regarded as one of the outstanding interpreters of **Elgar**'s Violin Concerto (another best-selling recording) and is also well-known for his jazz performances with **Stephane Grappelli**, among others.

*K*ENTNER, *Louis* (Born Karwin, Silesia, 1905; died 1987) ————

Hungarian-born pianist who became British in 1946. Several first performances of works by **Bartók**; noted interpreter of **Liszt**; many recitals in partnership with **Yehudi Menuhin**. CBE 1978.

*K*ERN, *Jerome* (Born New York 1885; died New York 1945) ————

American composer who founded the modern American **musical** with his masterpiece *Showboat*

(1927), written with librettist Oscar Hammerstein II: it had a serious, coherent story as well as a score of great distinction, including 'Can't help lovin' dat man' and 'Ol' Man River'. In partnership with Guy Bolton and P.G. Wodehouse in London, Kern produced many successful shows, among them *Sally* (1920), which included 'Look for the Silver Lining', *Sunny* (1925), *The Cat and the Fiddle* (1931), *Music in the Air* (1932) and *Roberta* (1933), with 'Smoke gets in your Eyes'. All these were filmed, as was *Showboat* (twice) and in 1934 Kern moved to Hollywood. There the artistry of Ginger Rogers and Fred Astaire inspired some of his best songs: 'Lovely to Look At' was added to *Roberta* (1935), and *Swing Time* (1936) included 'A Fine Romance' and 'The Way You Look Tonight'. Kern wrote complete scores for well over fifty theatre shows and films, and contributed numbers to at least as many others.

KEY

A small lever, depressed (usually by the fingers) to produce a note on a keyboard instrument. The word also refers to the practice whereby a passage or an entire work is based mainly on the notes of a particular scale, e.g. E major, C minor.

KHACHATURIAN, *Aram* (Born Tbilisi 1903; died Moscow 1978)

Armenian composer who blended his native folk idiom with the broad Russian tradition. Achieved international fame with the First Piano Concerto in D flat (1936). The **ballet** *Gayaneh* (1942) includes the much-played 'Sabre Dance', and the ballet *Spartacus* (1956), hailed in the Soviet Union as Khachaturian's masterpiece (it won the composer a Lenin Prize) has the famous **Adagio of Spartacus and Phrygia**.

KING'S COLLEGE, CAMBRIDGE

From its foundation in 1441, King's College was provided with a choir of twenty-four 'singing men and boys'; it is today one of the world's finest church choirs. The annual Festival of Nine Lessons and Carols is a great Christmas institution.

KING'S SINGERS

Highly skilled group of six male singers founded in 1968, when it consisted of five choral scholars from King's, Cambridge, and one from Christchurch,

Oxford. Personnel has changed, but the group continues to enjoy worldwide success in a huge variety of music from medieval times to twentieth-century popular tunes.

KIRKBY, *Emma* (Born Camberley 1949)

British **soprano** who studied classics at Oxford and taught before making her début in 1974. The voice has a boyish purity free from vibrato, and this has led to Kirkby's great success in **early music**.

KLEIBER, *Carlos* (Born Berlin 1930)

Argentinian conductor of German birth with the highest possible international reputation, though a reclusive nature and rigorous rehearsal demands make for rare appearances. Son of greatly respected conductor Erich Kleiber (1890–1956).

KLEMPERER, *Otto* (Born Breslau 1885; died Zurich 1973)

Outstanding German Jewish conductor who took Israeli nationality in 1970. Renowned for his noble readings of the Viennese classics, notably **Beethoven** and **Mahler**, whose assistant he was at the première of the Eighth Symphony in Munich in 1910. Left Germany to direct the **Los Angeles Philharmonic** 1933–39. Operation for brain tumour 1939 left him partly paralysed, but in 1955 was appointed Principal Conductor of London's **Philharmonia** orchestra; many distinguished concerts and recordings followed until Klemperer's retirement in 1972.

KÖCHEL NUMBERS

Ludwig von Köchel (1800–77) was an amateur botanist and mineralogist, so the business of classification came naturally to him; he listed all **Mozart**'s known works in a catalogue published in 1862 – hence 'Köchel numbers'.

KODÁLY, *Zoltán* (Born Kecskemét 1882; died Budapest 1967)

Very influential Hungarian composer, musicologist and educationalist. In 1905 he met **Béla Bartók** and joined him in folk-song collecting tours. Much of Kodály's output consists of choral pieces for adults or children: his teaching methods were adopted in Hungary's elementary schools and there are Kodály Institutes in the USA, Australia and Canada as well as

Hungary. Best known orchestral works are the **suite** from the **opera** *Háry János*, and *Dances of Galánta*.

KORNGOLD, *Erich* (Born Brno 1897; died Hollywood 1957) ————————

Austrian-born composer who became American citizen 1943. Child prodigy who at the age of ten was hailed as a genius by **Mahler**; at eleven he composed a **ballet** produced with great success at the **Vienna** Court Opera, and when he was twenty his opera *Die tote Stadt* was greeted as a masterpiece. Produced many **film scores** in Hollywood 1934 onwards: those for *Robin Hood* and *Anthony Adverse* won Oscars.

KOSTELANETZ, *André* (Born St Petersburg 1901; died Haiti 1980) ————————

Russian-born conductor and arranger (American citizen 1929). Guest conductor of **New York Philharmonic** who commissioned **Copland**'s *Lincoln Portrait* but best known as a populariser of the classics, and for his lush 'symphonic' arrangements of popular material.

KOUSSEVITSKY, *Serge* (Born Kalinin 1874; died Boston, Mass., 1951) ————————

Russian-born conductor. After early success as a solo double bassist, he established an important Russian music-publishing house and created his own **orchestra**. After the Russian Revolution, Koussevitsky created another orchestra in Paris, giving the première of **Ravel**'s arrangement of *Pictures at an Exhibition*. In 1924 succeeded **Monteux** as conductor of the **Boston Symphony Orchestra**, a post he retained for twenty-five years. Became an American citizen 1941, and in 1942, in memory of his wife, he set up the Koussevitsky Foundation which funded **Britten**'s *Peter Grimes*, among other compositions.

KREISLER, *Fritz* (Born Vienna 1875; died New York 1962) ————————

Austrian-born violinist (French citizen 1938, American citizen 1943) of incomparable charm and beauty of tone, also composer of charming **violin** pieces including 'Caprice Viennois', 'Liebesfreud', 'Liebesleid', 'Schön Rosmarin', 'Tambourin Chinois' and a number of short works in seventeenth- and

eighteenth-century style originally attributed to such composers as **Paganini**, Francoeur, et al. At the age of seven, Kreisler was the youngest student ever at the **Vienna** Conservatoire, and he won the gold medal when he was ten; after the age of twelve he never had another lesson. **Elgar** dedicated his Violin Concerto to Kreisler, who gave the first performance in 1910 with the composer conducting. Kreisler practised little, even at the height of his career, but achieved an effortless perfection which can still be appreciated on many recordings.

KRIPS, *Henry* (Born Vienna 1912) and *Josef* (born Vienna 1902; died Geneva 1974)————————

Austrian conductors and brothers. Josef played a leading part in reorganising Viennese musical life after the war and achieved a high international reputation. Henry went to Australia in 1938, becoming an Australian citizen in 1944. After appearing with **Sadler's Wells** Opera in 1967, he settled in London, specialising in Viennese light music.

KUBELIK, *Rafael* (Born Bychory 1914)————————

Czech-born conductor (Swiss citizen 1973). Principal Conductor of the **Czech Philharmonic** 1942–8, conducted the **Chicago Symphony Orchestra** 1950–3, was Music Director at **Covent Garden** 1955–8, and enjoyed a long term with the Bavarian Radio Symphony Orchestra 1961–79. Particularly identified with the music of **Janáček** (he gave the British première of *Jenůfa* in 1956), **Mahler** and **Britten**. Recorded the nine symphonies of **Beethoven** with nine different **orchestras**.

KUIJKEN FAMILY ————————

Sigiswald Kuijken (born 1944) is a Belgian violinist, **viol** player and conductor who in 1972 founded his own **early music** group, La Petite Bande, with his brothers, the viola de gamba player and cellist Wieland (born 1938) and the flautist and **recorder** player Barthold (born 1949).

KUNZ, *Erich* (Born Vienna 1909) ————————

Austrian bass-baritone greatly beloved in Vienna. Fine interpreter of such roles as Papageno in **The Magic Flute** and Beckmesser in *The Mastersingers* and delightful singer of Viennese *heurigen* songs.

L

LABÈQUE SISTERS, *Katia* (born Bayonne 1950) and *Marielle* (born Bayonne 1952) —

French pianists who play as a duo. Repertoire extends from twentieth-century classics to **jazz**, including a thrilling recorded account of **Gershwin**'s *An American in Paris*.

LALO, *Edouard* (Born Lille 1823; died Paris 1892)

After studying **violin** and **cello** in Lille and Paris, Lalo made a living teaching, while championing the **chamber music** of **Mozart, Haydn** and **Mendelssohn**, which had fallen out of favour in Paris. He finally found late success with his opera *Le Roi d'Ys* (1888), based on Breton myth. His other well-known work is the *Symphonie Espagnole* (1874), in fact a violin concerto with a Spanish flavour.

LAMBERT, *Constant* (Born London 1905; died London 1951) —

Composer, conductor, writer and friend of **Walton** and the Sitwells, Lambert's early promise was largely unfulfilled due to ill health. In 1931 he became the first, very influential, musical director of the Vic-Wells (later Royal) Ballet. Now most famous for his **jazz**-inspired *'The Rio Grande'* (1927), a setting of Sacheverell Sitwell's poem for **piano**, chorus and **orchestra**. He was also closely associated with Walton's *'Façade'*; the work was dedicated to Lambert, who often recited it.

LANCHBERY, *John* (Born London 1923) —

Ballet conductor, with **Sadler's Wells** (1951–60), the Royal Ballet and from 1972 the musical director of Australian Ballet. Wrote the **film score** for *The Tales of Beatrix Potter*; his Clog Dance for *La Fille mal gardée*, based on a tune from the earliest version of the ballet (1789), was the signature tune of Radio 4's *Home this Afternoon*.

'LAND OF HOPE AND GLORY'

Originally part of **Elgar**'s *Pomp and Circumstance* March No. 1, the tune was reused for Edward VII's coronation (1902) with words by A. C. Benson. Now a regular feature of the Last Night of the **Proms**.

'LAND OF MY FATHERS' ('Hen wlad fy nhadau') —

Welsh national **anthem**, composed 1856 by James James to words by Evan James, familiar to all from being sung at Welsh rugby football internationals.

LAND OF THE MOUNTAIN AND THE FLOOD

Popular overture composed at the age of seventeen by Hamish McCunn (1868–1916); the main theme was the signature tune of BBC-TV's *Sutherland's Law*.

LANDOWSKA, *Wanda* (Born Warsaw 1877; died Lakeville, Conn., 1959) —

Polish-born harpsichordist and teacher, Landowska helped revive interest in **baroque** and **classical** harpsichord music; also premiered new **concertos** by **Falla** (1926) and **Poulenc** (1929).

LANGRIDGE, *Philip* (Born Hawkhurst, Kent, 1939) —

English **tenor**, noted for his versatile voice and strong acting in opera from **Monteverdi** to **Schoenberg**. Married to the **soprano** Ann Murray.

LANNER, *Joseph* (Born Vienna 1801; died Oberdöbling, near Vienna 1843) —

Lanner is, with Johann **Strauss** the elder, the most important figure of the first generation of Viennese waltz composers. Largely self-taught, Lanner played in string bands with Strauss before the two became rivals for the affections of the public. With their lyrical melodies and skilled harmonies, many consider Lanner's waltzes subtler than the elder Strauss's, although they often lack the latter's compulsive rhythmic force.

LANZA, *Mario* (Born Philadelphia 1921; died Rome 1959) —

American **tenor** of Italian family, whose high early promise was marred by an intemperate lifestyle. Starred with great success in the film *The Great Caruso* (1951), and supplied the tenor voice for *The Student Prince* (1954).

LARGO

Tempo mark (Italian, meaning 'broad') which most often denotes a dignified and spacious mood rather than simply a slow beat, as in **Handel**'s *Largo*, the popular instrumental version of the **aria** 'Ombra mai fù' from Handel's opera *Xerxes*.

*L*ARROCHA, *Alicia De* (Born Barcelona 1923) ――――

Spanish pianist and teacher, often associated with the music of her compatriots **Granados** and **Albéniz**. In recent years, Larrocha has worked with **Sir Georg Solti** on the **Mozart** concertos.

'*L*AST ROSE OF SUMMER' ―――――――――――――

Famous **soprano aria** in Friedrich Flotow's **opera** *Martha* (1847), based on the Irish air 'The Groves of Blarney' with words by **Thomas Moore.**

*L*EDGER, *Philip* (Born Bexhill-on-Sea 1937) ―――

Conductor and keyboard player, Ledger was director of music at **King's College, Cambridge** (1974–82), before becoming principal of the Royal Scottish Academy of Music and Drama.

*L*EEDS (FESTIVAL AND COMPETITION) ――――――

The first Leeds Festival took place in 1858 to celebrate the opening of the new town hall. It became a regular fixture after 1880 under **Sir Arthur Sullivan** who, with his successor **Sir Charles Stanford**, built up a reputation for the highest standards. With the establishment in 1963 by a local teacher, Fanny Waterman, of the internationally-renowned triennial Piano Competition – whose most famous winner was **Murray Perahia** – as well as the foundation of Opera North in 1978, Leeds has become an even more important musical centre.

*L*EGRAND, *Michel* (Born Paris 1932) ―――――――

French conductor and composer. Oscar-winning writer of music for films, including *Les Parapluies de Cherbourg* (1964) and *The Thomas Crown Affair* (1968).

*L*EHÁR, *Franz* (Born Komáron, Hungary, 1870; died Bad Ischl 1948) ―――――――――――

Austrian composer of Hungarian extraction, Lehár was the leading twentieth-century composer of **operetta**. After studying at the Prague Conservatory, and service as a military bandmaster, he scored a hit in **Vienna** with the waltz 'Gold and Silver' (1902). After early attempts at writing operetta, a genre then falling out of favour, Lehár produced in 1905 his

masterpiece, *Die lustige Witwe* (*The Merry Widow*); with its witty and complex plot, flowing melodies and gentle waltzes, the work heralded a renewed international interest in Viennese light opera. Lehár followed this with other successes, notably in 1909 *Der Graf von Luxemburg* (*The Count of Luxembourg*). After the First World War his popularity began to wane, until he began a fruitful collaboration with the **tenor Richard Tauber**, most famously producing, in Berlin in 1929, *Das Land des Lächelns* (*The Land of Smiles*) with its song 'Dein ist mein ganzes Herz' ('You are my Heart's Delight'). Lehár became a close friend of **Puccini**, whose influence can be detected in Lehár's later works, particularly in *Giuditta* (1934).

*L*EHMANN, *Lotte* (Born Perleberg 1888; died Santa Barbara 1976) ――――――――――――――

German **soprano** (American from 1945). Lehmann was celebrated for her warmth and elegance, above all in the **operas** of **Richard Strauss**.

*L*EINSDORF, *Erich* (Born Vienna 1912) ―――――

Austrian, later American, conductor, Leinsdorf worked in Europe with **Bruno Walter** and **Toscanini**, finally to become closely associated with the **Boston Symphony Orchestra** in intelligent and restrained performances.

*L*EITMOTIV ―――――――――――――――――――――

German term, meaning 'leading motive', denoting a recurring theme which represents a character or idea, usually in symphonic or dramatic music. Most often used with reference to the **operas** of **Wagner**.

*L*ENYA, *Lotte* (Born Vienna 1898; died New York 1981) ――――――――――――――――――――

Austrian-born American singer who, in the Berlin of the 1920s, became closely associated with the works of Bertolt Brecht and **Kurt Weill** (whom she married), creating the role of Jenny in *Die Dreigroschenoper* (*The Threepenny Opera*).

*L*EPPARD, *Raymond* (Born London 1927) ―――――

Conductor and harpsichordist, prominent as a champion of **baroque** composers, in particular **Monteverdi** and Cavalli, of whose **operas** he made controversial editions.

James Levine, American conductor – dynamic and commanding in opera house, concert hall and on disc.

LEVINE, *James* (Born Cincinnati 1943) —————

Now perhaps the most prominent American conductor; after studying **piano** and conducting at the **Juilliard School**, Levine became assistant conductor of the **Cleveland Orchestra** under **George Szell**, moving in 1973 to become principal conductor at the **Metropolitan Opera**.

LEWIS, *Richard* (Born Manchester 1914; died Eastbourne 1990) —————

Fine English **tenor**, whose varied career began in 1947 at **Glyndebourne**, where he was a noted **Mozart** and **Britten** performer. He was also involved in important British premières, including **Walton**'s *Troilus and Cressida* (1954).

LIED —————

German for 'song' (its plural is *Lieder*). With a history stretching back to part songs from the fifteenth and sixteenth centuries, the lied is now most familiar in its nineteenth-century guise for voice and **piano**. Both **Mozart** and **Beethoven** wrote German songs, but it was **Schubert** who made the form his own. The songs in his three great song-cycles – *Die schöne Müllerin* (*The Beautiful Mill Girl*) (1823), *Winterreise* (*Winter Journey*) (1827) and *Schwanengesäng* (*Swan Songs*) (1828) – demonstrate a fertile inventiveness, and encompass all emotions, from wistful regret to violent joy or sorrow, while showing great sensitivity to the German text. Of Schubert's successors, **Schumann**, **Brahms** and **Hugo Wolf** are the most notable. While Schumann's lieder are more limited in range, they show a more complex dramatic and harmonic style. **Brahms** generally takes a simpler, often serene approach, while Wolf makes difficult technical demands on both pianist and singer, finally initiating the movement towards orchestral accompaniment, exploited in **Mahler**'s song-cycles *Lieder eines fahrenden*

Gesellen (*Songs of a Wayfarer*) (1884) and *Kindertotenlieder* (*Songs on the Death of Children*) (1902). These signal the removal of the lied from the drawing-room to the twentieth-century concert hall.

*L*ILL, *John* (Born London 1944) _____

One of the leading British pianists, Lill made his début in 1963 at the **Royal Festival Hall** playing **Beethoven**'s 'Emperor' Concerto. In 1970 he made musical history by winning the prestigious **Tchaikovsky** Piano Competition in Moscow, jointly with Vladimir Krainer. His formidable technical expertise matched by great stamina make him well suited to the large-scale works of **Chopin, Liszt** and **Rachmaninov**, although he is most famous for his complete cycle of **Beethoven** sonatas and concertos.

*L*INCOLN CENTRE FOR THE PERFORMING ARTS___

A complex of theatres, concert and lecture halls built in the 1960s and now the hub of New York cultural life. It includes: the **Juilliard School**, America's most prestigious college for music, drama and dance; the Avery Fisher Hall, housing the **New York Philharmonic**; and the smaller Alice Tully Hall, for **chamber** and solo concerts. The **Metropolitan Opera** moved there from Broadway in 1966.

*L*IND, *Jenny* (Born Stockholm 1820; died Wynds Point, Herefordshire, 1887) _____

'The Swedish Nightingale', as she became known, attracted ecstatic adulation wherever she went. She first appeared in London in 1847 in the presence of Queen Victoria and Prince Albert. Although she gave up the theatre in 1848 she continued giving concerts, settling in England in 1858 and becoming professor of singing at the **Royal College of Music** in 1883.

*L*IPATTI, *Dinu* (*Constantin*) (Born Bucharest 1917; died Geneva 1950) _____

Romanian pianist who, in 1934, became the centre of a musical scandal when he was not declared winner of the Vienna International Competition, causing the resignation of one of the judges, the distinguished French pianist **Alfred Cortot**. Lipatti was technically brilliant, and matched this quality with a rare sensitivity and nobility. He died from cancer at the age of 33.

Franz Liszt: probably the greatest pianist the world has known, and a visionary musical pioneer.

*L*ISZT, *Franz* (Born Raiding 1811; died Bayreuth 1868) _____

Liszt has been described as the greatest pianist of all time. Born in Hungary, Liszt studied **piano** in **Vienna** under **Czerny** and composition under **Salieri**, before settling in Paris in 1827, where he met **Berlioz** and **Chopin**, both at the forefront of the new **Romantic** movement. For most of his life, Liszt was uniquely famous across Europe, as a pianist, composer, centre of the musical avant-garde, and for his notorious affairs with women. His piano writing, including his ever-popular *Liebestraum* No. 3 and famous transcriptions of the orchestral and operatic works of Berlioz, **Beethoven** and **Verdi**, became ever .more innovative. He was an early champion of **Wagner** (for whom his daughter Cosima left her husband) and in some respects anticipated later composers such as **Debussy** and **Schoenberg**. In works like the Hungarian Rhapsodies (1852) he laid the foundations for a national Hungarian music, directly influencing

Bartók. Although no great orchestrator, his 'symphonic poems' (a term he himself coined) and the 'Faust' and 'Dante' Symphonies, with their use of a literary 'programme' or detailed subject-matter, provided a model for Romantic composers as far ahead as **Richard Strauss**.

'*L*ITTLE TRAIN OF THE CAIPIRA'

Colourful **toccata**, describing the journey of a country train, from the *Bachiana brasileira* No. 2 by the prolific Brazilian composer Heitor **Villa-Lobos** (1887–1959). The *Bachianas brasileiras* attempt to merge elements of **Bach**'s style with Brazilian folk rhythms.

*L*LOYD WEBBER, *Andrew* (Born London 1948)

Son of William Lloyd Webber, composer, organist and director of the **London College of Music**, Andrew Lloyd Webber's phenomenally successful career started when he teamed up with the lyricist Tim Rice. Together in 1969 they put together a fifteen-minute 'pop **oratorio**' for schools called *Joseph and his Amazing Technicolor Dreamcoat* – and the rest is history. *Joseph* expanded into a full-length stage show, by which time Lloyd Webber and Rice had produced one of the best-selling British LPs ever, the 'rock **opera**' *Jesus Christ Superstar*, later to become a blockbuster stage show and film (1973). Since then, Lloyd Webber (with various lyricists, including Alan Ayckbourn, Richard Stilgoe and Charles Hart) has created **musicals** for which audiences around the world seem to have an insatiable appetite: *Evita* (1978), *Cats* (1981, based on T.S. Eliot's cat poetry), *Starlight Express* (1984, then the most expensive musical ever staged), *The Phantom of the Opera* (1986, featuring his then wife Sarah Brightman and Michael Crawford), and *Aspects of Love* (1989). Other compositions include Variations on a Theme of Paganini (1986, for his cellist brother Julian, thereafter best known as the theme for LWT's *South Bank Show*), and the Requiem (1985) for his father, recorded with Brightman and **Placido Domingo**. Knighted 1992.

*L*LOYD WEBBER, *Julian* (Born London 1951)

Brother of Andrew Lloyd Webber. Since his début in 1972 he has become a distinguished cellist, playing with the world's leading **orchestras** and conductors,

including **Solti** and **Menuhin**, and making an award-winning recording of the **Elgar** concerto (1986).

*L*OEWE, *Frederick* (Born Vienna 1904; died Palm Springs, Fla., 1988)

Austrian-born American song-writer, Loewe's career only took off when he met the lyricist Alan Jay Lerner. Together, they made up one of this century's most successful musical-writing teams, creating *Brigadoon* (1947), *Paint Your Wagon* (1951), *Camelot* (1960), and *Gigi* (1973). But their greatest success was *My Fair Lady* (1956), based on Shaw's *Pygmalion* and featuring the songs 'The Rain in Spain' and 'Wouldn't It Be Loverly'. Loewe was the son of Edmund Loewe, the first leading man in **Franz Lehár**'s *The Merry Widow*.

'*L*ONDONDERRY AIR'

Anonymous Irish **air**, first collected and published in 1855, and described by Sir Hubert Parry as 'the most beautiful tune in the world'. The most famous words sung to it are by F. E. Weatherly – 'Danny Boy'.

*L*ONDON PHILHARMONIC ORCHESTRA

Founded in 1932 by **Sir Thomas Beecham** as his own **orchestra**, but self-governing since 1939. The orchestra has always been among the world's finest, making history as the first British orchestra to tour the USSR in 1956. Its connections with **opera** were confirmed in 1964, since when it has been resident at the **Glyndebourne** summer season. A distinguished list of principal conductors includes **Sir Adrian Boult, Sir John Pritchard, Bernard Haitink, Sir Georg Solti, Klaus Tennstedt,** and, from 1990, the Austrian Franz Welser-Möst. Now resident orchestra at the **Royal Festival Hall.**

*L*ONDON SYMPHONY ORCHESTRA

The oldest surviving London **orchestra**, formed in 1904 by deserters from **Sir Henry Wood**'s Queen's Hall Orchestra, and self-governing from the start. It was the first British orchestra to tour the USA and Canada (1912), and **Hans Richter** and **Elgar** were among its early conductors. After a decline in fortunes following the war, its reputation has steadily increased since the 1960s under a series of conductors including **Pierre Monteux, André Previn, Claudio Abbado,** and since 1988 **Michael Tilson**

Thomas. The orchestra is now resident at the **Barbican Centre**.

*L*ORENGAR, *Pilar* (Born Saragossa 1928) _____

Spanish **soprano**. Primarily associated with Italian *verismo* and Spanish **opera**, she has also been admired for her performances of classical roles, especially in **Mozart** and **Gluck**.

*L*OS ANGELES PHILHARMONIC ORCHESTRA ____

Los Angeles's top **orchestra,** founded in 1919. Its present principal conductor is the brilliant young Finn Esa-Pekka Salonen, whose predecessors include **Klemperer**, **Mehta**, **Giulini** and **Previn**.

*L*OTT, *Felicity* (Born Cheltenham 1947)_____

English **soprano**, internationally acclaimed for her roles in the **operas** of **Richard Strauss** and **Mozart**. Lott has also had a distinguished career as a concert performer, most famously singing at Prince Andrew's wedding in 1986.

*L*OUGHRAN, *James* (Born Glasgow 1931) _____

Scottish conductor; **Sir John Barbirolli**'s successor at the **Hallé Orchestra** in the 1970s. Perhaps best known for recording the nine Beethoven symphonies for the BBC in 1970.

*L*UDWIG, *Christa* (Born Berlin 1924) _____

German **mezzo-soprano** who has enjoyed a long career at the **Vienna** State Opera and other major houses. Specially successful in **Mahler**, **Mozart**, **Richard Strauss** and **Brahms**.

*L*ULLABY_____

Cradle songs are as old as music itself. Famous composed lullabies included the 'Wiegenlied' of **Brahms**, and there are many instrumental 'cradle songs' such as **Chopin**'s Berceuse for **piano**.

*L*ULLY, *Jean-Baptiste* (Born Florence 1632; died Paris 1687) _____

Born Giovanni Battista Lulli, he became a French citizen 1661 and the leading composer in the France of his day. He held a series of appointments at the court of King Louis XIV, and collaborated with Molière in *comédie-ballets*, among them *Le*

Bourgeois Gentilhomme (1670) in which Lully danced the role of the Mufti. From 1673, held royal licence to produce **opera** in Paris, where he introduced female dancers into **ballet**. Lully died from a gangrenous abscess, formed after he struck his foot with the staff he used for beating time on the floor during a service of royal thanksgiving.

*L*UMBYE, *Hans Christian* (Born Copenhagen 1810; died Copenhagen 1874)_____

'The **Strauss** of the North', Lumbye was the first music director of Copenhagen's Tivoli Gardens 1843–72; he composed much enjoyable music, including the 'Champagne Galop' and 'The Copenhagen Steam Railway Galop'.

*L*UPU, *Radu* (Born Galati 1945)_____

Highly regarded Romanian pianist who won the **Leeds** Piano Competition in 1969 and now enjoys a very successful international career. Specially distinguished in nineteenth-century romantics from **Schubert** to **Brahms**.

*L*UTE _____

Extremely ancient world-wide family of fretted stringed instruments which dates back at least to 2000 BC. Spread from the Arabic world into Spain in fourteenth century, popular throughout Europe till the eighteenth century; revived in twentieth century by virtuosi such as **Julian Bream**.

*L*UXON, *Benjamin* (Born Redruth 1937) _____

Versatile and popular British **baritone**. His repertoire extends from the title role in **Tchaikovsky**'s *Eugene Onegin*, and the title role in **Britten**'s television opera *Owen Wingrave* (1970), to the Victorian songs and duets he has recorded with **Robert Tear** and **André Previn**. Very active in support of Cornwall's own opera company, Duchy Opera. CBE 1986.

*L*YMPANY, *Moura* (Born Saltash 1916)_____

British pianist, Cornish by birth. Studied with **Tobias Matthay** and made her début at the age of twelve at Harrogate. Moura Lympany gave the first performance outside the USSR of **Khatchaturian**'s Piano Concerto, 1940, and was the first in the West to record all **Rachmaninov**'s Preludes for **piano**.

Yo-Yo Ma: one of the finest present-day cellists, and frequent partner of pianist Emmanuel Ax.

M

*M*A, *Yo-Yo* (Born Paris 1955) _____

French cellist of Chinese parentage. Gave first public recital aged five, went to New York with his parents, attended the **Juilliard School**, and gave famous concert when he was nineteen to mark hundredth anniversary of **Carnegie Hall**, playing all **Bach**'s unaccompanied **cello** suites.

*M*AAZEL, *Lorin* (Born Neuilly 1930) _____

American conductor and violinist. Aged nine, conducted at New York World Fair and Hollywood Bowl, later violinist in **Pittsburgh Symphony Orchestra**. First American conductor at Bayreuth 1960; Music Director of **Cleveland Orchestra** 1972–82. Director of **Vienna** State Opera 1982–4, resigning after controversy. From 1986 has been Music Director of **Pittsburgh Symphony Orchestra**. In London in 1988 conducted all **Beethoven** symphonies in a day for charity.

*M*cCORMACK, *John* (Born Athlone 1884; died Dublin 1945) _____

Irish-born **tenor** (American citizen 1917), whose numerous records helped to make him one of the world's most popular singers. After little training, won medal at the National Irish Festival of 1903; in 1905 studied in Milan with Vincenzo Sabatini, and a year later made his stage début at Savona under the name Giovanni Foli (his fiancée was a Miss Foley). Took part in every **Covent Garden** season 1907–14, often partnering **Tetrazzini** or **Melba**; he also became a favourite (1910–18) at the **Metropolitan Opera**. Realising he was a poor actor, he abandoned the stage in favour of concert work, developing a repertoire which extended from **Handel** and **Mozart** through German **lieder** to the sentimental Irish songs which occupied an ever larger share of his concert programmes. In the mid-twenties he returned to live in Ireland and in 1928 was made a Papal Count. He continued to tour the world, and gave a farewell recital in the **Royal Albert Hall** in 1938, though he continued to sing in aid of the Red Cross during the Second World War.

*M*cKELLAR, *Kenneth* (Born Paisley 1927) _____

Popular Scottish **tenor** who appeared in **opera** with the **Carl Rosa Company** from 1953 but has mainly concentrated on the lighter repertoire in concert and on records, particularly Scottish songs.

*M*ACKERRAS, *Charles* (Born Schenectady, New York, 1925)

Scholarly Australian conductor who began professional life as oboist in the Sydney Symphony Orchestra 1943–6. Studies in Prague led to special interest in **Janáček**: conducted first British performances of his *Katya Kabanová* (1951) and *The Makropoulos Affair* (1964). Has conducted own 'authentic' editions of works by **Handel**, **Mozart**, and **Gluck** and arranged two brilliant ballet scores: *Pineapple Poll* (from **Sullivan**'s music) and *The Lady and the Fool* (music by **Verdi**). Principal conductor, **Sadler's Wells** (later **English National**) **Opera** 1970–80. Conductor, Sydney Symphony Orchestra 1982–85, Music Director **Welsh National Opera** 1986–1992. Knighted 1979.

*M*ADAM BUTTERFLY _____

Puccini's *Madama Butterfly*, developed from a play by David Belasco which may have been based on a real-life story, was a fiasco at its first Milan performance in February 1904, but triumphed after amendments four months later at Brescia. An American naval lieutenant marries a Japanese child-bride, Cio-Cio-San, with no intention of remaining faithful. After a three-year absence, Lieutenant Pinkerton returns with a new American wife. The heartbroken Cio-Cio-San allows her to take the child and commits suicide. Butterfly's **aria** 'One Fine Day' ('Un bel dì vedremo') is universally beloved, as is the Love Duet, and the 'Humming Chorus'.

MADRIGAL

Name shared by a type of fourteenth-century Italian part song, and another type developed in Italy in the sixteenth century. This became very popular in England, where **Morley**, Weelkes and Wilbye, among others, produced superb examples.

MAGIC FLUTE, THE

Opera by **Mozart** with text by Emmanuel Schikaneder, first produced with great success at Schikaneder's theatre in Vienna in September 1791. Mozart and Schikaneder were Freemasons and the opera, based on an oriental fairy tale, reflects certain Masonic rituals. Schikaneder wrote a starring role for himself as the cheerful but brainless bird-catcher, Papageno. Favourite passages include Papageno's entrance **aria** 'Der Vogelfänger bin ich ja', Tamino's 'portrait' aria ('Dies Bildnis'), the two **coloratura** arias of the Queen of the Night, Pamina's lament 'Ach, ich fühl's' and Sarastro's prayer 'O Isis und Osiris'.

MAHLER, *Gustav* (Born Kalište, Bohemia, 1860; died Vienna 1911)

Austrian musician of monumental achievement both as composer and conductor. As a child he absorbed the idioms of popular folk-song which later permeated his musical vocabulary, and at fifteen entered the **Vienna** Conservatoire where his attention was divided between **conducting** and composition, as it was for the rest of his life. Mahler was imperious in his demands as a conductor, and uncompromising in his search for new ways to approach established masterpieces, which led him into many conflicts in a series of conducting appointments. The high point of Mahler's conducting career was his ten years at the Vienna Hofoper (now the State Opera) 1897–1907, now regarded as the golden era of that house. In 1902 Mahler married Alma Schindler; the death in

1907 of their daughter Maria at the age of four was a shattering blow. That year Mahler was hounded from office by Vienna's anti-Semitic press: he spent much time in New York during his last years, dying prematurely just before his fifty-first birthday of heart disease aggravated by a bacterial infection. Almost throughout his frenetically busy conducting career, Mahler spent his summer months composing. He produced ten huge **symphonies** (the tenth reconstructed long after his death by Deryck Cooke), *The Song of the Earth* (settings of Chinese poems) and many settings of poems from *Des Knaben Wunderhorn* (The Youth's Magic Horn), a collection of folk poems. From the 1950s Mahler's work has gained hugely in popularity; the slow movement of his Fifth Symphony became specially familiar as the theme music for the film *Death in Venice* (1971).

MALCOLM, *George* (Born London 1917)

British harpsichordist, pianist and conductor. Master of the Music, Westminster Cathedral 1947–59. Wide experience as orchestral conductor and brilliant keyboard recitalist.

MANCINI, *Henry* (Born Cleveland, Ohio, 1924)

American composer, conductor, arranger and pianist who wrote the famous theme for *The Pink Panther* (1963). Pianist in **Glenn Miller** orchestra before starting highly successful career producing **film scores**. Won an Oscar for *Breakfast at Tiffany's* (1961) which included 'Moon River'.

MANDOLIN

Instrument of the **lute** family, shaped like half a pear cut lengthways, usually with eight strings tuned in pairs. Played with a plectrum. Originated Naples, mid-seventeenth century. Appears in **Mozart**'s *Don Giovanni*; **Vivaldi** wrote mandolin **concertos** and **Beethoven** composed sonatinas for mandolin with **piano**.

MANTOVANI, *Annunzio Paolo* (Born Venice 1905; died Tunbridge Wells 1980)

Italian-born violinist and conductor, famous for the shimmering, echoing strings of the 45-strong Mantovani Orchestra whose huge recording success began with 'Charmaine' (1951), arranged by **Ronald Binge**. Awarded diamond-studded baton in 1966 by

Decca, with 50 million LP sales in the USA to his credit and 18 gold disc winners.

*M*ARCH

Form of music, certainly in use from ancient times, to accompany the orderly progress of groups of people, especially troops; sometimes in quick time, sometimes slow. Some of the best marches were composed by **John Philip Sousa** and Kenneth Alford (see **Colonel Bogey**), but march rhythm is also much used by major composers, e.g. **Beethoven**, **Chopin**, **Wagner**, **Tchaikovsky**, **Berlioz** and **Elgar**.

*M*ARIMBA

Percussion instrument like a **xylophone** made of strips of wood with resonators underneath; the wood-strips are struck by soft-headed hammers. Originated in South Africa as the Malimba.

*M*ARRIAGE OF FIGARO, THE

Le Nozze di Figaro, **opera** by Mozart, first produced in Vienna in 1786. Text by Lorenzo da Ponte, based on a play by the French playwright Beaumarchais which had been banned in Vienna on account of its supposedly seditious story. Famous numbers include Figaro's farewell to the page Cherubino ('Non più andrai'); 'Voi che sapete' (Cherubino's account of his youthful sufferings in love); the Countess's lament for lost love ('Dove sono?'); and the moving and brilliant Finale.

*M*ARRINER, *Neville* (Born Lincoln 1924)

British conductor. Principal second violin in the **London Symphony Orchestra** 1956–68. Music and Artistic Director Academy of St Martin-in-the-Fields, which he founded in 1959. Music Director of Los Angeles Chamber Orchestra 1969–79 and Minnesota Symphony Orchestra 1979–86. With the Academy and other orchestras, Marriner is one of the world's most-recorded conductors. Knighted 1985.

*M*ARSALIS, *Wynton* (Born New Orleans 1961)

American trumpeter of outstanding brilliance both in **jazz** and the **classical** repertoire. Many recordings include selection of nineteenth-century **cornet** solos. Often works with his saxophonist brother Branford Marsalis (born 1960).

*M*ARSEILLAISE, LA

French national anthem, written and composed in Strasbourg 1792 by army officer Rouget de Lisle, and officially adopted 1795. Acquired its name through its use by the Marseilles volunteers at the storming of the Tuileries (August 1792).

*M*ARTINON, *Jean* (Born Lyons 1910; died Paris 1976)

French conductor and composer. While a prisoner in Stalag IX during the Second World War, wrote music which won a prize awarded by the city of Paris. The Symphony No. 3 ('Irlandaise') was created while he was conductor of the Radio Eireann Orchestra 1948–50. Subsequent principal conducting appointments include the Concerts Lamoureux (Paris) 1951–7, **Israel Philharmonic** 1958–60, **Chicago Symphony** 1963–9 and French Radio Orchestra 1968–75. Specialised in French music, **Prokofiev** and **Bartók**.

*M*ASQUE

Highly elaborate form of court and theatrical entertainment, usually on a mythological theme and involving the use of masks, which developed in England in the seventeenth century. Masques often featured in plays and semi-operas for which **Purcell** wrote music.

*M*ASS

The ritual of the Eucharist in the Roman Catholic Church has been accompanied by music from early times. Five sections are most often chosen for musical settings: the Kyrie, Gloria, Credo, Sanctus (and Benedictus) and Agnus Dei. **Bach**, with his Mass in B minor and **Beethoven** with his Masses in C and D (the *Missa Solemnis*) are among composers who have extended settings of mass texts into **oratorio** form.

*M*ASSENET, *Jules* (Born Montaud, St Étienne, 1842; died Paris 1912)

French composer whose ability to please the public with a long succession of **operas** brought hostile attacks from the avant-garde, including **Debussy**. Among Massenet's major successes were *Manon* (1884), with a score notable for eighteenth-century delicacy, *Werther*, based on Goethe's story (1892),

Thaïs (1894), with its famous 'Méditation' for violin, reflecting the conversion of a courtesan, and *Don Quichotte* (1910). Massenet's tuneful genius also found expression in many songs and orchestral works such as *Scènes Pittoresques* (1874).

MASTER OF THE QUEEN'S (King's) MUSIC

Musical equivalent of the Poet Laureate. Post established under Charles I, entailing leadership of the royal band, but now with no fixed duties, though it carries an honorarium. Present incumbent is **Malcolm Williamson** (since 1975).

MASTERSON, *Valerie* (Born Birkenhead 1937)

This highly accomplished English **soprano** sang **Gilbert and Sullivan** with D'Oyly Carte Opera 1966–70, but has since won international renown in **Handel operas** and many others, perhaps most notably **Verdi**'s *La Traviata*.

MASUR, *Kurt* (Born Brieg, Silesia, 1927)

Highly esteemed German conductor. Became Musical Director of the Leipzig Gewandhaus orchestra in 1970 and, in 1992, of the **New York Philharmonic**.

MATHIESON, *Muir* (Born Stirling 1911; died Oxford 1972)

From 1934 music director of London Films, musically responsible for over 500 British films. Commissioned many leading composers from **Arthur Bliss** (*Things to Come* 1935) to **Richard Rodney Bennett** (*Interpol* 1956).

MATTHAY, *Tobias* (Born London 1858; died nr Haslemere 1945)

British musician of German descent, very influential piano teacher at **Royal College of Music** (1880–1925) and at his own school (from 1900). Advocated muscular relaxation and rotation of the forearm. **Myra Hess** was among many notable pupils.

MATTHEWS, *Denis* (Born Coventry 1919; died Birmingham 1988)

British pianist, scholar and admirable lecturer. Toured with RAF orchestra in the Second World War, thereafter established high reputation as pianist, especially in **Mozart** and **Beethoven**. Professor Newcastle University 1972–84. CBE 1975.

Zubin Mehta: Indian conductor born in Bombay who has achieved high international distinction.

MAUCERI, *John* (Born New York 1945)

American conductor mainly associated with **opera** in USA and Europe. Conducted first European performance of **Bernstein**'s Mass 1973 in Vienna; Music Director of **Scottish Opera** (1987–).

MAYER, *Robert* (Born Mannheim 1879; died London 1985)

Very influential British musical patron of German birth. With his first wife Dorothy, founded Robert Mayer Children's Concerts 1923, and Youth and Music (1954). Knighted 1939, CH 1973, created KCVO on his hundredth birthday.

MEHTA, *Zubin* (Born Bombay 1936)

Extremely successful Indian conductor. Son of Mehli Mehta, founder of Bombay Symphony Orchestra, Zubin studied at **Vienna** Academy and won Liverpool conducting competition 1958. Musical Director **Montreal Symphony Orchestra** 1961–7; raised **Los Angeles Philharmonic** to new heights 1962–77; Music Director **New York Philharmonic** 1978–91. Music Director for life of **Israel Philharmonic**.

MELBA, *Nellie* (Born Melbourne 1861; died Sydney 1931)

Helen Porter Armstrong (née Mitchell), who took her stage name from her native city, was the most famous operatic **soprano** of her day. After study in Paris and a début in Brussels, her career took off in 1888 at **Covent Garden** which she thereafter regarded as her musical home: her farewell to the house was in 1926. Also enjoyed long association with the **Metropolitan**, and organised Australian **opera** seasons 1911 and 1924. Gave her name to Pêche Melba and Melba Toast. DBE 1918.

MELODY

Sequence of notes arranged in organised pattern which, for some reason that eludes definition, pleases and satisfies the ear. Established local traditions and the element of rhythm have much to do with a melody's success.

'MEMORIES OF THE ALHAMBRA'

'Recuerdos de la Alhambra' is a haunting tremolo study by the Spanish guitarist and **guitar** composer Francisco Tarrega (1852–1909). Known as the '**Sarasate** of the guitar', he greatly influenced other players and composers.

MENDELSSOHN, (-BARTHOLDY) *Felix* (Born Hamburg 1809; died Leipzig 1847)

Felix made his solo début aged nine and, a year later, a psalm-setting of his was performed by the Berlin Singakademie. At twelve he met the great writer Goethe and established a lasting friendship. At seventeen he composed a masterpiece, the Overture to *A Midsummer Night's Dream*. When he was twenty he conducted the first performance of **Bach**'s *St Matthew Passion* since the composer's death and began the travels to England, Scotland, Italy and elsewhere which inspired the *Fingal's Cave* Overture and the 'Italian' and 'Scottish' Symphonies. Mendelssohn was conductor of the Lower Rhine Festival 1833–6 and of the Leipzig **Gewandhaus** Orchestra 1835–46. In 1843 he established the important Leipzig Conservatoire, and in 1846 conducted the first performance of his **oratorio** *Elijah* at the **Birmingham** Festival, for which it was written. His sister Fanny died suddenly the following year and the shock (coupled with years of overwork) hastened Mendelssohn's own premature death. Much of Mendelssohn's music remains extremely popular, including many of the 'Songs without Words' for **piano**, the First Piano Concerto, the Octet, the whole

of the *Midsummer Night's Dream* music, completed in 1842, and the Violin Concerto in E minor (1844).

MENOTTI, *Gian-Carlo* (Born Cadegliano 1911)

American composer of Italian birth who has written some of the most accessible **operas** of the twentieth century. *Amelia Goes to the Ball* (1937) and *The Medium* (1947) were both popular, but their success was eclipsed by *The Consul* (1950), a drama of struggle against a police state, which ran for eight months in New York and had great international success. *Amahl and the Night Visitors* (1951) was the first opera written for television and has enjoyed constant stage revivals worldwide. Founded the Spoleto Festival of Two Worlds in 1958.

MENUHIN, *Yehudi* (Born New York 1916)

American born violinist of Russian parentage; Swiss citizen 1970; British citizen 1985. A child prodigy, his performances were astonishingly mature, and at sixteen he recorded **Elgar**'s concerto with the 75-year-old composer conducting. He gave over 500 concerts for the Red Cross in the Second World War, played for the survivors of Belsen and, controversially, was the first Jewish artist to appear with the **Berlin Philharmonic** under **Furtwängler** after the war. Active in promoting an East–West *rapprochement* in politics and music, he gave many concerts with the Indian **sitar** player **Ravi Shankar**; another partner, in the cause of promoting a single world of music, has been the **jazz** violinist **Stephane Grappelli**. In 1958 he started his own **chamber** orchestra and has conducted many other orchestras round the world. He was appointed Director of the Gstaad Festival in 1956, the Bath Festival in 1958 and the Windsor Festival in 1969. Always a great encourager of young talent, he started the Yehudi Menuhin school at Stoke D'Abernon in 1962. Gave concerts with his pianist sister Hephzibah (born 1920; died 1981). His sister Yalta and son Jeremy are also pianists. KBE 1965; OM 1987; among many other honours, recipient of the Nehru Award for International Understanding.

MERRY WIVES OF WINDSOR, THE

The **overture** to this **opera**, successfully produced in Berlin in 1847, is the best-known work of Otto Nicolai (1810–49), German conductor and composer credited with the foundation of the **Vienna Philharmonic Orchestra** 1842.

*M*ESSAGER, *André* (Born Montluçon 1853; died Paris 1929) _____

At first a leading organist, his ballet *The Two Pigeons* was a big success in 1886; *Véronique* (1898) and *Monsieur Beaucaire*, which starred **Maggie Teyte** in 1919, are the best known of a series of operettas. Messager also excelled as a conductor. He was a notable champion of **Wagner**, and conducted the first performance of **Debussy**'s *Pelléas et Mélisande* in 1902. He was Musical Director at **Covent Garden** 1901–7, of the Paris Opéra 1907–14, of the Opéra-Comique for two periods, and of leading Paris orchestras.

*M*ETRONOME _____

Adjustable ticking device for establishing the speed of a composition according to the 'metronome marking' (sometimes suspect) on a score. Commonest type is clockwork model invented by Johann Maelzel (1772–1838).

*M*ETROPOLITAN OPERA HOUSE _____

Most prestigious American **opera** house, originally opened in 1883 with **Gounod**'s *Faust*. Present theatre, seating 3800, is part of New York's **Lincoln Centre** and was opened in 1966. Most of the world's greatest singers and conductors have appeared there: in 1910 **Toscanini** conducted the first performance of **Puccini**'s *The Girl of the Golden West*. **Rafael Kubelik** was the first Music Director at the house (1972–3). The current Artistic Director is **James Levine**.

*M*EYERBEER, *Giacomo* (Born nr Berlin 1791; died Paris 1864) _____

After early success as a pianist child prodigy and studies in Italy, Meyerbeer scored a massive success with his *Robert le Diable* (*Robert the Devil*) at the Paris Opéra in 1831. *Les Huguenots* (1836) and *Le Prophète* (1849) confirmed his position as the most successful **opera** composer of his day, renowned for spectacular scenes and what has been called 'massive monumentalism'. Helped **Wagner** as a young man, to be rewarded later with a virulent anti-Semitic attack.

Meyerbeer died while rehearsing *L'Africaine* which had occupied him for over twenty-five years.

*M*EZZO-SOPRANO _____

Voice whose range lies between that of the **soprano** and **contralto**. In **opera**, 'mezzos' are often cast in dramatic roles (e.g. Amneris in **Verdi**'s *Aida*) or as nurse or confidante (e.g. Suzuki in *Madam Butterfly*).

*M*ICHELANGELI, *Arturo Benedetti* (Born Brescia 1920) _____

Michelangeli won high acclaim as a pianist in London (1946) and New York (1950) for his brilliance and intellectual power. Subject to periodic bouts of illness which led him to cancel concerts. Founded **piano** school in Brescia.

*M*IGHTY HANDFUL _____

Group of nineteenth-century Russian composers (sometimes called 'the Five') dedicated to nationalist ideas. They were **Balakirev**, **Borodin**, César Cui (1835–1918), **Moussorgsky** and **Rimsky-Korsakov**.

*M*ILITARY BAND _____

Small bands often accompanied royal armies in the Middle Ages, while regimental bands originated in Germany about the middle of the seventeenth-century, the idea spreading to France and England in the 1670s. Apart from playing on the march, military bands are used for ceremonial occasions such as 'Beating Retreat', and frequently give concerts; their repertoire extends well beyond military music to include arrangements of orchestral pieces and the large number of concert compositions for military band.

*M*ILLER, *Glenn* (Born Clarinda, Iowa, 1904; died in air crash 1944) _____

Trombonist and legendary bandleader who formed the Glenn Miller Orchestra in 1938. With numbers such as 'Moonlight Serenade' and 'In the Mood', it became the world's favourite swing band. Miller formed a famous service band in the US Army 1942. Posted missing after presumed crash of aircraft between London and Paris, after which his band remained active under other leaders.

M OZART

I am inclined to agree with the great conductor **Sir Thomas Beecham** who said, 'If I were a dictator, I should make it compulsory for every member of the population to listen to Mozart for one quarter of an hour daily.' Mozart achieved a perfect blend of passion and form in his compositions which means he can offer profound consolation to minds like ours, overstretched by twentieth-century troubles.

Mozart lived in the days when most musicians had to rely for employment on aristocratic patrons. When Wolfgang began to show signs of musical genius (playing the clavier at three and composing from the age of five), his father Leopold decided to capitalise on his exceptional talent. Over a period of four years, Wolfgang was shown off in all the main musical centres of Western Europe. The strain of all this travel, however, told heavily on the health of the boy, who was seriously ill several times.

Still intent on establishing his son on the international scene, Leopold took him as a teenager on three successive visits to Italy. These did not result in the hoped-for court appointment and Wolfgang was forced to return to Salzburg. His time here was productive but the larger world still beckoned and in 1778 Mozart set off for Paris. Unfortunately, those who had been ready

to swoon over an infant prodigy responded coldly to a young man of twenty-two. His mother, deprived of adequate food and heat in poor lodgings, died during the visit, and once more Mozart was driven back to Salzburg.

Mozart accepted an appointment as court organist in 1779 but chafed constantly under the conditions of his employment by the Prince-Archbishop. Matters came to a head during a state visit to **Vienna**. The Archbishop, not unnaturally, expected Mozart to be available to perform for him, while Mozart thought he should be able to accept more lucrative engagements elsewhere in the city. High words were exchanged and Mozart, we are told, was literally booted out by the Archbishop's chamberlain. Now he was on his own, free to make his way as best he could.

Vienna was at that time the most musical city in the world and from 1781 to 1786 Mozart enjoyed great success as a keyboard performer, mainly in **concertos** of his own composition.

In 1782 Mozart married Constanze Weber, whose father and sister Aloysia were both singers. Constanze has been much criticised but she was kind-hearted and deeply loyal to her husband. After his death she did a great deal to promote the performance and publication of his works. As for Wolfgang, he came to adore Constanze and hated their periods of enforced separation.

Despite his prodigious output, Mozart's financial affairs became increasingly desperate. A contributory factor was that, as time went on, he preferred to devote himself to composing rather than playing in public. Alas, the rewards of composing in those days did not match the effort involved. For the composition of ***The Marriage of Figaro***, which was acclaimed in Vienna in 1786, he received 450 gulden – the sum he might have commanded for a single concert as a performer.

But the last five years of Mozart's life did bring some spectacular triumphs. The city of Prague went wild about *Figaro*, and he was commissioned to write **Don Giovanni** for the theatre there; in the last year of his life he experienced great popular success in Vienna with **The Magic Flute**. On the other hand, the last three of Mozart's forty-one **symphonies** were probably not performed while Mozart was alive, he failed to get the appointment he thought he deserved as *Kapellmeister* at the Emperor's court, and he died a few weeks short of his thirty-sixth birthday, probably of rheumatic fever compounded at the end by kidney failure. When all is said and done, no one can pretend that the world extended a very cordial welcome to the man who was perhaps its supreme musical genius.

Favourite works

The K numbers refer to the **Köchel** catalogue.

OPERAS *Idomeneo*, K366; *The Abduction from the Seraglio*, K384; *The Marriage of Figaro*, K492; *Don Giovanni*, K527; *Così fan tutte*, K588; *The Magic Flute*, K620.

SYMPHONIES No. 29 in A, K201; No. 31 in D ('Paris'), K297; No. 35 in D ('Haffner'), K385; No. 36 in C ('Linz'), K425; No. 38 in D ('Prague'), K504; No. 39 in E flat, K543; No. 40 in G minor, K550; No. 41 in C ('Jupiter'), K551.

LIGHTER ORCHESTRAL WORKS *The Sleigh Ride*, K605 No. 3; *Eine Kleine Nachtmusik*, K525; *A Musical Joke*, K522.

PIANO CONCERTOS No. 21 in C, K467 (contains the famous *Elvira Madigan* theme tune); No. 23 in A, K488; No. 24 in C minor, K491.

VIOLIN CONCERTOS No. 3 in G, K216.

OTHER CONCERTOS For Flute and Harp in C major, K299; for Clarinet in E flat, K622; for Horn No. 4 in E flat, K495.

CHURCH MUSIC *Exultate, Jubilate*, K165 (includes the famous 'Alleluia'); *Ave Verum Corpus*, K618.

CHAMBER MUSIC Clarinet Quintet in A, K581; Oboe Quartet in F, K370; String Quartet No. 17 in B flat, K458 ('Hunt'); String Quartet No. 19 in C, K465 ('Dissonance').

PIANO SONATAS Sonata in C, K545 ('for beginners').

Guglielmo (Bryn Terfel) and Ferrando (Peter Bronson) in a scene from Mozart's ever-popular Così fan tutte.

*M*ILSTEIN, *Nathan* (Born Odessa 1904) —————

Russian-born violinist whose playing combines passion with the utmost precision. American citizen 1942. Left Russia on a concert tour with **Vladimir Horowitz** 1925 and decided not to return.

*M*INUET (for description see **Dance**) —————

Two famous Minuets are the one which occurs in the String Quintet in E major by Boccherini (1743 –1805), and the Minuet in G by **Paderewski**, which is No. 1 of his *Six Humoresques de Concert*.

*M*ISERERE —————————————————

Part of the early morning service of Lauds in the Roman Catholic Church. The famous Miserere of Allegri (1582–1652) is said to have been written out from memory by the fourteen-year-old **Mozart**. A well-known operatic Miserere occurs in **Verdi**'s *Il Trovatore*.

*M*OFFO, *Anna* (Born Wayne, Penn., 1935) —————

American **soprano** specially famous as Violetta in **Verdi**'s *La Traviata*. She had a notable international career mainly at the New York **Metropolitan** until 1974 when she suffered a vocal breakdown. Began singing again in 1976.

*M*OISEIWITSCH, *Benno* (Born Odessa 1890; died London 1963) —————————————————

Russian-born pianist (British citizen 1937). An attractive character with a dry sense of humour; a very popular and expert concert artist, particularly in works by his friend **Rachmaninov**.

*M*ONCKTON, *Lionel* (Born London 1861; died London 1924) —————————————————

British musical comedy composer. Became a music critic, breaking through to the West End with a number called 'What will you have to drink?' in a burlesque of 1891. His most successful shows were *The Arcadians* (1909), composed with Howard Talbot, and *The Quaker Girl* (1910).

*M*ONTEUX, *Pierre* (Born Paris 1875; died Hancock, Maine, 1964) —————————————————

French-born conductor (American from 1942) of high distinction. As conductor for Diaghilev's Russian ballet company, conducted the premières of *Petrouchka* and *The Rite of Spring* (**Stravinsky**), *Daphnis and Chloë* (**Ravel**) and other major new scores, and championed contemporary composers throughout a long career with the **orchestras** of Paris, Boston, San Francisco, Amsterdam and elsewhere. Appointed chief conductor at the age of 86 of the **London Symphony Orchestra** on a 25-year contract; he conducted them in 1963 in a centenary performance in London of *The Rite of Spring*. Monteux's pupils include **Neville Marriner** and **André Previn**.

*M*ONTEVERDI, *Claudio* (Born Cremona 1567; died Venice 1643) —————————————————

Italian composer whose significance in music has been likened to that of Shakespeare in literature at the same period. His *Orfeo* (*Orpheus*) (Mantua, 1607) is the first **opera** to employ a full **orchestra**; many operatic scores have been lost, but *The Return of Ulysses* (1640) and *The Coronation of Poppaea* (1642) are acknowledged masterpieces. Monteverdi's huge quantity of church music includes the famous and beloved Vespers composed for Mantua in 1610; large numbers of madrigals and other short pieces have also survived.

*M*ONTREAL SYMPHONY ORCHESTRA —————

Since 1954 the Orchestre Symphonique de Montréal has had distinguished conductors: **Otto Klemperer**, Igor Markevitch, **Zubin Mehta** and **Raphael Frühbeck de Burgos** among them. Since 1978, under **Charles Dutoit**, it has become one of the world's most frequently recorded **orchestras**.

'*M*OONLIGHT AND ROSES' —————————

Popular song adapted from an Andante by Edwin Lemare (1865–1934), organist of St Margaret's, Westminster, 1897–1902, and thereafter very successful recitalist in Britain and USA.

*M*OORE, *Gerald* (Born Watford 1899; died Penn, Bucks., 1987) —————————————————

British pianist who, from 1925, developed a career as the world's most celebrated accompanist, partnering many leading artists. Wrote and lectured brilliantly on his chosen craft. CBE 1954.

The Magic Flute *brought popular success to Mozart in his last months. This is Thomas Allen as the birdcatcher Papageno for the Royal Opera, 1984.*

Punk or perfectionist? The two co-exist in Nigel Kennedy. Brilliant musician and self-appointed shocker, he is equally at home in jazz and the classics.

MOORE, *Grace* (Born Jellicoe, Tenn., 1901; died Copenhagen in air crash 1947) _____

American **soprano** who from 1928 sang **opera** at the **Met**, **Covent Garden** and in Paris, but chiefly famous for her musical films including *New Moon* (1931) with **Laurence Tibbett**, *One Night of Love* (1934) and *Love Me For Ever* (1936).

MOORE'S IRISH MELODIES _____

The Irish poet, reciter and singer Thomas Moore (1779–1852) published between 1808 and 1834 ten collections of *Irish Melodies* (mostly traditional) to which he added his own words. **'The Last Rose of Summer'** and 'The Minstrel Boy' are among the best known.

MORLEY, *Thomas* (Born Norwich 1557; died London 1602) _____

One of the greatest English **madrigal** composers. His most famous publication, *The Triumphs of Oriana* (i.e. of Queen Elizabeth I) included works by twenty-four composers, himself among them. Morley's 'It was a lover and his lass' may have been written for the original production in 1599 of Shakespeare's *As You Like It*.

MORMON TABERNACLE CHOIR _____

One of the most famous musical institutions in America, the choir derives its name from the 8000-seat Mormon Tabernacle completed in Salt Lake City in 1867. The choir specialises in sumptuous versions of mainly devotional music.

MORTIMER, *Harry* (Born Hebden Bridge 1902; died 1992) _____

Best-known member of famous **brass-band** family, champion **cornet** player and principal **trumpet** in symphony **orchestras** 1930–41. Brought together the country's best players in his 'Men O'Brass' band. CBE 1984.

MOTET _____

A form of short unaccompanied devotional choral composition, usually with Latin words, that flourished from the thirteenth to sixteenth centuries, though the term also described later, similar compositions.

MOUSSORGSKY, *Modest* (Born Karevo, Pskov district, 1839; died St Petersburg 1881) _____

One of the **'mighty handful'** of Russian composers who attached great importance to nationalism in music. Moussorgsky's major operatic achievement was *Boris Godounov*, premiered after much revision in 1874. An addiction to drink helps to account for the unfinished state of Moussorgsky's other theatre works, some of which were completed after his death by **Rimsky-Korsakov** and others. The Prelude ('Dawn on the Moscow River') to *Khovanschina* (1873) is very beautiful. Moussorgsky's best-known orchestral work is *Night on the Bare Mountain* (1867, revised and orchestrated by Rimsky-Korsakov 1886); the splendid piano work *Pictures at an Exhibition* (1874) was memorably orchestrated by **Ravel**.

MÜNCHINGER, *Karl* (Born Stuttgart 1915; died 1990) _____

German conductor, founder in 1945 of the highly esteemed Stuttgart Chamber Orchestra with which he toured worldwide and made many fine recordings. Münchinger's repertoire was centred on **Bach**.

MUNROW, *David* (Born Birmingham 1942; died Chesham Bois 1976) _____

British **recorder** player (professor at **Royal Academy of Music** from 1969) and performer on great variety of other early wind instruments. In 1967 he was founder and director of the Early Music Consort which performed much rediscovered **early music** in a highly attractive way. Munrow was a brilliant communicator whose 'Pied Piper' **BBC** broadcasts (1971–6) were very popular. By the time of his tragically premature death he had become one of the most influential musicians of his time.

MURRAY, *Ann* (Born Dublin 1949) _____

Irish **soprano**. Highly accomplished singer both in concert and **opera** work. Great success 1985 in title role of **Handel**'s *Xerxes* with **English National Opera**; also outstanding in **Mozart** and **Rossini**.

MUSIC HALL _____

A form of popular musical entertainment which flourished in Britain for just under a century from approximately 1850. It developed from the kind of

*T*HE MUSICAL

When **Noel Coward** was five years old his mother took him to see a musical comedy called *The Dairymaids* at the Grand Theatre, Croydon. 'It established in my mind', wrote Coward many years later, 'that musical comedy was gaily irrational to the point of lunacy, a conviction which I have staunchly upheld for over sixty years.'

The invention of Musical Comedy is credited to that impresario of genius George Edwardes. As a young man he had been Richard D'Oyly Carte's theatre manager at the Savoy; then in 1885 he set up shop on his own account at the Gaiety Theatre, where at first he produced comic burlesques. But Edwardes sensed that there was a market for something a touch more refined. At his other theatre, the Prince of Wales, Edwardes put on in 1892 a creation called *In Town*. This is usually referred to as the first musical comedy, though that precise term was used for the first time to describe *A Gaiety Girl*, produced in the following year. A long series of similar shows followed, most of them with 'girl' in the title: *The Shop Girl* was the first musical comedy to be produced at the Gaiety Theatre in 1894. The glamorous members of the chorus at that theatre soon became known as 'Gaiety Girls'; they were chaperoned with the utmost propriety and many of them married aristocratic 'stage-door Johnnies' who fell for their charms from the stalls.

George Edwardes had a third London theatre under his control, Daly's, and there he staged *The Geisha* with music by Sidney Jones in 1896: it ran for 750 performances. Other great musical comedy successes of the period were *Floradora* (1899) with a score by Leslie Stuart, and *The Arcadians* of 1909 with music by Howard Talbot and **Lionel Monckton**. All London's hit shows of the time were quickly transported to New York, where in 1903 the first all-Negro musical comedy appeared: *In Dahomey*.

The triumph of *The Merry Widow* in London in 1907 set a vogue for imported **operetta** and that influence was felt in many home-produced shows, including two great successes during the First World War: *Chu Chin Chow* and *The Maid of the Mountains*. It is difficult to categorise many of the musical shows of the present century, though the numerous lighter products of the twenties and thirties can properly be described as musical comedies. One of the most famous was *No, No Nanette*, whose score by Vincent Youmans included **'Tea for Two'**. It was typical of the two-way traffic in shows across the Atlantic at this time, though imports from the USA outweighed traffic in the other direction, starting with a show of 1919 called, on Broadway, *Oh, Boy!* and renamed *Oh, Joy!* for London. It had music by the great **Jerome Kern**. Alongside the quasi-operettas of Noel Coward and **Ivor Novello**, musical comedy continued to flourish in London in the thirties, culminating in *Me and My Girl* which opened at the Victoria Palace in 1937 and ran on well into the Second World War.

Meanwhile, Broadway was buzzing with the theatre music of **George Gershwin** and **Richard Rodgers** as well as Jerome Kern. One result of the Rodgers/Lorenz Hart collaboration, *On Your Toes* (1936), introduced a serious **ballet** sequence, 'Slaughter on Tenth Avenue', into a musical comedy. This was one indication of the way things would change on Broadway. Another important trend had already been signalled by Jerome Kern's *Showboat* of 1927. Here was a story of some weight which even dared to touch on the burning contemporary issue of colour.

So there were some precedents for the revolutionary impact of *Oklahoma!* in 1943. In collaboration with his new partner, Oscar Hammerstein II, Richard Rodgers produced a show which was a totally integrated blend of story and music, incorporating a dream-ballet by Agnes de Mille. This was the first of the major theatrical entertainments usually described simply as 'musicals'. In 1947 *Oklahoma!* came to London, to be closely followed by **Irving Berlin**'s *Annie Get Your Gun*, and another period of American domination in the musical theatre began.

The astonishing sequence of Rodgers and Hammerstein shows included *Carousel* (1945), *South Pacific* (1949), *The King and I* (1951) and *The Sound of Music* (1959), while among the long list of successes by other writers was *My Fair Lady* by Alan Jay Lerner and **Frederick Loewe**. In 1957 **Leonard Bernstein** produced one of the most brilliant and serious of all musicals – *West Side Story*, which transposed the story of *Romeo and Juliet* to twentieth-century New York. Bernstein's lyric writer in that show was **Stephen Sondheim** whose successes as composer and lyricist started with *A Funny Thing Happened on the Way to the Forum* in 1962 and continued through *Follies* (1971) and *A Little Night Music* (1973) to experimental shows such as *Into the Woods* (1987).

In the fifties, British musical successes included small-scale pieces such as Sandy Wilson's *The Boy Friend* of 1953, and Julian Slade's *Salad Days* the following year. **Lionel Bart** brought out the lastingly popular *Oliver!* in 1960, and in 1968 *Joseph and the Amazing Technicolor Dreamcoat* signalled the arrival of the man who now dominates the popular musical theatre worldwide, **Andrew Lloyd Webber**. His spectacular pieces include *Evita* (1978), *Cats* (1981) and *Phantom of the Opera* (1986). The musical today occupies a place somewhere between **opera** and musical comedy, with a work such as *Les Misérables* (1980) by the French composer Claude-Michel Schönberg bordering closely on the operatic, while the hugely successful revival in the West End of *Me and My Girl* proves that there is still a market which is not entirely nostalgic for the 'gay irrationality' of lighter musical entertainment.

Cast members of Andrew Lloyd Webber's spectacular Starlight Express.

entertainment offered at London's pleasure gardens and at the 'song-and-supper rooms' of the early nineteenth century. At this point enterprising publicans began to add special saloons, or 'music halls', to their premises: one of the first to open was the Mogul in Holborn in 1847. Within twenty years there were some 200 music halls in London alone, many of them specially-built theatres. A new breed of specialist music-hall entertainers grew up, among them, in the early days, George Leybourne (1842–84) who sang 'Champagne Charlie' and 'The Man on the Flying Trapeze'. Dan Leno (1860–1904), Albert Chevalier (1862–1923), Marie Lloyd (1870–1922) and Nellie Wallace (1870–1948) were among the major stars of later generations. The rise of radio and the cinema dealt a death-blow to the music hall, though it retains its nostalgic appeal, as the success of the **BBC's** *Good Old Days*, and countless amateur and professional imitations, proves.

*M*UTI, *Riccardo* (Born Naples 1941) ——————

Italian conductor, currently (1993) music director at **La Scala**. Principal conductor, **Philharmonia Orchestra** 1973–82, of the **Philadelphia Orchestra** 1980–92.

*M*UTTER, *Anne-Sophie* (Born Rheinfeldin 1963) —

German violinist who began recording with **Karajan** when only fifteen, having made her London début in 1977. Important worldwide career; at the age of only twenty-three appointed to International Chair at **Royal Academy of Music**.

N

'*N*ARCISSUS' ————————————————

Light **piano** piece by the American Ethelbert Nevin (1862–1901), memorably parodied on a record by Joyce Grenfell and Norman Wisdom; Nevin also wrote 'The Rosary' (1891) which sold over six million copies.

*N*ASH, *Heddle* (Born London 1896; died London 1961) ————————————————

Distinguished British **tenor**. Sang at the Old Vic in 1920s, at **Glyndebourne** 1934–8, at **Covent Garden** 1929–39 and later. Very famous in **Elgar's** *Dream of Gerontius* and **Handel's** *Messiah*. Son John Heddle Nash (born 1928) is a baritone.

*N*ATIONAL YOUTH ORCHESTRA OF GREAT BRITAIN ————————————————

Formed in 1947 by Dame Ruth Railton, who remained director until 1965, to provide training opportunities for gifted young musicians. Three rehearsal periods are held each year for around 150 young people between thirteen and nineteen, usually in a boarding school during holidays, followed by one or more public concerts, including an annual appearance at the **Proms**. Given their extra rehearsal time, the standard rivals adult orchestras, and many members enter the music profession.

*N*EVEU, *Ginette* (Born Paris 1919; died in air crash, Azores, 1949) ————————————

French violinist, one of the finest of her time. Début in Paris at seven, beat **David Oistrakh** to win **Wieniawski** Prize, Warsaw 1935. Her recordings include an outstanding version of the **Sibelius** concerto.

*N*EW YORK PHILHARMONIC ORCHESTRA ———

America's oldest symphony **orchestra**, founded 1842. Principal conductors have included **Mahler**, **Mengelberg**, **Toscanini**, **Barbirolli** and **Bernstein**, who in 1969 was made Laureate for life.

*N*IELSEN, *Carl* (Born Sortelung, Funen, 1865; died Copenhagen 1931) ————————————

The most important Danish composer of the twentieth century. Nielsen was little known outside Denmark until after the Second World War when his stature began to be widely appreciated. He devised his own approach to symphonic form in six **symphonies** based on the transformation of themes; No. 4 ('The Inextinguishable', 1915–16) and No. 5 (1921–2) are specially famous, the latter with its prolonged solo for the side-drummer who is instructed to drown the **orchestra**. The overture to the **opera** *Maskarade* is a lively concert item.

NIKISCH, *Arthur* (Born Lébényi Szent Miklós 1855; died Leipzig 1922)

Hungarian musician, the most famous conductor of his day. Appointed conductor of the **Boston Symphony Orchestra** 1889, and in 1895 of both the **Berlin Philharmonic** and Leipzig **Gewandhaus** orchestras, posts he retained to the end of his life. Toured in USA with **London Symphony Orchestra** 1912.

NILSSON, *Birgit* (Born West Karup 1918)

Swedish **soprano**, the finest and most famous Wagnerian soprano of her day, though also distinguished in **Strauss**'s *Electra* and **Puccini**'s *Turandot*. Retired 1986.

NOBLE, *Dennis* (Born Bristol 1899; died Jávea, Alicante, 1966)

British **baritone** who was in great demand as an **oratorio** singer (he sang the baritone solo part in the first performance of **Walton**'s *Belshazzar's Feast*, 1931) and was very effective in **opera**. He sang at **Covent Garden** from 1924 to 1938 and again in 1947. Also toured with the **Carl Rosa** company.

NOCTURNE

The Irish pianist and composer **John Field** was the first to use this title for a dreamy, romantic piece; **Chopin** and others followed suit.

NORMAN, *Jessye* (Born Augusta, Georgia 1945)

Beloved American **soprano** of glorious vocal gifts and ample figure. She made her operatic début in Berlin in **Wagner**'s *Tannhäuser*, appeared at **La Scala** 1972 and the same year at **Covent Garden** as Cassandra in *The Trojans* (**Berlioz**), but some of her greatest triumphs have been on the concert platform in works by **Schubert**, **Mahler**, Berlioz and others.

NORRINGTON, *Roger* (Born Oxford 1934)

British conductor (at first, professional **tenor**) much associated with the 'authentic instrument' movement. At Kent Opera (1966–84) revived several **Monteverdi** operas; founded London Classical Players 1978. CBE 1990.

NOVELETTE

Name given by **Schumann** to eight **piano** pieces (Op. 21) as a compliment to the British **soprano** Clara Novello, who was famous throughout Europe; the name was later adopted by other composers.

NOVELLO, *Ivor* (Born Cardiff 1893; died London 1951)

Welsh composer, actor, playwright and impresario, son of the singer and conductor Clara Novello-Davies. Ivor began writing songs when he was about fifteen, and in 1914 scored an instant success with 'Keep the Home Fires Burning'. In 1919 he appeared in his first film, *The Call of the Blood*, and in the twenties his famous profile won huge adulation in many romantic roles on stage and screen. He also contributed numbers to **revues** such as *A to Z* (1921). In the mid-thirties he started creating a series of spectacular musical plays which revived the spirit of Viennese **operetta** with immense success. *Glamorous Night* (1935) was followed by *Careless Rapture* (1936), *Crest of the Wave* (1937), *The Dancing Years* (1939), *Arc de Triomphe* (1943), *Perchance to Dream* (1945) and *King's Rhapsody* (1949). *Gay's the Word*, produced in February 1951, starring Cicely Courtneidge, was a send-up of Novello's high-flown romanticism in his earlier shows. He died shortly after a performance of *King's Rhapsody* in which he himself played the king.

NUNC DIMITTIS

Part of the service of Compline in the Roman Catholic Church and Evensong in the Anglican Church, frequently set to music. A well-known Nunc Dimittis by Geoffrey Burgon (born 1941) was the signature tune for the TV serial *Tinker, Tailor, Soldier, Spy*.

'NYMPHS AND SHEPHERDS'

Song written by **Purcell** for a play by Shadwell, *The Libertine* (1692), but now famous thanks to a recording made by a choir of Manchester schoolchildren in 1929. Later they formed a flourishing 'Nymphs and Shepherds' association.

OPERA

What is the point of opera? Samuel Johnson's famous definition of the art as 'an exotic and irrational entertainment' was neatly countered by W.H. Auden in 1961. 'No good opera plot can be sensible,' he wrote, 'for people do not sing when they are feeling sensible.' The true sphere of opera is the world where the language of words is no longer enough – the realm of love and death, mystery, imagination and eternal truth.

Opera was born in Italy at the time of the Renaissance and arose from the belief that the Greeks and Romans had enjoyed musical entertainments. **Claudio Monteverdi** was the earliest opera composer whose works have survived into modern times. He too chose classical subjects and contributed to the first public opera house which opened in Venice in 1637.

The new art-form was soon exported to other countries. The son of a Florentine miller called Lulli went to France where, as **Jean-Baptiste Lully**, he became music master to the French royal family. His works also dealt with antiquity, a fashion followed in English court **masques** of the period. The first English operatic masterpiece was *Dido and Aeneas* written in 1689 by **Henry Purcell**.

An opera company was set up in Hamburg in 1678, and it was there in 1704 that the young **George Frideric Handel** presented his first opera, *Almira*. In 1711 he came to London with *Rinaldo*; it was a triumph, and Handel followed it with a series of Italian operatic masterpieces.

In the early eighteenth century leading operatic singers could dictate terms to composers, demanding **arias** to show off their strong points and adding embellishments of their own invention. Dramatic truth suffered and reform was overdue; it came at the hands of **Christoph Willibald Gluck** with *Orpheus and Eurydice*, produced in **Vienna** in 1762. This set new standards of austere simplicity and integrity and 'opera seria' was born.

However, by this time another livelier strand of operatic entertainment had grown up in Italy and spread to other countries – *opera buffa*, which dealt in comic situations and modern stories. **Mozart**, in his Italian operas, was heir to both these traditions, composing several works in the *opera seria* mode for his teenage visits to Italy, and graduating in later years to the contemporary comedy of ***The Marriage of Figaro*** (1786). **Rossini**'s thirty-nine operas likewise included works in both the serious and comic vein, though today he is chiefly remembered for his comedies, supremely for ***The Barber of Seville*** (1816).

Both *The Marriage of Figaro* and *The Barber of Seville* derived from plays by the French writer Beaumarchais, who was regarded as dangerously subversive in the years before the French Revolution. **Beethoven**'s only opera ***Fidelio*** (first version 1805) was a thinly disguised attack on the tyranny of the Terror which followed the Revolution. Politics had entered the opera house.

Fidelio was an example of an operatic form which had grown up in Germany, the *Singspiel*, with passages of spoken dialogue. Mozart's German operas, including **The Magic Flute**, are cast in this mould. *Singspiel* was a symptom of a growing nationalism in opera, in Germany and elsewhere. **Carl Maria von Weber** looked to German legend for the story of *Der Freischutz*, anticipating the passionately Germanic **Richard Wagner**. No spoken dialogue for Wagner, however, but a continuous web of sound. Wagner sought the inner truth he felt to be lacking in the spectacular operas of **Giacomo Meyerbeer** which were beloved of the French. Some years went by before **Bizet**'s *Carmen* (1875) brought a new kind of emotional truth to the operatic stage in Paris.

Meanwhile, in Russia, the new national spirit found expression in *A Life for the Tsar* (1836) by **Mikhail Glinka**, **Mussorgsky**'s *Boris Godounov* (1874) and other works; **Bedřich Smetana** produced a Czech operatic manifesto in *The Bartered Bride* (1866), and in Italy **Giuseppe Verdi** stepped into the shoes left vacant by Rossini. He created a whole gallery of credible human characters, none of them more touching than the heroine of **La Traviata** (1853). **Giacomo Puccini**, Verdi's natural heir, portrayed a series of victimised women in his works, making his breakthrough with *Manon Lescaut* in 1894. This was the period of *verismo* or 'realism' in opera, two of the most famous examples being Mascagni's **Cavalleria Rusticana** (1890) and Leoncavallo's **Pagliacci** (1892).

The early twentieth century brought the opulent scores of **Richard Strauss** to the operatic stage. The violence of *Salome* (1905) and *Electra* (1909) was followed by the Viennese schmaltz of *Der Rosenkavalier* (1911) in a post-Wagnerian sunset of glorious colours. For though Wagner had his devoted followers, there were others who reacted against him. The delicate poetry of **Debussy**'s *Pelléas and Mélisande* (1902), for example, is far removed from the passion of *Tristan and Isolde*. Altogether more revolutionary in music and subject-matter were **Schoenberg**'s *Erwartung* (1909), **Béla Bartók**'s *Bluebeard's Castle* (1918), Berg's

Luciano Pavarotti in a scene from Verdi's Aida, *performed at Covent Garden in 1984.*

Wozzeck (1925) and **Stravinsky**'s *Oedipus Rex* (1928).

The last fifty years have been marked by an extraordinary growth of interest in opera in Britain. When **Benjamin Britten**'s *Peter Grimes* was produced in 1945 it was hailed as 'A real English opera that is going to live side by side with any of the great operas of the world.' Britten's far-ranging operatic achievement has been followed by the successes of **Sir Michael Tippett**, while the stage works of **Sir Peter Maxwell Davies** and Sir Harrison Birtwhistle have been among their most important achievements.

Bearing in mind recent developments, one can't help wondering whether the twenty-first century will finally tear apart that strange invention we call opera. Or perhaps it has already found a new lease of life in a different form – as the **musical**.

OPERETTA

The French novelist Émile Zola, famous for social realism, once remarked that operetta was 'a noxious infant that should have been strangled at birth.' He was speaking of a form of entertainment that was born and survived its infancy in France and, if he had had his way, the world would have been deprived of a great deal of light-hearted enjoyment and a storehouse of appealing melodies.

Operetta is an Italian word which simply means 'little opera' and it was used in just that sense in the seventeenth and eighteenth centuries. It was in the nineteenth century, with the growth of a moneyed middle class, that a taste grew up for something less demanding than **opera** in the way of musical entertainment, and **Jacques Offenbach**, who had served an apprenticeship as a cellist in the **orchestra** pit of the Opéra-Comique in Paris, hit on a winning formula. He opened the Théâtre des Bouffes-Parisiens in 1855 with a series of small-scale pieces, and achieved a huge hit with *Orpheus in the Underworld* in 1858. This treated a legend of classical antiquity with refreshing irreverence; witty spoken dialogue alternated with musical passages of great melodic appeal in a frothy confection which made no demands on the audience. Operetta as created by Offenbach, whose eighty-nine works in the genre included such famous pieces as *La Belle Hélène* (1864), *La Vie Parisienne* (1866), and *La Périchole* (1868), may have been thought somewhat naughty when it first appeared but it hardly deserved to be called noxious. The fashion for satire established by Offenbach eventually gave way in France to more escapist works such as Alexandre Lecocq's *La Fille de Madame Angot* (1872), Robert Planquette's **Les Cloches de Corneville** (1877) and **André Messager**'s *Véronique* (1898). Early twentieth-century French operettas include **Reynaldo Hahn**'s delightful *Ciboulette* (1923).

But Offenbach's appeal transcended the boundaries of France. Pirated versions of his early pieces began to appear in **Vienna** almost as soon as they were seen in Paris, and when Offenbach arrived in Vienna in person he took the city by storm. Over coffee, so the story goes, he told **Johann Strauss** he should turn his attention to the theatre, though Strauss took his time in taking up the challenge. Strauss realised what stiff competition he would have to face from Offenbach himself, and from **Franz von Suppé** who had produced the first truly Viennese operetta, *Das Pensionat*, in 1860 and went on to compose a long series of successful pieces in similar vein.

Operetta found perhaps its most congenial home in the city of wine, women and song, and a number of able composers were ready to turn their hands to the musical equivalent of Sachertorte, Vienna's succulent chocolate cake. Johann Strauss, after a shaky start with *Indigo* in 1871, produced perhaps the finest of all operettas in *Die Fledermaus* (1874), and another major success with *The Gipsy Baron* (1885). Suppé's best works included *The Beautiful Galatea* (1865) and *Boccaccio* (1879), while Carl Millöcker created a lasting success with *Der Bettelstudent* (1882).

In the first decade of the twentieth century, operetta in Vienna took on a new lease of life with works by **Franz Lehár, Oscar Straus, Leo Fall** and, a little later, Lehár's fellow Hungarian **Emmerich Kálmán**. *The Merry Widow*, first seen in Vienna, triumphed all round the world: at one time, it was said, the Widow could be found waltzing on any given night in no fewer than 400 theatres in Europe alone. Straus's *A Waltz Dream* and Leo Fall's *The Dollar Princess* were both hits in 1907 and Kálmán triumphed with pieces such as *The Gipsy Princess* (1915) and *Countess Maritza* (1924). What is sometimes called the Silver Age of Viennese Operetta continued with Lehár's fruitful collaboration with the tenor **Richard Tauber**, beginning with *Paganini* in 1925 and culminating with *Giuditta* in 1934. With this Lehár achieved his life's ambition to have one of his works produced at the Vienna State Opera: in his view, operetta had

Illustration of a scene from Franz Lehár's The Merry Widow *which appeared in a souvenir programme of 1907.*

to be taken seriously as an art form. Nowadays, however, with the exception of *Die Fledermaus*, the State Opera leaves operetta to another theatre which specialises in the lighter repertoire, the Volksoper, which might be described as Vienna's **Sadler's Wells**. There, operetta still attracts large and enthusiastic audiences.

A lack of enthusiasm in Vienna for one of Lehár's operettas, *The Yellow Jacket*, led to revisions and a change of title before the piece was produced in Berlin in 1929 with Richard Tauber in the leading role of Prince Sou-Chong. As *The Land of Smiles*, containing the most famous of all Lehár's Tauber songs, 'You are my Heart's Delight', it delighted audiences in Berlin

and most of the other musical centres of the world. Berlin in fact had by then developed its own brand of operetta, verging on revue. *Frau Luna* by Paul Lincke had a great success in 1899; *The Cousin from Nowhere* made the name of Eduard Künneke in 1921, while in 1930 two major successes, *White Horse Inn* by Ralph Benatsky and others, and *Victoria and her Hussar* by Paul Abraham may be said to signal the end of the line for operetta in Berlin.

In other countries, operetta flourished under different names. The success of Jacques Offenbach in London was seen as a challenge that demanded a British response: the triumphant series of **Gilbert and Sullivan** operas (they were never called operettas) began with *Trial by Jury*, presented in 1875 as a companion-piece to Offenbach's *La Périchole*. Sullivan was succeeded as a composer of light opera by **Edward German,** notably with *Merrie England* (1902), and some of the productions of **Ivor Novello,** such as *Glamorous Night* (1935), and **Noel Coward**, whose *Bitter Sweet* was a triumph in 1929, may be regarded as operettas with their nostalgia for a Ruritanian never-neverland.

Most of the major European operettas found their way to the United States, and expatriate composers created many such pieces for New York. Among them were Gustav Kerker's *The Belle of New York* (1898) and **Victor Herbert**'s *Naughty Marietta* (1910). **Rudolf Friml** achieved worldwide success (not least thanks to Hollywood) with *Rose Marie* (1924) and *The Vagabond King* (1925), as did **Sigmund Romberg** with *The Student Prince* (1924) and *The Desert Song* (1926).

By degrees the impossibly romantic heroes and heroines of operetta, the titled characters, the glamorous dresses and uniforms, began to be seen as unacceptably artificial and out of date: musical comedy and the more recent **musical** took its place. Now – and not only in Vienna – the best operettas are being revived with great success. With a few honourable exceptions the texts require careful revision, especially in translation (the writers on the whole did not have the gifts of W.S. Gilbert). The music, however, needs no such revision.

O

OBOE

Woodwind instrument, blown through a double reed, descendant of the shawm, and known in the seventeenth century as the hautbois or hautboy. Sounds the 'A' to which an **orchestra** tunes.

OCARINA

Small keyless wind instrument shaped rather like an egg (the Italian name means 'little goose'). Invented about 1860, it is sometimes known as 'sweet potato'.

OFFENBACH, *Jacques* (Born Cologne 1819; died Paris 1880)

German-born composer (French from 1860), regarded as the inventor of **operetta**. He composed ninety stage works in all. Born Jacob Eberst, he took the surname we know from the town of Offenbach-am-Main where his father was born. In 1833 Jacob went to Paris to study the **cello** and soon became known as Jacques. After playing in the **orchestra** at the Opéra-Comique (where he suggested to his partner that they should play alternate notes to save work), Offenbach became, in the 1840s, a cello virtuoso of international standing, playing for instance at a Windsor Castle banquet in Ascot week. After a few years as a theatre conductor, the Paris Exhibition of 1855 prompted Offenbach to offer programmes of light pieces at the Théâtre Marigny under the name 'Bouffes Parisiens', and the name remained when Offenbach took up permanent residence at the Théâtre Comte. The company had great success in London in 1857. Working at first on a small scale, Offenbach produced the ambitious *Orpheus in the Underworld* in 1858; it started a run of very successful shows, including *La Belle Hélène* (1864) and *La Périchole* (1868), which continued through the 1860s and won Offenbach great acclaim not only in Paris but in London, **Vienna** and elsewhere. While in Vienna Offenbach produced a waltz, 'Evening Papers', in competition with 'Morning Papers' by **Johann Strauss**. He gave forty concerts in the USA during World Exhibition year, 1876, undertaking the tour because his works had rather fallen out of favour in Paris, driving him for a time

into bankruptcy. In his last years Offenbach worked on a much more serious work, his masterpiece, *The Tales of Hoffman*, but he died before it could be produced. He was given a hero's funeral in Paris attended by many thousands.

OGDON, *John* (Born Mansfield Woodhouse, Notts., 1937; died London 1989)

British pianist whose career was blighted from 1970 by mental illness, though he recovered sufficiently to resume his career in his last years, particularly in a duo partnership with his wife Brenda Lucas (born 1935). London début at **Proms** 1958; won joint first prize with **Ashkenazy** in Moscow **Tchaikovsky** Competition 1962, after which he enjoyed an all-too-brief international career at the highest level playing a wide repertoire of challenging and often unusual works.

'O GOD, OUR HELP IN AGES PAST'

Very popular **hymn** with words published by Isaac Watts in 1719, and tune attributed to William Croft (1668–1727). He was organist of St Anne's, Soho, hence the tune is known as 'St Anne'.

OISTRAKH, *David* (Born Odessa 1908; died Amsterdam 1974)

One of the greatest violinists of his day. After coming second to **Ginette Neveu** in the **Wieniawski** Competition of 1935 and winning the Ysaÿe Competition in Brussels 1937, he developed a career first in the Soviet Union and later internationally, showing his mastery in a wide repertoire which included much new music. He was the principal teacher of his son Igor Oistrakh (born Odessa 1931), who won the Wieniawski competition in 1952. The two often appeared together in works by **Bach**, **Mozart** and others, and Igor also has his own flourishing international career.

'OLD HUNDREDTH'

Hymn tune that first appeared in a Dutch collection of 1540, so called because it was attached to the 100th Psalm. Published with the words 'All People that on Earth Do Dwell' in 1560. A massive ceremonial arrangement was made for the Coronation of 1953 by **Vaughan Williams**.

'ONAWAY, AWAKE BELOVED!'

Tenor song (sung by the musician Chibiabos) in **Coleridge-Taylor**'s *Hiawatha's Wedding Feast* first performed at the **Royal College of Music** 1898. The two other parts of the Hiawatha Trilogy (settings of words by Longfellow) are *The Death of Minnehaha* (1899) and *Hiawatha's Departure* (1900).

OPUS

Latin for 'work', word used in listing a composer's creations, e.g. Opus 20, though in some cases lists are identified with their cataloguers, such as **Köchel** for **Mozart**, Deutsch for **Schubert**, Longo and Kirkpatrick for **Scarlatti**.

ORATORIO

A large scale musical setting, usually of a religious text. The name derives from the Oratory of St Philip Neri in Rome, where religious plays were given in the mid-sixteenth century. The most famous oratorio is **Handel**'s *Messiah* (1741).

ORGAN

The oldest, and often the largest, keyboard instrument. It derives from the *hydraulis* invented by a Greek engineer called Ktesibios living in Alexandria in the third century BC, and over the centuries has existed in many shapes and sizes, ranging from the small 'portative' (portable) organs of the Middle Ages to the giant instruments of Henry Willis (1821–1901), who built the **Royal Albert Hall** organ, and the great French builder of nearly 500 organs, Aristide Cavaille-Coll (1811–99). The organist operates manuals (with the hands), on anything up to five keyboards, or pedals (for the feet) to admit, by mechanical, pneumatic or electrical means, a current of air from a reservoir to a series of tuned pipes. The tone is varied by the use of 'stops'.

ORMANDY, *Eugene* (Born Budapest 1899; died Philadelphia 1985)

Hungarian-born conductor (American from 1927). Child prodigy violinist in Europe till 1914, but now most famous for his long association with the **Boston Symphony Orchestra** (1936–80), after which he was Conductor Laureate. Hon KBE 1976.

ORTIZ, *Cristina* (Born Bathia, Brazil, 1950)

Brazilian-born pianist, British from 1977. First woman to win the prestigious Van Cliburn competition in Texas (1969). Flourishing concert and recording career.

OTELLO

Great **opera** by **Verdi** (libretto by Arrigo Boito) based on Shakespeare's *Othello*. First produced **La Scala** 1887. Also fine opera by **Rossini**, first produced Naples 1816.

OUSSET, *Cécile* (Born Tarbes 1936)

French pianist who gave her first recital at the age of five, won the Queen Elizabeth competition in Brussels and made her British début at the **Edinburgh Festival** in 1980. Many concerts and recordings.

OVERTURE

Term (from the French *ouverture*, opening) used to describe the orchestral introduction to an **opera** or **oratorio** or a concert work of similar length. In the eighteenth century, sometimes interchangeable with 'symphony' or 'suite'.

OZAWA, *Seiji* (Born Hoten, Manchuria, 1935)

Highly gifted Japanese conductor who intended to be a pianist until he broke two fingers playing rugby. Won Besançon **conducting** competition in France (1959) and scholarship to study with **Karajan** in Berlin. Toronto Symphony Orchestra 1965–9, San Francisco Symphony Orchestra 1970–6, **Boston Symphony Orchestra** from 1973 (at first with **Ormandy**). Also much **opera** internationally.

P

PACHMANN, *Vladimir de* (Born Odessa 1848; died Rome 1933)

Ukrainian pianist who specialised in **Chopin** and in his later career played little else. He was well known for his skill in quiet passages, which led to his being called not 'pianist' but 'pianissimist'.

ORCHESTRA

*T*here is probably no bigger musical thrill than to see and hear a great orchestra in action, but the use of that word to describe a body of musicians goes back no more than two and half centuries. The word is Greek, originally describing the semi-circular space in front of the stage in the classical Greek theatre, where the chorus sang and danced; in the eighteenth-century London pleasure gardens, the bandstand was known as the orchestra, and as late as 1728 the writer Roger North considered it 'improper' to use the word to denote a group of performing musicians. Now that 'orchestra' properly means an assembly of instrumental players, it can be applied to a group of almost any size and shape, ranging from Palm Court ensembles to the full-size symphony orchestra of a hundred or more instruments. A number of stringed instruments are always included in an orchestra; if they are absent the group is more likely to be called a band.

The early history of the orchestra is hazy. As early as 1607 **Claudio Monteverdi** used forty instruments of different kinds to accompany his opera *Orfeo*. They included fifteen **viols** and two **violins**, **flutes**, hautboys (early **oboes**), **trumpets**, **trombones**, two **harpsichords**, two small **organs** and a **harp**. No doubt these were the instruments he happened to have at his disposal in Mantua, and elsewhere things were similarly haphazard. Composers wrote for whatever instruments happened to be available.

Perhaps the biggest factor in the development of the orchestra as we know it was the displacement of the gentle-sounding viol by the more resonant violin. In 1626, the French king Louis XIII reorganised his string players as the '24 Violons du Roi', and Louis XIV's chief composer, **Jean-Baptiste Lully,** combined them in his **opera** and **ballet** productions with the oboes and **bassoons** of the king's outdoor band. Common to most groupings in those days was the **continuo**, frequently a harpischord with the addition of a **cello** or bassoon to supply a bass line. This was thought necessary to hold the ensemble together, an operation rendered even more secure when the composer was seated at the keyboard. **Handel** directed his **organ** concertos in this manner, and **Mozart** controlled opera performances. As late as the 1790s **Josef Haydn** 'presided at the **pianoforte**' when his **symphonies** were performed in London.

The finest eighteenth-century orchestra was probably the one established in Mannheim at the court of the Duke of Saxony. The Duke encouraged the composer and violinist Johann Stamitz to assemble the best musicians money could buy, and perhaps for the first time the potential expressive range of orchestral sound began to be explored. Mozart was hugely excited by the Mannheim orchestra when he visited the city in the 1770s, and the works produced by Mozart and other leading creators of the middle and late eighteenth century helped to stabilise the composition of what may be called the 'classical' orchestra. It consisted of a variable number of stringed instruments (violins, violas, cellos and sometimes the **double bass**), plus flutes, oboes, bassoons and, a relatively late arrival, the **clarinet**, together with trumpets, **horns** and **drums** on occasion. This was the orchestra inherited by **Beethoven.**

But whereas in 1824 Beethoven was content with an orchestra of sixty, by the end of the nineteenth century **Richard Strauss** was writing symphonic poems which called for an orchestra of over a hundred players.

The control of large numbers of players, however, presented a problem. In 1820 the composer Louis Spohr came to London to 'lead' a Philharmonic Society concert but elected to 'conduct' instead. 'I took my stand with the score at a separate music desk in front of the orchestra,' Spohr recalled later, 'drew my conducting stick from my pocket and gave the signal to begin. I also took the liberty when the execution did not satisfy me, to stop, and in a very polite but earnest manner to remark upon the manner of execution, which remarks Mr Ries (the first violin) interpreted to the orchestra.

Surprised and inspired by the result, the orchestra expressed aloud its collective assent to the new mode of **conducting**, and thereby overruled all further opposition.'

I have quoted at length from Spohr's recollections because they foreshadow the future role of the orchestral conductor, and neatly establish one function of the orchestra leader – to interpret the requirements of the maestro to the rest of the players. As the nineteenth century went on, the role of the conductor became ever more important and from the time of **Gustav Mahler**, perhaps the first 'great conductor', that role has been central to music-making on the concert platform and in the opera house. The result has been to make some conductors into musical stars of the first magnitude, not invariably with beneficial results for the music.

Baton-waving megalomania probably began with the great French musician **Hector Berlioz**, who was fond of employing vast orchestral forces in brilliantly subtle ways. In the **'romantic'** era, strikingly personified by Berlioz himself, the use of the orchestra to portray human emotions was extensively explored. **Wagner** was perhaps the nineteenth-century master of this, and the emotional canvas of ***The Ring*** required not only large numbers of all existing instruments in the orchestra pit but the creation of new ones too.

In the twentieth century a number of composers have continued to write for a large orchestra, sometimes with the addition of unusual instruments or electronic devices. But the growth of the **Early Music** Movement, coupled perhaps with a pressing need to economise, has led to a careful reappraisal of the way music of former times should be performed.

So what will be the future of the symphony orchestra in the twenty-first century? Will composers continue to write for it or will it become essentially a period piece, necessary only to reproduce the masterpieces of the late nineteenth and early twentieth centuries? Whatever happens, surely no one would like the big orchestra to disappear completely.

The Scottish Chamber Orchestra: an ensemble of this size is just right for the music of Haydn, Mozart and the early Beethoven.

*P*AVAROTTI

Luciano PAVAROTTI

1935	Born in Modena, northern Italy
1947	Nearly died of a blood infection
1961	Début in *La Bohème* at Reggio Emilia
1963	Début at Covent Garden
1965	Partnered Joan Sutherland in Australia and Miami; début at La Scala
1968	Début at the Met., New York
1973	First concert at Liberty, Missouri
1975	Survived plane crash, Milan
1990	'Nessun Dorma' became anthem of football World Cup; 'Three Tenors' concert, Rome
1991	'Free' concert in Hyde Park, London

*P*avarotti, with his immense bulk and beaming smile, has won the hearts of countless people who would never think of taking a seat at the **opera**. His name can fill the largest open-air arenas, and his records and videos sell in millions. Pavarotti is by no means the first Italian **tenor** to win adulation. **Enrico Caruso** achieved it, so did **Beniamino Gigli**. But now television makes the impact of a major star truly universal, with the result that Pavarotti has won the love of millions.

His main home is a large house on the outskirts of Modena in northern Italy. He was born in the same city; his father was a baker (a good singer too) and his mother worked in a cigar factory. The house was full of records of great tenors, and at five years of age Luciano would serenade his neighbours with the aid of a toy **mandolin**. The horrors of the Second World War and its aftermath affected him greatly but he sang in a church choir and in 1947, when he was twelve, managed to meet the great Gigli who was on a visit to Modena. Soon after the encounter, which made a great impression on Pavarotti, he nearly died of a blood infection: it was the first of two close encounters with death.

At the age of nineteen Pavarotti started serious study with a Modena singing teacher, Arrigo Pola, but his naturally fine voice took time to become a great instrument. In 1956 he was a member of a choir from Modena which took first prize at the Llangollen International **Eisteddfod**, but it was not until 1961 that individual success came with first prize in a local singing competition. This led to Luciano's début in one of his most successful roles, Rodolfo in **La Bohème**, at the nearby town of Reggio Emilia.

In 1963 Pavarotti was spotted singing the Duke in a Dublin Grand Opera Society production of *Rigoletto*, and this led to his first engagement at a major international house, deputising for the indisposed **Giuseppe di Stefano**. Here he made a great impression on **Joan Sutherland** and her husband, the conductor **Richard Bonynge**, who engaged the young tenor to take part in a tour of Australia in 1965. This was a triumph and introduced Pavarotti to leading roles in the **bel canto** operas of **Bellini** and **Donizetti,** which suited his voice to perfection.

By 1970 Pavarotti's star was shining very brightly in the operatic firmament, and as time went on he enlarged his repertoire to include new roles in **Verdi** operas and works by **Puccini.** But Pavarotti has always carefully studied the limitations as well as the strengths of his voice. 'God help me if I tried to sing **Wagner**,' he once said.

Meanwhile, two events of the 1970s had a profound effect on the singer's professional career and personal life. He has said that during the early seventies he experienced a deep depression, a sense that his life was not worth living. This desperate feeling vanished completely after the plane in which he was travelling crashed on landing at Milan airport on 22 December 1975: Pavarotti was, miraculously as he sees it,

Pavarotti in performance clasping his now familiar white handkerchief.

among the survivors, and his love of life has not deserted him since. The other event was Pavarotti's first concert appearance in the town of Liberty, Missouri, in 1973. Since then audiences of ever-growing size in most of the world's major auditoria have thrilled to the sight and sound of Luciano Pavarotti on the recital platform – always with that vast white handkerchief which helps, says the singer, to inhibit an excess of gesture. It also relaxes him, he says, and is 'my security blanket while on the concert stage'.

So the phenomenal career has continued to unfold. In demand all over the world, Pavarotti can naturally command astronomical fees, but the nervous strain of fulfilling the world's expectations is considerable. He speaks of the walk to the stage before another performance as 'the death march' and often won't appear till he's found a bent nail on the floor to bring him luck.

A compensating love of food and drink has resulted in an appalling weight problem. There were fears that when Pavarotti sang Cavaradossi in *Tosca* at Covent Garden in 1992 he would

have to be seated throughout, but this proved a false alarm. The maintenance of a public persona so massive in all respects is a full-time task, even with the help of a small army of professional advisers and the backing of a close-knit family headed by a devoted wife and three grown-up daughters.

Whatever engagements Pavarotti accepts or declines in the future, his fame will unquestionably endure. In addition to many best-selling records of opera and popular Italian **songs**, the recording of the 'Three Tenors' concert, given by Pavarotti, **Placido Domingo** and **José Carreras** has been a huge international chart-topper: the video is said to have sold at least three-quarters of a million copies. And the 'free' concert Pavarotti gave to tens of thousands standing in the pouring rain in London's Hyde Park in July 1991 will be seen and heard again by devoted admirers for generations to come.

*P*ACIFIC 231

Powerful and evocative 'symphonic movement' composed in 1923 by the Swiss composer Arthur Honegger (1892–1955), who gave it the name of a type of railway locomotive. Honegger also composed the symphonic psalm *King David* (1921).

*P*ADEREWSKI, *Ignacy Jan* (Born Kurylówka, Poland, 1860; died New York 1941)

Polish pianist, composer and statesman. After studies with the famous teacher Theodor Leschetizky in Vienna, Paderewski embarked on a career as a virtuoso pianist which took him frequently to London, Paris and the USA. During the First World War he worked ceaselessly for Poland's liberation, and in 1919 became Prime Minister of his newly independent country. He resigned after ten months and resumed his performing career. By far the best known of Paderewski's compositions is the Minuet in G from the *Six Humoresques de Concert*.

*P*AGANINI, *Niccolò* (Born Genoa 1782; died Nice 1840)

Italian **violin** virtuoso of unprecedented brilliance who also played the **viola** and **guitar** and composed numerous works, mainly for his own use. With his long hair and cadaverous features, Paganini was often thought to be in league with the devil: only superhuman intervention, it was thought, could account for such playing. Paganini did nothing to discourage such fantasies, which helped him to amass considerable fortunes – which he just as often lost. In 1833 he expressed his admiration for **Berlioz** by commissioning a work for viola and **orchestra** (*Harold in Italy*). Paganini never played it, but after attending a performance he sent his son Achille to the impoverished composer with a present of 20,000 francs. Paganini was idolised wherever he went: in Dublin one concert-goer went so far as to pawn his overcoat to pay for his seat. Paganini's influence, both on succeeding generations of violinists (for whom he set new standards of virtuosity), and on composers, was very extensive. **Schumann**, **Chopin** and **Liszt** were both inspired to express Paganini's technical expertise in terms of the **piano**: the last of his Twenty-four Caprices for unaccompanied violin has been the subject of famous variations by **Brahms**, **Rachmaninov**, Lutoslawski and **Sir Andrew Lloyd Webber**.

*P*AGLIACCI

Extremely popular one-act **opera** by Ruggiero Leoncavallo (1857–1919) first seen in Milan in 1892. Based on a real-life story, it tells of an actor who kills his wife out of jealousy during a performance. He expresses his desperation in the **aria** 'Vesti la Giubba' ('On with the Motley').

*P*ALESTRINA, *Giovanni Pierluigi da* (Born Rome c. 1525; died Rome 1594)

One of the greatest composers of the sixteenth century, Palestrina took his name from a small town where he was employed for a time as an organist; when the Bishop of Palestrina became Pope, Palestrina moved with him to Rome, where he held a variety of church appointments. His second wife had inherited a flourishing fur business in which Palestrina proved to be an able businessman; this helped make his last years highly prosperous. Palestrina composed well over 100 Masses and a huge number of other works, almost entirely religious. By succeeding generations he was revered as 'the saviour of church music'.

*P*ALMER, *Felicity* (Born Cheltenham 1944)

British **soprano** who studied at the Guildhall School in London and in Munich before winning the **Kathleen Ferrier** prize in 1970. Notably successful in French repertoire from **Gluck** to **Boulez**.

'*L*A PALOMA' ('The Dove')

Song published in 1859 by the Spanish composer Sebastian de Yradier (1809–65). It was, and is, enormously popular in Latin America and was inspired by Yradier's time in Cuba in the 1850s.

*P*ANPIPES

Series of pipes of varying length bound together and blown across their tops. The pipes can be made of a wide variety of materials. The Ancient Greeks, who called the instrument the Syrinx, credited its invention to the god Pan.

*P*ARKER-SMITH, *Jane* (Born Northampton 1950)

British organist who achieved early distinction and international fame following her début at

Welsh National Opera has enjoyed many successes. Here Alison Hagley and Neil Archer star in WNO's award-winning Pelléas et Mélisande *(Debussy) in 1992.*

One of the most accomplished and beloved musical personalities of our time, Jessye Norman, at the closing concert of the Edinburgh Festival, 1991. She is partnered by Philip Moll.

The BBC Symphony Orchestra is in the vanguard of adventurous music-making. Here it appears at the Royal Festival Hall under Sir John Pritchard, 1984.

Westminster Cathedral in 1970. Wide repertoire, but much identified with French **organ** music.

PARSONS, *Geoffrey* (Born Sydney 1929) ————

Australian pianist who came to London in 1950 as accompanist to **Peter Dawson** and settled in Britain. Gradually assumed the mantle of **Gerald Moore** as the most sought-after accompanist of his time.

PARTRIDGE, *Ian* (Born London 1938) ————

British **tenor** of high accomplishment in **oratorio** and as a recitalist; distinguished **Schubert** singer. Frequently partnered at the piano by his sister Jennifer (born 1942).

'PASSING BY'————

Most popular composition of Edward Purcell who died in 1932. His real name was Edward Purcell Cockram. Delightfully recorded by Alvar Lidell who had a good **baritone** singing voice, apart from being a leading **BBC** announcer.

PATTI, *Adelina* (Born Madrid 1843; died Craig-y-Nos Castle, nr Brecon, 1919)————

Italian **soprano** of phenomenal vocal talent, the highest-paid singer of her day, even if she were only engaged to sing '**Home, Sweet Home**' which became identified with her. Spectacular international career included twenty-five consecutive seasons at **Covent Garden** (1861–95).

PATZAK, *Julius* (Born Vienna 1898; died Rottach, Bavaria, 1974) ————

Austrian **tenor** who sang with Munich opera 1928–45 and **Vienna** State Opera 1945–60. Distinguished Florestan in **Beethoven**'s *Fidelio* and a charming interpreter of Viennese *heurigen* (Wine Festival) songs.

PEARS, *Peter* (Born Farnham 1910; died Aldeburgh 1986) ————

British **tenor**, closely associated in professional and private life with **Benjamin Britten**. Was a member of the **BBC** Singers when he met Britten in 1936. With **Sadler's Wells**, Pears was notably successful as the shy Vasek in *The Bartered Bride*, and in 1945 he had a major triumph in the title role of Britten's *Peter Grimes* – many of Britten's works were

conceived with the high, flexible voice of Pears in mind. Well known for the songs of **Schubert** and **Schumann**, performed in partnership with Britten and, later, **Murray Perahia**. Knighted 1978.

PEEL, *Graham* (Born Manchester 1877; died Bournemouth 1937) ————

British composer of many songs, including settings of Housman's *A Shropshire Lad* of which the best known is 'In Summertime on Bredon'.

PENILLION ————

Canu penillion is a type of Welsh traditional singing revived with the rise of the competitive **eisteddfod** movement from the late eighteenth century. The harpist plays a traditional melody, followed by variations; the singer improvises a kind of **descant** against the **harp** accompaniment which must not begin until after the harp has started and must end with it. The words may be either improvised or established verses.

PERAHIA, *Murray* (Born New York 1947) ————

American pianist of Sephardic-Jewish family who achieved international recognition when he won the **Leeds** Piano Competition in 1972. Since then he has developed a career of the highest distinction. Has made outstanding recordings of all **Mozart**'s **concertos**, conducting from the keyboard; also notable recordings of four-hand music in partnership with **Radu Lupu**. A director of the Aldeburgh Festival since 1973.

PERCUSSION INSTRUMENTS ————

The accidental striking of some resonating surface could well have produced man's first musical sound. The huge percussion family extends worldwide and is divided into instruments which produce definite notes and those which do not.

PERGOLESI, *Giovanni* (Born Iesi 1710; died Pozzuoli 1736) ————

Italian composer chiefly famous for comic **operas** composed for Naples. One of them, *La Serva Padrona* (*The Maid as Mistress*) produced in 1733 as an *intermezzo* in a serious opera, achieved great international success, as did his *Stabat Mater* which became the most frequently printed musical work of the eighteenth century.

THE PIANO

The pianoforte, to give it its full name, is the most useful and versatile of musical devices. I have never ceased to be grateful for the piano lessons I had when a boy. Though never likely to play a **concerto** at the **Proms** (my dream at the age of twelve or thereabouts) I have enjoyed all the social possibilities of the piano very much.

'The pianoforte', as Leigh Hunt neatly put it, 'is a harp in a box.' The wonder is that a **percussion** instrument such as this can produce such a range of music. Of course, everything depends on the way pianists strike or stroke the keys and how they control, by means of the sustaining or 'loud' pedal, the dampers which dictate how long a note sounds, and use the 'soft' pedal to reduce the volume of sound. This effect is accomplished either by moving the hammers nearer the strings (in most upright pianos) or by moving the hammers sideways (in grand pianos) so that they strike only two of the three strings used to produce most notes.

The piano has assumed various shapes in the three centuries of its existence. The man usually credited with its invention was a Florentine instrument-maker called Bartolomeo Cristofori (1655–1731). Although the tone of the **harpsichord** could be varied by various stopping devices, it was incapable of the subtle gradations of tone which could be achieved by hammers. In fact the piano is more nearly related to the **clavichord**, which has a tiny sound. Cristofori's 'gravicembalo col piano e forte' was altogether more robust.

In the course of the eighteenth century the harpsichord and clavichord were almost totally eclipsed by the new instrument and in the nineteenth century the piano reigned supreme. **Bach** certainly encountered pianos of the maker Gottfried Silbermann (1681–1753), and it was his sons **Carl Philipp Emmanuel** and **Johann Christian** who originated the piano **sonata**. Johann Christian deeply influenced the first great pianist-composer **Wolfgang Amadeus Mozart** when he visited London as a small boy.

It was as a pianist in his own piano **concertos** that Mozart conquered **Vienna** in the 1780s. He liked the pianos made by Andreas Stein in Augsburg. Mozart's rival **Muzio Clementi** settled in London where he was active as a piano manufacturer and publisher of piano music. Clementi's competitor John Broadwood sent a piano to a grateful **Beethoven** whose legendary strength at the keyboard had shattered many a previous instrument. Sebastian Erard, who set up shop in Paris, presented one of his pianos to Napoleon in 1801. At this time the pianoforte was often called the fortepiano, a term now associated with instruments which had a wooden rather than an iron frame, only two strings to a note and leather, not felt, on the hammer-heads.

Technical advances came rapidly. In 1800 Matthias Müller produced the first true upright piano to replace the cumbersome 'vertical grand'. Soon every household which aspired to gentility wanted a piano. A series of outstanding pianist-composers provided the amateur with inspiration and a flood of new music to attempt. The Irishman **John Field**, who invented the piano **nocturne**, was followed by **Frédéric Chopin**. **Schubert** hugely enriched the piano repertoire and confirmed its status as the supreme accompanying instrument with his **songs**; **Schumann** wrote wonderfully poetic piano music (his wife Clara was a virtuoso); **Mendelssohn** was a child prodigy as a pianist as well as a composer and invented the notion of 'piano recitals' given (in his case) in the presence of swooning admirers. **Brahms** was a fine pianist and composer for the keyboard. Later came **Anton Rubinstein** (1829–94), Ferruccio Busoni (1866–1924), **Sergei Rachmaninov, Claude Debussy** (though he was not a great performer) and **Maurice Ravel.**

Most of the major piano manufacturers were in business by the middle of the nineteenth century. The German Heinrich Steinweg changed his name to Steinway when he left Europe for the USA in the wake of the 1848 revolutions. He started making pianos according to the 'Steinway system' in America in 1855, and in 1880 opened a European factory in Hamburg. In 1856 Hans von Bülow played **Liszt**'s sonata on a piano made in Berlin by Carl Bechstein, another name destined to be world-famous; Julius Blüthner began operations in Leipzig at much the same time. Meanwhile, as early as 1828, Ignaz Bösendorfer had been granted the right to trade as a piano-maker in Vienna. Bösendorfer pianos emerged unscathed from the hammerings of Franz Liszt and their world reputation was secure. In Paris the maker Ignaz Pleyel built a concert hall and gave it his own name; notable names in England included Chappell, Challen, Brinsmead, Spencer and Rogers. It was not until the mid-twentieth century that the Japanese entered the field in a very big way, making the name Yamaha in particular a formidable force in the world of piano manufacture and keyboard teaching.

The piano as an instrument has been subject to some strange variations. **Drums** and **cymbals** actuated by pedals were attached to some early instruments; one of Clementi's uprights could be converted into a musical box, the ancestor of the **barrel organs** which were once so popular with street musicians. Later 'piano rolls' made of perforated paper were used to actuate the note mechanism with the aid of pneumatic pressure; 'player pianos', using a variety of systems, became hugely popular and were eventually capable of great subtlety.

In the middle and late twentieth century there has been a reaction against what might be called 'rampant pianism'. Technical accomplishment by pianists, stimulated by a network of major international competitions, has never been higher. On the other hand the American composer John Cage (b. 1912) invented the idea of the 'prepared piano' with bolts between the strings and strips of rubber passed over and under them. Others have followed him in instructing that the strings should be plucked with the fingers, hit with sticks or subjected to other abuse. Cage also 'composed' a piece called *Silence* with no notes at all: the pianist comes on, sits at the instrument for five minutes or so and walks off.

But somehow I think the piano will survive.

Vladimir Horowitz rehearsing Rachmaninov at the Royal Festival Hall, 1982.

*P*ERLEMUTER *Vlado* (Born Kaunas 1904) ————

French pianist of Polish birth famous for his playing of **Chopin** and of **Ravel**, whose complete **piano** works he memorised and played to the composer. Still gave concerts in his late eighties.

*P*ERLMAN, *Itzhak* (Born Tel-Aviv 1945) ————

Israeli violinist, one of the most accomplished in the world; plays seated as he was deprived of the use of his legs by polio at the age of four. Performs **chamber music** with **Ashkenazy** and **Lynn Harrell**; wide-ranging repertoire includes **Scott Joplin** rags recorded with **André Previn**.

*P*ETRI, *Michala* (Born Copenhagen 1958) ————

Danish **recorder** player, widely regarded as the world's finest; made her début with **orchestra** in 1969 and the same year formed a trio with her mother Hanne (keyboard) and brother David (**cello**).

*P*EYER, *Gervase de* (Born London 1926) ————

British clarinettist who studied under Frederick Thurston; founder member of the Melos Ensemble and principal **clarinet** of the **London Symphony Orchestra** 1955–71. Also conductor and notable teacher.

*P*HILADELPHIA ORCHESTRA ————

American orchestra founded in 1900 which became world famous for its rich sonority under the direction from 1912–38 of **Leopold Stokowski**. His successor for the next forty years was **Eugene Ormandy**, who was followed in 1980 by **Riccardo Muti**. The current Music Director (from 1993) is Wolfgang Sawallisch.

*P*HILHARMONIA ————

London **orchestra** founded 1945 by Walter Legge, mainly to make recordings. **Karajan**, **Klemperer** and **Giulini** were frequent conductors, and when Legge attempted to disband the orchestra in 1964 Klemperer stayed on to work with them as a self-governing body, the New Philharmonia. In 1977 the orchestra dropped the 'New'. **Sinopoli** principal conductor since 1984.

*P*HILLIPS, *Montague* (Born London 1885; died Esher 1969) ————

British composer who married the **soprano** Clara Butterworth. She starred in her husband's most successful work, the light **opera** *The Rebel Maid* (1921) which includes 'The Fishermen of England'.

*P*IANOLA ————

An instrument made by the Aeolian Corporation, but the term is commonly, if wrongly, applied to all player-pianos. The keys of a piano-like keyboard are operated by compressed air supplied through perforations in a moving paper roll.

*P*IBROCH ————

Gaelic-derived name for the 'great music' (*ceòl mór*) of the Scottish Highland **bagpipe**. Ceremonial in origin, it takes the form of a theme with variations based on the four categories of pibroch – salute, lament, march and 'gathering'.

*P*ICCAVER, *Alfred* (Born Long Sutton, Lincs., 1884; died Vienna 1958) ————

British **tenor** whose real name was Peckover. Entered audition for Prague Opera as a joke in 1907 and was engaged; subsequently (1910–37) long and distinguished career at State Opera in **Vienna**, where he was idolised. Given a rapturous reception when he returned to Vienna for the post-war reopening of the State Opera in 1955.

*P*ICCOLO ————

Italian word for 'small'; name of a small **flute** which sounds an octave above the ordinary concert flute. Its bright sound is prominent in **Sousa**'s march 'The Stars and Stripes For Ever'.

*P*INNOCK, *Trevor* (Born Canterbury 1946 ————

British harpsichordist and conductor who made his playing début in London in 1968 and has subsequently recorded, among other things, the complete keyboard works of **Rameau**. In 1972 founded the English Concert, an **orchestra** which has played a leading role in the 'authentic instrument' movement.

*P*INZA, *Ezio* (Born Rome 1892; died Stamford, Conn., 1957) ————

Italian **bass** with repertoire of nearly a hundred roles

who was a much-loved leading singer at the **Metropolitan** 1926–48, achieving special acclaim in the title role of **Mozart**'s ***Don Giovanni*** which he also sang at the Salzburg Festival. On his retirement from the Met. at the age of fifty-six, Pinza appeared with great success in musicals, notably *South Pacific*, which opened on Broadway in 1949.

*P*ITTSBURGH SYMPHONY ORCHESTRA

Originally formed in 1895, disbanded in 1910 and re-formed in 1926, the Pittsburgh is among the USA's leading **orchestras**. Conductors have included **Victor Herbert** (1904–10), **Richard Strauss**, **Elgar**, **Klemperer** and **Previn** and, since 1986, **Lorin Maazel**.

*P*IZZICATO

Instruction to play a stringed instrument by plucking the strings with the fingers. Famous pizzicato passages occur in the **ballet** *Sylvia* by **Delibes** and the third movement of **Tchaikovsky**'s Fourth Symphony.

*P*LAINCHANT

Plainchant (or Plainsong) was developed in the earliest years of the Christian Church as the standard form of ritual melodic singing in worship. The words are sung in unison in a free rhythm similar to speech. Pope Gregory is credited with reforms instituted in the sixth century (see **Gregorian chant**).

'*T*HE PLOUGHBOY'

Satirical verses about political advancement are combined with a tune composed by William Shield (1748–1829). It was memorably arranged by **Benjamin Britten** and memorably recorded by him with **Peter Pears**.

*P*LOWRIGHT, *Rosalind* (Born Worksop 1949)

British **soprano** who won the Sofia International Competition in 1979 and subsequently developed a major international career. Outstanding in **Verdi** and **Richard Strauss**.

'*P*OEM' (Fibich)

Much the most famous composition of the Czech composer Zdenek Fibich (1850–1900). He wrote numerous **operas** and melodramas, **symphonies**, **chamber music** and songs. 'Poem' is a movement from a symphonic poem called *At Twilight* (1893).

*P*OÈME (Chausson)

Beautiful and well-known work for **violin** and **orchestra** (1896) by Ernest Chausson (1855–99), French composer, whose other works include a Symphony in B Flat and several pieces featuring the violin.

*P*OGORELICH, *Ivo* (Born Belgrade 1958)

Yugoslav pianist, resident since 1982 in Britain. His failure to reach the final rounds of the Warsaw **Chopin** Competition in 1980 caused a furore and paradoxically launched his very successful career. The Ivo Pogorelich Piano Competition will be inaugurated in Pasadena, California, in December 1993.

*P*OLLINI, *Maurizio* (Born Milan 1942)

Italian pianist and (from 1982) conductor. At the age of eighteen he won the Warsaw **Chopin** Competition of 1960. High reputation in Chopin and **Schoenberg**.

*P*OLYPHONY

A word descended from classical Greek meaning 'many sounds'. It applies to the kind of music in which several melodic strands are played or sung simultaneously and are of more or less equal importance. Polyphony flourished between the thirteenth and seventeenth centuries and continued as an important factor in compositional technique thereafter. Monophonic music has a single melodic line; homophonic music (the most frequently heard kind of music) has a single melodic line with other parts acting as accompaniment.

*P*ONS, *Lily* (Born Draguignan 1898; died Dallas, Texas, 1976)

French-born **soprano**, American from 1940. Début in title role of *Lakmé* by **Delibes** 1928 (her recording of the 'Bell Song' is one of her best memorials). Sensational career at the **Metropolitan** 1931–59 exhibited her exceptional **coloratura** range. Married 1938–59 to **André Kostelanetz**.

*T*HE PROMS

*T*he Last Night of the Proms is surely one of the most popular of all musical occasions. Perhaps it is not surprising that this good-humoured orgy of patriotic songs should appeal to the British but thanks to radio and television the event is relished all round the world.

I have been presenting the Last Night (and from time to time other Proms) for the BBC for thirty years. My father took me to the Proms for the first time in 1937 so one way or another I feel I have a personal stake in this great series of concerts which will soon be a hundred years old.

I am writing, of course, about the **Henry Wood** Proms which originated at the new Queen's Hall in Langham Place. The manager, Robert Newman (1858–1926), was impressed by Wood as a theatre conductor and in February 1895 decided to run a ten-week season of promenade concerts, with Wood conducting a specially created Queen's Hall **Orchestra**.

Funds, however, were a problem. Wood was unable to contribute capital, as Newman requested, but his friend, Dr George Cathcart, agreed to put up the money on certain conditions. First, the lower pitch in use on the continent (known as 'diapason normal') had to be used: the doctor felt the higher pitch used in Britain was ruining English voices. Second, Wood had to conduct all concerts, including special **Wagner** nights; the third, a fountain should be installed in the arena to maintain some humidity in the atmosphere. The fountain is still with us, and 'diapason normal' became the rule throughout the British musical profession.

Henry Wood, then aged twenty-six, conducted the first of the Proms which now bear his name on 10 August 1895. The programme included Wagner's *Rienzi* Overture and **Liszt**'s Hungarian Rhapsody No. 2, but the rest of the programme featured such popular items as a **cornet** solo and familiar **ballads**. Gradually the programmes became more substantial, Monday Wagner nights were soon an institution, and **Tchaikovsky** and **Beethoven** evenings became regular features. As early as 1898 there was a British Composers' night including music by 'one of the most promising of the younger generation of English composers' – **Edward Elgar.**

Some hardy perennials of the Last Night were also heard quite early on. On 22 October 1901 a thick London fog oozed its way into the Queen's Hall but it did not stop the audience awarding an unheard-of double encore to Elgar's *Pomp and Circumstance* March No. 1, with the tune which was to become known as **'Land of Hope and Glory'.** On 21 October 1905 Henry Wood marked the centenary of the Battle of Trafalgar with the first performance of his *Fantasia on British Sea Songs*, incorporating the 'Hornpipe' whose accelerating rhythm still defeats the Last Night Promenaders, and **'Rule Britannia'**. 'Jerusalem' was introduced in 1953 in one of several doomed attempts to displace the *Sea Songs*. The audience wouldn't tolerate these efforts, and now we have both.

The management of the Proms has undergone a number of changes. When Newman got into financial trouble in 1901, Sir Edgar Speyer, a banker and privy councillor, stepped into the breach. Chappell's ran the Proms through the First World War and afterwards but they lost money. In 1927, after some hesitation, the **BBC** took the series over and has run it ever since with the exception of two years during the Second World War when the chief sponsor was Keith Douglas, honorary secretary of the Royal Philharmonic Society.

After the Queen's Hall was destroyed by enemy bombs on the night of 10 May 1941, Douglas took the decision to transfer the Proms to the **Royal Albert Hall**, and there they remained when the BBC resumed control in 1942.

Henry Wood – Sir Henry as he became in 1911 – conducted all the Proms until 1941 when, at the age of seventy-two, he agreed to share the task with Basil Cameron. **Sir Adrian Boult** was brought into the conducting team in 1942: he was on the rostrum for the Golden Jubilee Concert on 10 August 1944. Wood was terminally ill and died a few days later. **Constant**

Lambert and Stanford Robinson appeared as associate conductors in the 1940s, and in 1947 **Sir Malcolm Sargent** was engaged. The following year he became chief conductor of the Proms, greatly adored by the Promenaders and an incomparable master of the Last Night speech, until cancer forced his withdrawal from the 1967 season. He struggled to the hall to make a last appearance at the Last Night that year (conducted by **Sir Colin Davis**) and died two-and-a-half weeks later. Since then successive chief conductors of the BBC Symphony Orchestra have played a prominent role in the Proms but the conducting honours have been more and more widely shared.

The same applies to the orchestral forces involved. Until the Second World War, first the Queen's Hall Orchestra and then the BBC Symphony Orchestra carried the whole burden of the season but it became increasingly obvious that such an arrangement could not produce adequately rehearsed performances. The **London Philharmonic** was brought in to share the load in 1941 and the story since then has been one of ever more invitations to guest orchestras of high

Sir John Pritchard conducting the BBC Symphony Orchestra at the Last Night of the Proms in 1989.

quality from all around the world. Prom soloists are now also the best the international scene affords.

The development of the Proms into perhaps the most comprehensive music festival in the world began with the appointment of Sir William Glock as the BBC's controller of music in 1959. In 1961 **Glyndebourne** contributed the first of many subsequent full-length **opera** performances. Other venues were tried and, as for the Albert Hall itself, its infamous echo was silenced by the installation of acoustic 'saucers' suspended from the ceiling in 1968.

Under the direction of Robert Ponsonby and John Drummond the worldwide prestige of the Proms has continued to grow. Successive generations of young people have ensured that the audience remains as enthusiastic as ever.

The Henry Wood Proms are literally unique as a means of bringing music to the world at large, and long may they survive.

Cole Porter. His brilliant facility in music and words was 'Just One of Those Things'.

PONSELLE, *Rosa* (Born Meriden, Conn., 1897; died Green Valley, Baltimore, 1981)

American **soprano** of major importance who made her début in 1918 opposite **Caruso** in the first **Metropolitan Opera** production of **Verdi**'s *The Force of Destiny*. Retired to become outstanding teacher in Baltimore.

POPP, *Lucia* (Born Bratislava 1939)

Czech-born Austrian **soprano** whose career has been centred on the **Vienna** State Opera but extends to London, Salzburg, New York and elsewhere. Numerous recordings in a wide-ranging repertoire.

PORTER, *Cole* (Born Peru, Indiana, 1891; died Santa Monica, Calif., 1964)

American composer and lyricist, one of the wittiest of the twentieth century. He was born of a wealthy family who discouraged him from taking up music, but he soon gave up an intended law career in favour of attending Harvard School of Music. The revue *Hitchy-Koo of 1919*, for which Porter wrote the score, ran for two years, and through the twenties he continued to contribute to revues; in 1928 he collaborated on a great success, *Paris*, which

included 'Let's do it'. From then on Cole Porter produced a stream of successful theatre shows, several of which were filmed, including *Anything Goes* (1934) and *Kiss me, Kate* (1948). Lists of favourite Cole Porter numbers will depend on individual taste. 'Miss Otis Regrets' (1934), 'Just One of Those Things' (1936) and 'I get a Kick out of You' (1934), are personal favourites of mine, while the film *High Society* (1956) is full of brilliant Cole Porter numbers. One great song, 'Night and Day', written for *Gay Divorce* (1932), gave its name to a 1946 film biography which starred Cary Grant as the composer. Cole Porter's last years were unhappy. In 1956 he had to have a leg amputated as the result of a riding accident some years earlier; that same year his wife died, and he became something of a recluse.

POSTHORN

Brass instrument with or without keys, sometimes straight and sometimes coiled, formerly used for signalling on mail and other coaches. **Mozart**'s Serenade No. 9 in D is known as the 'Posthorn'. Koenig composed his famous *Posthorn Galop* in 1844.

POULENC, *Francis* (Born Paris 1899; died Paris 1963)

French composer (and pianist) whose music makes an immediate appeal. Born into a wealthy pharmaceutical family, Poulenc studied harmony but otherwise preferred to rely on instinct. Neatly described as part ragamuffin, part saint, he once admitted he was not a composer to make harmonic innovations. As a young man he was one of the group of young modern composers known as '**Les Six**'. The deceptively simple *Trois mouvements perpetuels* for **piano** (1918) first made his name internationally known, and *Les Biches* (1924), a **ballet** score for Diaghilev, contributed to his growing fame. A renewal of Poulenc's Roman Catholic faith led to a series of religious works, of which the *Gloria* (1959) is one of the best known, and to the biggest of Poulenc's **operas** *Les Dialogues des Carmélites* (produced **La Scala** 1957). But Poulenc also drew inspiration from popular music, from **jazz**, **music hall** and circus bands: an irrepressible wit often breaks the elegant surface of his music. It emerges, for example, in the *Concert champêtre*, a **harpsichord** concerto produced in the twenties for **Wanda Landowska**, in some of Poulenc's many songs, and in one of his most popular works, the version for piano and narrator of *Babar the Elephant* which was written to amuse some young nephews and nieces during the German occupation of France during the Second World War.

*P*RAELUDIUM

Latin for **prelude**, and the title of the best-known piece by the Finnish-born composer Armas Järnefelt (1869–1958) who became Swedish in 1910.

*P*RELUDE

A prelude is a composition which precedes or introduces something else, for example a **fugue**, a **suite**, or an **opera**. In earlier days, an introductory improvisation by, say, an organist. The name is also used to describe short **piano** pieces by **Chopin** and others which explore a single mood or musical idea. The Prelude to the *Te Deum* of **Marc-Antoine Charpentier** (*c.* 1645–1704) is well known as the Eurovision signature tune.

*P*RESTON, *Simon* (Born Bournemouth 1938)

British organist, harpsichordist and conductor. Organ scholar of **King's College, Cambridge**; made an outstanding **Royal Festival Hall** début as organist in 1962, and under the influence of **George Malcolm** established international career as harpsichordist. Organist of Westminster Abbey 1981–7.

*P*REVIN, *André* (Born Berlin 1929)

Emigrated with his family of Russian Jewish origin to the USA in 1939, obtained US nationality 1943. After early sucess as a **jazz** pianist and Hollywood composer and arranger, he studied with **Pierre Monteux** and embarked on a very successful career as a conductor, succeeding **Sir John Barbirolli** with the Houston Symphony, before becoming principal conductor of the **London Symphony Orchestra** 1968–79. Soloist in **Mozart** piano concertos. His compositions include the **musical** *The Good Companions* (1974) and an effective piece for actors and **orchestra** created with Tom Stoppard, *Every Good Boy Deserves Favour* (1977).

*P*REY, *Hermann* (Born Berlin 1929)

German **baritone** distinguished in the **operas** of **Mozart**, **Rossini** and **Wagner** among others: also

fine concert singer who in 1976 founded an annual **Schubert** festival at Hohenems.

*P*RICE, *Leontyne* (Born Laurel, Mississippi, 1927)

American **soprano** who graduated from the **Juilliard School** to sing Bess in a two-year world tour of **Gershwin**'s *Porgy and Bess*. Her 1955 *Tosca* on TV was a significant breakthrough for a black singer. Excels in **Verdi**.

*P*RICE, *Margaret* (Born Blackwood, Mon., 1941)

Welsh **soprano** who made her début in **Mozart** with **Welsh National Opera** in 1962; has since developed a major international career, especially in Mozart and **Verdi**. DBE 1993.

*P*RIMROSE, *William* (Born Glasgow 1903; died Provo, Utah, 1982)

The foremost **viola** player of his day, Primrose was **Toscanini**'s principal viola in the NBC Orchestra 1937–42, and henceforth lived in the USA. Partnered **Heifetz** and Piatigorsky in **chamber music**; commissioned and premiered **Bartók**'s viola **concerto** 1953. CBE 1953.

*P*RITCHARD, *John* (Born London 1921; died 1989)

British conductor: distinguished periods as Music Director at **Glyndebourne** 1969–78, of the Liverpool and **London Philharmonic** Orchestras, and as Principal Conductor of the BBC Symphony Orchestra 1982–9. Knighted 1983.

*P*ROKOFIEV, *Sergei* (Born Sontsovka, Ukraine, 1891; died Moscow 1953)

Countless young people have been introduced to the instruments of the **orchestra** through hearing *Peter and the Wolf*, composed by Prokofiev for children's concerts in Moscow in 1936; his 'Classical' Symphony of 1916, the **ballets *Romeo and Juliet*** (première 1938) and *Cinderella* (first performed 1945), the score for the films *Lieutenant Kijé* (1933) and *Alexander Nevsky* (1938), together with the Third Piano Concerto (completed 1921) and extracts from the **opera** *The Love for Three Oranges* (première 1921) are known and loved by millions around the world. One of the most important composers of the twentieth century, Prokofiev was

*P*UCCINI

Giacomo PUCCINI

1858	Born in Lucca, Tuscany
1893	*Manon Lescaut* triumphed, Turin
1896	*La Bohème* premiered, Turin
1900	*Tosca* first performed, Rome
1904	*Madam Butterfly* failed in Milan, succeeded in Brescia
1910	*The Girl of the Golden West* premiered, New York
1918	The Triptych, including *Gianni Schicchi*, premiered New York
1924	Died in Brussels
1926	*Turandot* first performed, Milan.

*P*uccini once said of himself, 'I have more heart than mind,' and it is because his melodies appeal directly to the emotions that his **operas** are among the most popular ever written.

Puccini's father, who died when Giacomo was five, was head of Lucca's music school, the Pacini Institute, and a church musician. Puccini's mother Albina, whom he adored, was left to bring up seven children on very little. Giacomo was no prodigy but at fourteen he astonished church congregations by including tunes from **Verdi** operas in his **organ** improvisations, and when he was eighteen he walked nineteen miles to Pisa to hear a performance of ***Aida***.

Puccini graduated from the Pacini Institute and went to the Milan Conservatoire at the age of twenty-two. For a time he shared a small room with three other students; they were perpetually hungry and often postponed their single daily repast 'so that it might not be over too soon'.

However, Puccini was fortunate in his teachers, Antonio Bazzini and Amilcare Ponchielli. Ponchielli introduced the young composer to the poet Ferdinando Fontana, who supplied Puccini with the libretto for his first opera, a one-acter called *Le Villi*. The piece was

staged in Milan on 31 May 1884, and resulted in Puccini being summoned to an interview with Giulio Ricordi, head of Milan's most powerful publishing house.

Ricordi held the key to performance in the world's leading opera houses. Over the years he was Puccini's mentor and perhaps his closest friend. It took Puccini five years to complete his first full-length opera, *Edgar*, which was received only politely at **La Scala** in April 1889. Ricordi's colleagues urged him to end the association. 'If you wish to close the door to Giacomo Puccini,' replied Giulio, 'I myself will exit by the same door.'

Ricordi had to endure another four years of uncertainty while Puccini battled with a series of writers over the libretto of his next chosen subject, the story of the Chevalier des Grieux and Manon Lescaut. But Ricordi's belief in the composer was sensationally vindicated at the first night of the opera in Turin on 1 February 1893; Puccini had to take twenty-five calls during the action and more than thirty after the final curtain.

Meanwhile the great love of Puccini's own life had begun. Shortly after his mother's death in 1884 he had become passionately involved with Elvira, the wife of a Lucca schoolfriend, Giuseppe Gemignani. Despite strong family disapproval Elvira left her husband with her daughter, Fosca, and in December 1886 gave birth to Puccini's son, Antonio. Before the triumph of *Manon Lescaut* the couple endured harsh financial problems, but in 1891 Puccini found a retreat for himself and his family in the small lakeside village of Torre del Lago, near Pisa. Elvira was desperately jealous, even of Giacomo's male friends; as far as other women were concerned, she had good reason for Puccini was highly susceptible. There were frequent violent quarrels but in 1904 the couple married, and remained faithful to each other in their fashion to the end.

The next stage heroine to win Puccini's heart was the consumptive Mimì in **La Bohème**. With its reflection of the impoverished companionship of the composer's own young life, it is perhaps

Giacomo Puccini, 1858–1924.

his supreme masterpiece. The opera achieved twenty-four sold-out performances in its first season at Turin in 1896.

For some years Puccini had been brooding about an opera based on the melodramatic *Tosca* by Victorien Sardou. Here was another victimised woman, for although Tosca kills the evil Scarpia he exacts a terrible revenge after his death. The opera is set in Rome, and the first performance took place there in 1900 to a mixed reception.

When Puccini was in London for the production of *Tosca* at **Covent Garden** he saw David Belasco's play **Madam Butterfly**. At once Cio-Cio-San, abandoned by her American sailor husband, appealed to him as an oriental Mimì. This time the work was offered to La Scala, Milan, which snapped it up. What followed on 17 February 1904 was a shock to all concerned: the audience howled its disapproval when it wasn't exploding with laughter. Puccini reworked the opera in three acts instead of two, and in May 1904 it began its subsequent conquest of the lyric stage at the Teatro Grande in Brescia.

Puccini saw another Belasco play when he was in New York in 1907, *The Girl of the Golden West*, and this was the basis of his next opera, staged at the **Metropolitan** in December 1910.

The death of Giulio Ricordi in 1912 was a bitter blow and may help to account for Puccini's difficulty in finding another subject to suit him. The **Vienna** State Opera wanted an **operetta** and supplied the libretto for *La Rondine*. The resulting lightweight piece was first produced at Monte Carlo in 1917. Puccini worked with unusual speed to complete his next work: a trio of three one-act operas for the Met. and staged there in December 1918. These were *Suor Angelica*, *Il Tabarro* and *Gianni Schicchi*, Puccini's only comic opera and the most successful piece of the three.

Then the composer's attention was drawn to the play *Turandot*. With its exotic oriental setting and its blend of high drama and comedy it was just what Puccini wanted. Struggling against worsening health, he battled with his librettists to find the exact form he wanted for the work. It was never finished. In the autumn of 1924 he died after an operation for cancer of the throat. The final love duet in *Turandot* was completed by Puccini's friend Franco Alfano, but when **Toscanini** conducted the first performance at La Scala on 25 April 1926, he stopped halfway through the third act, turned to the audience and said, 'At this point the maestro laid down his pen.' The curtain fell slowly.

Favourite works

Some of Puccini's **arias** have achieved huge popularity.

Manon Lescaut – 'Never Have I Seen Such a Woman'.
La Bohème – 'Your Tiny Hand is Frozen'; 'They Call Me Mimì'; and the duet 'Lovely Maid in the Moonlight'. Also 'Musetta's Waltz Song'.
Tosca – 'Strange Harmony of Contrasts'; 'The Stars were Brightly Shining'; 'Love and Music'.
Madam Butterfly – 'Humming Chorus'; Love Duet; 'One Fine Day'.
The Girl of the Golden West – 'Let Her Believe Me Free'.
La Rondine – 'Doretta's Dream'.
Gianni Schicchi – 'O My Beloved Father'.
Turandot – 'In this Kingdom'; 'None Shall Sleep' ('Nessun Dorma').

condemned in 1948 by the Soviet authorities for 'formalist perversions alien to the Soviet people' and during his last years had to struggle with ill health and public disfavour. Regarded when young as a shocking innovator, Prokofiev lived in the USA 1918–22, then in Paris, producing ballet scores for Diaghilev among other works. Homesickness inclined him to accept Soviet commissions from 1933, and from 1936 till the end of his life he lived mainly in Russia. During the Second World War he worked on his great opera based on Tolstoy's *War and Peace*. This was one of the works condemned by the authorities in 1948; it was not seen on stage until 1957, when official attitudes had softened. By then both Stalin and Prokofiev were no more: ironically they died on the same day in 1953. Prokofiev's large output includes eight operas, seven symphonies, five piano concertos and numerous other instrumental and vocal pieces.

*P*URCELL, *Henry* (Born London 1659; died London 1695)

'Fairest Isle' from Purcell's *King Arthur* (1691) was one of the songs chosen for unison singing in class when I was a boy, and this experience did nothing to convince me that Purcell was one of the greatest of British composers. That revelation came when I was involved in a Cambridge production of *Dioclesian* (1690). Purcell wrote incidental music for many plays like *Dioclesian*, among them *Abdelazar* (1695) which includes the theme used by **Benjamin Britten** for his *Young Person's Guide to the Orchestra*, and just one great **opera**, *Dido and Aeneas* (1689), as well as the 'semi-operas', plays which include a good deal of music and incorporate a **masque** which is wholly set to music: *The Fairy Queen* (1692), based on Shakespeare's *A Midsummer Night's Dream*, is perhaps the best known. Purcell produced great quantities of music for the church, and large numbers of secular songs. He was also a great master of instrumental music, including the famous Chacony in G minor (1680) and several Fantasias for Strings. Dido's wonderful dying lament from *Dido and Aeneas* can serve as a lasting epitaph to a musical genius who might have achieved even more if he had not died so young.

Q

*Q*UARTET

A composition for four voices or instruments; or a group of players or singers who perform such music. The string quartet (consisting of two **violins**, **viola** and **cello**) is the most common instrumental quartet, and its repertoire includes some of the greatest music ever written. The piano quartet (**piano**, violin, viola cello) also has a large and beautiful repertoire. There are works in which one violin is replaced by a wind instrument, such as a **clarinet** or **oboe**, and countless compositions for vocal quartet.

*Q*UILTER, *Roger* (Born Brighton 1877; died London 1953)

British composer of ample private means and great generosity, a founder of the Musicians' Benevolent Fund. Quilter's settings of Shakespeare songs, and of Tennyson's 'Now Sleeps the Crimson Petal' have remained very popular, and his *Children's Overture*, based on nursery rhymes and once very well known, is coming back into favour. Quilter wrote the incidental music for the children's play *Where the Rainbow Ends* which was staged annually at Christmas in the West End for many years.

R

*R*ACHMANINOV, *Sergei* (Born Semyonovo 1873; died Beverly Hills 1943)

Russian composer, pianist and conductor. Studied at the Moscow Conservatory, where he produced his First Piano Concerto in 1891, and graduated with the highest honours. The following year he wrote the Prelude in C sharp minor for **piano**, whose popular appeal became something of an embarrassment; it was demanded by audiences at all Rachmaninov's recitals. Disaster struck with the performance of his First Symphony: the orchestra was ill prepared and the conductor, according to one story, was drunk, leading to one critic's description of the work as 'a programme symphony on the Seven Plagues of Egypt'. Rachmaninov was thrown into a severe depression which only seems to have lifted after being treated by a hypnotist some three years later. In 1900, he began work on what was to be his most famous work, the Second Piano Concerto, whose unabashed **Romanticism** was later used to great effect in the film *Brief Encounter*. In 1909 Rachmaninov began extensive and exhausting touring as a virtuoso concert pianist, which provided a lucrative living, especially after his move to the USA following the 1917 Russian Revolution, but proved a distraction from composition. Nevertheless, he managed to produce two more piano **concertos**, the *Rhapsody on a Theme of Paganini* in 1934, and numerous **songs**, including the wordless *Vocalise*. By the time of his death from cancer in 1943, Rachmaninov was one of the most popular composers and performers in the Western world.

*R*ĀGA

From the Sanskrit for 'passion' or 'feeling', *rāga* denotes a melody-type or modal scale in Indian music, where each set of notes can produce a multitude of *rāgas* through differing ornamentation, repetition or omission. First classified as early as the eighth century, each *rāga* is traditionally associated with particular times of day, festivals or deities: legend has it that a sixteenth-century court musician was able to plunge the day into darkness by singing a night-time *rāga*. Musicians have considerable leeway in individual interpretation, with room to improvise and draw on local customs.

*R*AIMONDI, *Ruggero* (Born Bologna 1941)

Italian **bass**, noted for his beautiful and resonant voice, and his commanding performances of nineteenth-century Italian **opera**, especially **Verdi**, and also as a great **Don Giovanni** in Joseph Losey's 1979 film.

*R*ÁKÓCZI MARCH

Stirring Hungarian march, named after the eighteenth-century nationalist hero Prince Ferenc Rákóczi. Used by **Berlioz** in his *Damnation of Faust* (1846), and also by **Liszt** in his Hungarian Rhapsody No. 15 (1852).

*R*AMEAU, *Jean-Philippe* (Baptised Dijon 1683; died Paris 1764)

Leading French composer and theorist of his day. Nowadays, he is best remembered for his expressive **harpsichord** pieces and for his tragic **operas**, including *Hippolyte et Aricie* (1733) and *Castor et Pollux* (1737), which ensured the continuation of a specifically French style against the prevailing Italian fashion.

*R*AMEY, *Samuel* (Born Kolby, Kansas, 1942)

American bass **baritone**, made his début at the New York City Opera in 1973. Specialises particularly in roles by **Rossini** and **Verdi**; also a celebrated Figaro and **Don Giovanni**.

*R*AMPAL, *Jean-Pierre* (Born Marseilles 1922)

French flautist, regarded as one of the most outstanding in the world. Despite premiering modern works, Rampal is most closely associated with the eighteenth-century repertoire, and was an early advocate of authentic performance, making many award-winning recordings of, among others, **C.P.E. Bach** and **Mozart** as well as the complete **J.S. Bach** sonatas with the English harpsichordist **Trevor Pinnock**. He has also long been a champion of **chamber music** in France.

*R*AVEL, *Maurice* (Born Ciboure 1875; died Paris 1937)

Of Swiss and Basque ancestry, Ravel grew up in Paris, his musical talent spotted by his father early on. He entered the Paris Conservatoire in 1889, studying **piano** and later composition with **Fauré**, under whose sympathetic tutelage he wrote works for **orchestra** and piano, including the *Pavane pour une infante défunte*. Ravel cut a controversial figure in his youth, and in 1903 the old guard at the Conservatoire, who could see little merit in his works, forced him to leave, ironically at the same time that he produced his enduringly popular String Quartet. Throughout his life Ravel had an aching nostalgia for childhood, with a special fascination for clockwork toys. This is reflected in some of his music, such as the charming *Ma mère l'oye* (Mother Goose) Suite for piano duet. Ravel was a great orchestrator – it is his arrangement of **Moussorgsky**'s *Pictures from an Exhibition* that we most often hear, for example

RATTLE

Simon RATTLE

1955	Born in Liverpool
1970	Formed own orchestra for charity concert, Liverpool
1974	Won John Player International Conductor's Award
1980	Principal Conductor of City of Birmingham Symphony Orchestra
1986	*Porgy and Bess* at Glyndebourne
1987	Début with Berlin Philharmonic Orchestra
1991	Symphony Hall opened in Birmingham

Stuck in a traffic jam in 1986, Simon Rattle and the late Michael Vyner dreamed up the idea of celebrating the arts of the twentieth century in its last decade. Thus was 'Towards the Millenium' born. Each March and April until the year 2000, a series of concerts given in London and Birmingham by the London Sinfonietta and the City of Birmingham Symphony Orchestra will celebrate the successive decades of the present century. In 1992 the years from 1911–20 have been highlighted in a project which has won great public and critical interest.

Simon Rattle was the son of a businessman turned teacher with a spare-time passion for **jazz**. At the age of four, he was accompanying his father's piano-playing on a small drum-kit, and by the time he was eleven he was playing in the Merseyside Youth Orchestra. As a boy Simon was an ardent follower of the Royal Liverpool Philharmonic Orchestra concerts, and recalls being knocked out by George Hurst's conducting of **Mahler**'s Second Symphony: it was for him 'the road to Damascus', he said later. Under the guidance of Douglas Miller, he then developed a considerable talent for the **piano**, giving a performance of **Gershwin**'s *Rhapsody in Blue* with the Liverpool Concert Orchestra when he

was twelve. But it was the conductor's rostrum which really attracted him, and at the age of fifteen he put together an **orchestra** of his own to give a charity concert.

Simon Rattle spent the summer of 1971 with the **National Youth Orchestra** before entering the **Royal Academy of Music** that September at the age of sixteen. There he soon became involved in the preparation of **opera** performances. 'He could play the piano like a complete orchestra,' said a contemporary; 'he could tell the singers what to do and gave everyone confidence.' In 1973 Simon accepted the conductorship of the Merseyside Youth Orchestra and, on 6 December that year, conducted a performance of Mahler's Second Symphony at the Royal Academy which no one present has ever forgotten.

In 1974 Rattle entered for the newly-established John Player International Conductor's Award and won it against competition from two hundred other entrants. The award entitled him to work for two years with the Bournemouth Symphony Orchestra and Bournemouth Sinfonietta alongside their regular conductors. This tough apprenticeship gave him the chance to widen his repertoire out of the London limelight, and led in 1975 to his first association with **Glyndebourne** where, at the head of the Sinfonietta, he prepared and conducted the tour of **Stravinsky**'s *The Rake's Progress*. The following year, aged twenty-one, he made a striking **Royal Festival Hall** début with the New **Philharmonia** Orchestra, conducted the London Schools Symphony Orchestra on a United States tour, gave his first account of **Gershwin**'s *Porgy and Bess* with the Chelsea Opera Group, and made his début at the **Proms**, the youngest conductor ever to do so.

The years from 1977 to 1980 brought further opportunities to learn in twin appointments as associate conductor with the **BBC** Scottish Orchestra and the Royal Liverpool Philharmonic. Overseas, a concert with the Rotterdam Philharmonic led to the offer of its musical directorship, and Rattle's début with the **Los**

Angeles Philharmonic was followed by the offer of a post there, but these temptations were turned down.

In May 1976 Simon Rattle had conducted the City of Birmingham Symphony Orchestra for the first time at a **Beethoven** concert in Oxford. Two years later the orchestra found itself without a conductor and when Rattle was invited to conduct them in December 1978 it came as no surprise when he was asked to stay.

Since then it has been a source of wonder that a young man of such outstanding talent should have decided to stay at the head of a provincial orchestra. But in the Simon Rattle years a great deal has happened to **Birmingham** and the CBSO. From the start, Rattle was determined that the orchestra should rank alongside great civic orchestras like those of Chicago, **Vienna** and Berlin, and a memorandum of 1986 addressed to the Arts Council and the City of Birmingham laid out the means by which this was to be accomplished. Rattle's contract would only be renewed on four conditions; they included improved orchestral pay to attract the best talent, the enlargement of the string sections, a prestigious touring programme and the building of a new concert hall. The city, eager to become identified with a first-rate orchestra and maestro, responded with great generosity. How many other conductors, of whatever eminence, have been able to demand a brand new concert hall and get it?

But for all its importance, Birmingham is not the only string to Simon Rattle's bow. There are close ties with the London Sinfonietta and with the world of opera. Successes at Glyndebourne have included *Porgy and Bess* in 1986, and **Mozart** operas with an 'original instrument' orchestra. In 1985 Rattle made his début at **English National Opera** with **Janáček**'s *Katya Kabanova* and in 1990 he conducted the same composer's *The Cunning Little Vixen* at **Covent Garden**. Abroad, he confines himself to a small selection of prestigious appearances, including about three a year with the **Berlin Philharmonic**. When **Claudio Abbado** retires, perhaps around the millenium, there are many who think Simon Rattle is the person most likely to succeed him. That is, if he can bring himself to exchange Brum for Berlin.

Simon Rattle conducting the City of Birmingham Symphony Orchestra, 1992.

– painting brilliant colours with his music, nowhere more so than in the famous *Boléro* whose insistent single melody is sustained through masterful scoring.

RECITATIVE

Term describing speech-like passages in **operas** and **oratorios** of the seventeenth and eighteenth centuries (and some later works), often used to advance the plot. A recitative frequently introduces an **aria** which expresses an emotional state. Recitative can be either fully accompanied ('accompagnato') by the **orchestra**, or dry ('secco'), in which case a sparse chordal accompaniment is supplied, typically by a keyboard player.

RECORDER

Reedless woodwind instrument, with a whistle-mouthpiece, mainly found in descant, treble, tenor and bass sizes. Much used in the sixteenth to eighteenth centuries, it has enjoyed a revival since the 1930s.

REILLY, *Tommy* (Born Guelph, Ontario, 1919)

Canadian-born **harmonica** player and composer, resident in Britain since 1935. His expertise encouraged composers to write for the instrument, including **Robert Farnon**, whose Prelude and Dance for harmonica and **orchestra** he premiered in 1966.

REINHARDT *Django* (Born Liberchies 1910; died Fountainebleau 1953)

Belgian **jazz** guitarist who, despite suffering a badly burnt left hand, became an international star and leading exponent of European jazz. Worked mainly as a soloist and with **Stephane Grappelli** (in the Quintet of the Hot Club of France).

REMEDIOS, *Alberto* (Born Liverpool 1935)

The greatest English **Wagner tenor** of his generation, Remedios won international acclaim for his Siegmund and Siegfried in the **English National Opera**'s *Ring* cycle of the 1970s under **Reginald Goodall**.

REQUIEM

The Latin Mass for the Dead, popular with composers from the seventeenth century, partly because of the musical scope given by contrasting moods of each section, e.g. the terrifying Dies Irae (Day of Wrath) and the elegiac Agnus Dei (Lamb of God). The most famous Requiem is probably **Mozart**'s; others include the operatic settings by **Berlioz** (*Grande messe des morts*, 1837) and **Verdi** (1874), and in contrast the simple and restrained version by **Fauré** (1887–8). **Britten**'s *War Requiem* juxtaposed the Latin text with poems by Wilfred Owen condemning war; first performed at the consecration of the new Coventry Cathedral in 1961.

RESPIGHI, *Ottorino* (Born Bologna 1879; died Rome 1936)

The most successful Italian composer of his generation, Respighi studied in Bologna, then under **Rimsky-Korsakov** in Russia and with **Max Bruch** in Berlin. In 1913 he settled in the city with which he is most associated, Rome, becoming Professor of Composition at the St Cecilia Conservatory and, from 1924 to 1926, its Director. Although he wrote several **operas**, Respighi is best known for his two tone poems *Fontane di Roma* (*The Fountains of Rome*), composed in 1916, and *Pini di Roma* (*The Pines of Rome*), of 1924. The former depicts the four most famous Roman fountains at different times of day, while the latter focuses on various tree-lined roads and parks. Respighi was also an accomplished arranger, with a special interest in **Baroque** and **early music**. His suite *Gli uccelli* (*The Birds*, 1927) draws on themes from **Rameau**, and includes portraits of the dove, nightingale and cuckoo, while the *Ancient Airs and Dances* derives from early lute music.

REVUE

A topical show usually consisting of songs, dancing and sketches, often with a satirical edge. The revue originated in nineteenth-century France, with its golden age in the 1920s and 1930s, when the black dancer Josephine Baker was the toast of Paris and song writers like **Ivor Novello** and **Noel Coward** were working in London's West End on spectacular shows such as *A to Z* and *London Calling*. On Broadway the careers of **Irving Berlin**, **George Gershwin** and **Rodgers** and Hart were launched in revue; among the most famous shows of the kind was New York's Ziegfeld Follies, with huge sets and glamorous casts. Spectacular revue declined with the

Raina Kabaivanska as Cio-Cio-San in Puccini's Madam Butterfly. *One of the world's best-loved operas, it was booed at its first performance.*

Since winning the Leeds International Piano Competition in 1972, Murray Perahia has gone on to become one of the world's most distinguished pianists.

George Gershwin fulfilled his ambition to write a negro opera in Porgy and Bess. *At Covent Garden in 1992, Willard White and Cynthia Haymon led the cast.*

arrival of the talkies. More intimate shows continued to appeal, however, including London's 'Sweet and Low' series (1943–7) and the satirical *Beyond the Fringe* (1961).

*R*ICCI, *Ruggiero* (Born San Francisco 1918) _____

Virtuoso violinist, who made his **Carnegie Hall** début aged eleven, playing the **Mendelssohn** Concerto. Ricci excels in the demanding nineteenth-century repertoire, his formidable technique especially suited to **Paganini.**

*R*ICCIARELLI, *Katia* (Born Rovigo 1946)_____

Italian **soprano**, internationally popular as a strong actress in the **operas** of **Verdi** and **Puccini** especially; starred as Desdemona in Zeffirelli's 1986 film of Verdi's *Otello*.

*R*ICHTER, *Sviatoslav* (Born Zhitomir, Ukraine, 1915)_____

Russian pianist, who won much acclaim through his close association with **Prokofiev**'s music, giving the first performance of three of the **piano** sonatas and conducting the première of the Second Cello Concerto with **Rostropovich**. In the 1960s, Richter's fame spread to the West, both as a thoughtful and intense pianist, with a repertoire from **Bach** to **Shostakovich**, and as a sensitive accompanist to the singers **Dietrich Fischer-Dieskau** and **Elisabeth Schwarzkopf**, despite his notorious habit of cancelling concerts at short notice. He was also a friend of **Britten**, often playing at the Aldeburgh Festival.

*R*IMSKY-KORSAKOV, *Nikolay Andreyevich* (Born Tikhvin 1844; died St Petersburg 1908) _____

Rimsky-Korsakov's first career was as a naval officer, but he soon realised that this was the wrong choice, particularly after meeting **Balakirev** in 1861. This was a time of a great nationalist renaissance in Russian music, and Rimsky-Korsakov, who had always had a love for peasant culture, found a friend and ally in **Moussorgsky**, with whom he shared a study – Moussorgsky would use it in the mornings to write his **opera** *Boris Godounov* while Rimsky-Korsakov began composing his first opera, *The Maid of Pskov*, in the afternoons. Finally, in 1871, he became professor of composition at the St Petersburg Conservatory, and was able to resign his commission in the navy. There

followed collections of Russian folk-songs as well as a string of operas on folk themes, often with fantastic plots, including *May Night*, *The Snow Maiden* and *Christmas Eve*. Rimsky-Korsakov's music is celebrated for its brilliant orchestration, nowhere more so than in *Scheherazade* and in the famous 'Flight of the Bumble Bee', an orchestral interlude in the opera *The Tale of Tsar Saltan*, where the prince becomes a bee in order to sting his wicked aunts. Always a modest man, Rimsky-Korsakov was centrally important to Russian opera, and not only through his own work: following Moussorgsky's death, he used his formidable skills to prepare *Boris Godounov* for performance, and later completed **Borodin**'s opera *Prince Igor*.

*R*ING, THE _____

Wagner's great tetralogy of **operas** *Der Ring des Nibelungen* (*The Ring of the Nibelung*), comprising *Das Rheingold* (*The Rhinegold*), *Die Walküre* (*The Valkyrie*), *Siegfried*, and *Götterdämmerung* (*The Twilight of the Gods*). Wagner initially intended to write a single opera about the hero Siegfried, taken from medieval sagas, but over a period of twenty-six years (from 1848 to 1874) the project expanded into a huge dramatic cycle showing how the old order of the gods is destroyed through greed and lust for power. The story begins with the theft of the Rhinegold by the loveless dwarf Alberich, who forges a ring to obtain mastery over the world, only to be tricked out of it by the gods (under Wotan) to pay off the giants who have built for them the glorious palace, Valhalla. But the ring is cursed, and it is only through the adventures of the mortal Siegfried that the gold can be returned to its rightful owners, the Rhinemaidens, thus holding out the promise of a new order based on love. The complete cycle was first performed in 1876 at Wagner's new Bayreuth theatre (this was the first Bayreuth Festival). The cycle is the most extraordinary enterprise in operatic history, with parts of its music – including 'The Ride of the Valkyries' and 'Siegfried's Funeral March' – firmly entrenched in the popular consciousness.

*R*OBESON, *Paul* (Born Princeton, New Jersey, 1898; died Philadelphia 1976) _____

The most prominent black performer of his time, Robeson studied law at Columbia University before making a name for himself as an actor in the 1920s (he was powerful as Shakespeare's Othello). But it was his rich bass-baritone voice that was to make him internationally famous, as a singer of Negro spirituals and star of **musicals**, especially **Jerome Kern**'s *Show Boat*, featuring the song he made his own, 'Ol' Man River'. Outspoken Communist sympathies almost ended his career in the McCarthyite 1950s, although he gave one concert at the **Carnegie Hall** in 1958.

ROBLES, *Marisa* (Born Madrid 1937)

One of the world's most famous harpists, Robles studied at the Madrid Conservatory, where she also became one of the youngest professors. In 1959 she moved to Britain, making her concert début at the **Royal Festival Hall** in 1963, and winning a huge following through numerous recitals both on stage and television. She has also championed the **harp**'s place in **chamber music**, accompanying her then husband, the flautist Christopher Hyde-Smith, and founding her own chamber groups, the Robles Trio and later the Robles-Delme Ensemble.

RODGERS, *Richard* (Born Long Island 1902; died New York 1979)

Rodgers was among the greatest composers of **musicals**, with a breathtaking list of successes to his name. New York born and bred, he teamed up with his first great collaborator, the lyricist Lorenz Hart, in 1919. In 1935 they had their first big break with the circus-based musical *Jumbo*, followed by successes like *Babes in Arms*, *The Boys from Syracuse* and *Pal Joey*. After the death of Hart, Rodgers started working with the lyricist Oscar Hammerstein II in what was to be an even more fruitful partnership, beginning with the seminal show *Oklahoma!* in 1943. The Rodgers and Hammerstein team went on to create *Carousel* (1945) – featuring the song 'You'll Never Walk Alone', since taken up by supporters of Liverpool Football Club – *South Pacific* (1949), *The King and I* (1951), and *The Sound of Music* (1959), all of which were made into popular films. After the death of Hammerstein in 1960, Rodgers never again achieved such heights, but a rich legacy remains to delight us.

RODRIGO, *Joaquin* (Born Sagunto 1901)

Blind from the age of three, Rodrigo nevertheless studied composition in Valencia, then under **Dukas** in Paris, where he met **Falla**. After the Civil War, he returned to Spain to settle in Madrid, taking up a professorship at the Conservatory in 1947. Rodrigo is best known for his **concertos** – for **flute**, **piano**, **violin**, but above all for **guitar**, especially the *Concierto de Aranjuez*, which nostalgically recalls the old Spain and was immediately popular. Other pieces for guitar followed, including the *Fantasia for a Gentleman*, premiered by **Andrès Segovia** in 1954.

ROGÉ, *Pascal* (Born Paris 1951)

French pianist, entered the Paris Conservatoire aged eleven, giving his first recitals in 1969. Best known for French repertoire: he recorded all the **Saint-Saëns** concertos with the conductor **Charles Dutoit**.

ROLFE JOHNSON, *Anthony* (Born Tackley 1940)

Rolfe Johnson gave up farming to become one of Britain's leading **tenors**, singing at **Glyndebourne** from 1974 and **Covent Garden** from 1985. Primarily associated with eighteenth-century **opera** and **oratorio**.

ROMANCE

Term originally denoting a **ballad** from France or Spain, but since used rather loosely, usually for slow movements of a tender, lyrical quality – for example, the slow movement of **Mozart**'s D minor Piano Concerto, and **Vaughan Williams**'s *The Lark Ascending*.

ROMANIAN RHAPSODIES

Two glittering orchestral works (1901) by the Romanian composer George Enescu. Inspired by **Liszt**'s Hungarian Rhapsodies, the works employ melodies derived from native folk-tunes.

ROMANTIC/ROMANTICISM

'Romantic' is a somewhat catch-all label, derived from the term for an extravagant or fanciful story, and used in music to distinguish nineteenth-century compositions from their **classical** precursors, so covering virtually all music written between about 1790 and about 1914. 'Romanticism' was first and foremost a reaction against the formal constraints of classicism; the individual's imagination and emotion were now emphasised over order and reason, with a renewed interest in nature, the supernatural and the past. The artist was no longer simply a skilled entertainer but a hero, struggling for a better world. Composers took inspiration from painting and literature, often giving their music specific descriptive subject-matter. Some romantic elements are evident as early as the **symphonies** of **Beethoven** (with the 'Eroica' based on the heroic deeds of the individual (originally Napoleon), and the 'Pastoral' (using music to depict the countryside), in **Schubert**'s **lieder**, often about the suffering of the individual soul, and in **Berlioz**'s *Symphonie fantastique*, which bears the subtitle 'Episodes in the life of an artist'. Romantic music is often characterised by its emphasis on long, lyrical melodies and lush orchestration, as can be found in **Tchaikovsky** or **Wagner**, for example. Another important facet of Romanticism was its interest in nationalism, with the aim of forging specifically national styles, often using folk-songs.

*R*OMBERG, *Sigmund* (Born Nagykanizsa 1887; died New York 1957) ⸻

Hungarian-born composer who emigrated to the USA after training as an engineer. Romberg's first stage success came with the **operetta** *Blossom Time*, based on the life of **Schubert**, and using the composer's melodies for the score. This was followed by *The Student Prince* (1924), set in old Heidelberg, with the famous 'Serenade' and chorus 'Gaudeamus Igitur'. On other stage shows Romberg teamed up with **Gershwin**, **Rodgers**, and the lyricist Oscar Hammerstein II, as well as writing **film music** and leading his own touring **orchestra**.

*R*ONDO ⸻

From the Italian for 'round', a composition with a recurring section (A) sandwiched between contrasting themes (B,C), i.e. ABACA or similar. Often used for the last movement of a **sonata** or **concerto**, for example the 'Turkish Rondo' in **Mozart**'s Piano Sonata K. 331.

*R*OSSINI, *Gioachino* (Born Pesaro 1792; died Passy 1868) ⸻

Born into a musical family, Rossini studied at the Liceo Musicale in Bologna, where he was given a rigorous training in traditional **harmony** and **counterpoint**. He started writing **operas** in his mid-

teens, soon receiving commissions from the great opera houses, including **La Scala**, and it was not long before he had established himself as Italy's leading composer, excelling at comic operas (*opera buffa*), which he seemed to dash off effortlessly, often reusing parts of his earlier works. When, in 1815, he was commissioned to write *The Barber of Seville*, Rossini completed the task in three weeks. However, the première in Rome was a disaster, disrupted by the supporters of a rival setting of Beaumarchais's play, although it soon became, and has remained, his most popular work, typically combining strong melodies and lively rhythms with brilliant comic effects: **Verdi** called it 'the most beautiful *opera buffa* there is'. In 1824 Rossini moved to Paris, which became his permanent home. Here he wrote his last and, to many, his greatest opera, *William Tell*, with its ever-popular overture. It was a great success, but although Rossini lived for another forty years, he composed little except for two religious works, the *Stabat Mater* and the *Petite messe solennelle*, and a collection of **piano** pieces he called 'sins of my old age'.

*R*OSTROPOVICH, *Mstislav* (Born Baku 1927) ⸻

Russian cellist and conductor, Rostropovich was a brilliant student and later professor at the Moscow Conservatory. In 1956 he began touring in the West, impressing audiences with his faultless technique and daring repertoire; he has inspired some of the greatest modern works for **cello**, including pieces by **Prokofiev**, **Shostakovich** and **Britten**, with whom he formed a lasting friendship in 1960. In 1978 the Soviet authorities stripped him of his citizenship for supporting the dissident writer Solzhenitsyn, and he moved to the West with his wife, the **soprano Galina Vishnevskaya**. Appointed KBE 1987.

*R*OTHENBERGER, *Anneliese* (Born Mannheim 1924) ⸻

German **soprano** who studied in Mannheim before working with the Hamburg State Opera from 1946, making her British début at **Glyndebourne** in 1959 as Sophie in **Richard Strauss**'s *Der Rosenkavalier*, a role she was to repeat in the film version.

*R*OYAL ACADEMY OF MUSIC ⸻

Founded in 1822 under the patronage of George IV, and moved from Hanover Square to its present site in Marylebone Road in 1912. The Academy offers training to the highest standard in all aspects of the musical profession.

ROYAL ALBERT HALL

Since it opened in 1871 as a memorial to the Prince Consort, the hall has housed a huge variety of events; best known musically for the summer **Proms**, which have been held there since the Queen's Hall was bombed in 1941.

ROYAL COLLEGE OF MUSIC

Founded in 1883 under the patronage of the Prince of Wales (later Edward VII), moving to Prince Consort Road in 1894. Like the Royal Academy, a school of excellence for performers, teachers and composers; it houses a fine reference library and collection of musical instruments.

ROYAL FESTIVAL HALL

The main concert hall of the South Bank complex, built for the 1951 Festival of Britain, with a capacity of 2895. Its acoustics were improved in 1964 after much criticism. The resident orchestra is the **London Philharmonic**.

ROYAL PHILHARMONIC ORCHESTRA

Founded by **Sir Thomas Beecham** in 1946, and controlled by him until his death in 1961, after which it was self-governing. The RPO has a largely popular repertoire in the concert hall. Principal conductors since Beecham have included **Kempe**, **Dorati** and **Previn**. **Vladimir Ashkenazy** has been Music Director since 1987.

ROYAL SCOTTISH ORCHESTRA

Founded in 1891, originally as the Scottish Orchestra; 1950–91 named the Scottish National Orchestra. Based in Glasgow, its conductors have included **Max Bruch**, **Sir John Barbirolli**, **Sir Alexander Gibson** and **Bryden Thomson**.

ROZHDESTVENSKY, *Gennady* (Born Moscow; 1931)

Russian conductor whose mother was a professional **soprano**; his father, Nikolay Anosov, was a conductor and professor at the Moscow Conservatory,

where he taught his own son. Rozhdestvensky was a precocious student, and was invited to conduct at the **Bolshoi** when just twenty, having led at short notice a rehearsal of *The Sleeping Beauty* from memory. Associated with the Bolshoi until 1970, introducing many new works to the Russian repertoire, since when he has been principal conductor of the Stockholm Philharmonic, and the **BBC** and the **Vienna** Symphony Orchestras.

RUBINSTEIN, *Anton* (Born Vikhvatinets 1829; died Peterhof 1894)

Russian pianist, composer and teacher, Rubinstein's prodigious talents were apparent early on, and he gave public concerts from the age of ten. He met **Chopin** and **Liszt** (with whom he was often compared), and played before Queen Victoria. As a composer, Rubinstein was less successful – he is remembered mainly for the popular Melody in F (1852) for **piano**. His lasting achievement was helping to found important institutions such as the Russian Musical Society and the St Petersburg Conservatory (of which he was the first director). His brother Nikolay (born Moscow 1835; died Paris 1881) was also a gifted pianist and teacher, and founded the Moscow Conservatory. A well known *bon viveur*, Nikolay championed the works of **Tchaikovsky**. Despite at first calling the First Piano concerto 'worthless and unplayable', he later became a noted performer of the solo part.

RUBINSTEIN, *Artur (Arthur)* (Born Lodz 1887; died Geneva 1982)

Polish-born pianist (American citizen 1946), Rubinstein studied in Berlin under **Max Bruch** among others, after establishing himself as a young prodigy. He made his London début in 1912, accompanying the great Spanish cellist **Casals**, and remained in London during the First World War. His long career (he was still playing in his eighties) was characterised by an increasing self-discipline. He made many recordings, notably of Spanish music and of the complete works of **Chopin**, which he interpreted with brilliance and sensitivity. Hon. KBE 1977.

'RULE, BRITANNIA'

Written by **Thomas Arne**, to words by the poet James Thomson, and originally part of the masque

Alfred (1740). The melody has since been used by many composers, including **Handel**, **Beethoven** and **Wagner**. One of the highlights of the Last Night of the **Proms**.

*R*USSIAN RONDO————————————

The catchy last movement of a flute concerto in E minor, by the Italian composer Saverio Mercadante (1795–1870) who was mainly famous for his sixty **operas**. It was the signature tune for several years of **BBC** Radio 4's *Baker's Dozen*.

*R*USTLE OF SPRING (*Frühlingsrauschen*) ————

The third of Six Pieces for Piano by the Norwegian composer Christian Sinding (1856–1941), written 1896. Always a popular concert and parlour piece, this restless and evocative work has been rearranged many times.

*R*UTTER, *John* (Born London 1945) ————————

English composer and conductor, Rutter studied at Cambridge, becoming director of music at Clare College. He now has his own choir, the Cambridge Singers. Best known for his works for children and for church music. Christmas would be incomplete today without **carols** written or arranged by John Rutter.

S

*S*ADLER'S WELLS ————————————

On the site of a pleasure garden with music rooms, the present theatre was opened in 1931. The first resident companies were the Vic-Wells Opera (becoming Sadler's Wells Opera and, following a move to the Coliseum in 1968, **English National Opera**), and the Sadler's Wells Ballet (now based in **Birmingham**). The theatre was reopened after the war with the première of **Britten**'s *Peter Grimes*, inaugurating a new era in British **opera**. Nowadays, Sadler's Wells hosts visits by opera and dance companies from Britain and abroad.

Polish-born pianist Artur Rubinstein, who continued to delight the world in his late eighties.

*S*T JOHN'S COLLEGE CHOIR ————————

One of the finest college choirs at Cambridge. It enjoyed a flourishing period under the direction of George Guest which continues under the present Director of Music, Christopher Robinson.

*S*AINT LOUIS SYMPHONY ORCHESTRA ————

The second-oldest orchestra in the USA, dating back to the 1880s and based in St Louis, Missouri. Principal conductors have included Vladimir Golschmann, Georg Semkov and, until 1989, Leonard Slatkin.

*S*AINT-SAËNS, *Camille* (Born Paris 1835; died Algiers 1921)————————————

Saint-Saëns was taught **piano** by his great-aunt, composed his first piece when he was three, and gave his first public performance aged ten, playing **Mozart** and **Beethoven** piano concertos. Studied

Sir Malcolm Sargent in his element at the Last Night of the Proms, 1966, the year before he died.

piano, **organ** and composition at the Paris Conservatoire, then took various posts as a professional organist, an instrument he loved (one of his best-known pieces is his Third Symphony, in fact a great organ **concerto**), and **Liszt** called him 'the world's greatest organist'. Saint-Saëns introduced French audiences to modern German and forgotten **Baroque** music, and founded the Société Nationale de Musique specifically to encourage native composers such as **Franck** and his own pupil **Fauré**, although later he became disenchanted with music's new directions, disliking **Debussy** and positively horrified by the notorious first performance of **Stravinsky**'s *The Rite of Spring* in 1913. He travelled widely, in Russia, Africa, and to England, where he played before Queen Victoria, and where he was greatly admired (the Philharmonic Society commissioned the Third Symphony, and he wrote his **oratorio** *The Promised Land* for the 1913 Gloucester Festival). Remembered for his opera *Samson and Delilah* and his dazzling concertos, his most popular works remain the witty and irreverent *Carnival of the Animals*, which he himself thought frivolous, and would not allow to be performed in public in his lifetime, and *Danse macabre*.

SALIERI, *Antonio* (Born Legnago 1750; died Vienna 1825)

Son of a wealthy merchant, Salieri learned **violin** and **harpsichord** as a child in Italy before moving to **Vienna** in 1766, where he began to compose **operas**. A protégé and close friend of **Gluck**, he became court composer and conductor, and was so influential that he was known as Vienna's 'musical pope'. He was a prolific if rather conservative composer, and as a teacher he earned the affection and respect of **Beethoven**, **Schubert** and **Liszt**. Salieri seems fated to remain the diabolical figure of myth (as in the film *Amadeus*) who thwarted and finally poisoned the young genius **Mozart**. In fact, he did neither, though his success certainly made it difficult for Mozart to achieve the official recognition he sought.

SANKEY AND MOODY

Ira David Sankey (1840–1908), an evangelical singer and composer, collaborated with the preacher Dwight L. Moody (1837–99) to compile collections of hymns (including *Sacred Songs and Solos*, 1873) used in their revivalist meetings in the USA and Britain.

SARASATE, *Pablo De* (Born Pamplona 1844; died Biarritz 1908)

Spanish virtuoso violinist and composer. A child prodigy, he gave numerous concerts in Europe and the Americas from 1859, visiting London in 1861 and 1874, and impressing his audiences with a formidable technique and ability to produce an extraordinarily sweet tone. **Bruch**, **Saint-Saëns**, **Dvořák** and **Lalo** all wrote works for him. As a composer, he is best known for his transcriptions for **violin** of Spanish dances and the dazzling *Carmen Fantasy* based on **Bizet**'s opera.

SARGENT, *Sir Malcolm* (Born Ashford 1895; died London 1967)

Sargent grew up in Lincolnshire, where he learned **piano** and **organ**. His conducting of his own *Impression on a Windy Day* at the **Proms** won the admiration of **Sir Henry Wood**, and in 1924 he settled in London to teach at the **Royal College of Music**. During the 1939–45 war, Sargent became famous for his morale-boosting concerts with the **Hallé** and **London Philharmonic**. Chief conductor with the Liverpool Philharmonic and then the BBC

Symphony Orchestra, he was idolised at the Proms from 1948 until his death. As well as being a great populariser of music, Sargent is remembered for his work with the Royal and the **Huddersfield** Choral Societies: **Beecham** called him 'the greatest choirmaster we have produced'. Knighted 1947.

SAXOPHONE

Patented in 1846 by the Belgian inventor Adolphe Sax, with a mouthpiece similar to a **clarinet**'s and keys like a **flute**, the saxophone comes in seven sizes, from contrabass to sopranino. **Bizet** was one of the first to use the instrument (in his *L'Arlésienne*), since when it has often found a place in the **orchestra**, and it is, of course, a mainstay of **jazz**.

SCALA, LA (Teatro alla Scala)

Italy's most important **opera** house, opened in Milan in 1778. La Scala has premiered some of the most famous Italian operas, but its golden age was under the masterful direction of **Toscanini** (off and on between 1898 and 1929), who widened the scope of the house to include operas by **Wagner** and **Richard Strauss** as well as French and Russian works.

SCARLATTI, *Alessandro* (Born Palermo 1660; died Naples 1725) and *Domenico* (Born Naples 1685; died Madrid 1757)

Little is known of Alessandro's childhood; he moved to Rome at the age of twelve, where he was to enjoy the patronage of Queen Christina of Sweden, writing many **operas** and **oratorios**. He left Rome for Naples to work for the Spanish Viceroy in 1684 and, apart from an abortive attempt to secure the patronage of the powerful Medici court in Florence and a short period back in Rome, remained in Naples for the rest of his life. His surviving output consists of around 70 operas and over 600 **cantatas**, as well as oratorios and instrumental works. Taught by his father, Domenico was sent to study in Venice in 1705. He proceeded to Rome, where he met **Corelli** and the young **Handel**, and in 1714 he was employed by the Portugese ambassador to the Vatican. He soon took the opportunity to escape Alessandro's domineering interference by moving to Lisbon, and thence to Madrid, where he was court composer. Domenico is best known for his 500-odd innovative **sonatas** for the **harpsichord**, which enjoyed great popularity in

Britain thanks to the efforts of his friend Thomas Roseingrave, the English publisher.

'SCENES THAT ARE BRIGHTEST'

Popular song from the **opera** *Maritana* (1845) by the Irish composer **Vincent Wallace**, to words by Edward Fitzball. *Maritana* was one of the three operas of 'The English Ring', the others being *The Bohemian Girl* (**Balfe**) and *The Lily of Killarney* (**Benedict**).

SCHERZO

Italian for 'joke', the term was first applied to light-hearted **madrigals**, but in the **classical** period was used to describe a light, brisk inner movement in **symphonies** and **chamber music** (replacing the normal Minuet), and usually with a contrasting middle section (the 'Trio'). **Beethoven** established it as an integral part of the symphony – seven of his symphonies have a Scherzo. **Mendelssohn** used the form to depict the fairy-world in *A Midsummer Night's Dream*, but later composers have generally been attracted by its potential for the grotesque and bitter, notably **Mahler** and **Shostakovich**.

SCHERZO (Litolff)

Henry Litolff's *Concerto symphonique* No. 4 (1852), the fourth of his five piano concertos, was admired by **Liszt** but is now neglected, except for its famous Scherzo which remains a popular 'lollipop'.

SCHIFF, *András* (Born Budapest 1953)

Hungarian pianist, studied in Budapest, then in Britain with **George Malcolm**. After winning prizes in the mid-1970s at the Moscow **Tchaikovsky** and **Leeds** Piano Competitions, he is now one of the world's leading interpreters of **Bach** on **piano**, and a fine **lieder** accompanist.

SCHIPA, *Tito* (Born Lecce 1888; died New York 1965)

Italian **tenor**, studied in Lecce and Milan. Début at **La Scala** in 1915. From 1919 he was one of the top tenors appearing in the USA, and continued to perform in Italy well into the 1950s. Schipa specialised in lyrical roles – he created the role of Ruggero in **Puccini**'s *La Rondine* and was a famous Alfredo in **Verdi**'s *La Traviata*.

SCHUBERT

Franz SCHUBERT

1797	Born in Vienna
1815	Composed nearly 150 songs, including 'The Erlking'
1817	Met singer Michael Vogl
1819	'Trout' Quintet composed
1822	Called on Beethoven; composed 'Unfinished' Symphony
1823	*Rosamunde* produced
1825	Probably composed Symphony No. 9 (the 'Great' C major)
1827	Composed *Winter Journey*; visited dying Beethoven
1828	Composed String Quintet in C major
1828	Died in Vienna

*T*o me as to countless others, Schubert is the most sympathetic of composers. Apart from his creative genius he possessed a rare gift for friendship, and in his short life one convivial occasion after another provided relief from hours of lonely hard work.

Franz Schubert was the son of a parish schoolmaster in **Vienna**. At the age of eleven he won a choral scholarship to the Imperial choir school; one of the adjudicators was **Antonio Salieri**, who instructed the boy in composition for four years. Almost more important, Schubert won the friendship of a richer student nine years his senior, Josef von Spaun, who provided him with a copious supply of manuscript paper when funds ran short.

In 1814 Franz took up a teaching appointment at his father's school. He hated the work but there was the consolation of music in his spare time. He played **viola** in a family **quartet**, composed a **Mass** which impressed Salieri, and was drawn into a circle of young Bohemians where musical evenings quickly became known as Schubertiads. Spaun was perhaps the most conformist of the friends; among the rest were Franz von Schober, and the poet Johann Mayrhofer whose verses inspired forty-seven of Schubert's songs. In 1815 Schubert produced a total of almost 150 **songs**, including the famous 'Erlking' to words by Goethe.

Franz escaped from his teaching job in 1815 and for the rest of his life survived as a freelance musician, sustained by friends such as Schober. When he was twenty, the composer met the **baritone** Michael Vogl. He was nearly thirty years older than Schubert but the two became close companions and Vogl was the first singer to introduce his friend's songs to the public. In the summer of 1819 Schubert went off with Vogl on a summer tour of Upper Austria where Schubert was inspired to write the 'Trout' Quintet. On his return to Vienna, Schubert's hopes were concentrated on operatic success and in June 1820 his **operetta** *The Twin Brothers* was enthusiastically received but only for six performances.

Two major works of 1822 were the Symphony in B minor (the 'Unfinished'), which was not performed until 1865, and the 'Wanderer' **Fantasia** for **piano**. That year Schubert made contact with **Beethoven**, whom he revered. According to one account Beethoven was out when Schubert called so he left his compositions with a servant. It was only on his deathbed that Beethoven read through more of Schubert's music and realised its greatness: 'Truly this Schubert has the divine fire,' he said. At that moment Schubert was ushered into the presence of the dying giant; he was a torch-bearer at Beethoven's funeral (March 1827).

During 1823 Schubert suffered a first bout of severe illness, the treatment for which resulted in the loss of all his hair. It seems probable he was suffering from venereal disease. A summer holiday with Vogl improved his health but this was a year of disappointment. Schubert's hopes for a theatrical success were dashed when the play *Rosamunde* flopped in December, though the composer's incidental music was praised.

Schubert (in the glasses) and the singer Johann Michael Vogl perform at the piano during a 'Schubertiad'.

1825 brought the realisation that his music was becoming well known outside Vienna. The Ninth Symphony in C major may have been composed at this time. Prospects for a permanent appointment came and went, but in 1826 the composer was elected a member of the Philharmonic Society, who voted him 100 florins as a testimonial.

More important publishers began to show an interest in Schubert's works, but in 1827 Schubert composed a bleak sequence of twenty-four songs, *Winter Journey*, and his circle of friends began to break up.

In his last year Schubert produced a number of major works, including the String Quintet in C major and a final series of songs. But his health was getting worse. After a final walking holiday in October, he took to his bed, unable to eat or drink. He wrote to Schober, spoke of completing his latest opera and corrected the proofs of *Winter Journey*. On 19 November he died, according to his doctor of typhoid fever. He was buried near Beethoven in the Währing cemetery and words by his poet friend Franz Grillparzer were inscribed on his grave: 'Music has entombed here a rich treasure, but still fairer hopes'.

Favourite works

SYMPHONIES No. 8 in B minor (the 'Unfinished'); No. 9 (the 'Great' C major); No. 5 in B flat.

SONGS 'Ave Maria'; 'Death and the Maiden'; 'The Erlking'; 'Hark, Hark the Lark'; 'Shepherd on the Rock'; 'To Music'; 'To Sylvia'; 'The Trout'; 'The Wanderer'.

PIANO MUSIC Eight Impromptus, especially Impromptu in G flat; *Moments musicaux*, especially the one in F minor; Fantasy in F minor (duet).

OTHER MUSIC Overture, entractes and incidental music from *Rosamunde*; Trio in B flat; Trio in E flat; String Quintet in C major; Quintet in A major ('The Trout').

SCHMIDT, *Josef* (Born Bavideni 1904; died Zürich 1942)

Romanian **tenor** who studied in **Vienna**, and whose diminutive stature (he was less than five feet tall) debarred him from a stage career. However, his concerts, radio recitals and recordings won him international acclaim, not least in Germany. As a Jew, however, he had to flee the Nazis and settle in Switzerland, where he died in an internment camp.

SCHNABEL, *Artur* (Born Lipnik 1882; died Axenstein 1951)

Austrian pianist, who made his début aged eight. Schnabel was one of the greatest **Beethoven** interpreters: for the Beethoven centenary in 1927 he played all thirty-two **sonatas** in concerts in Berlin, later making recordings of the complete sonatas and **concertos**. Schnabel especially loved the late sonatas – music, in his words, 'better than it could be played' – and was also a champion of **Schubert**'s sonatas, then largely neglected. In 1933, he had to flee Nazi persecution, and after the war he lived in Switzerland. His own works include **symphonies**, string **quartets** and a **piano** concerto.

SCHOENBERG, *Arnold* (Born Vienna 1874; died Los Angeles 1951)

Austrian-born composer, whose influential abandonment of the established key-system changed the course of twentieth-century music. Of his many pieces, among the best known are his early string sextet *Verklärte Nacht* (*Transfigured Night*) and the huge and demanding (unfinished) **opera** *Moses and Aaron.*

SCHRAMMEL QUARTET

A group consisting typically of two **violins**, accordion and **guitar**, playing a repertory of light Viennese music and songs. The original Schrammel Quartet was formed by the brothers Johann and Joseph Schrammel in the late 1870s, at first with a **clarinet** instead of an accordion.

SCHREIER, *Peter* (Born Meissen 1935)

German **tenor**, made his début in *Fidelio* at the Berlin State Opera in 1961. Renowned for his interpretations of **lieder**, his singing in the **Bach** *Passions*, and for **Mozart**.

SCHUMANN, *Elisabeth* (Born Merseburg 1888; died New York 1952)

German **soprano**, who made her début in Hamburg 1909, joining the **Vienna** State Opera ten years later. Schumann is associated with the music of **Richard Strauss**; she was a famous Sophie (*Der Rosenkavalier*), and in 1921 toured the USA with the composer, singing his songs. Following the Nazi annexation of Austria, Schumann settled in the USA to escape persecution. She was a **lieder** singer of great distinction, and her charm in **Mozart** roles and as Adèle in *Die Fledermaus* made her a favourite with audiences throughout her long career.

SCHUMANN, *Robert* (Born Zwickau 1810; died Endenich 1856)

Schumann entered Leipzig University in 1828 as a somewhat unwilling law student, not attending lectures but spending his time drinking and composing songs and **piano** works in imitation of his great idols **Schubert** and **Beethoven**. Eventually, he was allowed to study music, but his life was plagued by disaster: his career as a pianist was hampered by troubles with his fingers, caused in part by using a mechanical stretching device and also due to mercury poisoning from a syphilis cure, and in 1833 he suffered his first bout of a recurring mental illness. However, he founded an influential music periodical, which he edited for ten years, and composed a great deal of splendid music. His greatest happiness derived from his love for Clara Wieck, the daughter of his piano teacher and herself a brilliant pianist, whom he married in 1840; she was to provide continuing musical, financial and emotional support. Apart from composing, Schumann pursued an unsuccessful career as a conductor; in 1854 he fell seriously ill and threw himself into the Rhine, only to be rescued by fishermen. He was taken to a private asylum near Bonn, where he remained until his death. Despite a tempestuous life, Schumann's music is often gentle and highly lyrical; he is remembered for his four **symphonies**, his brooding **song cycles** and perhaps above all for his sensuous and reflective piano music.

SCHWARZKOPF, *Elisabeth* (Born Jarotschin 1915)

German **soprano**. Following her first solo recital in 1942, she was invited by **Karl Böhm** to join the

Vienna State Opera, and made regular appearances after the war at **Covent Garden**, **La Scala**, San Francisco and Salzburg. On stage, she was a renowned interpreter of **Mozart** and **Strauss** as well as **Wagner** and **Puccini**, and her performances of **Wolf** and Strauss **lieder** were almost without parallel. She was married to Walter Legge, who masterminded her recording career. DBE 1992.

SCOTTISH OPERA

Founded by **Sir Alexander Gibson** in 1962, and since 1975 based at Glasgow's Theatre Royal; from there it tours Scotland and northern England. Its celebrated 1971 *Ring* cycle was the first outside London for forty years.

SCOTTO, *Renata* (Born Savona 1934)

Italian **soprano** who studied in Milan and joined **La Scala** in 1953, winning international acclaim when she stood in for **Callas** at the 1957 Edinburgh Festival. Her dramatic power is especially well suited to **Puccini**'s vulnerable heroines.

SEA FEVER

John Ireland's celebrated 1913 setting for voice and **piano** of John Masefield's poem, with the first line 'I must down to the seas again'.

SEGOVIA, *Andrés* (Born Linares 1893; died Madrid 1987)

Segovia taught himself the **guitar**, and by the age of fifteen he was giving recitals in Granada, followed by concerts in Barcelona and Madrid, and a tour of South America in 1916. More than anyone else, Segovia led the revival of interest in the classical guitar: his lack of formal teaching had enabled him to develop his own virtuoso technique and, as well as composing his own pieces, he widened the repertory for guitar (which had largely consisted of popular Spanish music) by making arrangements of **lute** music and other well-known pieces by composers such as **Bach**, **Handel**, **Mozart** and even **Chopin**. Moreover, he inspired contemporary composers to write for him, including **Villa-Lobos**, **Falla** (*Homage for the Tomb of Debussy*, 1920) and **Rodrigo**, whose *Fantasia for a Gentleman* he premiered in 1954. As a teacher in Spain and at Berkeley in California, Segovia was a source of encouragement and inspiration to many young guitarists, including **John Williams**, and his unceasing energy enabled him to give recitals and master classes well into his eighties.

SERAFIN, *Tullio* (Born Rottanova di Cavarzere 1878; died Rome 1968)

Italian conductor, began his **conducting** career in 1898. In 1902 he became assistant to **Toscanini** at **La Scala**, where he worked more or less continuously until 1918, introducing works by **Humperdinck**, **Rimsky-Korsakov** and **Strauss**. From 1924 he worked for ten years at the **Metropolitan**, giving the first US performances of *Turandot* as well as **operas** by **Moussorgsky** and **Falla**. He encouraged some of this century's finest singers, including **Gigli**, **Rosa Ponselle**, **Joan Sutherland** and especially **Maria Callas**, and was largely responsible for the revival of the *bel canto* repertoire.

SERENADE

From the Italian for 'calm', a song of love or greeting usually sung in the evening, often to a **guitar**. There are many serenades in **opera** (e.g. *Don Giovanni*, *The Barber of Seville*), and in the **classical** period there was a fashion for instrumental serenades, including **Mozart**'s *Eine Kleine Nachtmusik*. Twentieth-century examples include **Vaughan Williams**'s *Serenade to Music* and **Britten**'s *Serenade for Tenor, Horn and Strings*.

SERENADE (Drigo)

Famous **serenade** from the **ballet** *Les Millions d'Arlequin* (1900) by the Italian composer Riccardo Drigo (1846–1930), existing in many arrangements, and a favourite of light-music concerts.

'SERENATA' (Toselli)

Song, written 1900, by the Italian composer Enrico Toselli (1846–1916) to verses by Alfredo Silvestri. Its fame was partly due to Toselli's 'scandalous' marriage to the Archduchess Louise of Austria-Tuscany in 1907.

SERKIN, *Rudolph* (Born Eger 1903)

Austrian-born pianist (American citizen 1939). Best known for his **chamber music** performances with the violinist Adolf Busch, and his unsentimental interpretations of **Bach** (often accompanied by his own grunting and singing).

SHAKESPEARE AND MUSIC

Shakespeare's works have exerted a huge influence on composers, who have set his **songs**, turned his plays into **operas**, or used them as the basis for incidental and **film music**, **symphonies** and **overtures**. Among the host of song-setters, **Schubert** is perhaps the greatest, especially for 'Who is Sylvia?' (from *The Two Gentlemen of Verona*). Of those who wrote operas based on the plays, the best known include **Rossini** (*Otello*, 1816), **Wagner** (*Das Liebesverbot*, 1836, from *Measure for Measure*), **Berlioz** (*Béatrice et Bénédict*, 1862, from *Much Ado*), **Britten** (*A Midsummer Night's Dream*, 1960) and above all **Verdi**, who composed *Macbeth* (1847), and crowned his career with the two great masterpieces, *Otello* and *Falstaff* (1887 and 1893). Berlioz, who worshipped Shakespeare, wrote a symphony based around *Romeo and Juliet* (1839). He was followed by **Liszt** (*Hamlet*, 1858) and **Elgar** (*Falstaff*, 1913), while **Tchaikovsky** also wrote fantasy overtures for *Romeo and Juliet* and *Hamlet* (1869 and 1888). Shakespearean incidental music includes **Mendelssohn**'s magical *A Midsummer Night's Dream* and **Walton**'s famous scores for the Olivier films *Henry V* (1944), *Hamlet* (1947) and *Richard III* (1954). **Prokofiev**'s *Romeo and Juliet* (1936) is perhaps the best-known Shakespearean ballet. The fascination of Shakespeare for musicians shows little sign of abating.

SHANKAR, *Ravi* (Born Varanasi, Uttar Pradesh, 1920)

Indian **sitar** player and composer, largely responsible for popularising Indian music in the West, partly in association with **Yehudi Menuhin** and George Harrison. Compositions include the **film score** for *Ghandi*, 1983.

SHANTY

Sailors' work song, to accompany and facilitate hard labour on sailing ships, the shanty-man singing the verse, and the sailors participating in the chorus.

SHARP, *Cecil* (Born London 1859; died London 1924)

Collector and editor of English **folk music**, who began his huge survey of folk-dances, songs, **carols** and **shanties** in 1899, and profoundly influenced the work of composers such as **Vaughan Williams**, **Holst** and **Percy Grainger**.

SHELLEY, *Howard* (Born London 1950)

English pianist, studied at the **Royal College of Music**, making his début in London 1971. Also known for **piano** duets with his wife Hilary Macnamara, and for **chamber music**.

SHIRLEY-QUIRK, *John* (Born Liverpool 1931))

Leading British **baritone**. In the 1960s and 1970s worked in the English Opera Group with **Britten**, creating roles in *Owen Wingrave* and *Death in Venice*. Noted song, **lieder** and **oratorio** performer.

SHOSTAKOVICH, *Dmitri* (Born St Petersburg 1906; died Moscow 1975)

Shostakovich's early career was characterised by the air of optimism that followed the Bolshevik Revolution – his first precocious **symphony** (a graduation piece for the Petrograd Conservatory) was followed by two others celebrating workers' struggles. His 1934 **opera** *Lady Macbeth of the Mtsensk District* was an immediate success, but *Pravda* attacked the work's modernism in an article entitled 'Chaos instead of Music', marking the beginning of Shostakovich's troubled and ambiguous relationship with the Soviet authorities. He responded by writing his Fifth Symphony ('the creative reply of a Soviet artist to justified criticism'), which has remained his most popular work. During the war Shostakovich recorded the suffering and heroism of the long and brutal siege of Leningrad in his Seventh Symphony, but after the war he once again fell foul of the authorities, who accused him of creating an 'anti-people art'; once again he seemed to toe the party line, withholding his more complex music. In the thaw following Stalin's death, however, Shostakovich was recognised as the Soviet Union's finest composer, and in 1962 his once reviled *Lady Macbeth* was revived to great critical acclaim. Shostakovich's prolific output encompassed grand public works but also many pieces expressing searchingly private emotions, including his fifteen String Quartets and the enigmatic Fourteenth Symphony (dedicated to his friend **Britten**).

*S*HUMSKY, *Oscar* (Born Philadelphia 1917) _____

Perhaps the leading American violinist of his generation, Shumsky gave his first concert at the age of eight with the **Philadelphia Orchestra** under **Stokowski**. In 1938 he joined **Toscanini**'s NBC Symphony Orchestra, and soon became familiar as a virtuoso soloist and leader of the Primrose String Quartet. Shumsky was also a conductor, and the Musical Director of the Stratford Festival, Ontario, between 1959 and 1967.

*S*IBELIUS, *Jean* (Born Hämeenlinna 1865; died Järvenpää 1957) _____

Born into a Swedish-speaking family in a small town in southern Finland (then part of the Russian Empire), Sibelius learned the **violin** and **piano** as a child, composing his first piece when he was ten. He became familiar in his teens with the national legends that were to provide so much of his inspiration; his dedication to a national culture was consolidated by his travels, particularly to the Karelia region, which inspired the **suite** of the same name. By 1899, with his First Symphony and the tone poem *Finlandia*, Sibelius had established himself as the country's leading composer, and had been awarded a small state pension. Fame at home was followed by increasing acclaim abroad, especially in Britain and America: **Henry Wood** introduced his work during the 1901 **Prom** season, and Sibelius himself visited England five times before the First World War. He composed the last four of his seven **symphonies** (an eighth was destroyed) at a villa in the countryside near Helsinki, and there he lived for the rest of his long life, although his composing career stopped in the mid-1920s. Each of his symphonies has its own character, and they remain among the best loved orchestral works for their distinctive and atmospheric sound, evoking the austere northern landscape and, in Sibelius's words, 'pure spring water'.

*S*IDE DRUM _____

Also known as the snare drum, a small **drum** with strings or snares (made of gut, plastic or metal) stretched across the bottom end, which makes an incisive rattling when the drum is hit (the snare can be released). Played with two sticks, usually giving rolls.

*S*ILLS, *Beverly* (Born Brooklyn, New York, 1929) __

American **soprano** whose international operatic career includes the **coloratura** roles of **Donizetti** and **Bellini**. From 1955 a star of New York City Opera, of which she was a distinguished director 1979–88.

*S*INOPOLI, *Giuseppe* (Born Venice 1946) _____

Italian conductor, initially closely involved with contemporary music. He began conducting **opera** in the mid-1970s in Venice, then in Berlin, Hamburg and **Vienna**. Principal conductor of the **Philharmonia** from 1984, and since 1990 of the West Berlin Opera.

*S*ITAR _____

Indian **lute** consisting of a long, broad and fretted neck attached to a body often made from a dried gourd, with three sets of strings: four principal strings for the melody, two or three drone strings, and nine to thirteen strings to increase resonance. A major instrument in classical Indian music, popularised in the West by **Ravi Shankar** in the 1950s and 1960s.

*S*IX, LES _____

Name coined in 1920 by the critic Henri Collet for the group of young French composers inspired by the anti-**romantic** ideas of Cocteau and the music of Satie. The 'members' were Auric, Durey, Honegger, Milhaud, **Poulenc** and Germaine Tailleferre, although their paths diverged considerably.

*S*METANA, *Bedřich* (Born Litomyšl 1824; died Prague 1884) _____

Smetana was taught **piano** by his father, and attended school in Prague (where in 1840 he saw **Liszt** perform) and Plzeň, after which he continued to study composition and compose. His plans for a career first as a concert pianist and then as director of his own music institute met with little success, and so in 1856 he left Bohemia for Göteborg in Sweden, where he opened a music school, organised **chamber** and **choral** concerts at which he introduced audiences to contemporary music, and continued to

Sir Georg Solti: compelling Hungarian-born maestro of almost unrivalled world stature.

compose, producing in 1858 his Lisztian symphonic poem *Richard III*. Although from a German-speaking family, Smetana was an ardent nationalist and in 1861, despite his eminence in Sweden, he returned home. In 1866, following the success of his first two **operas** (one was *The Bartered Bride*, still regarded as *the* great Czech comic opera), he was appointed principal conductor of the Provisional Theatre, where he encouraged new Czech works, finding time to compose the great symphonic cycle *Má Vlast* (*My Fatherland*), inspired by Czech legend and landscape. Increasingly stricken by syphilis from 1874, resulting in deafness, Smetana's life ended wretchedly some ten years later in a Prague lunatic asylum, although the crowds at his funeral bore witness to his importance as one of the founders of modern Czech music.

*S*ÖDERSTRÖM, *Elisabeth* (Born Stockholm 1927)

Swedish **soprano**, studied at Royal Academy of Music and Opera School (Stockholm), joining Swedish Royal Opera in 1950. Her large repertory includes **Monteverdi**, **Mozart**, **Strauss** and **Janáček**. A great favourite at **Glyndebourne**.

*S*OLEMN MELODY

Popular piece for **organ** and strings by the Welsh composer and organist **Walford Davies**, written in 1908, and often heard in an arrangement for solo organ.

*S*OLOMON (*Cutner*) (Born London 1902; died London 1988)

Great English pianist, known by his first name only, who made a precocious début, aged eight, in London's Queen's Hall, playing **Tchaikovsky**'s First Concerto. Renowned for his sensitive and unmannered playing. Premiered the Piano Concerto of **Arthur Bliss**, 1939.

*S*OLTI, *Georg* (Born Budapest 1912)

Born into a Hungarian Jewish family, Solti studied piano and composition at the **Liszt** Academy in Budapest under Hungary's most distinguished musicians, **Bartók**, **Dohnányi** and **Kodály**. His long career in **opera** began when he was employed as a repetiteur (teaching the singers their parts) with the Budapest Opera. In 1936 and 1937 he worked with **Toscanini** at Salzburg, making his **conducting** début the following year in Budapest with *The Marriage of Figaro*. As war and the Nazi threat loomed, Solti left for Switzerland in 1939; after the war he became Musical Director of the Bavarian State Opera (1946–52), and then in 1952 of opera and concerts in Frankfurt. Solti's long association with Britain began with the **London Philharmonic** in 1949; between 1961 and 1971 he was an outstanding Music Director of **Covent Garden**, going some way to realise his avowed intention of making it 'the best opera house in the world'. Solti has made many remarkable recordings, exploiting new stereo techniques with the first complete *Ring* cycle (1966), and including much of the great operatic repertoire as well as masterful accounts of **Beethoven** and **Mahler symphonies**. Awarded a knighthood in 1971, he became a British citizen in 1972. The great affection with which Solti is held in Britain was confirmed when he conducted **Verdi**'s *Otello* in a gala celebration of his eightieth birthday at Covent Garden.

SONATA

'Sonata' simply means played, or sounded (as opposed to the sung **cantata**). The term was first used around 1600, although the form was first popularised later in the century by **Corelli**, who composed over sixty suites of movements for instrumental ensembles, which he divided into two types: the *sonata da chiesa* (church sonata), alternating slow and fast movements of a dignified nature, and the *sonata da camera* (chamber sonata), a suite of dances. Both kinds were led by the **violin** with a **continuo** accompaniment consisting of **harpsichord** and often **cello** and **bassoon**. The sonata really came into its own in the **classical** period, when **sonata form** became the archetypal structuring device for instrumental compositions. Best known from this time are the sonatas for keyboard, or solo instrument with keyboard accompaniment, of **Clementi**, **Haydn** and **Mozart**, usually consisting of three movements (fast, slow, fast). With **Beethoven**'s thirty-two **piano** sonatas the formal constraints of the classical sonata were stretched to their limits, with works like the 'Moonlight' and 'Hammerklavier' expressing a new emotional intensity. After **Schubert**, the sonata lost favour with **Romantic** composers who wanted more flexible forms, although both **Chopin** and **Liszt** wrote great virtuoso piano sonatas. The sonata has since been revived by many composers consciously imitating classical forms, notably in France (**Fauré**, **Debussy** and **Ravel**) and Russia (**Prokofiev** and **Shostakovich**), but many twentieth-century examples are sonatas in name only.

SONATA FORM

Developed in the late eighteenth century, and most often used for the first movements of **symphonies**, **chamber** works and **sonatas**, 'sonata form' consists of three sections: (1) Exposition, stating the main theme in the tonic key (first subject), with a second subject in a related, contrasting key; (2) Development, playing around with the thematic material, modulating between keys to lead to (3) the Recapitulation, which repeats both first and second subjects in the tonic key, often concluding with a **coda**.

SONDHEIM, *Stephen* (Born New York 1920)

With early encouragement from Oscar Hammerstein II, a family friend, Sondheim was already writing prize-winning **musicals** while a student, and after further study at Princeton University he was approached to write the lyrics for **Bernstein**'s *West Side Story* (1957). His contribution to this great musical was widely admired, and he worked as a lyricist with composers Jule Styne and **Richard Rodgers** before achieving his first solo success with *A Funny Thing Happened on the Way to the Forum* in 1962 (featuring the song 'Comedy Tonight'), which went on to win a Tony award. Since then, Sondheim has written a succession of musicals renowned for their innovative subject matter and sophisticated music and lyrics, including *Follies* (1971), *Sweeney Todd* (1979) and *Assassins* (1990). His best-known works have drawn on a mixture of sources: *A Little Night Music* (1973, with the song 'Send in the Clowns') is based on the Bergman film *Smiles of a Summer Night*; *Pacific Overtures* (1976) incorporates elements of traditional Japanese theatre; and *Into the Woods* (1987) derives from Grimm fairy tales. In 1975, the musical *Side by Side by Sondheim* was assembled to celebrate his achievements.

SONG, SONG CYCLE

As far as we know, all cultures have used song, with some of the earliest extant examples to be found in the Bible and in Ancient Greek texts, though little is known of how they were performed. With the development of musical notation in the Middle Ages, songs became more widely transmitted thanks partly to groups of travelling **troubadours**, and from varying courtly, religious and folk traditions emerged **polyphonic** songs and **motets**. By the late sixteenth and early seventeenth centuries, with the rise of the amateur musician and printing, the modern song appeared in the form of **madrigals** (by **Monteverdi** and **Byrd**, for example). Great English successors to Byrd included Henry Lawes (who set poems by Milton and Herrick) and **Purcell**. By the eighteenth century song-writing had become a sizeable leisure industry, with composers like William Boyce and **Thomas Arne** writing for the pleasure gardens, drawing-rooms and the stage. The **Romantic** era was dominated by the German **lied**, but across Europe composers looked to the great poets for a more elevated and emotionally sophisticated kind of lyric: in France, particularly, the songs of **Berlioz** and the *mélodies* of **Fauré** and **Debussy** expressed a new kind of sensitivity to the setting of texts. At the same time, the new interest in folk culture inspired composers as diverse as **Moussorgsky**, **Grieg** and **Vaughan Williams**. Songs written in this century range from the modernist works of Berg and **Schoenberg** to songs from **musicals** and pop songs. A song cycle is a group of songs with a common theme or narrative. Developed in the nineteenth century, famous examples include **Schubert**'s *Winterreise* (1828), **Schumann**'s *Dichterliebe* (1840), **Mahler**'s *Das Lied von der Erde* (1909) and Vaughan Williams's *On Wenlock Edge* (1909).

'SONG OF THE FLEA'

Dramatic setting of Mephistopheles's **song** from Goethe's *Faust*, for voice and **piano**, by **Moussorgsky** (1879); made widely famous by the Russian bass **Feodor Chaliapin**.

'SONGS MY MOTHER TAUGHT ME'

The fourth of **Dvořák**'s *Gipsy Songs* (1880), with words by Heyduk, for **soprano** or **treble** and **piano**. The haunting melody has been arranged in many different ways.

SOPRANO

From the Italian *sopra* (above), the highest female voice (boy sopranos are known as **trebles**, and male sopranos, originally **castrati**, sing **falsetto**). The different kinds of soprano include **coloratura**, lyric, dramatic and soubrette (light or lively), depending on the qualities and role of the voice. Also used to describe high instruments, e.g. soprano **saxophone**.

SOR, *Fernando* (Baptised Barcelona 1778; died Paris 1839)

Spanish composer and guitarist, known as 'the **Beethoven** of the **guitar**'. Following the political turmoil of the Napoleonic invasion, Sor left Spain for Paris and then London, where he lived for several years, achieving great popular success with his songs and works for piano and guitar. Now perhaps best known for his ballet *Cendrillon* (1822 – used for the opening of Moscow's Bolshoi Theatre in 1823), the Fantasies and the Mozart Variations for guitar. His studies form part of the repertory of any serious

guitarist, even today, and his teaching manual *Method for the Guitar* (1830), has long been the standard work.

SORCERER'S APPRENTICE, THE (L'Apprenti sorcier)

Orchestral **scherzo** (1897) by Paul Dukas (1865–1935), based on Goethe's poem describing the apprentice's disastrous attempts at casting spells, vividly portrayed in Disney's *Fantasia* with Mickey Mouse as the hapless novice.

SOUSA, *John Philip* (Born Washington, DC, 1854; died Reading, Penn., 1932)

American composer and bandmaster. After a teenage apprenticeship in the US Marine Band (of which his father was a member), Sousa worked with various theatre **orchestras** until in 1880 he returned to the Marine Band as Director. Formed the legendary Sousa's Band (1892–1931), which gained international popularity through constant touring. Sousa is remembered as the 'March King' for his many rhythmically and melodically catchy patriotic marches, including 'Hands across the Sea' and 'The Stars and Stripes For Ever'.

SOUVENIR

Very popular piece for **violin** and **piano** composed in 1904 by the Czech composer František Drdla.

SOUZAY *Gérard* (Born Angers 1920)

French **baritone**, highly acclaimed for his **song** and **lieder** recitals, specialising in the French repertoire, from **Lully** and **Rameau** to the nineteenth century.

SPINET

Small keyboard member of the **harpsichord** family (similar to a virginal), popular between the late fifteenth and seventeenth centuries, especially with amateur musicians. It has one set of strings, which are plucked, and a range of four octaves.

SPIRITUAL

Religious song developed by the black slaves of the American Deep South, popularised during the evangelical movements of the late nineteenth century and later by singers such as **Paul Robeson**. Often concerning death and release from oppression.

The trumpet – once a signal for battle but in the hands of a master like Louis 'Satchmo' Armstrong, it gives voice to the human soul.

Sir Andrew Lloyd Webber's Requiem *was a tribute to his father. The prodigiously successful composer is seen at the première in St Thomas's Church, New York, 1985.*

STADE, *Frederica von* (Born Somerville, New Jersey, 1945)————————

American **mezzo-soprano**; rose from a humble 1970 **Metropolitan** début as Third Boy in *The Magic Flute* to an international career, specialising in the lyric roles of **Bellini**, **Rossini**, **Mozart** and **Strauss**.

STANFORD, *Charles Villiers* (Born Dublin 1852; died London 1924)————————

Anglo-Irish composer, teacher and conductor. He learned **piano**, **organ** and **violin** as a child, studying in Dublin and at Cambridge, where he became an innovative conductor of the University Music Society. After further studies in Leipzig and Berlin, he was appointed professor of composition at the newly-founded **Royal College of Music** (1883) and also at Cambridge (1887): his many subsequently famous students included **Vaughan Williams**, **Holst**, **Bliss** and **Ireland**. His numerous compositions include the popular 'Songs of the Sea' and 'Songs of the Fleet', and the beautiful part-song 'The Blue Bird'. Knighted 1902.

'THE STAR-SPANGLED BANNER'————————

Since 1931, the official US national **anthem**. The words were written by Francis Scott Key in 1814 (inspired by an incident in the war with Britain), and sung to the tune of John Stafford Smith's 'To Anacreon in Heaven'.

STERN, *Isaac* (Born Kremenets 1920)————————

Russian-born American violinist, made his solo début in 1935. Following the war (during which he regularly played for Allied troops), Stern undertook extensive world tours, winning much praise for his warm and characterful playing of **Beethoven** and **Brahms** in particular, and for his part in a **trio** with pianist **Eugene Istomin** and cellist Leonard Rose. Much involved in education, he also led the campaign in the 1960s to save the **Carnegie Hall**. His many recordings include the 1971 soundtrack for *Fiddler on the Roof*.

STOKOWSKI, *Leopold* (Born London 1882; died Nether Wallop, Hants., 1977)————————

British-born conductor (American from 1915). Stokowski studied with Parry, **Stanford** and **Walford Davies** at the **Royal College of Music**, the

Leopold Stokowski conducting the LSO in a special sixtieth anniversary programme from the Royal Festival Hall, 1972.

youngest student to have been admitted. He made his conducting début in Paris in 1908, on the strength of which he was invited to become the conductor of the Cincinnati Symphony Orchestra. In 1912 he began his long and legendary association with the **Philadelphia Orchestra** which, by dint of his exacting technical and artistic demands, he made into one of the world's finest and most famous orchestras, creating the so-called 'Philadelphia sound'. Stokowski's idiosyncratic and forceful personality soon made him a celebrity: he would often conduct from memory, discarding the baton and addressing the audience directly; he once scolded some women for knitting. He had a passion for contemporary music (despite the protests of audiences and a cautious management), but more than anything he was a great populariser, notably in his 1941 collaboration with Disney on *Fantasia*. More controversially, he often 'touched up' the orchestration of composers from **Bach** to **Puccini**, which led to many a raised eyebrow. From the 1940s, he was associated with many other orchestras in the States, and also the **London Symphony Orchestra**, which he continued to conduct after 1972, when he returned to Britain.

THE STRAUSS FAMILY

Johann Strauss 1 (1804–49)

Johann Strauss 2 (1825–99) – 'The Waltz King'

Josef Strauss (1827–70)

Eduard Strauss (1835–1916)

Strauss is a common name in Germany and Austria – it means 'nosegay' or 'bunch' (of flowers) – but to lovers of light music the world over, it is associated with one family dynasty which came to power in the ballrooms of **Vienna** in the nineteenth century and retains unrivalled popularity to this day.

The capital of the Austrian Empire was already waltz-mad when the Congress of Vienna assembled in the city in 1814–15, and a **quartet** formed by **Josef Lanner** was able to cash in on the craze. The quartet's **viola** player was the young Johann Strauss, three years junior to Lanner, and when Lanner expanded the quartet first into one **orchestra** and then into two, Strauss became his assistant. When he was twenty-one, Strauss set up his own orchestra, and the supposed enmity between the two men (who seem, in fact, to have remained good friends) kept rival factions at each other's throats in fashionable Viennese society until Lanner's death in 1843. **Chopin**, eager to attract attention in Vienna in 1831, complained that 'Lanner, Strauss and their waltzes obscure everything,' while **Richard Wagner** reported that 'the extraordinary playing of Johann Strauss often made the audience almost frantic with delight'.

In the wake of triumphant successes at the Sperl Pleasure Gardens and elsewhere in Vienna, Johann Strauss the Elder toured widely in Europe with his orchestra. He paid two highly successful visits to Britain in 1837 (the year of Queen Victoria's coronation) and 1849. He had the reputation of treating his musicians generously. 'He always rents the most elegant hotels,' wrote one of them; 'In short, Strauss cares for his men just as a fond father cares for his children.'

Unfortunately his own family affairs were less admirable. In the mid-1830s Strauss's wife Anna, who had just given birth to their son Eduard, learned that her husband had admitted paternity of a daughter by his mistress Emilie Trambusch: she bore him a total of seven illegitimate children. Eventually abandoned in favour of Emilie, Anna resolved that her eldest son, Johann, should be well trained to take over the role of family breadwinner, though his father was strongly opposed to him entering the musical profession.

Of the three sons, we know that Johann and his younger brother Josef showed early musical talent, winning praise from their father for their piano-playing. But Johann was also secretly learning the **violin**, which he practised in front of a mirror 'in order to grow accustomed to an elegant bearing', and when he was nineteen applied to the Viennese authorities for permission to form his own orchestra. Very quickly he made his mark. He is, said one critic, 'a waltz incarnate', and before long Vienna was debating the rival merits not of Lanner and Strauss but of Strauss father and son.

The year of revolutions, 1848, found the two Johanns on opposite sides. Johann senior wholeheartedly supported the old régime, writing his most famous piece, the Radetsky March, to celebrate the victories of a repressive Imperial general. Young Johann, however, was on the side of the students and liberals who wanted reform. In September of the following year, Johann senior died of scarlet fever contracted from one of his illegitimate offspring; Johann junior, at the age of twenty-four, found himself in undisputed charge of the Strauss orchestra and all that implied.

With amazing rapidity, his political views underwent a change. Passed over for his father's job as conductor of the music at court, he soon began producing marches and other pieces to recapture the Emperor's favour. It was not withheld for long, though Strauss had to wait until 1863 before the coveted title of Director of the Imperial Court Balls was bestowed on him.

Meanwhile, in the 1850s Johann Strauss junior was in demand on all sides, so much so that he suffered repeated breakdowns in health. A prolonged and total rest cure was prescribed in 1853, and in July that year Johann's younger brother, Josef, was forced to make his début at the Sperl as conductor of the family orchestra.

Josef, at twenty-six, was a brilliant young man. Poet, playwright, architect, artist and pioneering engineer (he designed Vienna's first street-cleaning machine), he seemed destined for success in spheres other than music. But family loyalty was strong and when the call came his musical talents, so far disregarded, proved more than adequate: 'Pepi is the more gifted of us two,' said Johann. The fact is that over the years until Josef's premature death in 1870, the two brothers were perfect foils for each other: Johann with his fiery, extrovert personality, Josef the courtly charmer with his dreams and attractive vein of melancholy. The Viennese loved them both.

Nor were their activities confined to the Imperial capital. Johann in particular was in demand all over the world. From 1856 to 1865 he appeared every summer at the resort of Pavlovsk, not far from St Petersburg, and was back there again in 1869 (with Josef) and 1886. In 1867 Johann conducted a spectacularly successful season of promenade concerts at London's **Covent Garden**, and in 1872 he faced what he regarded as the terrors of transatlantic travel to appear at the World's Peace Jubilee in Boston, USA, where he conducted 20,000 performers (with the help of 100 sub-conductors) in 'The Blue Danube'. After that he couldn't wait to get home again.

The first of Johann's three wives, Jetty, was foremost among those who urged the Waltz-king to try his hand at **operetta**, and from 1871 until the end of his life Strauss devoted much of his time to the theatre. He produced one unquestioned masterpiece in *Die Fledermaus* and many other works for the stage, culminating in the grand **opera** *Ritter Pasman*. Thus preoccupied, Johann deputed the running of the Strauss orchestra to his youngest brother, Eduard, after the sadly premature death of Josef in 1870. Eduard remained responsible for the orchestra until its disbandment in 1901. He was a

Johann Strauss the Younger, 1825–99.

glamorous and popular figure, known as 'handsome Edi' to the Viennese, and achieved particular success as a composer with his quick polkas. He was the father of Johann Strauss III who continued the family traditions well into the twentieth century.

Favourite works

JOHANN STRAUSS 2

(dances) 'The Blue Danube'; 'Tales from the Vienna Woods'; 'Wine, Women and Song'; 'Voices of Spring'; 'Thunder and Lightning Polka' and 'Perpetuum Mobile'.
(operetta) *Die Fledermaus; The Gipsy Baron.*

JOSEF STRAUSS (dances) 'Village Swallows from Austria'; 'Music of the Spheres'; 'The Dragonfly'.

EDUARD STRAUSS (polkas) 'Line Clear'; 'Steam Up'.

STOLZ, *Robert* (Born Graz 1880; died Berlin 1975)

Austrian conductor and composer from a musical family, Stolz studied in **Vienna** and in Berlin with **Humperdinck**, working in various provincial theatres until in 1905 he was appointed chief conductor of the Theater an der Wien, Vienna. In Vienna, he composed popular **operettas**, **lieder** and marches, and, after moving to Berlin in 1924, **film scores** too. An opponent of the Nazis, he left for Paris in the 1930s, and spent the war in Hollywood (where he wrote Oscar-winning scores), afterwards returning to Vienna. His operettas include *Whirled into Happiness* (1921) and *Wild Violets* (1932); he also contributed to the score of White Horse Inn (1930).

STRADIVARIUS

Family of **violin**-makers from Cremona in north Italy, the most famous of whom was Antonio Stradivari (*circa* 1644–1737). He made over a thousand instruments (including some **cellos** and **violas**), whose design and unique tone make them the most sought after (and expensive) to this day.

STRAUS, *Oscar* (Born Vienna 1870; died Bad Ischl 1954)

Austrian composer, studied in **Vienna** and Berlin (with **Max Bruch**), conducting in various theatres in Germany and Austria, before turning his hand to composing **operettas** and cabaret. His first success came with *A Waltz Dream* in 1907, swiftly followed by the work for which he is best remembered, *Der Tapfere Soldat* (*The Chocolate Soldier*, based on Shaw's *Arms and the Man*). Other works include the operettas *The Last Waltz* (1920) and *Three Waltzes* (1935, incorporating music by the two **Johann Strausses**), and the score for the 1950 film *La Ronde*.

STRAUSS, *Richard* (Born Munich 1864; died Garmisch-Partenkirchen, Bavaria, 1949)

Strauss began composing as a child, and by his early twenties was already being likened both to **Wagner** (his great hero) and **Brahms** on the strength of his Violin and Horn Concertos, and his tone poems *Aus Italien* and *Don Juan*. After two attempts at **opera**, and other instrumental works including *Also sprach Zarathustra* (1896) and *Sinfonia Domestica* (1903), he attracted international notoriety in 1905

with *Salome*, based on Oscar Wilde's play: the opera was attacked as blasphemous and obscene, but audiences flocked to see Salome remove her seven veils and hear the bold music, both sensual and violent. He again courted scandal with *Elektra* (1909), taken from Sophocles; it was his first collaboration of many with the skilled librettist Hugo von Hofmannsthal. *Der Rosenkavalier* (1911) proved to be their most enduring success, sumptuously set in eighteenth-century **Vienna**, with a rich score employing the anachronistic waltz. Many of his later operas – including *Ariadne auf Naxos* (1912, revised 1916), *Die Frau ohne Schatten* (1919), *Arabella* (1932) and *Capriccio* (1942) – have also found a regular place in the operatic repertory. Strauss's reputation was badly damaged by his naïve and seemingly compliant attitude to the Nazis, although after the war his mellow late works, including the lyrical Oboe Concerto and the *Four Last Songs* did much to reinstate him in favour around the world.

STRAVINSKY, *Igor* (Born Oranienbaum (now Lomonosov) 1883; died New York 1971)

Stravinsky learned the **piano** as a child, later taking lessons in composition from **Rimsky-Korsakov**. In 1910, he went to Paris with Diaghilev's Ballets Russes, where he met **Debussy** and **Ravel**, and composed two dazzling **ballet** scores, *The Firebird* and *Petrushka*. In May 1913, the company premiered his *The Rite of Spring*. In what was to become a legendary scandal of twentieth-century music, the audience rioted, appalled both at the violent and disjointed rhythms and harmonies and at the portrayal of an ancient Russian pagan ritual (choreographed by Nijinsky): to many others, however, the occasion marked the exciting arrival of modernity. After the First World War, Stravinsky turned to the eighteenth century to provide formal and stylistic models for his compositions (often known as 'neo–**classical**'). His **oratorio** *Oedipus Rex* (1927) drew on **Handel**, although its Latin text (by Cocteau) and frequent dissonance made it coolly modern, while his later opera *The Rake's Progress* (1951), inspired by the famous Hogarth prints and with a sophisticated libretto by W.H. Auden and Chester Kallman, was an updated ***Don Giovanni***. Reversion to the Orthodox Church also influenced his music, notably the 1930 *Symphony of Psalms*. Taking American citizenship in 1945, Stravinsky worked into his eighties and was always keen to experiment.

STREICH, *Rita* (Born Barnaul, Russia, 1920; died Vienna 1987)

German **soprano**, with Berlin State Opera (1946–51) and from 1953 the **Vienna** State Opera, often appearing at **Glyndebourne**, Salzburg and Bayreuth. Acclaimed **coloratura** singer, particularly strong in **Mozart** and **Strauss**.

SUITE

A series of instrumental movements often based on dances, popular in the eighteenth century (e.g. **Handel**'s *Water Music* and **J.S. Bach**'s **Violin** and **Cello** Suites), and revived in the twentieth century by composers such as **Debussy** and **Stravinsky**. Also a rearrangement of numbers taken from theatre works (e.g. **Grieg**'s *Peer Gynt* Suite).

SULLIVAN, *Arthur* (Born London 1842; died London 1900)

Sullivan studied at the **Royal Academy of Music** and in Leipzig (where he was a contemporary of **Grieg**), then worked as an organist and teacher. He met W.S. Gilbert in 1869, creating perhaps the most famous partnership in English music (see **Gilbert and Sullivan**). Their first collaboration was a Christmas piece for the Gaiety Theatre in 1871, *Thespis*, but phenomenal success really arrived with *Trial by Jury* in 1875, which did so well that the impresario Richard D'Oyly Carte set up his company exclusively to perform their works: *HMS Pinafore* (1878) ran for over seven hundred successive performances, followed by *The Pirates of Penzance*. In 1881, the company moved to the Savoy Theatre (hence the name 'Savoy Operas'), where success continued with *Patience* (a satire on the aestheticism of Oscar Wilde), *Princess Ida* (poking fun at Tennyson), *The Mikado* and *The Gondoliers*. Sullivan's relationship with Gilbert was sometimes strained, however, as he felt his music was subservient to Gilbert's witty lyrics, and in 1891 he made an attempt at serious **opera**, with his version of Sir Walter Scott's *Ivanhoe*. This never achieved the popularity of the light operas, and the Gilbert and Sullivan team reunited for *Utopia Limited* (1893) and

The Grand Duke (1896). Sullivan was also committed to 'serious' music, both as conductor of the Philharmonic Society and **Leeds** Festival and for his **choral music**, including the famous **hymn** 'Onward, Christian Soldiers'. Knighted 1883.

'SUMER IS ICUMEN IN' ('Summer is a'coming in')

One of the earliest surviving secular compositions, this canon or round was written around 1250, possibly by the Reading monk John of Fornsete (hence its other name, the 'Reading Rota'). Properly for four **tenors**, with two **basses** providing accompaniment. Incorporated by **Britten** into the last movement of his *Spring Symphony*.

SUPPÉ, *Franz von* (Born Spalato (now Split) 1819; died Vienna 1895)

Suppé's father was an Austrian civil servant who was not enthusiastic about his son's musical aspirations; nevertheless, the young boy learned the **flute**, composed a **Mass** at the age of thirteen, and when he was sent to study law at Padua, spent much time in Milan where he met and saw the **operas** of **Donizetti** (a distant relative), **Rossini** and **Verdi**. In 1835, following the death of his father, Suppé moved to **Vienna**, and after studying at the Conservatory became assistant conductor at the Theater in der Josefstadt, where his first attempts at **operetta** were well received. Occasionally appearing as a singer himself, from 1845 he conducted at the Theater an der Wien (where he worked with **Jenny Lind** on a production of **Meyerbeer**'s *Les Huguenots*), and from 1865 until his retirement in 1882 at the Carltheater, by which time he was one of Vienna's most respected musicians, and was granted the Freedom of the City. Inspired by the satirical and witty French operettas of **Offenbach**, Suppé's thirty or so stage works set the style of the classic Viennese operetta. His great successes included *Die Schöne Galatea* (1865) and *Boccaccio* (1879). The overtures to plays such as *Light Cavalry*, *Poet and Peasant* and *Morning, Noon and Night in Vienna* have remained popular.

SUTHERLAND, *Joan* (Born Sydney 1926)

Taught **piano** and singing initially by her mother, and then professionally after winning singing

SYMPHONY

To us the word symphony suggests the grandest form of instrumental music, an expression in terms of sound of universal truth, but it was not always so ambitious. 'Symphony' is derived from two words in ancient Greek which simply mean 'sounding together', and in earlier times it was applied to vocal works such as **Giovanni Gabrieli**'s *Sacrae Symphoniae* of 1597. In the seventeenth and early eighteenth centuries 'symphony' or 'sinfonia' often described the instrumental introduction to an **opera**, or an instrumental interlude in an otherwise vocal work, such as the 'Pastoral Symphony' in **Handel**'s *Messiah*. The symphony settled into its characteristic classical four-movement form in the middle of the eighteenth century, a development of the three movement (fast-slow-fast) operatic **overtures** of **Alessandro Scarlatti** and others. In 1740 the Viennese composer M.G. Monn inserted a **minuet** before the finale of one of his symphonies, and this soon became a customary procedure; meanwhile Johann Stamitz, creator and director of the finest **orchestra** in Europe, at Mannheim, was busy developing the symphony as a means of showing off the corporate talents of his musicians. In Paris and London too, the orchestral symphony, employing relatively modest forces, was becoming popular in the mid-eighteenth century. It was the wonderfully inventive **Joseph Haydn**, however – forced to produce a steady stream of works for immediate performance by the Esterházy orchestra from 1761 – who firmly established the symphony at the heart of the orchestral repertoire.

Haydn was fond of surprises, and there was nothing cast-iron about his procedures, but the characteristic Haydn symphony consists of a **sonata-form** first movement, a slow or slowish second movement, a minuet and **trio** to provide a lighter interlude, and an exuberant finale. Haydn wrote at least 104 symphonies, including the famous 'Surprise', 'Military' and 'Clock' symphonies (Nos 94, 100 and 101). **Mozart** as a symphonist was influenced by Haydn, but Haydn

learned from Mozart too. Before he went to London there is some evidence that Haydn was acquainted with Mozart's mature symphonies which run from the 'Haffner' (No. 35) through the 'Linz' (36) and 'Prague' (38) to the trio of great masterpieces (No. 39 in E flat, No. 40 in G minor, and No. 41 in C – 'Jupiter') produced in the summer of 1788.

When I was a boy I used to play Mozart's symphonies with my mother in **piano** duet arrangements – not a bad way of getting acquainted with the symphonic repertoire. I remember being hugely taken with the opening theme of Symphony No. 40 in G minor so I was not altogether surprised when it rocketed to the top of the charts in a 'pop' arrangement in 1970. By the 1780s the first movement had come to bear the main weight of a symphony: the two contrasting themes which are the basis of sonata form provide the seeds of dramatic conflict, and in 'Mozart 40' the conflict already assumes the stature of classical tragedy.

Beethoven was to carry that process much further. Though the first two of his nine symphonies were written for the relatively modest orchestra of Haydn's day, they already bear Beethoven's heroic stamp. The Symphony No. 3 in E flat of 1803 was actually called 'Eroica' by the composer; monumental in scale and intention, it set the pattern for the symphony of the nineteenth century. Beethoven's Symphony No. 5 in C minor foreshadowed the 'programme' symphony – one that tells a story of some kind. He said of the arresting four-note summons at the start: 'that is how fate knocks at the door'. Beethoven introduced the **scherzo** in place of the minuet in his symphonies: in the mighty 'Choral' (No. 9) it comes second.

The mighty achievement of Beethoven weighed heavily on his successors. **Brahms** was forty-three before he managed to complete the first of his four symphonies and not altogether flattered when the critics called it 'Beethoven's tenth'. The great symphonies of Brahms have no particular story to tell, though they convey an eloquent enough message. **Hector Berlioz**, on the other hand, (a passionate devotee of Beethoven) was the first to use symphonic form for musical biography: his *Symphonie fantastique* of 1830 is subtitled 'Episodes from the Life of an Artist' and culminates in the pictorial nightmare of the Witches' Sabbath. Other Berlioz symphonies, such as *Harold in Italy*, with its solo viola, and *Romeo and Juliet*, are closely based on literary sources.

In a manner far removed from the **classical** spirit **Tchaikovsky** coloured his last three symphonies with elements from his own bitter experience of life, leaning heavily on Beethoven's notion of a malignant Fate. There is also a strong autobiographical thread running through the nine completed symphonies of **Gustav Mahler**, who followed Beethoven in using voices whenever it suited him to do so. The deeply moving *Song of the Earth* for tenor and alto soloists with orchestra is consistent with Mahler's definition of symphony as 'the building of a world by means of every available technical resource.'

The development of the orchestra in the nineteenth century led to ever more mighty concepts. **Franz Liszt** was the first to develop the symphonic idea into the symphonic poem, and his two symphonies clearly reveal their literary origins – *Dante* and *Faust*. **Richard** **Strauss** preferred the tone-poem, as he called it, to the symphony. *Death and Transfiguration*, *A Hero's Life* and *Thus Spake Zarathustra* are on a massive scale, while Strauss's *Don Juan* dates from almost the same time as another very popular symphonic poem, *The Sorcerer's Apprentice* by Paul Dukas, written in 1897.

Epic symphonists of the twentieth century include **Jean Sibelius**, the Dane **Carl Nielsen, Dmitri Shostakovich** and **Ralph Vaughan Williams**. Among other British composers, **William Walton** made a notable contribution with his two symphonies, and **Sir Peter Maxwell Davies** produced a major work in 1977 which, after much hesitation, he decided to call a symphony.

The very name 'symphony', with the heroic implications it has acquired over the years, is enough to daunt many a composer. Way back in 1916 the Russian composer **Serge Prokofiev** found a way of reversing the trend. Using the kind of orchestral forces that would have been familiar to Haydn, he produced a brand new, and still immensely refreshing, small-scale Classical symphony.

The London Symphony Orchestra with Principal Conductor Michael Tilson Thomas at its home in the Barbican Centre, London.

competitions, Sutherland made her début as **Purcell**'s Dido in Sydney in 1947, moving to London to study at the **Royal College of Music** and the Opera School. In 1952, she was accepted by **Covent Garden**, where she created the role of Jennifer in **Tippett**'s *Midsummer Marriage*, and sang for the first time two of her best-known roles, Gilda in **Verdi**'s *Rigoletto* and **Handel**'s Alcina. Meanwhile, in 1954 she had married her accompanist and compatriot **Richard Bonynge**, who encouraged her in the Italian *bel canto* repertory, an encouragement which came to fruition in Zeffirelli's 1959 production of **Donizetti**'s *Lucia di Lammermoor*: Sutherland won the highest praise in the title role, and launched her international career as the leading **coloratura** and dramatic **soprano** of her generation, a worthy successor to **Callas**. In 1965, she formed her own company, with her husband, to take to Australia, where she was hailed as that country's greatest singer since **Melba**. Sutherland was known above all for the clarity and brilliance of tone she brought to the florid coloratura music of Donizetti, **Bellini** and Verdi, but she also excelled as a Handelian and in **operetta**, particularly in **Offenbach** and in *Die Fledermaus*, one of the last roles she sang before her retirement in 1990. DBE 1979.

SWEDISH RHAPSODY

The orchestral piece *Midsommervaka* (Midsummer Vigil), written in 1904 by the Swedish composer Hugo Alfvén (1872–1960), is the first and best known of his three Swedish Rhapsodies. It was successfully produced as a **ballet** in Paris in 1920.

SYNCOPATION

Device to vary a regular rhythm, e.g. by stressing weak beats, putting rests in or suspending notes through the strong beat (sometimes known as an off-beat). Although the device has been widely used for centuries, its most dramatic effects can be heard in **jazz** and in modern music (e.g. **Stravinsky**'s *The Rite of Spring*).

SZELL, *George* (Born Budapest 1897; died Cleveland, Ohio, 1970)

Hungarian-born American conductor, who studied in **Vienna** and was engaged by **Richard Strauss** to work at the Berlin State Opera (1915). Conducted the (**Royal**) **Scottish Orchestra** 1937–9, and the **Cleveland Orchestra** (1946–70), which he made into one of the world's finest.

SZERYNG, *Henryk* (Born Warsaw 1918; died Kassel, Germany, 1988)

Polish-born violinist, studied composition with Nadia Boulanger in Paris before settling in Mexico during the war, after which he championed the music and musicians of his adopted country. A virtuoso concert performer, best known for playing **Paganini** and **Mozart**.

T

TALLIS, *Thomas* (Born *c*. 1505; died Greenwich 1585)

English composer who was granted, jointly with **William Byrd**, a monopoly of music printing. Much of his harmonically rich music, mainly for the Church, has survived, including the forty-part **motet**, *Spem in Alium*, for eight five-part choirs.

TAMBOURINE

Percussion instrument of ancient origin consisting of a shallow wooden hoop with parchment or plastic stretched across one side and metal jingles in slots in the hoop. Common in music of Spanish or gypsy character. Dropped on the floor, it signals the death of Petrouchka in **Stravinsky**'s ballet of that name.

TAN, *Melvyn* (Born Singapore 1956)

Singaporean keyboard player who studied at the **Yehudi Menuhin** School and **Royal College of Music** and has specialised in playing early-nineteenth-century music (e.g. **Beethoven**, **Schubert**) on the fortepiano.

TATE, *Jeffrey* (Born Salisbury 1943)

British conductor who, despite spina bifida, has developed a brilliant career. Principal conductor of **English Chamber Orchestra** 1985, and at **Covent Garden** 1986. Musical Director Rotterdam Philharmonic from 1991. CBE 1990.

*T*AUBER, *Richard* (Born Linz 1891; died London 1948)

Austrian-born **tenor** (also conductor and composer) who took British nationality in 1940. After studies in Frankfurt and Freiburg he made his début in *The Magic Flute* and soon became well-known, especially for his **Mozart** roles, throughout Germany. Famous for his ability to sing in high, hushed tones (mezza-voce), his unique voice revived the fortunes of **Franz Lehár** who wrote a series of **operettas** with Tauber in mind after his success in *Paganini* (1925). The most successful was *The Land of Smiles*, produced under that title in Berlin in 1929 with the most famous of all the 'Tauber songs' – 'You are my Heart's Delight' ('Dein ist mein ganzes Herz'). This work made Tauber's name in London in 1931 and in 1938 he fled from the Nazis to make his home in Britain, where he continued to appear in operettas, producing one of his own, *Old Chelsea*, in 1943. He also became active as a conductor. Tauber's monocled good looks and suave charm made him successful in musical films, starting with *Blossom Time* (1934), in which he played **Schubert**. During his operetta years with Lehár, he was also prominent at the **Vienna** State Opera, and he made a last appearance with that company during their visit to **Covent Garden** in 1947.

*T*AUSKY, *Vilem* (Born Perov 1910)

Czech-born conductor (British from 1948), Principal Conductor of the BBC Concert Orchestra 1956–66. Director of Opera, Guildhall School of Music, 1966–86; also Artistic Director of Phoenix Opera. CBE 1981.

*T*AVENER, *John* (Born London 1944)

English composer whose deeply-held religious beliefs (he is a convert to Greek orthodoxy) are central to his creative life. Many of his works involve voices. Among his instrumental works, 'The Protecting Veil', premiered at the 1989 **Proms** by the cellist Steven Isserlis, drew a warm public response.

'*T*EA FOR TWO'

Hit **song** with music by Vincent Youmans (1898–1946) and words by Irving Caesar, from the 1924 Broadway **musical** *No, No, Nanette*. Memorably orchestrated (1928) as the 'Tahiti Trot' by **Shostakovich**.

*T*EAR, *Robert* (Born Barry, South Glamorgan, 1939)

Welsh **tenor** who made many **Britten** roles his own with the English Opera Group. He is now artistic adviser to the Faculty of Voice jointly operated by the **Royal Academy of Music** and **Royal College of Music**. CBE 1984.

*T*EBALDI, *Renata* (born Pesaro 1922)

Italian **soprano** who, despite an attack of polio at the age of three, became the outstanding lyric soprano of her generation. In 1946, she appeared at the reopening of **La Scala** at **Toscanini**'s invitation. Regarded for a time at La Scala as the arch-rival of **Maria Callas**.

*T*ELEMANN, *Georg Philipp* (Born Magdeburg 1681; died Hamburg 1767)

Hugely productive and gifted German composer of whom his lifelong friend **Handel** said that he could write an eight-part **motet** as easily as most people could write a letter. From 1721 until his death, Telemann was music director at Hamburg, where he was responsible for the music in the city's five main churches, and for a period directed the Hamburg Opera. He wrote 1943 church **cantatas**, 44 Passion settings, 40 **operas** and a vast amount of instrumental music, and in his lifetime was considered the outstanding German composer with a reputation far exceeding **Bach**'s. However, his work quickly went out of fashion, and in the nineteenth century his very fluency went against him in an age which thought of composition as a kind of sacred struggle. In recent times, however, Telemann's great qualities have been more adequately recognised. His music is consistently charming and delightful, and in many cases has previously unsuspected depths. A few years after Handel wrote his *Water Music*, Telemann also produced a most attractive *Water Music* Suite to celebrate the centenary of Hamburg's College of Admiralty. Among other well-known works are the Viola Concerto in G major, the Suite in A minor for recorder and strings, and the very descriptive *Don Quixote* Suite; also famous are the three sets of *Tafelmusik* (table music) produced in 1733, each set containing an orchestral **suite**, a **concerto**, a **quartet**, a **trio** and a solo **sonata**.

185

T C H A I K O V S K Y

Pyotr Ilyich TCHAIKOVSKY

1840	Born in Votkinsk, Vyatka province
1850	Entered School of Jurisprudence in St Petersburg
1854	Mother died
1859	Clerk in Ministry of Justice
1863	Began full-time musical career
1869	Composed *Romeo and Juliet*
1876–90	Pen-friendship with Nadezhda von Meck
1877	Marriage. Composed *Eugene Onegin*, Fourth Symphony
1886–9	Works included Fifth Symphony, *The Sleeping Beauty*
1893	Composed 'Pathétique' Symphony
1893	Died in St Petersburg

*T*chaikovsky's prodigious gift for melody coupled with his instant appeal to the emotions brought him great popularity in his lifetime and he remains one of the world's best-loved composers.

Pyotr (Peter) was the second son of a civil servant; his mother was of aristocratic French descent and the boy adored her. Early music lessons were spasmodic, thanks to a series of family moves, and at the age of ten, Peter became a boarder at the School of Jurisprudence in St Petersburg. He long remembered the pain of parting from his mother, and when he was fourteen she died of cholera. During a subsequent family holiday on the Gulf of Finland, Tchaikovsky found escape from his grief in music and produced his earliest compositions.

At this stage he showed no very remarkable talent but after seeing a production of **Mozart**'s *Don Giovanni* at the age of twelve he secretly decided to devote his life to music. His father was in no position to provide him with an allowance, so when he left school, Peter became a clerk in the Ministry of Justice. He did, however, take lessons in composition, and when St Petersburg acquired a new conservatoire of music in 1862, under the direction of **Anton Rubinstein**, Tchaikovsky became a student.

Anton thought highly enough of the young man to suggest he be employed by his brother **Nicholas Rubinstein** as professor of composition at the new conservatoire he was about to open in Moscow. In 1866 Tchaikovsky took up this post and two years later his First Symphony, 'Winter Daydreams', was performed with great success. With its use of folk-song, it made a great impression on **Mily Balakirev** and the **'Mighty Handful'** of Russian nationalist composers which also included **Borodin**, Cui, **Mussorgsky** and **Rimsky-Korsakov.**

In fact it was Balakirev who suggested the subject of *Romeo and Juliet* to Tchaikovsky: it was the first of many works concerned with frustrated love and was to prove his first masterpiece. Another symphonic **fantasia** on a Shakespearean subject, *The Tempest*, attracted much praise in 1873. Meanwhile, Tchaikovsky produced a series of early **operas**, *The Voyevode, Ondine, The Oprichnik* and *Vakula the Smith*, which were variably received.

His middle thirties were climactic years for Tchaikovsky. In 1875 Hans von Bülow gave the first triumphant performance of the Piano Concerto No. 1 in B flat minor in Boston. In 1876 Tchaikovsky was overwhelmed by a performance of *Carmen* in Paris, and bored by **Wagner**'s *Ring* at the first Bayreuth Festival. Another fine work, the *Rococo Variations* for **cello** and **orchestra**, was completed in December 1876.

A day or two later Tchaikovsky received his first letter from Nadezhda von Meck. She was so in love with Tchaikovsky's music that she immediately responded when Tchaikovsky asked her for a loan of three thousand roubles. The money was offered as a gift, and Madame von Meck soon made Tchaikovsky an annual allowance which enabled him to devote himself entirely to composition. The only condition was that the two of them should never meet.

Meanwhile, in April 1877 Tchaikovsky received a letter from Antonina Milyukova, declaring that she loved him. Later she threatened suicide if the composer would not meet her. At that time Tchaikovsky was obsessed with the fate of the heroine of his latest opera, *Eugene Onegin*, and felt he could not treat Antonina in the heartless manner of Onegin towards Tatiana. Coupled with a desire to contradict rumours about his homosexuality, this was enough to make Tchaikovsky agree to a meeting and make a proposal of marriage to Antonina. He promised nothing more than a platonic relationship, and the marriage, which took place in July 1877, was a catastrophe from the start. Tchaikovsky fled to his sister Sasha's estate in the Ukraine; then, after trying to live with his wife in Moscow, attempted suicide. The doctors decreed that, if the composer was not to lose his reason, the couple must separate. Antonina spent her last years in a mental hospital, while her husband unsuccessfully tried to come to terms with his own sexual nature.

In the next few years Tchaikovsky travelled a great deal abroad. He found refuge from his troubles first in Switzerland, then in Italy. He composed the beautiful Violin Concerto and was inspired by the carnival season in Rome to write his cheerful *Italian Caprice*. The lovely Serenade for Strings and the big Piano Trio in A minor, written in memory of Nicholas Rubinstein, were other major works of this relatively fallow period. In 1884 Nadezhda von Meck's feelings were strangely sublimated in the marriage of her second son Nicholas to Sasha's daughter Anna Davydova.

A year later Tchaikovsky decided to rent a house of his own not far from Moscow. It was the beginning of a fruitful period which produced the 'Manfred' Symphony, the Fifth Symphony and the second of his three great ballet scores, *The Sleeping Beauty*.

By now Tchaikovsky was famous throughout the musical world. He developed an international reputation as a conductor mainly of his own works, and enjoyed great success in the United States as well as in many countries of Europe.

But these worldly successes provided no lasting distraction from private misery. In 1890,

Tchaikovsky towards the end of his life.

when he was working on his opera *The Queen of Spades*, Tchaikovsky was stunned to receive a letter from Madame von Meck putting an abrupt end to the composer's allowance and to their relationship. This was an appalling blow to Tchaikovsky and it is probably true to say that he never recovered from it.

Tchaikovsky's last major work was his Sixth Symphony, for which his brother Modest suggested the title 'Pathétique'. It is in fact deeply tragic; and not long after the composer conducted the first performance he himself was dead. It is now well established that he died of self-inflicted arsenic poisoning; he was fifty-three.

Favourite works

BALLET SCORES *Swan Lake; The Sleeping Beauty; The Nutcracker*.

SYMPHONIES Nos. 1, 2, 4, 5 and 6.

OVERTURES *Romeo and Juliet; 1812*.

OPERA *Eugene Onegin*.

CONCERTOS Piano Concerto No. 1 in B flat major; Piano Concerto No. 2 in G; Violin Concerto in D.

OTHER MUSIC *Capriccio Italien; Variations on a Rococo Theme*; Serenade for Strings; String Quartet No. 1 in D.

*T*E KANAWA

*S*ome years ago I was introducing a Christmas gala for BBC-TV in which Kiri Te Kanawa was the star guest. She was singing 'Rejoice Greatly' from **Handel**'s *Messiah*, and in the performance she looked, as well as sounded, suitably divine. But it so happened she was in the middle of having her hair done when she was required for rehearsal, so she appeared on the set in dressing gown and curlers and decided to add to the sleazy effect with a fag dangling from her lips. Not of course that she smokes – it was just a bit of fun, and there's been a lot of that in the course of a career which has taken Dame Kiri (as she became in 1982) to superstardom.

Kiri Te Kanawa broke through to world fame when the Prince of Wales invited her to sing at his wedding in St Paul's Cathedral in 1981. She gave us Handel's 'Let the Bright Seraphim' and, as Jean Rook put it in the *Daily Express*, 'Heaven was brushed by Maori **soprano** Kiri Te Kanawa's dome-splitting top A'. Some people were less flattering about her appearance in a bright, multicoloured, high-necked dress and peacock-blue hat. She was wearing, wrote Clive James unkindly in the *Observer*, 'what may have been the last surviving example of Maori national dress'. But the dress and its wearer were seen in 600 million homes worldwide, and ten years later when a **theme** song was needed for the World Rugby Cup, it was Dame Kiri who recorded the best-selling 'World in Union'.

A love of sport and the open-air has been part of Kiri Te Kanawa's nature from the start. She was born in 1944, the daughter of a Maori and a woman of European origin, but five weeks later she was adopted by a childless couple of the same racial mix, Tom Te Kanawa and his wife Nell. After Kiri had sung 'Daisy, Daisy' and 'When I Grow too Old to Dream' on a local radio talent show, Nell realised that her voice was worth developing. In due course she moved the whole family to Auckland so that Kiri could attend a convent school, St Mary's College, where the music department was headed by a famous teacher of singing, Sister Mary Leo.

Kiri went to St Mary's when she was fourteen and left two years later: it was thought she was not bright enough for GCE 'O' levels. She took a series of temporary jobs but continued singing lessons with Sister Mary and was soon in demand on the local cabaret circuit. She enjoyed living it up, but Nell knew there was more to the future for Kiri than that and secured a grant from the Maori Trust Foundation which meant her daughter could devote herself fulltime to singing studies for a year. There was still some doubt as to which direction her career would take – would she find herself in **opera**, one contemporary wondered, or go in for 'Shirley Bassey' music? But whichever way she chose to go, her friends felt she had the Maori gift of 'stickability' and would eventually win through. By the time Kiri was twenty-one she was hailed as 'the undisputed queen of **song** in New Zealand', returning after her victory in the *Melbourne Sun* **aria** competition in Australia to a traditional Maori welcome at Auckland airport, followed by a sold-out concert in Auckland Town Hall.

In her native country, Kiri was in great demand. One of her records had won a golden disc, she had appeared on television and made a couple of films. What next? Her mother and Sister Mary decided she must study abroad and James Robertson, who had heard Kiri sing at a New Zealand competition, agreed to take her on at the new London Opera Centre. With the help of a grant from the New Zealand Arts Council and after a triumphant series of six farewell concerts, she was seen off by hundreds of well-wishers singing the Maori song 'Now is the Hour'. Kiri and Nell arrived in London on Kiri's twenty-second birthday, 6 March 1966.

London, and study at the Opera Centre, came as a shock to the young New Zealander. On the one hand there was fun and there were parties; on the other a lot of hard work for someone who found herself suddenly unknown after a taste of stardom down under. In 1967 Kiri escaped from the irksome discipline of the Opera Centre for a visit home. Once again she gave a triumphant series of concerts and on 30 August at St Patrick's Roman Catholic Cathedral she married, as 'the Bride of the Year', an Australian engineer, Desmond Park. Desmond became Kiri's manager, and the partnership was just what was needed to provide a steady sheet anchor during Kiri's meteoric rise to world fame. They have two children, both adopted like Kiri herself.

In her early years, Kiri had sung as a **mezzo**, but during the late sixties she developed the upper reaches of her voice. When in 1969 she was taken on by Vera Rosza, her singing teacher to this day, she was securely established as a soprano. She was noticed in operatic productions at the Opera Centre and elsewhere and, after deeply impressing **Sir Colin Davis** and Sir Peter Hall at an audition, was given a three-year contract at **Covent Garden** starting with the 1970–1 season. She started work there after another triumphant tour in New Zealand, in the course of which she sang at a special concert for the visiting Royal Family. Then it was back to London to sing minor roles at the opera house, and understudy or 'cover' major roles. But it was intended from the start that Kiri should sing the Countess in *The Marriage of Figaro* at Covent Garden in December 1971, under the musical direction of Colin Davis, and this marked her breakthrough to top-rank critical recognition. 'The new star', wrote Andrew Porter in the *Financial Times*, 'is Kiri Te Kanawa.' She gave us 'such a Countess Almaviva as I have never seen before'. It has remained one of her finest interpretations.

During the twenty years or so since that spectacular success in London, Kiri Te Kanawa has starred at most of the world's major opera houses. In 1974 she conquered the **Met.** in New York as Desdemona in **Verdi**'s *Otello*, stepping in at the last moment to replace Teresa Stratas, and she has extended her opera repertoire to include three more **Mozart** roles, four by Verdi and three **Puccini** heroines, Rosalinde in *Die Fledermaus*, and three **Richard Strauss** operas. No **Wagner**. 'The operas are sometimes too long and I lose interest a bit, so I say "why bother?"'

Why bother indeed? Kiri Te Kanawa's success on the opera stage is matched by a

Kiri Te Kanawa in Richard Strauss's Capriccio *at Covent Garden, 1992.*

sensationally successful recording career embracing lighter repertoire as well as opera, and she can fill the largest arenas for concert appearances. 'I do half light, half serious in these concerts,' she says. 'I'm having fun.' Long may she continue to enjoy bringing such enjoyment to others.

*T*EMPERAMENT

Musically this means not the tantrums of an operatic diva, but the slight adjustment in the tuning of musical intervals necessary in keyboard (and wind) instruments. Strictly speaking, for example, G sharp and A flat should sound differently, but since both notes have to be accommodated on the same black key on the keyboard, the tuning of each has to be adjusted, though such an adjustment does not trouble the normal ear.

*T*EMPO

Italian for 'time'. Used in music to describe the speed at which a passage of music is to be played. 'A tempo', meaning 'resume original speed', is one of many phrases using the word.

*T*ENNSTEDT, *Klaus* (Born Merseburg 1926)

German conductor, hailed as one of the foremost interpreters of the Austro-Germanic repertoire, particularly **Mahler**. Succeeded **Solti** as principal conductor at the **London Philharmonic** 1983, but in 1987 throat cancer caused him to reduce his activities.

*T*ENOR

Apart from the rare **countertenor**, the highest male voice. Many types of tenor voice exist, e.g. light, lyric or dramatic. The *Heldentenor* ('heroic tenor'), bordering on baritone, is much used by **Wagner**.

*T*ERTIS, *Lionel* (Born West Hartlepool 1876; died London 1975)

Distinguished British **viola** player who won wide recognition for the viola as a solo instrument. Using a large viola of his own design, Tertis produced a **cello**-like sound of great beauty, and inspired many new works, including **Walton**'s Viola Concerto. Transcribed many works, including **Elgar**'s Cello Concerto, for his own instrument. Made his performing farewell at the age of eighty-seven. CBE 1950.

*T*ETRAZZINI, *Luisa* (Born Florence 1871; died Milan 1940)

Celebrated Italian **coloratura** soprano whose dazzling agility and fullness of tone earned her a large fortune, though on the **opera** stage she barely attempted to act. Her fame, like **Melba**'s, attached her name to food, e.g. 'Chicken Tetrazzini'.

*T*EYTE, *Maggie* (Born Wolverhampton 1888; died London 1976)

English **soprano**, chosen and trained by **Debussy** to sing Mélisande in the 1908 production of *Pelléas et Mélisande*, and thereafter much associated with French **song** which she interpreted with the utmost distinction. She brought her unique artistry to a wide range of work in **opera**, **operetta**, musical comedy and the recital platform. To a voice of the finest purity she added a touching spontaneity which was all her own. DBE 1958.

*T*HALBEN-BALL, *George* (Born Sydney 1896; died London 1987)

Australian-born British organist, appointed in 1923 to the Temple Church in London where he remained until 1981; he was civic and university organist of **Birmingham** 1949–82. In 1926 he made the famous recording of **Mendelssohn**'s 'O For the Wings of a Dove' with the boy treble Ernest Lough. Prominent as a recitalist for over half a century, and the inspiration for succeeding generations of organists. Knighted 1982.

*T*HEME

The melody or phrase which forms the basis of a composition. The 'Theme with Variations' is a common musical form; a 'theme-song' sometimes runs through a musical play or film, often providing its title, or it can be associated (like a signature tune) with a particular performer.

*T*HIBAUD, *Jacques* (Born Bordeaux 1880; died Mont Cemet 1953)

French violinist spotted by the conductor Colonne while playing in the Café Rouge in Paris, who thereafter developed a major career in Europe and America. A member of the famous **trio** with pianist **Alfred Cortot** and cellist **Pablo Casals**; their 1926 recording of **Schubert**'s B flat Trio remains a classic. Founded, with pianist Marguerite Long, the famous Long-Thibaud Competition (1943). Thibaud was killed in an air crash on the way to a concert tour in French Indochina.

THOMAS, *Ambroise* (Born Metz 1811; died Paris 1896)

Berlioz once remarked: 'There are three kinds of music: good, bad, and composed by Ambroise Thomas.' Unoriginal and conservative, Thomas was nevertheless greatly honoured in France in his lifetime, becoming head of the Paris Conservatoire in 1871. He is now chiefly remembered as the composer of the successful opera *Mignon* (1866), with its famous Gavotte.

THOMAS, *Michael Tilson* (Born Hollywood 1944)

Appointed the youngest-ever assistant conductor of the **Boston Symphony Orchestra** at the age of twenty-four and principal guest conductor of the **Los Angeles Philharmonic** in 1981, Thomas became principal conductor of the **London Symphony Orchestra** in 1988.

THREE CHOIRS FESTIVAL

The oldest choral festival in England, involving the cathedral choirs of Gloucester, Hereford and Worcester and held alternately in each city in late August. It began about 1715 as a 'meeting' of the three choirs lasting two days, but has since expanded into a comprehensive festival involving many events apart from choral performances in the cathedrals. It has been a great source of patronage to British composers since the 1860s: **Elgar** was prominently featured between 1902 and 1933, and major works from contemporary composers are still regularly commissioned.

TIBBETT, *Lawrence* (Born Bakersfield, Calif., 1896; died New York 1960)

Outstanding American **baritone**. After early experience as an actor and amateur singer, he made his début at the **Metropolitan** in 1923 and appeared there in leading roles until 1950. With his handsome looks, he also starred in films such as *New Moon* and *The Rogue Song* which both appeared in 1930.

TIPPETT, *Michael* (Born London 1905)

Widely regarded as the greatest living British composer, Tippett was a relatively late starter. He played the **piano** without distinction as a boy, but when he was fourteen a concert conducted by **Sir Malcolm Sargent** fired him with an ambition to

Sir Michael Tippett, doyen of British composers, conducting the English Chamber Orchestra in his own music, 1980.

become a composer. He studied at the **Royal College of Music** 1923–8 and then took a further rigorous course in **counterpoint**. It was not until 1944, when his **oratorio** *A Child of our Time* was first performed, that Tippett's name became widely known. This deeply moving account based on a contemporary story (interspersed with Negro **spirituals**) about the killing of a German official in Paris in 1938 by a Jewish boy remains Tippett's most popular work. During the 1940s he was a very significant Director of Music at Morley College in South London. His compositions include five **operas**, four **symphonies**, four string **quartets**, four piano **sonatas** and a number of other large-scale works; the operas, perhaps, have attracted most attention. *The Midsummer Marriage* of 1952 was very successfully revived in 1970; *King Priam* of 1962 was seen as representative of Tippett's second, dissonant, period of composition, and *The Knot Garden* of 1970 inaugurated a third period which reconciled his earlier styles and embraced other elements such as the **blues** and **early music**. Knighted 1966.

'TO A WILD ROSE'

No. 1 of ten Woodland Sketches (1896) for **piano** by the American pianist and composer Edward

MacDowell (1860–1908), the best-known American composer before the twentieth century and the first to be internationally recognised.

TOCCATA

From the Italian *toccare*, to touch, the term has been used since the sixteenth century chiefly to describe a brilliant keyboard showpiece. Famous examples are **Bach**'s Toccata (and Fugue) in D minor for **organ**, **Schumann**'s Toccata (for **piano**) Op. 7, and the last movement of the Fifth Organ Symphony by **Widor**.

'TOM BOWLING'

The best-known **song** of the English composer, impresario and singer Charles Dibdin (1745–1814). The name was taken from Smollett's *Roderick Random*, but the song commemorates Dibdin's brother Tom, captain of an East Indiaman. Dibdin also wrote 'The Bells of Aberdovey'.

TOMLINSON, *John* (Born Oswaldtwistle 1946)

British **bass**. Bayreuth's Wotan in *The Ring* since 1988; he will sing the role again in a new production there from 1994. Also appears in other major roles elsewhere, and has sung in over forty **operas** with **English National Opera**.

TORTELIER FAMILY

Paul Tortelier (1914–90) was one of the world's foremost cellists, a notable teacher (for example of **Jacqueline du Pré**), an accomplished communicator in TV master classes, a composer and an author. He married another cellist, Maud Martin; of their three children, Yan Pascal Tortelier (born 1947) became Principal Conductor of the Manchester-based BBC Philharmonic in 1992, and Maria de la Pau (born 1950) is a pianist. She adopted her surname from her godfather Pablo (Pau) **Casals**.

TOSCANINI, *Arturo* (Born Parma 1867; died New York 1957)

One of the greatest conductors of modern times, famous for the vivid intensity and meticulous preparation of his performances, but sometimes criticised for an almost brutal vehemence. Reputed to be a tyrant towards his performers, he resigned from **La Scala** in 1903 in protest at a demonstration when he refused to allow a **tenor** an encore in a **Verdi** opera, yet he also had great magnetic power and inspired remarkable devotion. Toscanini was famous for committing all his scores to memory, a procedure made necessary partly by short sight. After conducting the premières of *Pagliacci* (1892) and *La Bohème* (1896), Toscanini was principal conductor at La Scala 1898–1903 and 1906–8, returning 1921–9 as Artistic Director; but his career in the USA attracted even wider fame. He was principal conductor of the **Metropolitan Opera** 1908–15 and permanent conductor of the **New York Philharmonic** 1928–36, with electrifying results. In 1937 the NBC Symphony Orchestra was specially created for him, and he continued to give concerts and record with them until his final public appearance on the rostrum in April 1954, at the age of eighty-seven. Fiercely anti-totalitarian in politics, Toscanini refused to conduct in Nazi Germany or Fascist Italy and showed his sympathies by conducting the inaugural concert of the Palestine Symphony Orchestra in Israel in 1936.

TOY SYMPHONY

The most famous *Toy Symphony* is by Leopold Mozart (1719–87), **Mozart**'s father. Often performed at fund-raising concerts where the toy instruments are played by musical (and non-musical) celebrities.

LA TRAVIATA

The Fallen Woman, **opera** by **Verdi** based on the play *La Dame aux Camélias* by Dumas, and first performed (disastrously) in Venice in 1853. Now one of the most beloved of all operas. Alfredo, a young man of good family, falls in love with a famous Parisian courtesan, Violetta, who abandons her way of life to live with him. Alfredo's father pleads with her to give up his son, as their relationship is damaging his daughter's chance of a respectable marriage. Violetta complies and returns to her former life. Too late Alfredo discovers why she has abandoned him, and she dies of consumption in his arms. The score contains some of Verdi's best-loved music.

TREBLE

Name of the highest singing voice, once given to the highest part of any vocal group but now reserved for a child's unbroken voice, most often a boy's. Also refers to the highest-pitched member of an instrumental family, and the upper part of a composition. 'Treble clef' refers to the uppermost of the two sets of five lines on which **piano** music is most commonly written.

TRIO

Any group of three singers or instrumentalists, or a piece of music for such a group. Because the middle, contrasting, section of **minuets**, etc., were often written in **Baroque** times for three instruments, such passages continued to be called Trios – e.g. **Scherzo** and Trio in **Beethoven** symphonies.

TROMBONE

Brass instrument of noble but penetrating tone with a slide to alter the length of the cylindrical tube, thus allowing all the notes of the chromatic scale to be played. Its predecessor was the sackbut. The first symphonic use of the trombone was in **Beethoven**'s Fifth Symphony.

TROUBADOUR

Poet-musicians often of noble birth (hence not professional minstrels or *jongleurs*) who flourished in southern France in medieval times. In northern France called *Trouvères*, in Germany *Minnesingers*, their main subject was courtly love.

IL TROVATORE

The Troubadour, **opera** by **Verdi** first produced in Rome in January 1853, two months before the première of *La Traviata*. The plot of *Il Trovatore* is notoriously complicated. In fifteenth-century Spain, Manrico (the troubadour) leads a rebel force against the king's army headed by the Count of Luna. They both love the same woman, Leonora. Thinking that the gipsy woman Azucena (whom Manrico supposes to be his mother) murdered his brother years before, Luna has her arrested, and Manrico is caught trying to rescue her. Leonora poisons herself rather than submit to Luna's embraces, and in revenge Luna executes Manrico in Azucena's presence; after which she reveals that he has just slain his own brother. The score abounds in famous numbers, of which the 'Anvil Chorus' is one of the best known.

TROYANOS, *Tatiana* (Born New York 1938)

American **mezzo-soprano** who, from 1976, became a leading singer at the **Metropolitan**. Extraordinary versatility has enabled her to excel in **Handel**, **Richard Strauss** and **Bernstein**.

TRUMPET

Brass instrument which originated in ancient times, when it sounded only a few notes for signalling in battle. The 'natural' trumpet of the **Baroque** era was superseded by the three-valved trumpet in the early nineteenth century which could play all the notes in the scale.

TRUMPET VOLUNTARY

Title given by **Sir Henry Wood** to his arrangement of a keyboard piece called *The Prince of Denmark's March* by Jeremiah Clarke (*c*. 1673–1707), a contemporary of **Purcell**, who was long thought to have composed the tune.

TUBA

Family of low-voiced **brass** instruments which includes the **euphonium**, but the name most commonly refers to the orchestral tuba in F. First included in the **orchestra** by **Berlioz**. A '**Wagner** tuba' represents the dragon in his opera *Siegfried*.

TUCKWELL, *Barry* (Born Melbourne 1931)

The leading **horn** player of his generation, Tuckwell was playing in the Sydney Symphony Orchestra at the age of sixteen. After coming to Britain in 1950 he became principal horn with the **London Symphony Orchestra** in 1955, leaving in 1968 to pursue a flourishing solo career. Toured China (1984) with the Tuckwell Wind Quintet. Has latterly become internationally successful as a conductor. OBE 1965.

TURNER, *Eva* (Born Oldham 1892; died London 1990)

Perhaps the greatest British dramatic **soprano**, Eva Turner was appearing with the **Carl Rosa** Opera company in 1924 when she was invited to appear at **La Scala** under **Toscanini**. Famous above all as **Puccini**'s Turandot. An inspirational character, she remained active as a teacher and encourager of the young until just before she died. DBE 1962.

U

UCHIDA, *Mitsuko* (Born Tokyo 1948)

Japanese pianist who, after study in **Vienna**, won a **Beethoven** Piano Competition in 1969. An exceptionally fine **Mozart** player, she has recorded his piano **concertos** and complete piano **sonatas**.

UKULELE

Although this small four-stringed guitar-like instrument originated in Portugal, its name comes from Hawaii where it was patented in 1917. Made very popular in Britain by the Lancashire comedian George Formby (1904–1).

ULSTER ORCHESTRA

Symphony **orchestra** of Northern Ireland, formed in 1966 and since expanded. Under a series of fine conductors, especially Bryden Thomson (1977–85), **Vernon Handley** (1985–9) and **Yan Pascal Tortelier** (1989–92), the orchestra's quality has steadily improved.

V

VAN DAM, *José* (Born Brussels 1940)

Belgian bass-baritone of worldwide reputation, partly thanks to an extensive list of complete **opera** recordings. Début at **Covent Garden** 1973 as Escamillo in **Bizet**'s *Carmen*; he was Leporello in Joseph Losey's film of *Don Giovanni*.

VAUGHAN WILLIAMS, *Ralph* (Born Down Ampney, Glos., 1872; died London 1958)

Vaughan Williams was the most important English composer of his generation; he believed that a composer should 'make his art an expression of the whole life of the community', and to a remarkable degree his music expresses the spirit of England in his day. He studied at the **Royal College of Music**, with **Max Bruch** in Berlin and later with **Ravel** in Paris. In 1902 he began collecting English folk-songs, and that experience entered deeply into his compositions. Though himself agnostic, he edited in 1906 the refreshing *English Hymnal*, writing tunes for some **hymns** himself, including 'For all the Saints'. Very important was his close friendship with **Gustav Holst**, and for forty years the two men regularly criticised each other's work. Much of Vaughan Williams's life was spent in Surrey where he involved himself in the community by conducting the Leith Hill Musical Festival at Dorking for fifty years. From early **songs** such as 'Linden Lea' (1901) to the **film score** for *Scott of the Antarctic* (1948) Vaughan Williams wrote music that went to the hearts of the general public and has remained there. The Overture to *The Wasps* (1909), the violin romance *The Lark Ascending* (1914), the *English Folk Songs* Suite for military band (1923) and the *Fantasia on Greensleeves* (1934) have all remained very popular, but the composer's large output also includes nine **symphonies**, some very challenging, and stage works which perhaps – apart from the Masque for Dancing, *Job* (1931) – have not received their due. OM 1935.

VERISMO

Italian for 'realism'; the term applied to certain operas produced around the turn of the century with 'down to earth' stories and ordinary human characters. Prime examples are *Cavalleria Rusticana* (Mascagni) and *Louise* (**Charpentier**).

VERRETT, *Shirley* (Born New Orleans 1931)

American **mezzo-soprano** capable of some **soprano** roles. Sang the title role in *Carmen* at the Spoleto Festival 1963 and thereafter very successfully elsewhere. **Covent Garden** début as Ulrica in **Verdi**'s *A Masked Ball* 1966.

VIBRAPHONE

Not unlike the **marimba**, the vibraphone has tuned metal bars struck by padded hammers; under the bars are resonators with lids which are constantly opened and closed electrically, creating a pulsating sound.

VIENNA

The importance of Vienna as a musical centre over the centuries is unique. As far back as the twelfth century, famous minstrels frequented the court of the Babenburg dukes; the Vienna Boys' Choir was formed in 1498 to provide music for the Imperial chapel (it still does); **opera** came to Vienna in 1633, and the city witnessed the premières of many of **Mozart**'s major theatre works as well as **Beethoven**'s operatic masterpiece, *Fidelio*. The new Opera House on the Ring was opened in 1869 to house the Court Opera (later the State Opera); under **Mahler** it enjoyed a golden decade, but since then (it was rebuilt after the Second World War and reopened in 1955) it has continued to display high musical distinction. The Vienna Philharmonic Orchestra serves the opera but has its own concert life as one of the world's finest **orchestras**. Founded in 1842, the orchestra is self-governing and has invited a series of world-famous conductors to preside over it. The Vienna Symphony Orchestra is the city's municipal orchestra, also of very high standard. The light music of the **Strauss** family and others, which brought another kind of fame to Vienna in the nineteenth century, is taken seriously in the city. The Vienna Philharmonic give New Year concerts in the beautiful Golden Hall of the Musikverein which are entirely devoted to Viennese light music; they are prestigious social events and broadcast worldwide.

VIERNE, *Louis* (Born Poitiers 1870; died Paris 1937)

French organist, almost blind, who was organist at Notre Dame 1900–37 and died at the organ console there. Toured Europe and the USA. Wrote a piece called *Carillon de Westminster* based on the chimes of Big Ben.

VIEUXTEMPS, *Henri* (Born Verviers 1820; died Mustapha, Algeria, 1881)

Outstanding Belgian **violin** virtuoso compared by **Schumann** to **Paganini**. In 1834, at the age of fourteen he learned **Beethoven**'s Violin Concerto and performed it to great acclaim in **Vienna**. Wrote seven violin **concertos** and many other works, mainly for violin.

VIGNOLES, *Roger* (Born Cheltenham 1945)

British pianist who has concentrated on the art of accompanying and in that role has partnered some of the world's leading soloists.

Known to the jazz world as 'Vibes', the vibraphone was born in the USA during the early twenties.

VILLA-LOBOS, *Heitor* (Born Rio de Janeiro 1887; died Rio 1959)

Brazilian composer of great importance in the development of Brazilian music and musical education: he founded the Brazilian Academy of Music in 1945. Mainly self-taught, but influenced both by Brazilian **folk music** and by avant-garde composers of the twenties such as Darius Milhaud. In the *Bachianas Brasileiras* Villa-Lobos combined the style of **Bach** (whom he revered) with Brazilian dance rhythms. 'The Little Train of the Caipira' from No. 2 and the lovely **Aria** from No. 5 are specially well known.

VIOL

Type of bowed stringed instrument, with fretted fingerboard, which originated in the fifteenth century. English composers from **Byrd** to **Purcell** wrote great music for a **consort** of viols (two treble, two tenor and two bass instruments). Viols were eventually superseded by the **violin** family but are still employed for the performance of **early music**.

V ERDI

Guiseppe VERDI

1813	Born in Le Roncole
1836	Married Margherita Barezzi (who died 1840)
1842	*Nabucco* at La Scala, Milan
1847	*Macbeth* in Florence
1848	Bought estate at Sant' Agata, lived with Giuseppina Strepponi
1851	*Rigoletto* in Venice
1853	*Il Trovatore* produced in Rome; *La Traviata* in Venice
1859	Married Giuseppina Strepponi
1867	*Don Carlos* in Paris
1871	*Aida* produced, Cairo
1874	Requiem performed, Milan
1887	*Otello* at La Scala, Milan
1893	*Falstaff* at La Scala, Milan
1901	Died in Milan

*T*o the world at large Verdi is one of the greatest of all **opera** composers, but in Italy they also revere the memory of a great patriot.

He was the son of the innkeeper at the small village of Le Roncole, near Busseto in what was then the duchy of Parma. At the age of twelve he was organist in the village church and a year later the Busseto merchant Antonio Barezzi engaged him as an apprentice and took the boy into his own house. At fifteen Verdi had an **overture** performed by the local Philharmonic Society and at sixteen he became conductor of the town band.

Barezzi arranged (and contributed to) a scholarship which enabled the eighteen-year-old Verdi to go to Milan and try for admission to the Conservatoire. He was rejected as too old but studied composition privately. In 1836, at the instigation of Barezzi, he was appointed 'master of the music' in Busseto and that same year married Barezzi's daughter, Margherita. Three years later, Verdi moved back to Milan and in November 1839 his first opera, *Oberto*, was produced with some success at **La Scala**. The theatre director, Bartolomeo Merelli, immediately commissioned three more operas from the young man, but a series of personal tragedies – the loss of his infant son and daughter as well as his wife within three years – robbed Verdi of all desire to compose. With much difficulty Merelli persuaded him to set a story concerning the exiled Hebrews in Nebuchadnezzar's Babylon, and the resulting opera, *Nabucco*, gave Verdi his first taste of triumph in the theatre. What is more, the great Hebrews' Chorus soon became the unofficial hymn of the Italian resistance movement against the Austrians, who then occupied much of northern Italy.

There then followed what Verdi was later to call his 'years in the galleys'; fourteen operas in nine years. Quite different from the melodramatic vein of most of them was *Macbeth*, staged in Florence in 1847. Verdi loved **Shakespeare**, referring to him as 'Papa'; the great playwright, he once said, 'did nothing less than invent the truth'.

In 1848, the 'year of revolutions' when the Austrians were temporarily thrown out of Milan, Verdi was in Paris, where he renewed acquaintance with Giuseppina Strepponi, the prima donna of the first production of *Nabucco*. The pair set up house together at the small estate of Sant' Agata near Busseto. Even the loyal Barezzi was critical of what he regarded as an immoral relationship, but Verdi told him to mind his own business. It was a situation paralleled in one of the three great operas of the early 1850s, *La Traviata*, when the hero's father persuades his son's live-in lady friend to move out for the sake of respectability, and breaks her heart in the process. The other outstanding works of this period were *Rigoletto*, a thinly disguised account of evil promiscuity on the part of a French king, and that splendid mixture of Gilbertian improbability and great tunes, *Il Trovatore*.

Verdi married Giuseppina in 1859; she was to share his life for some fifty years in all and it is hard to imagine a more devoted companion. In the 1860s Verdi took a break of five years from

Engraving of Guiseppe Verdi, based on the striking portrait by Boldini.

the theatre to devote himself to politics (as a Deputy in the Italian parliament) and country life. Then he composed a spectacular account of the revolt of the Netherlands against Spanish tyranny in the sixteenth century, *Don Carlos*. Verdi claimed to hate the Paris Opera, which he thought was riddled with false values. If, however, the money was right, he could often be tempted, and when the Khedive of Egypt promised to pay 150,000 gold francs into the Rothschild bank in Paris without delay, Verdi agreed to consider the composition of an opera for the new Opera House in Cairo, *Aida*.

The first interpreter of the leading role was the gifted singer Teresa Stolz. Verdi admired her art and loved her as a person; he invited her to Sant' Agata to study *Aida*, thus making Giuseppina's life very difficult. But all three of them survived their *ménage à trois* to remain friends into old age.

At the first performance of *Aida* at La Scala, Verdi took thirty-two curtain calls but after that,

as far as new music for the theatre was concerned, there was silence for fifteen years. The composer's earlier works were revived, however, and they put up a statue to him at La Scala.

Then Verdi fell victim to what Giuseppina described as 'a bit of a conspiracy'. The publisher Ricordi, the poet and composer Arrigo Boito and Giuseppina persuaded him to consider the subject of Shakespeare's *Otello*. Verdi worked on the opera secretly, referring to it as 'the chocolate project'. When it opened at La Scala it was a sensational success; in his mid-seventies Verdi had echoed the truth of Shakespeare with music of an altogether new power and inventiveness. He was able to repeat the miracle six years later at the age of eighty with his only operatic comedy, *Falstaff*.

In 1897 the faithful Giuseppina died at the age of eighty-two, and after four unhappy years of loneliness Verdi followed her. At his funeral the vast crowd burst spontaneously into singing 'Va Pensiero' from *Nabucco*.

Favourite works

The achievements of so great a master of the musical theatre can only be appreciated by hearing the operas as a whole but here are just a few of the best known exerpts from Verdi's works.

Nabucco – Chorus of the Hebrew Slaves ('Va Pensiero');
Rigoletto – 'La Donna è mobile'; the Quartet; 'Caro Nome';
Il Trovatore – the Miserere; the Anvil Chorus; 'Di Quella pire';
La Traviata – Violetta's monologue beginning 'Ah, fors è lui …'; 'Di Provenza il Mar'; 'Parigi, O Cara';
La Forza del Destino – Overture;
Don Carlos – 'Dio, che nell'alma infondere';
Aida – 'Ritorna Vincitor'; 'O Patria Mia'; 'Celeste Aida';
Otello – 'Iago's Creed'; 'Willow Song';
Falstaff – Ford's monologue.

Verdi's Requiem Mass – written to honour the memory of Alessandro Manzoni who wrote the first great novel in Italian, *The Betrothed*. It is a fitting memorial to two heroes of the Italian Risorgimento.

VIOLA

The **violin**'s larger brother, lower in pitch and sometimes known as 'alto' or 'tenor' it has an important place in the **orchestra** and the string **quartet**.

VIOLIN

One of the finest and most versatile of all instruments, capable of great subtlety, brilliance and dramatic power, the violin seems to have originated (quite independently of the **viol** family) in the early sixteenth century. The first great maker was Andrea Amati of Cremona who supplied the French king with thirty-eight instruments. Amati taught Andrea Guarnieri (*c.* 1626–98) and probably Antonio **Stradivari** (1644–1737); the violins made in their workshops have never been surpassed for beauty of tone, and those which have survived command astronomical prices. In parallel with the creation of great instruments, a succession of violinist-composers appeared on the scene in Italy and an abundance of music for solo violin and for string orchestra began to be written. The nineteenth century brought a series of dazzling solo performers in the wake of the legendary **Paganini**. The twentieth century has also seen a number of outstanding virtuosi; advancing technical skill has matched the growing demands made on the violin soloist. But that is only part of the violin's importance. With its larger relatives, the **viola**, **cello** and **double bass**, it is indispensable in the **orchestra**, and is required in a vast amount of **chamber music**, not to mention its importance in the light salon orchestra and its role in **folk music** and dancing. The accomplished violinist can make his or her instrument speak to the listener with an eloquence that is incomparable.

VISHNEVSKAYA, *Galina* (Born St Petersburg 1926)

Russian dramatic **soprano**, wife of one of today's greatest cellists **Mstislav Rostropovich**, with whom she left the USSR in 1974. The soprano part in Britten's *War Requiem* was written for her, but she was prevented from singing the first performance in Coventry in 1962.

VIVALDI, *Antonio* (Born Venice 1678; died Vienna 1741)

The most important and influential Italian composer of his time, Vivaldi is universally known for the violin concertos known as *The Four Seasons* (not least thanks to the sensationally successful **Nigel Kennedy** recording). They are the first four concertos in a set of twelve (Op. 8) called *The Contest between Harmony and Invention* and represent only a tiny fraction of Vivaldi's output of over 760 works, including over 500 **concertos**. He was ordained as a priest in 1703, and his startlingly red hair earned him the nickname *il prete rosso* (the red priest). Music, however, took precedence. He was a brilliant violinist, and at the age of twenty-five was appointed Head of Violin at a Venetian orphanage for girls (the Ospedale della Pietà) which prided itself on its music. He remained on the staff for the rest of his life, becoming director of instrumental music in 1716, though he exasperated the governors by his frequent absences which took him on visits to Rome, Prague, Amsterdam, **Vienna** and elsewhere, and was criticised for his supposed relationships with the contralto Anna Girò and her sister Paolina who were both members of his entourage. But Vivaldi achieved a great international reputation in his lifetime (**J. S. Bach** made a number of transcriptions of his works) and his unquenchable enthusiasm inspired great loyalty in high-ranking patrons as well as fellow-musicians.

VOCALISE

A wordless song or vocal exercise. Famous examples are the *Vocalise* Op. 34, No. 14, by **Rachmaninov**, and *The Nightingale and the Rose* by **Saint-Saëns**.

W

WALDTEUFEL, *Emil* (Born Strasbourg 1837; died Paris 1915)

Why should a man whose family name was Levy change it to Waldteufel (wood-demon)? No one knows, it seems, and indeed not a great deal is known about the man who was second only to the **Strauss** family as a composer of **dance music** in the nineteenth century. Waldteufel studied **piano** at the Paris Conservatoire and worked as a demonstrator for a **piano** manufacturer. The Empress Eugénie heard him play, and in 1865 engaged him as court pianist and conductor of the court balls. After the collapse of the Second Empire he once again struggled for recognition, but fortunately Coote and Tinney's band included a waltz of his at a Buckingham Palace state ball in 1874. When, soon afterwards, the Prince of Wales attended a soirée in Paris, where Waldteufel played a waltz called *Manolo*, he asked for the composer to be presented to him, and thereafter Waldteufel's success, first in London and then in Paris, was assured. Some three hundred dance compositions by Waldteufel were published. Among his best-known waltzes are *Les Patineurs* (*The Skaters*) 1882, *Estudiantina* (1883), *España* (1886), based on Chabrier's Rhapsody of that name, and *The Grenadiers* (1886).

WALKER, *Sarah* (Born Cheltenham 1943)

British **mezzo-soprano** of great character and skill. Made a big impression with her Union Jack dresses in two appearances at the Last Night of the **Proms**, but also distinguished in **operas** from **Handel** to **Tippett**, expert in recitals and admirable in cabaret songs.

WALLACE, *Ian* (Born London 1919)

Scottish **bass** who has also achieved fame as a broadcaster and raconteur, chiefly on the **BBC** quiz programme *My Music*. Widely known for his exuberant renderings of Flanders and Swann songs (his memoirs have the title *Promise Me You'll Sing Mud*), Wallace had a distinguished career in **opera**, appearing regularly for some years at **Glyndebourne** where he so impressed conductor Vittorio Gui that he was engaged for Rome, Venice and the Bregenz Festival. He sang César in the musical *Fanny* at Drury Lane 1956–7.

WALLACE, *Vincent* (Born Waterford 1812; died Vieuzos, Hautes-Pyrénées, 1865)

Irish composer who in his day won worldwide fame as a pianist and virtuoso violinist. He emigrated to Tasmania in 1835, moving on to Sydney where he was hailed as 'the Australian **Paganini**'. Abandoning his first wife and small son, he toured throughout the Americas and was said in New York to be 'decidedly the first violinist and pianist in this country'. He appeared in London in 1844 and in the following year enjoyed a triumph with the **opera** *Maritana* written

with the librettist Edward Fitzball. Further travels followed, but Wallace was destined never to repeat this success.

WALTER, *Bruno* (Born Berlin 1876; died Beverly Hills 1962)

German-born conductor, American from 1946, specially associated with the music of **Mozart** and **Mahler**. After being Mahler's assistant in Vienna he conducted in 1911 the first performance of Mahler's *Song of the Earth*. Walter was prominent at the Salzburg Festival 1925–37 and conducted the German seasons at **Covent Garden** 1924–31. The Nazis forced him to flee first to France, then to the USA, where he enjoyed a flourishing career. In the early days of the **Edinburgh Festival**, Walter befriended and accompanied **Kathleen Ferrier**, engaging her for **Vienna** and launching her international career.

WALTON, *William* (Born Oldham 1902; died Ischia 1983)

British composer who inherited **Elgar**'s mantle as a creator of ceremonial music such as the two coronation marches *Crown Imperial* (1937) and *Orb and Sceptre* (1953). He wrote **film music** of great skill, including the scores for Laurence Olivier's *Henry V* (1944) and *Hamlet* (1948), created a major twentieth-century oratorio in *Belshazzar's Feast* (1931), composed two **symphonies** and three **concertos**, two **operas**, and, as a young man of twenty, the work by which he is perhaps best known, the brilliant *Façade*. Though born in Lancashire, Walton felt more at home as an adopted brother of the Sitwell family whose Chelsea home he shared in the early twenties after leaving Oxford. *Façade* is a series of settings of poems by Edith Sitwell, and was first performed in the family drawing-room. In 1923 it created a public scandal at the Aeolian Hall. Marrying the Argentinian Susana Gil in 1946, Walton made his home on Ischia, where his ashes were buried under a rock in the garden with an inscription taken from the seventeenth-century mystic Thomas Traherne: 'All Bliss consists in this, to do as Adam did.' Walton's work as a serious composer has perhaps not received all the recognition it deserves – the opera *Troilus and Cressida* (1954) is a case in point. But many of his compositions have become

WAGNER

Richard WAGNER

1813	Born in Leipzig
1836	Married Minna Planer
1840–1	Composed *The Flying Dutchman*
1843–5	Composed *Tannhäuser*
1846–8	Composed *Lohengrin*
1848–74	Creation of *The Ring*
1857–9	Composed *Tristan and Isolde*
1862	Separation from Minna
1862–7	Composed *The Mastersingers*
1870	Married Cosima von Bülow
1876	First Bayreuth Festival
1877–82	Composed *Parsifal*
1883	Died in Venice

An unpromising start in life may help to explain some of the less attractive characteristics of Richard Wagner. His father was probably the actor and painter Ludwig Geyer and uncertainty about his true father's identity, coupled with the suspicion that Geyer had Jewish blood, no doubt contributed to the composer's poisonous anti-Semitism.

When Wagner was fourteen he wrote a tragedy called *Leubald* and it was the desire to set this to music which led him to take lessons in composition and to study the works of the great composers, especially **Beethoven**. Despite a dissipated life-style, he composed **overtures**, piano **sonatas** and a **symphony** while a student at Leipzig University.

A period as chorus-master of the theatre at Würzburg gave the young man experience of the operatic repertoire; in 1834 he became musical director of a travelling theatre company, marrying one of the actresses, Minna Planer, in 1836. Wagner always regarded an extravagant style of living as necessary to his art, and after two years as musical director of a theatre in Riga, he and Minna were forced to flee to escape their creditors. They stowed away on a stormy sea journey which supplied inspiration for *The Flying Dutchman*.

The Wagners came to rest for a time in Paris where Richard was helped and encouraged by **Giacomo Meyerbeer** whose spectacular **operas** were all the rage in Paris at this time. Wagner responded by addressing Meyerbeer as his 'noble protector', though later he would vilify him in a notoriously racist pamphlet entitled *Jewishness in Music*. Meanwhile, thanks to Meyerbeer, Wagner became *Kapellmeister* at the Dresden court. There he conducted a notable performance of Beethoven's Choral Symphony and the premières of his own first masterpieces, *The Flying Dutchman* and *Tannhäuser*.

Wagner conceived of his art as a means of promoting the unification and spiritual regeneration of Germany, and he played an enthusiastic part in the revolutionary activities of 1848 in Dresden. A warrant for his arrest was issued and Wagner fled to an exile which lasted eleven years. Consolation came from **Franz Liszt** who was an ardent champion of Wagner's 'new music'; he was rewarded by Richard over the years with a mixture of adulation and abuse.

The 1850s were a time of great activity for Wagner. He completed the text of his massive four-part work based on Nordic legend, ***The Ring***, and composed the first opera in the cycle, *The Rhinegold*. Wagner accepted the patronage of Otto Wesendonck, who provided the Wagners with a house in Zürich and moved into the villa next door with his own wife, Mathilde. Wagner and Mathilde promptly assumed in real life the roles of the tragic lovers Tristan and Isolde, whose story Wagner was busy creating.

In 1861 the first performance of *Tannhäuser* in Paris provoked a riot because it lacked the traditional **ballet**. The following year Richard finally parted from Minna and was also allowed to return to Saxony; but after a successful visit to Russia (1863) he set up house near **Vienna**, where once again he lived beyond his means and was forced to flee or face imprisonment for debt. At the age of fifty-one he was

penniless, work on *The Ring* had come to a halt, and he contemplated suicide.

Rescue came from the eighteen-year-old King Ludwig of Bavaria who had a passion for Wagner's works and for the composer himself. During the remaining years of Wagner's life, the king supported him to the tune of almost a million marks. Such were the king's feelings that Wagner had to conceal from him the nature of his relationship with Liszt's daughter, Cosima von Bülow; they lived together and had three children before Cosima divorced her husband to marry Wagner in 1870. Meanwhile, *Tristan and Isolde* had been premiered (1865) and Hans von Bülow, despite his marital problems, conducted the first performance of *The Mastersingers* to great acclaim in Dresden in 1868. *The Rhinegold* and *The Valkyrie*, the first of the four *Ring* operas, were produced in 1869 and 1870.

But Wagner had decided that only a specially built theatre could house *The Ring* adequately; he settled on Bayreuth in Bavaria as the perfect setting. In 1874 the Wagners moved into their Bayreuth home, and *The Ring* score was finally completed. Two years later the vast work was performed at the first Bayreuth Festival.

He then became involved with a new admirer, Judith Gautier, and worked for five years on his last opera, *Parsifal*, premiered at Bayreuth in 1882. By this time Wagner's health

Scene from The Valkyrie, *with Gwyneth Jones (side on to camera), at Covent Garden, 1991.*

had begun to fail and in February of the following year he died of a heart attack.

Favourite works

Although Wagner's greatness cannot be fully appreciated in short excerpts from his operas, such extracts were the means of making his name known to the musical public at large. Some favourites follow:

Rienzi – Overture;
The Flying Dutchman – Overture; Senta's Ballad;
Tannhäuser – Overture; Grand March; Venusberg Music; 'O Star of Eve';
Lohengrin – Prelude to Act 3;
Tristan and Isolde – Prelude; 'Liebestod';
The Mastersingers – Prelude; Prize Song; Monologue of Hans Sachs.
THE RING OF THE NIBELUNGEN:
Entry of the Gods into Valhalla *(The Rhinegold)*;
Ride of the Valkyries *(The Valkyrie)*;
Forest Murmurs *(Siegfried)*;
Siegfried's Journey to the Rhine *(The Twilight of the Gods)*;
Parsifal – Good Friday Music;
Siegfried Idyll.

securely established, and to the British listener he found a way of expressing, time and again, a deep patriotism that is devoid of bombast. Knighted 1951. OM 1967.

WARSAW CONCERTO

Clever pastiche of a romantic piano **concerto**, composed by Richard Addinsell (1904–77) for the film *Dangerous Moonlight* (1941). It was about a Polish pianist (played by Anton Walbrook) who loses his memory after fighting in the Battle of Britain.

WATER WAGTAIL

Well-known impressionistic **piano** piece by Cyril Scott (1879–1970), once dubbed the 'English **Debussy**'. The quality of Scott's music is now winning overdue recognition.

WEBER, *Carl Maria von* (Born Eutin 1786; died London 1826)

There is no denying that Weber was the forerunner of **Wagner** in the creation of German **opera**, but this is to understate his own considerable achievement, which might have been even greater had he not died from tuberculosis in his fortieth year. A brilliant pianist as well as a composer of high gifts, his precocious talent won him the post of *Kapellmeister* at Breslau before he was eighteen. Credited with being perhaps the first true conductor in the modern manner, he instituted sweeping reforms against strong opposition, and he had to battle hard for his ideas: both in Prague and, later, Dresden he was charged with creating a German as opposed to an Italian operatic repertoire. His opera *Der Freischütz* (*The Freeshooter*), based on German legend, was a triumph throughout Europe following its Berlin première in 1821. *Euryanthe*, for Vienna, followed, and in 1826 Weber went to London to direct the first performance at **Covent Garden** of his fairy opera *Oberon*. Seven weeks later he died, and his body was brought back to Dresden for a hero's funeral at which Wagner gave the oration. The overtures to Weber's operas have long been concert favourites, and his *Invitation to the Dance* (1819) for piano is universally known. All his music has great and instant appeal, not least the delightful works for **clarinet** and **orchestra**.

WEDDING MARCH

For many years it was traditional for British brides to enter the church to the strains of the bridal march from **Wagner**'s *Lohengrin* and to leave it to the accompaniment of the wedding march from **Mendelssohn**'s incidental music to *A Midsummer Night's Dream*. But wedding marches were written and used long before these two pieces found favour, and the tendency now is to be more unconventional in choosing wedding music.

WEILL, *Kurt* (Born Dessua 1900; died New York 1950)

Prolific German-born composer, American from 1943, who in 1928 wrote in collaboration with Bertolt Brecht *Die Dreigroschenoper* (*The Threepenny Opera*), a savagely satirical updating of John Gay's **The Beggar's Opera**: the popular 'Ballad of Mack the Knife' from that piece epitomises the bitter-sweet sharpness of Weill's Berlin manner in the twenties. He married the singer Lotte Lenya and with her settled in the USA after being driven from Germany by the Nazis. In America, Weill lost some of his bite, but for the film *Knickerbocker Holiday* (1944) he wrote the haunting 'September Song'.

WEIR, *Gillian* (Born Martinborough, New Zealand, 1941)

New Zealand organist who played **Poulenc**'s Concerto for Organ at the First Night of the **Proms** 1965, and excels in contemporary music. Also harpsichordist and teacher.

WEISSENBERG, *Alexis* (Born Sofia 1929)

French pianist of Bulgarian birth who went to Israel as a refugee in 1945, subsequently studying at the **Juilliard School**. Won Leventritt Competition 1947. Flourishing international career punctuated by further period of study 1956–66.

WELL-TEMPERED CLAVIER

Title given by **Bach** to his set of twenty-four Preludes and Fugues in all major and minor keys composed at Cöthen 1722, and extended to include a further set of twenty-four composed in Leipzig 1744. The whole collection is known as 'the Forty-eight'. It was intended to demonstrate the advantages of the new 'equal **temperament**' system of tuning keyboard instruments whereby all semitone intervals were made the same, thus making it possible to play in every key.

WELSH NATIONAL OPERA

Opera company based in Cardiff and founded in 1946, which was soon associated with rare **Verdi** operas. In conjunction with **Scottish Opera** it gave a cycle of **Janáček** operas, and is greatly admired for **Britten** productions. It tours widely, and its musical directors have included **Sir Charles Groves**, James Lockhart and Richard Armstrong. Currently (1993), Carlo Rizzi is Musical Director and **Sir Charles Mackerras** is Conductor Emeritus. The company promoted the early careers of such singers as **Dame Gwynneth Jones**, **Dame Margaret Price** and Dennis O'Neill.

WESLEY FAMILY

The founder of Methodism, John Wesley (1703–91), believed in adapting popular or operatic songs to religious words. His brother Charles Wesley (1707–88), who wrote 'Hark, the Herald Angels Sing', called this 'plundering the carnal lover'. Charles's eldest son, another Charles (1757–1834), showed early promise, and his youngest son, Samuel (1766–1837), was regarded as a great organist and promoted the **Bach** revival. Samuel's illegitimate son Samuel Sebastian Wesley (1810–76) was considered the finest church musician of his day: his many compositions include the **anthem** 'Thou will keep him in perfect peace'.

WHITE, *Maude Valérie* (Born Dieppe 1855; died London 1937)

British composer, and the first woman to win the **Mendelssohn** Scholarship at the **Royal Academy of Music** 1879. Her songs include a memorable setting of Byron's 'So we'll go no more a-roving'.

WHITE, *Robert* (Born New York 1940)

American **tenor** of Irish descent who has specialised in Irish song, reviving much of the repertoire of **John McCormack** with great success.

WHITE, *Willard* (Born St Catherine, Jamaica, 1946)

Jamaican **bass** who won a scholarship to the **Juilliard School** and thereafter developed major international career. An outstanding Porgy in *Porgy and Bess*, his many other roles include Wotan in **Wagner**'s *The Valkyrie* for **Scottish Opera**, 1989.

WIDDOP, *Walter* (Born Norland, nr Halifax, 1892; died London 1949)

British **tenor** (nicknamed 'The Merry Widdop' by **Beecham**) who achieved high distinction in **oratorio** and on the **opera** stage, notably in **Wagner** roles such as Siegmund, Lohengrin and Tristan.

WIDOR, *Charles-Marie* (Born Lyons 1844; died Paris 1937)

Creator of the organ symphony (he wrote ten in all; the Fifth includes the universally known **Toccata**), Widor was a superb organist as well as a composer: he was the organist at St Sulpice in Paris 1870–1933, and was still performing at the age of ninety. He was particularly famous as a **Bach** interpreter.

WIENIAWSKI, *Henryk* (Born Lublin 1835; died Moscow 1880)

One of the greatest violinists of the generation after **Paganini,** Wieniawski was a child prodigy who, despite ill health (he suffered from a heart condition and sometimes could not complete his concerts), toured widely to great acclaim. Specially significant were his years in St Petersburg (1860–72) when he composed some of his best works and helped to create the Russian **violin** school. As a performer he believed in taking risks, but more often than not the results were sensational.

WILBRAHAM, *John* (Born Bournemouth 1944)

Distinguished British trumpeter who has occupied the Principal's desk in the New **Philharmonia**, **Royal Philharmonic** and BBC Symphony Orchestras. He is also a brilliant soloist who specialises in **Baroque** music.

WILLCOCKS, *David* (Born Newquay 1919)

British conductor and organist who was Director of Music at **King's College, Cambridge**, 1957–73, and Director of the **Royal College of Music** 1974–84. His compositions include famous carol arrangements. Knighted 1977.

WILLIAMS, *John* (Born New York 1932) _____

American composer especially of **film music** (e.g. *Star Wars*, 1977) and conductor, since 1980, of the Boston Pops Orchestra.

WILLIAMS, *John* (Born Melbourne 1942) _____

Australian guitarist, son of emigrant British guitarist Leonard Williams. Début in London 1955; studied with **Segovia** in Siena 1957–9. John's distinguished career (which includes teaching at the Royal and Royal Northern Colleges of Music) embraces music of many kinds and reflects his interest in **folk music**, **jazz**, pop and non-Western idioms as well as the repertoire of the classical **guitar**. He is a frequent duo partner of **Julian Bream**, and formed his own cross-over group, Sky. OBE 1980.

WILLIAMSON, *Malcolm* (Born Sydney 1931) ____

Australian composer, appointed **Master of the Queen's Music** 1975. His prolific output includes many works for voices and (following **Britten**) a number of pieces involving children and amateur performers.

WOLF, *Hugo* (Born Windischgraz, Styria, 1860; died Vienna 1903) _____

Austrian composer of an opera *Der Corregidor* (1895), on the same story as the **ballet** *The Three-cornered Hat*, and of **chamber music**, including the delightful *Italian Serenade* (1887), but Wolf is chiefly famous for his many **lieder**. Wolf set dozens of poems by Mörike, Eichendorff and Goethe among others, and composed large numbers of settings of Spanish and Italian poems in German translation. Highly strung, charming but unstable, Wolf spent his last years in a mental hospital, the outcome of venereal disease.

WOLF-FERRARI, *Ermanno* (Born Venice 1876; died Venice 1948) _____

The son of a German father and Italian mother, Wolf-Ferrari scored his greatest successes as a composer in the musical theatre. He achieved international fame with *I quattro rusteghi* (1906) (usually called in English *The School for Fathers*) based on a comedy by Goldoni, and *Susanna's Secret* (1909). *The Jewels of the Madonna* (1911) was a less successful melodramatic piece but it does contain a famous **intermezzo** that shows Wolf-Ferrari's art at its graceful best.

WOOD, *Haydn* (Born Slaithwaite, Yorks., 1882; died London 1959) _____

British composer named by his musical father after the famous **Joseph Haydn**. Haydn Wood wrote a large amount of attractive light music and many songs, including the famous 'Roses of Picardy' (1916) and 'A Brown Bird Singing' (1922).

WOOD, *Henry* (Born London 1869; died Hitchin 1944) _____

British conductor chiefly identified with the annual season of London **Proms** which now bear his name. After early experience as an **opera** conductor (assisting **Sullivan** with *Ivanhoe* in 1890 and conducting the first English performance of **Tchaikovsky**'s *Eugene Onegin* in 1892) he was engaged by Robert Newman in 1895 to direct the new Promenade Concerts at the Queen's Hall. During almost fifty years with the Proms, Wood introduced 'novelties' (new or unknown works, especially by British composers) and gave opportunities to large numbers of solo performers. His own compositions included his arrangement (under the pseudonym Klenovsky) of **Bach**'s Prelude and Fugue in D minor and the famous *Fantasia on British Sea Songs* first performed in 1905 to mark the centenary of the Battle of Trafalgar. Knighted 1911.

X, Y, Z

XYLOPHONE _____

Percussion instrument consisting of tuned wooden bars struck with hammers. Originating in Java, a rudimentary xylophone appeared in Europe in the early sixteenth century. Used by **Saint-Saëns** in his *Danse Macabre* to represent skeletons dancing.

YEPES, *Narciso* (Born Lorca 1927) _____

Spanish guitarist who made the first recording of **Rodrigo**'s *Concierto de Aranjuez*. Since 1961 he has used a ten-string **guitar** of his own creation.

Yepes has recorded the complete **lute** works of **Bach**, and has researched and transcribed for his instrument much little-known **early music**. He has also written **film scores**, notably for *Jeux Interdits* (*Forbidden Games*), 1952; this includes a very popular Romance which Yepes himself recorded.

ZABALETA, *Nicanor* (Born San Sebastian 1907)

Basque harpist of the highest distinction who has done perhaps more than anyone to promote the **harp** as a solo instrument in the twentieth century. He has explored, performed and recorded much eighteenth-century music, and **Rodrigo** arranged his *Concierto de Aranjuez* for harp at Zabaleta's request.

ZARZUELA

A word derived from the Spanish for Bramble-bush (*zarza*), used to describe a type of Spanish theatrical entertainment combining singing, dancing and speech, usually (but not necessarily) light in character. It originated as a diversion at the royal palace of La Zarzuela in the seventeenth century, but reached a high point of popularity in the nineteenth century when pieces by Barbieri and others became as beloved in Spain as **Gilbert and Sullivan** in Britain. Distinguished twentieth-century *zarzuelas* include *Luisa Fernanda* (1932) by Federico Torroba. **Placido Domingo**'s parents were *zarzuela* singers, and he has recorded a selection of *zarzuela* numbers.

ZELLER, *Carl* (Born St Peter in de Au 1842; died Baden 1898)

After early promise as a boy **soprano**, Zeller became a career civil servant, but he won fame as an Austrian composer of **operettas**. *Der Vogelhändler* (*The Bird Seller*) of 1891 revived the fortunes of Viennese operetta, and *Der Obersteiger* (The Master Miner) of 1894 was hardly less successful, with its delightful cautionary song 'Sei nicht bös'('Don't be Cross').

ZIEHRER, *Carl* (Born Vienna 1843; died Vienna 1922)

Austrian military bandmaster and prolific composer of dance music, a serious rival to the **Strauss** family, absorbing many Strauss musicians into his new civilian **orchestra** in 1878. He wrote twenty-four **operettas** including the successful *Die*

The Basque Nicanor Zabaleta: perhaps the most influential harpist of the twentieth century.

Landstreicher (1899), many waltzes, of which *Wiener Bürger* (*Vienna Citizens*) is perhaps the most famous, and a number of fine marches, such as *Der Zauber der Montur* (*The Magic of the Uniform*).

ZITHER

Folk instrument descended from the medieval psaltery. Four or five melody strings and thirty-seven accompanying strings are stretched over a flat wooden soundbox; they are plucked with the fingers or sounded with a plectrum. Used by Anton Karas in his **theme** music for the film *The Third Man* (1949).

ZUKERMAN, *Pinchas* (Born Tel-Aviv 1948)

Israeli violinist of Polish descent, also **viola** player and conductor. After early studies in Israel he entered the **Juilliard School** under the guardianship of **Isaac Stern**, and in 1967 was the joint winner with **Kyung-Wha Chung** of the Leventritt Prize in New York. He has a brilliant international career as soloist and in **chamber music** and in 1980 he became director of the St Paul Chamber Orchestra in Minnesota.

CONTENT:

Timeline years: 1500 1510 1520 1530 1540 1550 1560 1570 1580 1590 1600 1610 1620 1630 1640 1650 1660 1670 1680 1690 1700 1710 1720 1730 1...

Composer life-spans:

- 1525 PALESTRINA 1597
- 1543 BYRD 1623
- 1557 G. GABRIELI 1612
- 1567 MONTEVERDI 1643
- 1632 LULLY 1687
- 1653 CORELLI 1713
- 1659 PURCELL 1695
- 1668 COUPERIN 1733
- 1675 VIVALDI 1...
- 1681 TELEMANN
- 1683 RAMEAU
- 1685 J. S. BACH
- 1685 HANDEL
- 1714
- 17...

KEY

Baroque era
circa 1580–1750

Classical era
circa 1750–1810

Romantic era
circa 1810–1914

This chart shows the life-spans of some of the leading creators of music set against an indication of three of the main musical eras. Such divisions, and the labels attached to them, are quite arbitrary, and there is a good deal of overlap between them. When, for example, does the brief 'Classical' period end and the 'Romantic' period begin? We've placed the change-over around 1810, in the middle of Beethoven's creative life, but you could argue about it for ever.

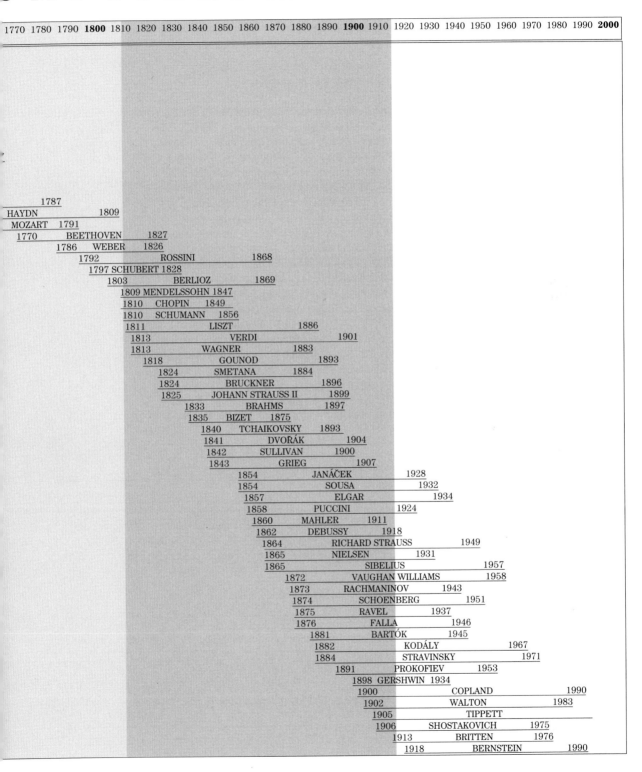

1770	1780	1790	**1800**	1810	1820	1830	1840	1850	1860	1870	1880	1890	**1900**	1910	1920	1930	1940	1950	1960	1970	1980	1990	**2000**

1787
HAYDN 1809
MOZART 1791
1770 BEETHOVEN 1827
1786 WEBER 1826
1792 ROSSINI 1868
1797 SCHUBERT 1828
1803 BERLIOZ 1869
1809 MENDELSSOHN 1847
1810 CHOPIN 1849
1810 SCHUMANN 1856
1811 LISZT 1886
1813 VERDI 1901
1813 WAGNER 1883
1818 GOUNOD 1893
1824 SMETANA 1884
1824 BRUCKNER 1896
1825 JOHANN STRAUSS II 1899
1833 BRAHMS 1897
1835 BIZET 1875
1840 TCHAIKOVSKY 1893
1841 DVOŘÁK 1904
1842 SULLIVAN 1900
1843 GRIEG 1907
1854 JANÁČEK 1928
1854 SOUSA 1932
1857 ELGAR 1934
1858 PUCCINI 1924
1860 MAHLER 1911
1862 DEBUSSY 1918
1864 RICHARD STRAUSS 1949
1865 NIELSEN 1931
1865 SIBELIUS 1957
1872 VAUGHAN WILLIAMS 1958
1873 RACHMANINOV 1943
1874 SCHOENBERG 1951
1875 RAVEL 1937
1876 FALLA 1946
1881 BARTÓK 1945
1882 KODÁLY 1967
1884 STRAVINSKY 1971
1891 PROKOFIEV 1953
1898 GERSHWIN 1934
1900 COPLAND 1990
1902 WALTON 1983
1905 TIPPETT
1906 SHOSTAKOVICH 1975
1913 BRITTEN 1976
1918 BERNSTEIN 1990

ACKNOWLEDGEMENTS

The publishers would like to thank the following
for supplying photographs:

Aldeburgh Foundation p. 28 (Stephen Cotgrove); Archiv für Kunst
und Geschichte, Berlin p. 167; Catherine Ashmore pp. 119, 125, 189,
201; Clive Barda/P.A.L. pp. 31, 37, 51, 52, 55, 69, 70 (Robbie Jack),
79, 83, 87, 88, 121, 129, 137, 140 *top* (Robbie Jack), 140 *bottom*
(Clive Barda), 143, 147, 155, 157, 158 *bottom* (James McCormick),
163, 176, 191, 205; BBC Picture Library p. 177; BFI Stills, Posters &
Designs p. 67 (Keystone 1914); Birmingham Symphony Hall p. 34
top; Dat's Jazz Picture Library pp. 85, 101 (Max Jones Files), 195;
Decca pp. 33, 93 (Gerald Schomitz), 172 (Vivianne Purdom); Deutsche
Grammophon pp. 103 (S. Lauterwasser), 108 (Jorg Reichardt);
Zoë Dominic p. 15; Mary Evans Picture Library pp. 49, 59, 109,
131, 151, 179; John Foster Black Dyke Mills Band p. 34 *bottom* (S. C.
Platten); Gimell Records Ltd p. 41 (Clive Barda); Huddersfield Choral
Society pp. 96/7 (Selwyn Green); Hulton Deutsch Collection pp. 7, 11,
32, 35, 39, 42, 50, 56, 71, 77, 91, 148, 164; London Symphony
Orchestra p. 183 (Robert Hill); Musée d'Orsay, Paris, p. 65; Redferns
pp. 24 (William Gottlieb), 73 (Steve Gillett), 81 (David Redfern), 122
(Tim Hall), 175 (David Redfern); The Royal College of Music pp. 21,
61, 95, 187, 197; Scottish Chamber Orchestra pp. 27, 135; Sony
Classical pp. 25, 112, 115 (Christian Steiner), 158 *top*; Warner
Music/Erato p. 16; Welsh National Opera Ltd p. 139 (Clive Barda).